TRANSFORMING DEVELOPMENT

Women, Poverty and Politics

MARGARET SNYDER

INTERMEDIATE TECHNOLOGY PUBLICATIONS 1995

Intermediate Technology Publications
103–105 Southampton Row, London WC1B 4HH, UK

© IT Publications 1995

A CIP catalogue record for this book
is available from the British Library

ISBN 1 85339 302 9

Typeset by J&L Composition Ltd, Filey, North Yorkshire
Printed by SRP, Exeter, UK

Contents

PART TWO: UNIFEM at Work in the World: Case Studies

Dedication

To the women in this story of strength, justice and hope, who band together to change their own lives and the lives of their families, communities and nations.

Acknowledgements

When I spoke about my interest in looking at questions of sustainable development through writing a history of UNIFEM, Ingrid Reed, then at Princeton University, Susan Berresford, John Gerhardt and June Zeitlin of the Ford Foundation and Joyce Moock of the Rockefeller Foundation all supported the idea. They made it possible for me to spend a year in study and research and six months travelling to listen to and learn from those who had been partners in our UNIFEM venture: grassroots women, Members of Parliaments, leaders of women's organizations, and former United Nations colleagues. UNDP Administrator Bill Draper gave his blessing to the work, as did my successor at UNIFEM, Sharon Capeling-Alakeja.

At Princeton, Henry Bienen, Dean of the Woodrow Wilson School, John Waterbury, Director of the Center of International Studies, Jeri Horner and others were welcoming and helpful. My research assistants, Kathy Larin at Princeton and Marie Duggan at the New School for Social Research were the best one could dream of. Nancy Murray smoothed my English once again, and Rosemary Kalapurakel typed and proofread.

UNIFEM staff briefed me at headquarters and in the field. Former colleagues Joann Vanek and Erlinda Go of the UN Statistical Office gave us all the data we needed from the WISTAT. Teresa Spens, one of the first members of UNIFEM's Consultative Committee, produced records from 1975, the moment her UK delegation proposed the creation of a development fund for women at the Mexico City Conference.

The UNDP officers in the countries that I visited during my interview period found the people with whom we had worked a decade ago, set appointments and fixed accommodations. I was accompanied on field visits and was invited to people's homes. Some 150 people were interviewed; they shared their development experiences, their relationships with UNIFEM, and their visions for the future. Many of them are quoted herein.

Just over two years since I started, there are already two books and many renewed and new friendships. I cannot think of a more enriching experience. I am proud, not only of my colleagues, but of everyone who made those first eleven years of UNIFEM formative and fruitful. And I am proud of the many donors and advocates of UNIFEM–countries, NGOs, individuals–who put their trust in us. They too must take pride when they read this book.

Women *have* transformed development. Given the opportunities discussed in this book, they will be ready to do much more for themselves, their families and their countries.

MARGARET SNYDER
Makerere University
Kampala, February 1995

ix

Acronyms

ACW	African Centre for Women (formerly ATRCW)
AIP	Africa Investment Plan
APDEV	Asia and Pacific Development Strategy
ASG	Assistant Secretary–General
ATRCW	African Training and Research Centre for Women
BCC	Bolivian Committee of Cooperation
CC	Consultative Committee
CILSS	The Permanent Interstate Committee for Drought Control in the Sahel
CSDHA	Centre for Social Development and Humanitarian Affairs
CSD	Commission on Social Development
CSW	Commission on the Status of Women
DIESA	Department of International Economic and Social Affairs
DAWN	Development Alternatives with Women for a New Era
DAC	Directors Authorization Ceiling
DTI	Department of Trade and Industry
ECA	Economic Commission for Africa
ECOSOC	(UN) Economic and Social Council
ECLAC	Economic Commission for Latin America and the Caribbean
ECOWAS	Economic Community of West African States
ESCAP	Economic and Social Commission for Asia and the Pacific
ESCWA	Economic and Social Commission for Western Asia
FAO	Food and Agricultural Organization
FLA	Forward Looking Assessment
GA	General Assembly
GNP	Gross National Product
IBTA	Bolivian Institute of Agricultural Technology
GUSW	General Union of Syrian Women
IFAD	International Fund for Agricultural Development
ILO	International Labour Organization
ILPES	ECLAC Regional Planning Institute
IMF	International Monetary Fund
INSTRAW	International Training and Research Institute for the Advancement of Women
ISST	Institute of Social Studies Trust (Delhi)
IWTC	International Women's Tribune Centre
IWY	International Women's Year
ITDG	Intermediate Technology Development Group
JPO	Junior Professional Officer
KWAHO	Kenya Water for Health Organization
MCH	Maternal and Child Health
NATCAP	National Assessment of Technical Cooperation Assistance Programmes

NCRFW	National Commission on the Role of Filipino Women
NGO	Non-Governmental Organization
NIEO	New International Economic Order
NORAD	Norwegian Agency for Development
NOW	National Organization for Women (Barbados)
PAC	Project Advisory Committee
PAPLAC	Participatory Action Plan for Latin America and the Caribbean
RC	Regional Commission
RIC	Rural Improvement Clubs
SADC	Southern African Development Community
SADCC	Southern African Development Co-ordination Conference
SAP	Structural Adjustment Programme
SETAM	Appropriate Technology for Rural Women (Bolivia)
SEWA	Self-Employed Women's Association (India)
SIDA	Swedish International Development Authority
SWPO	Senior Women's Programme Officer
TADD	Tribal Area Development Department
UN	United Nations
UNIFEM	UN Development Fund for Women
UNDTCD	UN Department of Technical Cooperation for Development
UNDP	UN Development Programme
UNFSTD	UN Fund for Science and Technology for Development
UNICEF	The United Nations Children's Fund
UNFPA	United Nations Population Fund
UNHCR	UN High Commission for Refugees
UNRWA	UN Relief and Works Agency
UNSO	UN Sahelian Organisation
USAID	US Agency for International Development
UWI	University of the West Indies
VFDW	Voluntary Fund for the UN Decade for Women
VIC	Vienna International Centre
VITA	Volunteers in Technical Assistance
WAFT	Women and Food Technologies
WAHA	Water for Health Assistant
WAND	Women and Development Unit (West Indies)
WFP	World Food Programme
WID	Women In Development

Introduction

The unique identity of UNIFEM calls for flexibility in order to retain its capacity to innovate. This implies the ability to take risks . . .

UNIFEM Consultative Committee
16th Session

WHEN I ARRIVED at the United Nations headquarters in 1978, I was assigned a tiny office with a clear view of the brick wall of the United States Mission to the UN. For a moment I pondered: Why, why, had I left the open spaces of Africa?

I knew the answer. The women of a hundred and thirty-three nations who had come together for the first time in history at Mexico City in 1975 had determined to create a Fund that would be used to reach out to the poorest women in the world. They knew that the benefits of progress went disproportionately to men, even though women contributed more than their fair share of economic work while also caring for their families and households.

The idea for a fund was now a reality and my new job was to find ways to reach those women and to assist in their empowerment. To that end it was necessary to identify a unique role for the Voluntary Fund for the UN Decade for Women (VFDW), one that would attract interest in and resources for women, but would not overlap the work of other UN funds and agencies. The Voluntary Fund was later named the UN Development Fund for Women (UNIFEM) and the work of that entity is the major focus of this book.

I have chosen to write the history of UNIFEM for several reasons. First, there is widespread disillusionment with 'foreign aid' as a stimulant to development. 'Why does poverty still prevail after all those years of foreign aid?' is a question commonly posed in the capitals of donor countries. It needs an answer. It seemed to me that the time had come to look beyond the usual and necessary determinant of project-effectiveness, by which the donor(s) measure(s) achievements against a list of set goals when a project is finished. One way to do that was to find out what had happened after a project was off the accounting books and off the minds of development-aid representatives. I determined to discover how people were faring now that five to ten years or more had passed since their foreign aid had begun. What works, I wondered? And why does it work? I would search for the answers.

Also emerging from disillusion with the results of foreign aid is a quest for new development paradigms. The UN General Assembly is even now debating ways to transform the concept of development in order to move it away from the prevailing preoccupation with economic growth and markets. The necessity for that search intensified in the early 1990s when wealth increasingly flowed to the few and turned the gap between the haves and have-nots into a chasm.

UNIFEM is a relevant partner in those discussions for many reasons, most vividly because of the structural changes in given societies that have caused the economic responsibility for the family to shift from the men to the women. Just one result of that shift is that women and their dependent children are now disproportionately represented in the population categorized as 'the new poor'. UNIFEM's rich experience in creating economic opportunities and in augmenting family well-being is thus pertinent to the pursuit of corrective action through fostering economic democracy–the logical follow-up to the political democracy that has taken hold in the twentieth century. UNIFEM attacks poverty at its source, by means of the immediate and far-reaching effects of its efforts to ensure that women have a more democratic access to the means of creating wealth.

The rationale for finding such new paradigms becomes even clearer when one learns that the costs of emergency assistance have eaten into development assistance. They have risen from 25 per cent of UN assistance in 1988 to 45 per cent in 1993. That fact strongly suggests that it would be worth trying to target development aid as a preventive to poverty, civil unrest and even to war. Aggravating that trend in assistance is the debt crisis that still faces many developing countries. Debts and interest, accumulated in the 1970s and 1980s when petro-dollars floated freely, must be paid to overseas private and multilateral banks. Today millions of poor people who had no democratic say in incurring those debts must pay for them instead of sending their children to school. The effects of poor or little education are devastating.[1]

That brings us to my second reason for writing this book. The prevailing prescriptions to assure the repayment of those debts are profoundly undemocratic and often cruel. They were laid down by the World Bank and the International Monetary Fund (IMF), and are supported by the G7 industrial nations. *The UNIFEM experience offers an alternative* to those prescriptions which have an impact that is often compounded by the globalization of the economy and the lingering effects of colonialism on countries that have less than a generation of experience with self-govern-ance and consequently lack strong political and administrative systems. Now there is also the cold war heritage and the fall of the Berlin Wall to turn our attention and our investments away from the 'Third World' to the former 'Second World'–Eastern Europe.

The World Bank and the IMF readily admit that the prescriptions for debt repayment exacerbate poverty and place excessive burdens on women.[2] Yet they continue their pursuit of economic growth and the global market economy without the balance that the pursuit of human well-being could give. In addition, the estimated cost of US$60 billion in aid given annually by the industrial countries is offset by their earnings of about US$125 billion from the sale of armaments. That statistic needs to be factored into the adjustment equation relative to debt repayment.

Structural adjustment is necessary but, as presently practised, it evinces a failure not only of compassion but even of reason. Compounding the anomaly even further, the Bank, by its own admission 'did not sufficiently analyse the impact of specific macro-economic and sectoral policies on the poor'. Its poverty-focused adjustment lending then fell sharply from eighteen loans in 1992 to just six in 1993.[3]

A third reason I have for writing is not a new but a persistent one. Nearly a decade ago Administrator Bradford Morse of the United Nations Development Programme (UNDP) said succinctly: 'Programmes that fail to pay adequate attention to productive activities are not only morally indefensible but economically absurd'.[4] Yet the cold hard fact nearly a decade later is that the bulk of international development assistance still bypasses women. A Norwegian evaluation states that 'Information on how women have so far gained from NORAD programmes is poor and scanty, but what is available indicates rather few benefits for women'.[5] The Dutch put it in a more devastating way: 'Economic and political development processes have in general had no beneficial effect on the position of women'.[6]

In short, women's access to development resources is still found more often in the speeches than in the field projects of major funding agencies. Why have women been given such meagre assistance from development co-operation organizations, including UN, bilateral and voluntary? Why do hard facts fail to move policymakers from words to action? Why does the flow of resources to women fall so woefully short of being commensurate with their responsibilities? Why is it that only some 15 per cent of development resources reach women? Much of that 15 per cent can be categorized as 'welfare' or basic needs assistance like maternal health care. Such care is critical indeed and should grow, but it does not begin to embrace the variety of supports that women need today. Alternatives to that neglect do exist and must be introduced more widely to meet today's challenges; the UNIFEM experience that I record in this book is a very valuable starting point.

UNIFEM is a pioneering fund that has been instrumental in creating an alternative development strategy that has worked effectively against poverty; it can be called grassroots economic empowerment. The strategy is grounded in UNIFEM's mandate to give special attention to rural and poor urban women, and in the hard facts of women's economic responsibilities: they produce 60–80 per cent of the food and comprise 70 per cent of the entrepreneurs in the informal employment sectors of developing countries, to name but two. When we asked those women what their needs were, the overwhelming response was, and has continued to be, increased incomes to provide for themselves and their children.

The significance of a development fund for women was apparent from the very beginning. It was most unusual for women as women to be the subject of a UN fund. There had been the establishment of the UNDP in response to the poverty of post-colonial countries, and the innocent faces of children affected by war had attracted support to UNICEF. The concern that a population explosion would exhaust the earth's resources brought bounteous contributions to UNFPA. At the same time, women and their concerns remained subsumed within such categories as 'poverty' and 'family'.

Why should women be separated out? It is now known that any development that does not channel resources to women will not only fail but will contribute to the decline of the larger society. Historically, women's substantial contributions to family and national well-being were so familiar as to be invisible. In fact, even though there was already a limited knowledge base about women's lives, many countries emerging from colonialism continued to identify men as the sole breadwinners. Men were perceived as economically active, while the prevailing mythology regarded women as doing household and motherly work only. The result of this oversight was that development specialists, who were almost all men, dealt only with men, while most of the work done by women was simply listed as 'unpaid family labour'.

There was an honest concern for the wellbeing of children, so the good will toward women was directed almost exclusively toward their role as mothers. That approach overlooked the profound reality that children needed more from their mother than milk and whatever love she had time to give. Income was needed; the mother's health had to be safeguarded; her education had to be guaranteed: those were the things that would enhance a woman's life and the lives of her children. Yet sons were the favoured students; daughters accounted for only a small percentage of primary and secondary students and they were barely visible at the universities. The result was that two of every three illiterates were women.

Those facts, among others, made the challenge for the Voluntary Fund a daunting one. We knew that it would take time to generate action based on women's centrality to the success of development. The fund for women would have to defy conventional UN approaches to assistance if it was to meet women where they lived and with the support they wanted and needed. In the 1960s and early 1970s, when and if assistance reached them, it was either through maternal and child health programmes (MCH) like those of UNICEF, or through programmes for wives, sponsored by FAO. The latter were appendages to agricultural projects and taught women home economics modelled on the needs of European housewives. Some of my FAO colleagues called that 'stitchin' and 'stirrin'.

The primary challenge for the Fund was to devise innovative ways to reach out to women's productive activities. From my years of working at the UN Economic Commission for Africa (ECA), I knew that bureaucratic attitudes could not be easily changed, but I had also learned that procedures could be altered. Women in poor communities were ready and willing to tell us what they needed. They were already experienced as managers of community self-help projects through their informal groups and organizations. I was convinced that such groups could be used by the Fund as channels for financial assistance. UNFPA had broken ground for that method by using international NGOs as executing agencies.

The Voluntary Fund, and later UNIFEM, would have to go beyond that model and create procedures to finance *national* NGOs. We would have to devise the types of development co-operation that would deal with women as agents of change rather than as victims of circumstances. And we would have to assist in the strengthening of national institutions–whether governmental or voluntary–to sustain that work. UNIFEM would have to be flexible, innovative and experimental; it would have to take risks.

UNIFEM's strategy remains uniquely appropriate at this present moment in history: a time in which the democratization of both civil society and the private economic sector has become a popular concept. Ever since its beginning, UNIFEM has worked within the civil society, interacting with governments and with people involved in the democratic process at the local level. Recognizing women as economic agents, the Fund does not merely provide for material needs but insists that people participate in its activities in order to increase their self-reliance and gain self-confidence. UNIFEM maintains a delicate balance between imparting skills and empowering group solidarity on the one hand, and being attentive to macro-economic policies on the other.

Since UNIFEM is the only UN fund with a holistic approach to women (as more than one of my interviewees said), it is time to learn from the economic democracy that women have developed. It is time to consider what corrective actions can be taken and how to breathe new life into the present economic system. I was, and still am convinced that transforming action is possible. We can reverse the current trends that push more and more people and families into poverty. The result could then be a reversal in global poverty and a safer world.

When one recalls that women and their dependents constitute the vast majority of the world's poor, it then becomes obvious that the findings contained in this book can have broad applications. To at last understand the underlying causes of poverty and to grasp the potential solutions–as revealed to us by women–is to take a giant step for *all* of the poor: men, women, and children. In the words of the UN General Assembly: 'General questions of development and access by women to development resources have as a common objective the creation of conditions that will improve the quality of life for all.'[7]

This study of UNIFEM makes use of the experience of non-governmental organizations and of the African Centre for Women (ACW), which is comprehensively described in *African Women and Development: A History*.[8] Formerly called the African Training and Research Centre for Women, ACW was the first women's centre to be established as an integral component of a UN institution. Its special importance also arises from its origins in the advice of women of the Africa region in the 1960s who directed ECA's work toward the 80 per cent of women who lived in rural areas, and from the continuing guidance those women give to its work.

Initiated as a programme to operationalize the resolutions adopted at conferences of African women during the 1960s, the Women's Programme/Centre of the UN Economic Commission for Africa was a pioneer in the United Nations system. It utilized African women's identification of the mechanisms causing their marginalization in modern societies, as well as their proposals for policies and actions that would benefit not just themselves but men and children too.

Moving beyond those footsteps, so to speak, UNIFEM originated as the only multilateral fund directed specifically to women. Created in the mid-1970s because the resources of the major development co-operation funds were not reaching rural and poor urban women, UNIFEM has continued to provide financial and technical assistance to hundreds of programmes and projects benefiting women for nearly 20 years.

The history of UNIFEM, like that of ACW, bears witness to the leadership given by the UN to the concept of, and the movement devoted to, women and development. The histories also testify to the ease with which the poor become political pawns–particularly poor women and the organizations that espouse their interests.

The approach of this book

After a section on the tools I use for analysing the impact of UNIFEM-assisted activities, this book places the women and development movement in its broad historical context, i.e. the independence of nation after nation in the period after the Second World War. I will describe the factors that interfaced to form the underlying concepts for the movement as it arose in developing countries.

Institution-building toward ending poverty is the overall theme of Part I of this book, under the heading 'Global Poverty and the Politics of Development'. UNIFEM's creation, the search for structure, definition of policy, and securing independent management comprised the institutional thrust of the Fund during the early years. The Consultative Committee and staff were determined that the Fund would be a unique 'special window' in the UN development co-operation system, and that it would have guidelines of its own and not overlap with other funds. It would be innovative and experimental–a risk-taker–and would act as a catalyst for change, strengthening women's access to mainstream resources and supporting their involvement in shaping the future of their societies.

Using a case-by-case approach to policy formulation, the Consultative Committee and the Secretariat developed strategic approaches and forged partnerships within the UN system and among voluntary organizations. Outreach to low-income women was a constant concern as UNIFEM sought to increase women's productivity, lessen their burdens, and enhance their participation in the decision-making processes of their nations.

The delivery system was also of utmost importance because we had to transfer resources efficiently to more than a hundred developing countries. We soon discovered that the UN itself was ill-equipped for operational activities of that kind; it had no direct delivery system to countries. UNDP was on the whole far more appropriate because it had a string of offices around the world.

As a new and still fragile UN development Fund, UNIFEM had to ride the political waves. There were those who wanted to see it prosper and those who didn't; among the latter were powerful bureaucrats. There were also plenty of politicians who saw the Fund as unimportant and who thought it could be used as a political pawn. A firm tripartite alliance between diplomats, NGOs and Fund staff, however, kept the Fund not only afloat but moving forward through the political storms. Some of these stories are told here.

Part II of this book describes and analyses 'UNIFEM at Work in the World'. I evaluate the impact UNIFEM has had on poverty by examining a selection of activities assisted by the Fund; I visited most of them between 1993 and 1994. Focusing primarily on women, they range from village-level projects aimed at increasing incomes and/or involving women in decision-making, to national-level policy and strategy interventions through ministries of planning, and then to regional and inter-regional analyses of the impact of global economic factors on women. By assessing the impact of the various projects up to ten or more years after their initial implementation, I will draw some conclusions about the effectiveness of UNIFEM support and the direction future development assistance should take to reduce poverty worldwide.

One premise of this book is that there is now enough hard evidence about the workability of strategies already employed. What is needed is to close the gap between the vast amount of knowledge available in the community of women, from grassroots to the global level, and the narrowness of ideas that are put into practice by 'mainstream' development agencies, where rhetoric still outstrips action. That closure can be achieved because now there are experienced senior women and cadres of educated young women in developing countries who are creative and committed to change. They are ready for action. With a modicum of support, they can transform societies in their own countries and in the world.

This study presumes that people of good will want to put an end to poverty. We can learn from experience in order to transform development and to halt the haemorrhaging of people into poverty. The irony is that we have not yet given women the chance to make life better for their families, and so to make life better for everyone. UNIFEM has demonstrated that the goal is reachable if we have the collective will and commit enough resources to the task. The case studies in this book reveal how women have been and still are contributing to that effort.

The major thesis of this book is that the experience in development co-operation with women provides a basis for reversing global poverty trends, thereby increasing the prospects of global security. Poverty is therefore the given reality, or it can be seen as the landscape within which I analyse UNIFEM programme and project interventions. The basic elements of the Fund's major mandates provide the variables for my assessment: namely, innovative/catalytic effects, sustainability and empowerment. Those elements were set out in General Assembly Resolutions A/RES/31/133 and A/RES/39/125 (see Annexes 1 and 2). They set the course for implementing the plans of action for the advancement of women, particularly in the least developed countries. That was our mission from the start.

I use the phrase 'women and development' in this book, with the definition that my colleague Mary Tadesse and I assigned to it, namely:

Women and development is an inclusive term that signifies a concept and a movement whose long-range goal is the wellbeing of society–the community of men, women and children.

Its formulation is based on the following suppositions:

○ 'Development', in accordance with the International Development Strategy for the Second Development Decade, means 'to bring about sustained improvement in the wellbeing of the individual and to bestow benefits on all'.

○ As women comprise more than half of the human resources and are central to the economic as well as the social well-being of societies, development goals cannot be fully reached without their participation.

○ Women and development is thus a holistic concept wherein the goal of one cannot be achieved without the success of the other.

○ Women, therefore, must have 'both the legal right and access to existing means for the improvement of oneself and of society'.[9]

A final note

In the field of women and development, theoretical feminism has tended to dominate the literature. As my graduate assistant commented after coming from a class on that subject, 'It's often difficult to fit the theory with the reality I faced overseas'. In contrast to the theoreticians, I have been both an 'insider' and a 'practitioner', deeply engaged in institutionalizing women's concerns in three major UN organizations. I thus approach the subject in a pragmatic way, with fresh perspectives and some unique sources of information. I believe that women like myself, who were pioneers in building institutions benefiting women, have an obligation to new generations to record and analyse that experience, including an account of the politics surrounding poverty issues.

The reader should note a limitation of this book as regards its parameters. The book does not embrace everything that women have done in the field of women and development. It speaks mainly to international support to women's own work for development, and almost always uses activities assisted by UNIFEM.

I visited fifteen countries to assess the projects that UNIFEM has assisted, and I interviewed women and men whose lives UNIFEM has touched since its initiation in 1977. Through listening to and learning from those people who made projects work, through careful examination of the projects and their sustainability, and making use of an abundance of documentation found in the projects' periodic monitoring and evaluation reports, I sought to increase my understanding of the dynamics of poverty, with a view to more effective interventions in the future.

PART ONE

GLOBAL POVERTY
AND THE POLITICS OF DEVELOPMENT

CHAPTER ONE
Toward a New Development Paradigm

Theoretical development models work at universities in Europe and in Chicago, but nowhere else in the world. Industrial countries would never have done what they now propose developing countries must do.

Edouardo Ishi Ito, Peru

THIS CHAPTER IS a preamble to the history and case studies that are set forth in the narrative that follows. As such, it provides the background and rationale for the methodology used to explicate UNIFEM's role in the worldwide struggle against poverty. Basic to an understanding of the text is an awareness of the impact that certain dimensions of the social order have on the lives of the poor, particularly on rural and urban women. It is to strengthen the whole society by stimulating productivity and increasing family incomes that UNIFEM selects and supports projects that empower and that create sustainable institutions.

A fundamental question begins this study and, in some sense, everything else flows from it. How do we define poverty? Most analysts view it in purely economic terms, defining 'poverty lines' in terms of income only. Using income as the measurement appears to have several advantages: it is quantifiable, easily understood, and data are available because it is the prevailing method used around the world.

The World Bank's *World Development Report 1990: Poverty*[1] defines the concept of poverty in the most general terms as 'the inability to attain a minimal standard of living'. The report notes the importance of considering many factors, including the cost of essential goods and services, the added cost of culturally determined necessities and other more subjective measures of well-being, such as health and education. However, the Bank's analysis, like others, is based on poverty lines defined exclusively in economic terms, e.g. having a household income of less than US$250 to $370 a year. That range encompassed the official poverty lines of eight developing countries at the time the report was written.

With the exception of the period in the mid-seventies when World Bank President Robert MacNamara distinguished between 'absolute and relative poverty' and when the International Labour Organization (ILO) addressed 'basic needs', multilateral and bilateral donors have traditionally endorsed a development strategy which focused on increasing economic productivity growth.[2] Little attention was paid to poverty *per se*, under the 'trickle-down' assumption that was actually discredited as early as the 1960s, but which has persisted; it holds that as economic growth increases within a given country, incomes will rise and poverty will be reduced.

Over the past thirty years it has become increasingly clear that the focus on growth-oriented development strategies has *not* led to the expected

3

reductions in poverty, nor has it benefited women. In fact, there has been an increase in structural poverty. The economic systems that have emerged from growth-led development strategies have left entire segments of the population in developing countries disenfranchised, without access to education, training, credit, or technologies, and hence with minimal, if any, access to the benefits of economic growth.

It has become clear that considering poverty in exclusively economic terms simplifies analysis, but is also unrealistic and unjust. In order to understand how poverty can be reduced and even eliminated, a more comprehensive understanding of its dynamic and multi-dimensional nature must be used. Poverty is not purely an economic phenomenon that can be captured in simple income measures. Consequently, some of the major development organizations have begun to revise and modify their approaches and to use a more 'people-oriented' perspective. The new approaches do not completely abandon the concept of productivity growth as a driving principle in the reduction of poverty, but they do address the issue more directly by specifying that both productivity and growth require investments in people and in their basic needs such as land and water, as well as access to credit, employment and social services.

UNDP has played a leading role as a conceptualizer of this newly articulated orientation. Its annual *Human Development Report* defines the goal of sustainable development as:

> development that not only generates economic growth but distributes its benefits equitably; that regenerates the environment rather than destroying it; that empowers people rather than marginalizing them. It is development that gives priority to the poor, enlarging their choices and opportunities and providing for their participation in decisions that affect their lives.[3]

Despite that definition the Report's Human Development Index shockingly fails to include gender disparities or income distribution. Although the authors have been alerted to that weakness, the creation of *separate* indices in those two critical human development areas continues, leading the reader to conclude that they are peripheral to sustainable human development itself.[4]

The extent to which the human development approach is put into practice or is simply rhetorical must of course be judged on a case-by-case basis, but there is little evidence from major donors that they have consistently and comprehensively included women in their programmes as producers and breadwinners. In countries where debt burdens are high and Structural Adjustment Programmes (SAPs) are in place, even willing governments unfortunately have few resources with which to promote human development.

As mentioned earlier, the global market emphasis has been questioned for its concentration of productive assets in the hands of the few while the majority of the people are marginalized. Moreover the export emphasis has neglected the productive activity that meets the needs of citizens and ignored the importance of building a sustainable national production base. Studies show that the rigorous conditions imposed by the IMF since 1980 for obtaining international credit, such as retrenchment of civil service employment, education and health services, impact negatively on human well-being, and especially so on women. Poverty then multiplies, as will be seen in several case studies in this book.[5]

In sharp contrast, UNIFEM takes a unique approach that starts with the basic assumption that women are central economic actors. Because it pays attention to the dynamics of local economies in which people strive to earn a living, this approach has been called economic democracy. Therein lies UNIFEM's distinction: it promotes productivity in a way that tackles poverty while simultaneously seeking to accelerate growth. Its work toward ending poverty has three dimensions, namely economic productivity, human development and participation in decision-making. By working with women, the Fund provides opportunities to the very ones who invest their income in the next generation. It seeks to gain a wider access to those resources whereby wealth can be produced rather than just redistributed.[6]

Project analysis

Each of the projects discussed in Part II of this book responds appropriately to the three dimensions of the social order that have an impact on poverty.

For the purpose of my analysis, economic productivity projects relate to formal and informal sector employment, including micro- and medium-scale industries, agriculture, sericulture, food processing, animal husbandry, garment production, brickmaking and handicrafts. The current economic adjustments undertaken by many developing country governments are also discussed.

Projects with social justice as their primary concern promote self-reliance and well being. Their principal focus is to increase people's access to the amenities necessary for a dignified existence, often called social or basic needs. Factors that foster human development include education, training, opportunities for health care and employment; those of a community service nature include provision of pure water and fuel, afforestation and sanitation.

Political participation and planning activities involve skills in decision-making, from the household to the national level; ways to gain representation in legislative bodies; training development planners and managers and consultants to formulate and evaluate programmes. In addition, they foster co-operation with others to ensure that a 'women's perspective' is included in macroeconomic planning exercises, such as country programmes and donor round-tables.

Depending on the type of individual project, the activities may be conducted in the civil society or by government institutions, by non-governmental organizations or national machineries. Project components often include technologies and training; some also involve workshops, seminars and the preparation of publications.

In my examination of specific interventions, and using poverty as my overriding concern, I analyse how those dimensions interact not only at the

5

project level but in the arena of macroeconomic policies. In other words, it is impossible to address one dimension without recognizing the effect it has on the others. It is only through an understanding of their interrelationship that we come to understand why women represent the majority of the poor throughout the world, and how strategies can best be designed to address that problem.

Through the examination of specific case studies in a number of different countries, organized within the categories mentioned above, I hope to offer a deeper understanding of what constitutes poverty and to identify some strategies that have proven most effective in alleviating it. As the analysis will show, there exist fundamental conflicts between different development priorities and strategies which must be faced if we are to develop more effective ways to deal with the issue of poverty.

Because the best of project interventions can fail when external forces intervene, I have recorded in this text the physical, economic, political and social environments in which people actually live: those that constitute the manifold causes of poverty at every level. It is necessary to take the broader environments into account, even those that are external to a particular country, because the trends within those areas have often caused the further marginalization of women, of low-income countries, and of certain population groups within countries. Therefore, women themselves, or gender for that matter, should not be considered in isolation, although a number of studies have done just that.

To determine the Fund's impact on poverty, my final analysis is based on three variables: empowerment, sustainable institutions, and innovative and catalytic effects.

Empowerment

Empowerment is defined by community workers as 'the state of persons (women and men) being enabled to take their destiny into their own hands'.[7] Empowerment came into the women and development vocabulary in the mid-1980s, championed by the women's group DAWN–Development Alternatives with Women for a New Era.[8] Personal autonomy, also called self-reliance, is at its core because women, the poor, and numerous nations in the developing world have limited abilities to exercise autonomy by making choices in political, social and economic arenas. Empowerment has three elements: first there is the economic one, namely access to productive assets such as land, credit and technologies that can produce income. The second aspect is human development, augmented by access to basic needs such as education and health services, pure water, fuel and shelter. The third element is participation in decision-making.

Any programme or project must have elements of both the empowerment of its participants and the sustainability of its organization's strength if it is to be effective; I use both as variables in assessing UNIFEM's assistance.

6

Sustainable institutions

As empowerment is to individual strength, sustainability is to organizational strength. The term 'sustainable' means here that the organizational or institutional aspects of a project or programme have the capacity for self-reliance and endurance.[9]

Strengthening local/national groups and institutions and contributing to non-governmental organizations' autonomy in the civil society are among the most important methods of promoting development, and also the most challenging to achieve. It is much more likely that water pumps will fail, seeds will arrive late, and markets will collapse after the donor departs if, as too often happens, institutional sustainability has been neglected. As Robert Chambers said: Without an organized power base, and without outsider's support, the rural poor remain vulnerable'.[10]

Noeleen Heyzer, UNIFEM's Director since 1994, identifies the need for strong grassroots organizations as a major sustainability issue and she deplores 'differential access of men and women . . . especially to newly created organizations and channels of decision-making.'[11]

To enhance their sustainability, UNIFEM has provided organizational support to various types of women's groups: women's bureaux of governments; 'traditional' professional and/or service-oriented NGOs; worker-based organizations; non-profit advisory groups; co-operatives; grassroots groups; and research organizations. While most are local or national organizations, some are global, and many have worldwide network affiliations. The primary objective of my country visits described hereafter was to gain greater insight regarding the issues of sustainability. How could it best be achieved?

Innovative and catalytic effects

Another element of the Fund's mandate that I use as a variable in analysing programme and project interventions is the catalytic and innovative impact of the activity. Use of these terms began at the very first session of the Fund's Consultative Committee and they were re-interpreted during the decade that followed. In 1987, Deputy Director Olubanke King-Akerele of the Fund Secretariat defined innovative and catalytic activities as 'those which open or strengthen women's access to 'mainstream' resources and other involvement in shaping the future of their societies'.[12]

UNIFEM made it clear that it is difficult to know in advance whether or not projects will actually stimulate women's mainstream participation, and to estimate whether they will be adopted by other sectors or continued or replicated by other donors. With that having been said, some criteria for selecting innovative and catalytic projects were identified. My own assessment is aided by analyses undertaken by the UNIFEM secretariat, and by the excellent monitoring and evaluation data that are available on projects assisted.

During my travels to the various projects, I sought the answers to four questions about UNIFEM assistance over the twenty years since it was created. These questions are:

- Did UNIFEM reach poor women?
- Did UNIFEM enable women to empower themselves?
- Were activities sustainable, building institutions and organizations that survived and thrived?
- Was UNIFEM innovative and catalytic, influencing policies and attracting other resources to women?

CHAPTER TWO
Women Create a New Scenario

Development is a process which enables human beings to realize their potential, build self-confidence, and lead lives of dignity and fulfillment . . . It is a process of self-reliant growth, achieved through the participation of the people acting in their own interests . . . and under their own control. Its first objective must be to end poverty, provide productive employment, and satisfy the basic needs of all the people.

Report of the South Commission, 1990, p.13

IN THE MID-TWENTIETH CENTURY, fifty-four newly self-governing countries joined the world community and colonialism became history. The anticipation of independence re-enlivened women's earlier experience of leadership and aroused their hopes that they could join men in shaping their new nations. Having personally shared in that sense of expectation as two new countries–Kenya and Tanzania–came into being, and having learned about others, I am convinced that neither the women and development concept nor the movement itself can be understood outside the context of the independence and post-independence period.

This chapter traces how the movement arose as an indigenous one, firmly grounded in women's past history and integrally tied to national development struggles in many countries. Several global influences converged to propel it forward, and while it was evolving in many countries, the Africa region became the pioneer in giving the women and development movement an institutional framework in the United Nations.

Origins of women and development: four factors interface

As the initial decades of independence were ended in 1970, four factors interfaced to transform the international community's perceptions of development; they constitute the foundation for the concept, and later the movement, called 'women and development'. Coming as it did in the second half of the twentieth century, that convergence took place during a period of massive global change highlighted by the following:

(1) Multiplication of the number of member states in the United Nations as colonialism was relegated to history. Both women and men joined United Nations delegations, bringing developing countries' perspectives to that body.
(2) Disillusionment with the modernization theories of the 1960s, with their industrial models and GNP goals of development that had been widely expected to 'trickle down' and thereby benefit whole societies.
(3) Clear and convincing evidence of women's centrality to productive

processes and thus to the economic as well as the social progress of the developing nations.

(4) The rebirth of the women's movement in industrial countries at a time when those countries were giving plentiful aid to developing nations and which, with political pressure, could support women's interests and concerns.[1]

An examination of each of those factors reveals how it contributed to the women and development concept and movement.

Multiplication of UN member states

Thirteen colonies became independent in the 1950s, and another forty-one in the 1960s as the colonial period halted abruptly after World War II. The membership of those new countries transformed the UN into a democratic and global body.[2]

Women were among the new delegates and they brought to the General Assembly, ECOSOC, and other bodies their first-hand experience in efforts to stimulate economic growth and social progress in their countries. The Commission on the Status of Women (CSW), for example, had six representatives from developing countries in 1960 and nineteen in 1969. These delegates influenced the CSW and other UN agendas, by speaking in ways seldom heard before in the UN. They told of women farmers, merchants and entrepreneurs, and spoke of women as the backbone of rural economies. Aida Gindy, who worked both at ECA and UN head-quarters during that decade, speaks of the 1960s as 'the initiating years' for women.[3]

Some of CSW's studies and reports show how its perspectives evolved over time. At its sixteenth session in 1963, CSW reported as a general consensus of opinion that 'there were sufficient facilities and programmes available to provide the assistance needed to further advance the status of women'.[4] Having added women from developing countries to its membership after 1963, CSW's 1969 study of replies from 65 governments about the participation of women in national economic and social development, showed that many countries were interested in women's participation in community development but 'they did not know how to achieve that effectively'.[5]

Evidence of further change can be seen in 1970, when CSW approved and sent to the General Assembly a 'Programme of Concerted International Action for the Advancement of Women'. That document set objectives and minimum targets for the advancement of women in the Second UN Development Decade, the 1970s. The draft of the Programme had languished since the early 1960s.[6] In the view of Helvi Sipila, who was a member and one-time Chair of CSW, the change had come about as a direct result of the presence of women from developing countries.[7]

Women's participation in United Nations deliberations reflected their long and rich experience in their own countries, dating back decades and even centuries. In every area of the world the pages of history are replete with accounts of women as leaders, decision-makers, and innovators of

10

new systems and organizations. What they reveal is that the roots of women's activism in the late twentieth century are embedded in the lives and stories of Asian, Latin American, Middle Eastern and African women of the past. Women and development flowered from that rich soil.[8]

From glimpses into history, it can be seen that women were well prepared for the next step in the twentieth century–the women and development concept and movement. Some case histories of the rise of the movement come from the present-day accounts of African women.

As their country's independence approached, Kenya women, led by Margaret Kenyatta, daughter of the future first President, organized two national seminars in 1962 and 1963, and an East Africa regional seminar in 1964. Asked thirty years later why she did it, Kenyatta replied:

> We organized to make women realize that they had roles to play in their independent countries, and they could organize to seek ways and means to train and educate themselves to become useful citizens for the development of their young, free nations. Women in East Africa began thinking that we could do something to assist development. African women were meeting everywhere. Before that, we had no contact because we were under colonial rule, and we had no right to meet as African women.[9]

The keynote address at the first Kenya seminar is also illustrative of the indigenous origins of the concept. Pumla Kisosonkole, a South African living in Uganda, had this to say:

> These days, the cry of the 'role of women' is being heard in Africa from East to West, and from North to South. What is the answer for East Africa? It is this: times have changed and are changing very fast, and woman must change with them in order that she does not become the 'forgotten factor' and in order that she will be ready and willing to play the fullest part in shaping the destinies of her country.[10]

Mabel Mulimo of Zambia explained how independence fervour was transformed into gender consciousness:

> The women's movement has been growing gradually from the time of the struggle for independence, though in those days it was just known as nationalism; gender was not an issue. But gradually the women's movement started agitating for an improvement in the situation of women. By 1971–72 we began to make our voices heard and government responded.[11]

Further evidence of women's mobilization during the independence period was the All African Women's Conference (later called the Pan African Women's Organization), that held its first meeting in Tanganyika in 1962.

For Phoebe Asiyo, who worked with Kenyatta in planning the early 1960s seminars, the dates are critical:

> This notion that we picked up the women and development issue from

11

western women is not at all true. It was here before 1968 (when feminism was revived in the West). You can't remove those dates.[12]

Ideas of contemporary women's roles in economic development were stirring in other regions as well. In the 1960s and early 1970s, for example, women's issues became important again in the Philippines, and this time their economic contributions were underlined. It was within the big thrust toward rural development, said Mary Racelis, that 'women and development' arose. People began to realize that women were playing economic roles but those roles needed to be recognized. Josefa Francisco added that in the 1970s development was promoted in the form of huge programmes like the Green Revolution and urban settlements, as well as through basic services and family planning.[13] Indian women pressured their government to form a National Committee on the Status of Women in 1971; the movement from a welfare to a development approach in that country's development plans is reflected in similar evolutions in other countries.

Disillusionment with industrial models
The second factor that made the women and development concept and movement possible was the failure of imported development paradigms. The notion of 'national development' and the practice of development co-operation as we understand them today began with the sudden increase of concern among the victorious nations of World War II for the countries that emerged from colonialism in the 1950s and 1960s. Expecting to duplicate the success of the Marshall Plan in reconstructing severely war-damaged European countries, US President Harry Truman launched the 'Point IV' programme in 1949, to transfer that experience to low income countries.[14]

Point IV offered American technical resources (not capital), to the new countries that were at the time called 'underdeveloped'. It posited that poor countries' poverty resulted from a technical backwardness that could be easily remedied by technical assistance from the West. Without dwelling on the causes of the socio-economic condition of the new nations, President John F. Kennedy, in his inaugural address, spoke to their need for justice:

> To those peoples in the huts and villages of half the globe struggling to break the bonds of mass misery, we pledge our best efforts to help them help themselves, for whatever period is required–not because the communists may be doing it, not because we seek their votes, but because it is right. If a free society cannot help the many who are poor, it cannot save the few who are rich.[15]

Despite Kennedy's compassion and eloquence, the motivation of many people in western nations was the fear that they would not be safe while poverty prevailed in poor countries. Even more threatening was the assumption that the poor countries would be charmed by the dreaded communism. It was thought that a flow of resources from the West would make countries immune to such a fatal attraction.

The early theories of development that devolved from the 'technical

12

backwardness' concepts of the Truman and Marshall Plan era gave way to a subsequent set of theories on how to stimulate economic growth and end poverty in the former colonies. Further external investment would be needed–this time financial–to put poverty into recession. By the time that the United Nations named the 1960s 'The Development Decade', as proposed by President Kennedy, it was believed that growth in the gross national product (GNP) was the primary means of ending poverty.[16] Therefore, the theory went, the formerly colonized countries were to industrialize, using capital-intensive technologies that in time would produce a 'take-off'. This approach to stimulating growth through finance featured both domestic saving and monetary inputs from the assisting countries. Such investment was presumed to create wealth and effect its distribution because benefits would 'trickle down' to the poorest people.

Even while capital-intensive industrialization was the overriding thrust of 'modernization' or 'dual economy' theories, other ideas were emerging in the UN as the struggle against poverty continued. At the UN Economic Commission for Africa headquarters in Addis Ababa, Ethiopia, Executive Secretary Robert Gardiner (Ghana) envisioned a new and complementary approach. He called for 'multiple small-scale investments . . . of a labour-intensive type . . . small- or medium-scale industries geared to national consumption patterns, and transportation and communications links between the farmer and the consumer.'[17] It would take nearly a decade, however, for Gardiner's foresight to be widely understood and implemented.

Keretse Adagala described women's response to modernization theory in the years immediately following Kenya's independence:

> The first Kenya development plan was about industrialization. Somehow women were supposed to benefit from 'trickle-down' effects. But it didn't trickle down. So women fell back on what you would call the sister organizations in society. It was a further struggle against colonialism in that it was a struggle against neo-colonial policy. Women sat and said: 'Wait a minute! How are we going to benefit from *uhuru* (independence)?' By about 1965 there was a spontaneous movement all over the country. Women built houses, grew crops to sell . . .[18]

At that time, 'under-development' or 'neo-marxist' theories were being proposed, mainly from the Latin American experience, by scholars such as Paul Baran and André Gunder Frank. The most important was the 'dependency' theory, which held that global capitalism operated to *under-develop* the Third World.[19] While most poor countries were politically independent, the theory said, they remained economically bound to and thus dependent upon the trade channels and systems set up during the colonial era. Even though it made no mention of women, the action plan founded on dependency theories–the New International Economic Order (NIEO)–would enter the women and development movement in the mid-1970s.[20]

Yet to be considered within the context of these major development issues was the preponderance of women in productive activities, such as agriculture, food security and trade, and their school-building and other community-based actions. In fact, the theories of the time gave scant attention to any human factor in development.

A UN organ that would eventually contribute to the undermining of modernization theory was the Commission on Social Development (CSD) that, like the CSW, reported to the Economic and Social Council. CSD members Ruda Mohamed of Nigeria, Lucille Mair of Jamaica, Inga Thorssen of Sweden and James Riby-Williams, observer and Chief of ECA's Social Development Division, were among those who urged the Commission to give greater consideration to women. The competition that was stimulated between CSD and CSW increased the influence that Third World women had on CSW, which helped to lessen its heavily legal emphasis and to make room for development concerns. By 1969 the CSW was looking for expertise in the development field and invited CSD to co-operate in organizing seminars and country studies to advance the status of women.[21] That CSD was also influenced can be seen when, in the following year, the key roles played by women became central to its discussions on popular participation.

As interest in promoting small- and medium-scale enterprise, farm to market linkages, people's development of their own communities, and women's participation in development gathered momentum in the United Nations system; the United Nations undertook a comprehensive review of all the efforts of the 1950s and 1960s, the first Development Decade. The review confirmed that, even when growth happened, it failed to fulfill its proponents' expectations that benefits would raise the standard of living for the poor. 'Underdevelopment' was beginning to be seen as far more complex than a technical plus financial approach could remedy.

The global search began for alternative paradigms to replace the failed economic growth model. That search intensified during the meetings held to prepare the International Development Strategy for the Second United Nations Development Decade, in the 1970s. UN Secretary General U Thant led the critics of the First Decade, and Government delegates agreed that the GNP-directed strategies not only failed to 'trickle down' but often worsened the situation of the poorest peoples. The CSD added that GNP–a strictly financial indicator–was an 'inadequate measure' of development.[22] Parallel with and influencing those concerns were the tensions and fears arising from the increasingly rapid population growth and the earth's finite capacity to sustain it.

As a result of the deliberations, the International Development Strategy for the Second Development Decade identified the ultimate purpose of development as: 'to bring about sustained improvement in the well-being of the individual and to bestow benefits on all'.[23] Gloria Scott from the Social Development Secretariat proposed an addition to the resolution that encouraged the 'full integration of women in the development effort'.[24] It was a phrase that would reverberate for decades. Women's programmes would thrive on this radical change in theory, from industrial growth to human equity (called populism), because women as women and their

14

sustained well-being were not at that time part of the development agenda.[25]

As the decade of the 1970s progressed, different dimensions of the new emphasis on human beings would be spelled out, including the 'absolute and relative poverty' concepts of the World Bank's Robert MacNamara and the 'basic needs' strategies of the International Labour Organization. The latter called for sufficient food, clothing, clean water, shelter, health care, employment and self-determination for all. Women's productive labour and domestic work were recognized in the ILO Strategy and rural women were singled out and identified as being overworked rather than underemployed.[26] Furthermore, peoples' well-being, once achieved, would lessen the possibility of a population crisis; healthier children would undoubtedly mean fewer children.[27]

Evidence of women's centrality to productive processes

The third interfacing factor that formed the foundation for the women and development concept and movement was factual evidence of women's productive roles. Anecdotal knowledge of women's economic activity in peasant and in 'modern' societies was abundant, but systematic data and research on their work in agriculture, trade and commerce were still scarce in the 1960s. This knowledge gap was filled in a timely way by the publication of the landmark volume *Woman's Role in Economic Development* by Danish economist Ester Boserup.[28] The potential for considering women, along with men, as human resources for development was greatly strengthened because Boserup was the highly respected author of *Conditions for Agricultural Growth* and was an adviser to the UN Secretary-General on Development Planning. She assembled hard data that defined women's critical yet usually unacknowledged economic activity. Boserup warned that the introduction of new agricultural technologies to men and the migration of men to towns for wage employment had induced 'a new sex pattern of productive work . . . for better or for worse . . . The whole process of growth would be retarded if women were deprived of their productive functions', she said.[29]

In the context of the industrial orientation of development theorists at that time, and of the largely welfare-driven assistance being provided by the UN to women, Boserup's revelations and commentaries were revolutionary. They clearly and indisputably situated women as critical to productive–as well as reproductive–processes and so to the economic and social progress of developing nations. Examples of Boserup's compilation of data are in Table 2:1 entitled *Work input by women and men in agriculture in some Asian countries*.

The value of *Woman's Role in Economic Development* was grasped immediately by United Nations' women; among them was Aida Gindy of the Social Development Division who had met Boserup in Africa. The UN soon provided the concept and movement of women and development with a political and organizational framework. First to take action was the Social Development Division at United Nations headquarters. By eliciting a request from the Commissions on Social Development and on the Status

15

Table 2.1: Work input by women and men in agriculture in some Asian countries

Country in which sample villages are located	Percentage of women in family labour force in agriculture	Average hours worked per week on own farm:			Percentage of work in farm performed by:		
		by active female family members	by active male family members	female hours as percent of male hours	active female family members	active male family members	hired labour of both sexes
Western India[a] { A	32	16	33	48	17	50	33
{ B	39	19	35	54	14	57	29
{ C	21	18	27	64	20	56	24
Central India[b] { A	27	15	29	52	6	21	73
{ B	40	20	30	67	7	20	74
Southern India		31			25	37	38
Delhi territory		7	17	45			
Malaya[a] { A		9	14	68			
{ B		30	43	70			
Philippines	21			50	13	69	18
China[b], average	30			41	13	72	15
Northern China	27			58	9	75	16
Southern China	31				16	69	15
of which: sub-region with multi-cropping of paddy	42			76	30	62	9

[a]The A sample refers to a village with one annual crop of paddy; The B sample refers to three villages with multi-cropping of paddy. The farm families were smallholders and both men and women had much wage-labour in addition to their work in own farm.
[b]The figures refer to the period 1929–33.

Source: Ester Boserup, 1970 Women's Role in Economic Development, New York: St. Martin's Press.

of Women, Gindy was able to plan an Expert Group Meeting in 1972 to 'advise on broad policy measures regarding women's role in economic and social development'.[30] The major working document for the Meeting and its report were prepared by Boserup. ECA's *Five-Year Programme for Women* (see below) was appended to the major document as a guide to practical actions on the subject of the meeting.

The Chair of the sessions was the respected Princeton University economist and UN Development Planning adviser Sir Arthur Lewis, who was at the time the President of the Caribbean Development Bank. Inga Thorssen, former Director of Social Development, returned as the Swedish delegate and was joined by Aziza Hussein (Egypt), Annie Jiaggie (Ghana) Vida Tomsic (Yugoslavia), Mina Ben Zvi (Israel), Leticia Shahani (Philippines) and Elizabeth Koontz (USA), among others. I was the ECA Observer. The meeting was 'the first occasion on which experts on development and those on the status of women came together to discuss common strategies to achieve effective integration'.[31] It was in fact the first global meeting on women and development.

Evidence was now building worldwide that women were more than mothers and wives; they were also productive workers, farmers, merchants and community mobilizers. Because of their multiple roles, in the home and in the economy, women would be key to every effort to break the cycle of poverty.

Rebirth of the women's movement in the West

The fourth and final factor in the foundation for the women and development movement was the rebirth of the women's movement in Western countries. While this new feminism reflected and reacted to discrete cultures, it fostered a readiness to support women's interests in other societies as well. Western women began to pressure their governments to extend development co-operation resources to women as well as to men. An example had been set by Sweden's Thorssen, who, after an Africa visit, inspired her Parliament to enact legislation as early as 1964 that mandated government support to women in foreign assistance programmes.[32] Thorssen also persuaded her government in 1969 to finance the two posts at the UN Economic Commission for Africa which would have the responsibility for designing a women's programme.

In the United States and other Western countries the revitalization of the women's movement was energized in 1968 when Betty Friedan's book *The Feminine Mystique,* published in 1963, reached a wide audience.[33] Three years after the 1970 convergence of the Western feminist movement with the other factors mentioned above, American government employee Mildred Marcy persuaded Senator Charles Percy to introduce an amendment to the US Foreign Assistance Act. Once passed, the Percy Amendment mandated USAID to give 'particular attention to integrating women' in projects they financed. Prior to that, US Women's Bureau staff members Mary Hilton and Kay Wallace had visited the ECA Women's Programme in Addis Ababa in 1972. We discussed with them the possibility of the US Department of Labor supporting ECA-designed programmes on national commissions on women and development and women's bureaux–an assistance that was soon provided.[34]

The efforts of many women, such as those mentioned above, and Western feminism itself thus facilitated the availability of financial and human resources for research, training, technical meetings and innumerable other development interventions favouring women. In addition, they contributed to a sense of solidarity among women throughout the world.

That overview delineates the key historical factors that interfaced in 1970 to create the 'women and development' concept, and later the movement. It is portrayed in Table 2:2. Several features of the origins merit reiteration. One is that women's concerns were, and still are, tightly interwoven with the political, social, and economic trends and events of a given time. Another is that, at the time when the development and the women's agendas converged, the latter had deep historical roots in developing countries. It cannot be said, therefore, that the women and development agenda was simply a clean slate waiting to be filled by the Western women's liberation movement. The final feature to be remembered is that the movement was given a political and organizational impetus and framework by women working in and with the United Nations. In the words of Lucille Mair:

> I give great credit to the United Nations. It helped. It provided the political and organizational framework for the international feminist movement at a fundamental stage of its development.[35]

A pioneering centre in the United Nations

Africa was the first of the developing regions to create a comprehensive Programme and a Centre for women and development within the UN framework.[36] There, the new seeds–woman's roles in economic development–fell on very fertile soil, prepared since the early 1960s when the UN Economic Commission for Africa (ECA) based in Addis Ababa, Ethiopia, sought to integrate social planning with overall development planning, both urban and rural. Among its activities in member states at that time was a regional conference entitled 'Urban Problems: the Role of Women in Urban Development', in 1964.

A total of eight regional conferences took place in Africa under UN auspices during the decade of the 1960s. Those gatherings were sponsored by ECA or in conjunction with UN headquarters and with others such as the German Foundation for Developing Countries, the Swedish International Development Authority (SIDA) and UN agencies.[37] Concurrent with them was the study on the 'Status and Role of Women in East Africa' that Boserup later used. The study credited women with carrying a major portion of the economic burden, and cited the great part they played in independence movements. Despite these facts, it found that only a few ECA member countries involved women in the early days of their community development programmes.[38]

The resolutions adopted by women's conferences in the region contained

18

concerns that the failure to acknowledge and support women's economic and social activities in their families, communities and nations had a negative effect on overall productivity and allowed opportunities for development to be missed. Whether one was a pragmatist or a humanist, women's participation was necessary for development to succeed in Africa.

Based on those findings, ECA established its own 'Women's Programme' in 1972 and began to speak of women as Africa's 'neglected' human resources.

Giving women access to development resources was thus aimed to benefit 'not just women but the nation as a whole' in the words of James Riby-Williams, the ECA official who most strongly supported the Commission's work with women.[39] That holistic approach to issues made confrontation with men undesirable. An understanding of the dire effects of poverty was yet another fundamental building-block for the concept of women and development that would form the basis for a women's programme.

Forty 'Country Womanpower Studies' that had been requested by the Rabat Conference in 1971, provided the information for 'The Data Base for Discussion on the Interrelation Between the Integration of Women in Development, their Situation and Population Factors in Africa'. The Data Base was a major milestone among documents on low-income women and was the first ever to set out a regional perspective. Its popular version: *Women of Africa Today and Tomorrow*–was the most quoted booklet on women of the first half of the 1970s[40] Another source of background data for the women's programme was the study 'Towards Full Employment of Women in Ethiopia', the first of its kind to be included in a Full Employment Mission by the ILO.

Armed with the indisputable evidence contained in those documents, ECA prepared its first operational document on women 'The Five Year Programme on Pre-Vocational and Vocational Training of Girls and Women, Toward Their Full Participation in Development, 1972–1976'.[41] It was soon adopted by ECA's Conference of Ministers.

The Five Year Programme included research and training projects in five major areas: modernization and its impact on rural women; women in wage employment; self-employed women in marketing, industry and the services; pre-vocational and vocational training of school-leaver girls; and national planning with women as resources for development. Those areas were chosen because 'few women had access either to the skills or to the resources to do their work most effectively, most usefully for themselves, their families and their countries'.[42]

Agricultural production was Africa's paramount concern, and over 90 per cent of the female labour force lived and worked in rural areas. With heavy male out-migration from farms, women's dependency ratios rose; production became more difficult. Under such circumstances, training women to meet the challenges of rural life became the highest priority of the Programme. ECA Executive Secretary Gardiner clinched the matter: 'There is no point in teaching our women to embroider pillows with "sweet dreams"', he said, 'when the malaria mosquitos won't let our people

Table 2.2: Where did women accomplish it first? A comparative time-line of South, North, and United Nations action

Year	The South	The North	The United Nations
1962	1st Kenya Women's Seminar All Africa Women's Conference: 1st regional organization		
1963		*Feminine Mystique* written	
1964	East African Women's Seminar	Sweden: legislation mandates assistance to women	
1965			ECA study on women and development
1968		Western feminism movement launched	
1970		Ester Boserup writes *Women and Economic Development*	
1972			ECA: 1st regional UN Women's Programme UNHQ: 1st global meeting on women and development
1973	CARIWA: Caribbean Women's Organization	USA Legislation: the Percy Amendment mandates assistance to women	

20

1975	ECA: African Training and Research Centre for Women International Women's Year Conference, Mexico City UNIFEM legislation: 1st UN Development Fund for Women INSTRAW legislation: 1st UN Research and Training Centre for Women
1976	Association of African Women for Research and Development (AAWORD)
1978	Association for Women in Development (AWID) USA
1979	1st global feminist meeting, Bangkok
1980	2nd global Women's Conference: Copenhagen
1982	Dakar Conference of women in the South
1984	Development Alternatives with Women for a New Era (DAWN)
1985	3rd global Women's Conference: Nairobi
1995	4th global Women's Conference: Beijing

sleep'.[43] By 1977, rural training workshops had been held in 22 countries, and ECA had broken new ground by asking host governments to allow NGOs to nominate one-fourth of the trainees. This was exceptional in a United Nations system that concentrated almost exclusively on governments.

Micro-enterprise had been identified as an area of concern in the employment sector of the Five Year Programme. Again, there was little documented information available, despite the fact that women represented 60 per cent or more of the traders in many West African markets and engaged in trade in other countries as well. Field surveys provided an analytical basis for examining the issue and designing technical and training programmes.

In the planning sector of the Five-Year Programme, a package of activities was designed to promote the establishment of government machinery, especially national commissions on women and development, plus their permanent secretariats or technical women's bureaux.

Reflecting later, Terry Kantai, the first head of the Kenya Women's Bureau, said that the seminars 'made a great impact in terms of sensitizing and training women in leadership positions'. She described the Women's Programme as 'a vital source of data and information, and a sustained contact which contributed significantly to ongoing leadership growth'.[44]

During the early 1970s, the Women's Programme drew many partner organizations into its work, to the extent that Dr Marilyn Carr, who was financed by the Intermediate Technology Development Group (ITDG) of the UK, remarked that it was the 'only genuine inter-agency programme' she knew. By the end of 1974, the Women's Programme had a strong intellectual, programmatic, financial and administrative foundation, plus the support of government officials and non-governmental leaders in the member states of ECA. In its brief life, the Programme achieved the readiness to become a full-fledged Centre. The African Training and Research Centre for Women was established on 30 March 1975. In recent days it has been renamed the African Centre for Women (ACW). A former staff member summed up the Centre's significance:

> I think the greatest strength of ATRCW is its position at the heart of the UN Regional Economic Commission for Africa. It can speak with a tremendous amount of authority . . . It can cite the backing, the support of member States. It can speak in the name of the United Nations, and from both of those bases, it has a tremendous amount of access and credibility.[45]

Initial concepts and an international model

As the ECA Women's Programme matured to become ATRCW, a new impetus for the global women and development movement was provided by the UN Commission on the Status of Women. CSW proposed to proclaim 1975 International Women's Year (IWY) and to hold a global conference to celebrate it. As a model institution for the women and development movement, including the Asia and Pacific Centre for Women and Development, ECA/ATRCW was cited time and again at international meetings as preparations gained momentum for the century's path-breaking event, the Mexico Conference of IWY.

The UN was becoming the political and organizational vehicle for the women's movement for several reasons. It had worldwide outreach; more women now served as their countries' diplomats at the UN; and women NGOs, diplomats, and a tiny group of women who were international civil servants at headquarters and worldwide, formed a unique, trilateral partnership. All of them understood that the freedom and well-being of people, called development, could not be achieved unless women's lives were transformed.

Global interdependence: a shifting agenda

Even as women prepared for their first global assembly, international development theory and practice were subjected to political and economic events. Countries of the South pointed out that despite its many merits, the International Development Strategy for the Second Development Decade, the 1970s, had neglected macro-economic issues. They then called for a New International Economic Order (NIEO). Doubts were expressed about the sincerity of the basic needs theory, which appeared both to distract attention from broader economic issues and to shift 'second-class technologies' on to the poor.

In the latter 1970s, poverty, equity, human development, basic needs *and* the NIEO were shoved off the global agenda. Western strategic self-interest took precedence over the productivity and well-being that characterized President Kennedy's appeal to justice and the East-West conflict became the context for development assistance. Military expenditures soared in both rich and poor countries. For example, the industrial countries expended 4 per cent of their GNP on the military; that was ten times more than they gave as official aid to the 'third world'.

Complicating the scene for the developing countries were the early oil price shocks that led them to borrow money on private and public international markets; the population growth that slowed per capita growth; the new oil price shocks of 1979–80 that led industrial countries to cut back on imports from poorer countries; and the downturn of the global economy. Then, in 1980, the World Bank and the IMF set stabilization and structural adjustment programmes (SAPs) as conditions for further loans to developing countries. As one result, the 1980s saw a reversal of net transfers with more money going from South to North to pay debts and debt interest than from North to South as development assistance to the poorer countries. Low income countries were repeatedly advised to adjust to the global market, a move that was effective for some but disastrous for many.

The Western strategy of promoting the 'free market' that was a feature of the calls for adjustments exacerbated the effects of the plummet of prices of developing country exports. Those events contributed to what has been called structural poverty, i.e., there was no room for millions of people either in the 'traditional' or the 'modern' sector. That would seem to have been reason enough to create a development fund for women but to add to

23

that imperative, research on the social impact of the stabilization and adjustment policies began to recognize their social costs, especially to women.[46]

If the 1980s were the lost decade for development, they were surely intensely so for women. In 1985, women of the world said: 'The critical international economic situation since the end of the 1970s has particularly adversely affected developing countries and, most acutely, the women of those countries.'[47] It was during those years of global economic uncertainty that UNIFEM would be created and begin its work.

CHAPTER THREE
A Unique Fund for Women

UNIFEM started the women and development issue in our region. We never would have survived without UNIFEM. It was the first to open the way.

Miriam Krawczyk, ECLAC, Santiago

FIVE YEARS AFTER the women and development concept had reached the UN's global agenda in 1970, a fledgling women and development movement came into being in Mexico City at the World Conference of the International Women's Year, 1975. The movement's financial instrument was to be the Voluntary Fund for the UN Decade for Women (VFDW, later renamed the UN Development Fund for Women or UNIFEM). During that decade, 1976–1985, while projects were being supported in countries worldwide, there was a protracted controversy over the Fund's nature and location. That dispute, however, did not distract the staff from putting policies, procedures and systems for reaching the poorest women into place or from putting pressure on the UN General Assembly and the UN regional offices to appoint women as programme officers. The Fund successfully rode through the political storms and established firm foundations for its new life after the Decade for Women.

At the IWY Conference, women from all of the world's regions and countries met each other for the first time and shared ideas, experiences, and hopes. IWY also marked the beginning of the UN's role as principal advocate and guardian of the global women and development movement. One thousand two hundred delegates from 133 countries attended that first inter-governmental women's meeting; its parallel NGO Tribune drew another four thousand women.

There was much to agree on in Mexico despite profoundly differing views on the scope of the women and development concept.[1] Delegates spoke of the conditions of women in rural areas, of poverty, popular participation, and of women's need for access to financial credit lines and grants. They described women's central position in their countries' economic and social life, and how their concerns were being institutionalized in the public and private sectors. National machineries, such as women's bureaux and ministries of women's affairs, were already established or in the process of being established to promote government policies favouring women. Recommendations on such issues were set out in the Declaration of Mexico, the World Plan of Action and a number of resolutions adopted by the Conference.[2]

Participants brought with them a great deal of evidence showing that most of the existing planning and development co-operation organizations and funds had not served women well. The outreach from those funds to the grassroots and to the poor communities where most women lived and

25

worked was severely limited. As a result, the huge amount of productive work performed by women in agriculture, fuel supply, self-help community improvements and the like, remained nearly invisible to most development co-operation organizations. On the occasions when women were recognized by developers, they were seen almost exclusively as mothers. As a result, they were offered services like maternal and child health care and training for home economics which, while necessary, were in no way sufficient to make it possible to reach national development goals.

Delegates were very specific. Women were actually farmers, merchants and entrepreneurs and should be recognized as such when national decisions were made and resources were distributed. The momentum of the African Training and Research Centre for Women, the World Food Conference and the Population Conference of 1974, and the Mexico Conference itself, had to be maintained. All of the analyses led to the same clear conclusion: institutions were needed to assure that women's concerns were placed permanently on national and international agendas; otherwise, those concerns would fade in the aftermath of the Conference.

A two-pronged approach was devised to meet that goal. The first was to target and challenge existing funds, foundations and agencies across the private, multi- and bilateral spectrum to 'make deliberate and large-scale efforts' to ensure that high priority was placed on giving women the skills, training and other opportunities they needed to improve their situations and to participate fully and effectively in the total development effort.[3]

Attaining that goal–getting a fair share of development resources for women–would prove to be an elusive task. The effort would stimulate a continuing flow of impressive rhetoric from heads of development agencies, but only a trickle of real support for women during the next decades.

The second approach was to create new, women-specific institutions that would ensure a long life for the movement. In the quarter-century since the Commission on the Status of Women held its first session in 1946, no new global institution in the UN system was assigned specifically to women. It was clear that in the development co-operation field, and in that of research, new institutions were necessary. They had to be empowered to provide assistance directly to women and to serve as catalysts for generating institutional transformation in the overall UN and in other international development co-operation systems.

Dr. Shirley Summerskill, head of the UK delegation, expressed the sentiments shared by many:

> There is evidence that women have not always benefited from changes introduced in the name of development and, indeed, that their position in relation to men has sometimes deteriorated. A positive effort is needed to redress the balance: not only constant vigilance to ensure that women share equitably in growing prosperity but also a more dynamic approach to widen the options which are open to women and to involve them more fully in the destiny of their countries.

Summerskill added:

It is because we attach so much importance to providing additional resources for women who live in the rural areas and in the poorest countries that my Government has decided that it is in principle prepared to contribute to the UN, subject to the consent of Parliament, £200 000 a year for three years beginning 1 January 1976 . . . We shall wish it to be used specifically to help women in the poorest countries, and especially rural women . . . We hope it will be used in particular for small, innovative 'grassroots' activities.[4]

Princess Ashraf Pahlavi of Iran generously offered another US$500 000 for such a fund. She then added $1 million for a research and training institute for the advancement of women and $500 000 for an Asia-Pacific Centre for Women and Development similar to that of ECA.

Stimulated by the financial offers from the UK and from Princess Ashraf, the delegates at Mexico City took swift action to correct institutional deficiencies. They proposed a special fund for the period of the Decade for Women 1976–85. That action would bring the Voluntary Fund for the UN Decade for Women (VFDW) into existence. They also moved to create another multilateral institution: the International Training and Research Institute for the Advancement of Women (INSTRAW). Two non-governmental organizations were also proposed at Mexico: Women's World Banking and the International Women's Tribune Centre.[5]

Delegates included certain provisos in the World Plan of Action:

Special measures should be envisaged to assist governments whose resources are limited in carrying out specific projects or programmes. The Fund for IWY established under ECOSOC Resolution 1851 (LVI) of 16 May 1974, in addition to multi- and bilateral assistance which is vital for the purpose, should be extended provisionally pending further consideration of its ultimate disposition in order to assist governments whose resources are limited in carrying out specific programmes and projects.[6]

The drafters of the Conference Resolution, entitled Special Resources for the Integration of Women in Development were led by Mr Chris Gerard and Dr Teresa Spens of UK.[7] When those delegates learned that there would be money left over in the IWY Trust Fund that had financed the Conference, they requested the Secretary-General to transform that fund into a development fund that could then attract additional voluntary contributions from governments. Resolution 12 of the Conference contained those recommendations.

Despite a letter from Summerskill to Sipila, nothing had materialized when the General Assembly met at its Thirtieth session in September of 1975. The sponsors of Resolution 12 were advised that procedural difficulties and the pressure of work had delayed the secretariat's action. However, after representatives of the UK, US, Sweden, and Iran consulted with Sipila, the General Assembly (GA) made the decision to extend the International Women's Year Trust Fund for the period of the Decade for Women, 1976–1985, and asked the Secretary General to make the report on the Resolution available to the Economic and Social Council.[8] In the following year, the GA delineated the criteria and management mechanisms for the Fund, and adopted them in its resolution 31/133, entitled Voluntary Fund for the UN Decade for Women (VFDW). See Annexe 1.[9]

The mandate given to the Fund in that resolution left no doubt that its resources were intended for the poorest women in the poorest countries. The monies were to supplement activities designed to implement the goals of the UN Decade for Women: Equality, Development, and Peace. Giving priority to the least developed, the land-locked and island countries, the Fund would finance: technical co-operation activities; regional and international programmes; inter-organizational programmes; research, data collection and analysis relevant to the preceding activities; and communications and public information activities relative to the goals of the Decade for Women. Special consideration would also be given to programmes and projects that benefited rural women, poor women in urban areas, and other marginal groups of women. Recognizing that the Fund would need an operational system, delegates added that the Secretary-General was to consult the Administrator of the UN's central development funding organization, the UNDP, when using the Fund for technical co-operation activities.

Management of the Fund was placed with the UN Comptroller, although the day-to-day activities would be administered by the UN's Centre for Social Development and Humanitarian Affairs (CSDHA) which had planned the Mexico Conference and administered the IWY Trust Fund. CSDHA's Branch for the Advancement of Women served as the secretariat to the Commission on the Status of Women and its Social Development Division backstopped the Commission on Social Development.

Thus the Fund in its initial conception had a complex bureaucratic system of operations: approvals had to be gained from the Director of BAW, the ASG/CSDHA, and the USG/DIESA, and all of their finance officers. Located in the CSDHA/DIESA that was financed from the 'regular budget' i.e., the assessed contributions of member states, it was seen by some to be easy prey to the recurring needs for supplementary money for those activities, rather than for activities in developing countries.

The Resolution that created VFDW also created a unique system for inter-governmental guidance. Five member States would be selected by the President of the GA to advise the Secretary-General on the application of the criteria for the Fund's use. Those States would appoint representatives to serve on the Consultative Committee (CC) on the Fund, with each member representing all of the countries in his or her geographical region. The five regions were those commonly considered by the General Assembly, namely African, Asian/Pacific, East European, Latin American/Caribbean, and West European and others.

This unusual Committee came to serve as a protective buffer between the Fund secretariat and the bureaucracy; it also provided a way for educating members of the General Assembly about the work of the Fund and thereby helped to raise contributions to it. Technically, the Committee was only advisory; actually, it could mobilize the whole General Assembly on issues. More than one person who came before it judged the Committee to be a 'nice small group' of five (mostly women) but then experienced its power in the General Assembly at a later time.

The effectiveness of the Committee would later be recognized by Under-Secretary Shuaib Uthman Yolah, who said 'the Consultative Committee's efforts played a critical part in creating the positive image of the Fund'.[10] Among the many reflections on its excellence was the recognition that the Fund was 'an innovative force for sustained international assistance to women in developing countries'.[11]

Policy development and the search for structure: three principles

At the first session in March 1977, the Consultative Committee members included Dr Lucille Mair of Jamaica and Leticia Shahani of the Philippines, who was selected by her colleagues to be Chairman/Rapporteur. There were also representatives of the German Democratic Republic, Nigeria, and the United Kingdom. Members reviewed the history of the Fund's creation and studied its mandate. They considered that the mandate to advise the Secretary-General on criteria should be interpreted 'in the widest possible sense' and should include advice on the screening, appraisal and selection of projects to be funded, as well as on the amounts to be allocated to those projects.[12]

The Committee then adopted three principles:

○ First, responsibility would be decentralized, because the United Nations regional commissions in Asia/Pacific, Africa, Latin America/Caribbean and Western Asia were 'in the best position to know the needs of their respective regions.'[13]

○ Second, the Fund would be a catalyst. 'In spite of its small size, the Fund should serve as a catalyst for carefully selected specific projects benefiting women in the developing countries.' It should be 'a supplement to and not a substitute for' other programmes undertaken within the UN system on behalf of women.

○ Third, high priority would be given to field projects, to be sure that 'the poorest women in the least developed, landlocked and island developing countries' would have priority on the Fund's resources.

The Fund was thus set on a pre-determined course to fight poverty. The strong guiding principles that continued to evolve both enhanced its functions and kept it from being submerged in political quagmires.

A pattern of decentralization

In those early discussions on the overall philosophy and systems of the Fund, the Consultative Committee, conscious of ATRCW's focus on poverty, emphasized the importance of involving the UN Regional Economic Commissions (RCs) in every stage of the process, starting with their taking responsibility for defining each region's own priorities. Even proposals made by the Centre for Social Development and Humanitarian Affairs were referred to the Regional Commissions for comments. This arrangement evidenced the tensions that were building up between the CSDHA secretariat and the Committee over the use of the Fund.[14]

The Committee advised that bloc allocations be awarded from the more than two million dollars, including the interest, that remained in the IWY Trust Fund after the Mexico City Conference bills had been paid. Each regional commission would get an allocation of US$400 000, to be transferred on the basis of acceptable project requests. There would be $300 000 for CSDHA, some of which was already committed to a national study on social development indicators undertaken by the UN Research Institute for Social Development (UNRISD), to publications like *Law and the Status of Women,* and to summary copies of the global and regional *Plans of Action for the UN Decade for Women.* Consultant Danielle Bazin (Haiti) would be employed to design the operations of INSTRAW. After the bloc allocations, nearly $100 000 still remained available for contingency cases. At the same time, other field-oriented UN agencies were encouraged to assist in identifying the country-level projects that would be submitted to the RCs for review and forwarding to headquarters.[15] Thus every possible step was taken to ensure a 'grassroots' approach to project formulation in order to reach the poorest women most directly.

Empowering the system: regional and headquarters staffing and management

In the view of the Consultative Committee, technical co-operation required appropriately qualified and experienced personnel at both regional and headquarters levels. The first to be examined were the UN regional commissions. Aside from ECA, it was found that they were not appropriately staffed to take on the innovative responsibilities delegated to them; another drawback was that among all of the Commission staff, only a few women were employed at senior professional levels. The Fund had to make an early commitment to strengthen the Commissions' capacity to deal effectively with women and development activities. The outcome of that commitment was the creation of a strong institutional framework for the women and development movement at the regional level that has lasted nearly two decades.

The fact that productivity-enhancing resources had not previously reached poor women showed the need for a new technical specialist, the senior women's programme officer (SWPO). The position called for a person trained in a development field, such as economics, sociology, agriculture or communications, and who also understood the nuances of programming for and transferring skills to women. The Fund therefore financed a full-time senior women's programme officer in each Commission for an initial period of two years, as proposed by the Committee at its second session. The programme officers were to be recruited 'from among women of the region'. Members stated firmly that this action 'should not be regarded as a precedent for budget support in an area of programme activity for which the commissions have mandated responsibilities.'[16] In other words, the regional commissions were expected soon to deploy their own posts to women's programmes.

A year later, in September 1978, the United States earmarked a contribution to VFDW for a second senior women's program officer in each region for two years. A forerunner of the snags that would often entangle such appointments came when ECLA forwarded to UNHQ the résumé of its candidate–a man. It was 'consistent with UN staff regulations' said ECLA, that the sex of the staffer not be a condition for appointment. Several cables later, and with our reference to the lack of women in senior–or any–professional posts at the Commission concerned, the matter was amicably resolved and a woman was appointed.

I have always believed that, if it had done nothing else, the Fund's contributions toward creating women's programmes at the regional commissions would have justified its existence. ESCAP said as much when reporting to its regional conference in 1984:

> Over the years, among the scant resources available for development programmes for women, the largest contribution has come from the VFDW.[17]

Miriam Krawczyk of the Economic Commission for Latin America and the Caribbean expressed the view of many when she told me in 1993 :

> UNIFEM started the women issue in our region. We never would have survived without UNIFEM. It was the first to open the way. Now it is 'legal' to speak about women. But when we started in the 1970s UNIFEM was absolutely essential.[18]

The Fund played an essential role at ECA as well, leading the General Assembly movement to pressure the Executive Secretary to appoint a permanent Chief of ATRCW. Mary Tadesse explained:

> Everybody knew that the permanent appointment would give a lasting place to the Women's Centre at ECA and would make it difficult to tamper with. I believe that UNIFEM too was anxious that its generous grants benefited a stable, self-sustaining programme.[19]

Experienced management

UN Headquarters in New York, where the Fund was located, also needed specialized staff who were experienced in working with development co-operation with women. During the Third Session of the Consultative Committee, 1977, members Balogun, Mair, Shahani, and Spens advised that a senior post be created and strongly recommended my appointment to the ASG/CSDHA and I took up the post in May, 1978.[20] A second professional post, also paid from the resources of the Fund, was filled in March 1982 by Liberian economist Olubanke King-Akerele, who literally stepped off a plane and into a UN conference chamber to serve as Secretary to the Consultative Committee.

Junior Professional Officer Kyo Naka was initially paid by his government (Japan), then in 1985 became a member of our core staff.

Obviously, such a small staff could not possess all of the technical knowledge that was necessary to appraise and monitor the hundreds of requests that came to the Fund. As I will discuss in more detail later in this book, we identified specialists in technology, forestry, agriculture and other areas who were working with UNICEF, UNDP, and NGOs, to enlist their help with project appraisals. Thanks to Administrator Bradford Morse, we were also able to borrow UNDP staff who were between assignments, to help us prepare for the Consultative Committee.[21] Even with the technical problems resolved, however, the sheer quantity of work was daunting. Requests had jumped to 175 a year and ongoing projects rose to 200 between 1980 and 1982.

We finally got action, thanks in good part to Akerele's workload study: *Programming Elements and Staffing Requirements for 1983.*

Projects
> 172 project proposals were processed
> 204 ongoing projects were monitored and serviced

General, project related communications
> 193 incoming interoffice memos
> 196 outgoing interoffice memos
> 654 telexes
> 438 incoming memos
> 388 outgoing memos
> 250 responses to queries about the fund
> 1000 revolving loan fund books sent out

Finance-related communications
> 42 interoffice memos
> 22 cables prepared for UNDP transmittal
> 50 other finance-related communications

Other indicators
> 147 interviews with visitors, potential users, donors
> 31 meetings with representatives of Permanent Missions
> 46 national committee/NGO meetings

Preparation of reports
> Documentation for the eleventh session of the Consultative Committee

In addition, there were record-keeping requirements, resource mobilization responsibilities, information activities and official missions.

Figure 3.1: *VFDW Secretariat Workload: January–June 1982*

She showed the professional work-months in four units, namely, management, the project cycle, administration/finance, and information; the heaviest workload fell within the project cycle. Her study confirmed that the workload demanded and resulted in an unreasonable amount of overtime for professionals (unpaid), interns, and secretaries. For 1983 we proposed a staffing pattern of five professionals for the VFDW coordination office.

Workload indicators for the six-month period January–June 1982 are cited in Figure 3.1 because they are not atypical of a women's office in a large bureaucracy.

We finally got the needed staff when the Administrative Management Service (AMS), reviewed the data and agreed with our view that a serious risk to the efficiency of the Fund was posed by the prevailing workload.[22] AMS credited the 'dedicated and hard-working group of staff' with achieving 'a great deal, with relatively little resources'.[23] and recommended immediate appointment of two additional project officers. This had the full support of the then head of UN Administration, Kofi Annan.

The Senior Women's Programme Officer quagmire

As the number and complexity of projects supported by the Fund continued to expand, the policy of decentralizing functions to the regions continued to be part of the very determined effort of the Fund to respond to the needs of the poorest women. But it was time for political action. Under the aegis of the General Assembly, the Consultative Committee pressed the regional commissions to support women's programme officers from their own regular budgets. Commission officials protested, however, that if the posts were to be discontinued it would be impossible to adequately compensate for their absence 'without running the risk of jeopardizing the overall programme of work'.[24]

VFDW ceased financing Women's Programme Officers in 1984 when two posts each were finally financed from the regular budget allocations of ECA and ECLAC and one each of ESCAP and ESCWA; the Secretary-General made temporary arrangements through 1985. But contracts were often still limited to two years. This meant that valuable resources continued to be wasted in efforts to maintain the posts and to ward off threats of discontinuation. The uncertainty of their tenure left the women's programme officers on the look-out for secure positions every year or so. Unfortunately, at least two of the commissions were in countries experiencing civil unrest, which further complicated life for the staff and made the task of hiring personnel even more difficult.

Over the course of six years, five General Assembly Resolutions urged the regional commissions to give priority to resolving the question of senior women's programme officers and to ensure that all posts would be maintained with regular budget resources. All of these Resolutions were initiated by the Fund's Consultative Committee, in the interest of sustaining the regional capacities to serve and lead their member States.[25]

Unlike most funds, VFDW was supposed to be an experimental and innovative risk-taker; the average value of its national-level projects was US$85 000 in 1982 and rose to $100 000 in 1985. Deliberate risks, however, required staff to monitor the projects closely. Clearly, VFDW was caught on the horns of a dilemma: its financial resources were too modest to justify large expenditures on staffing; yet, it had to invest staff time on small- and medium-scale projects because they were experimental. The Fund's effectiveness as a catalyst depended heavily on establishing a track record that would produce substantial growth.

As an illustration of the different weight given to discrete entities in the United Nations in terms of staffing patterns, the contrast between VFDW/ UNIFEM and UNFPA is striking. UNFPA started with six employees, not one, and three of them were senior.[26] UNFPA then financed other staff to represent population interests within many UN organizations, and helped to create whole Divisions in the regional commissions.

The difference between the two funds related in part to the fact that the mission of VFDW was unique. The donors to the fund, and we women ourselves, did not envision how many resources are required to effect profound social change. The potential women's lobby has always understood the need for economic empowerment of grassroots women but has as yet not carried that concept to global level.

At this writing, UNFPA and UNICEF, with their large-scale budgets, have proven that the policies and practices of governments can be changed when adequate resources are provided.[27] Although this book testifies to UNIFEM's positive impact throughout the world, the Fund has never had the human and financial resources to operate on the scale that its mission actually calls for.

Donors to the Fund and to other multilateral funds were very resistant to what they judged to be 'disproportionate' expenditures on staff. The fact was that VFDW was only using 4 per cent to 7 per cent of its resources for 'overheads' while other funds expended up to 13 per cent or 14 per cent.[28] The intention of placing a ceiling on overhead costs is logical and good: a maximum amount should reach field projects. Yet, as senior official Dudley Madawela (Sri Lanka) said when reviewing the work of the Fund: 'the volume of administrative, substantive and managerial activities of a fund depends not so much on the level of resources as on the number of projects

Table 3.1: Ratios of projects to staff at three United Nations Funds

Fund	Projects:staff
VFDW	102:1
Capital Development Fund (CDF)	33:1
UNFPA	22:1

to be serviced'.[29] See Chapter 5. We calculated the ratios of projects to staff for VFDW and other funds as shown in Table 3.1.

Not only were our resources severely constrained, but the proposal to move the VFDW staff to Vienna, where CSDHA had relocated, provoked tensions about hiring at headquarters. Yet the numbers of ongoing projects and the number of newly submitted ones had jumped by 67 per cent and 70 per cent respectively in the years 1980–82. Despite that expansion, CSDHA was asserting that there was an overload of VFDW staff at UN headquarters and it was reluctant to create more posts in New York.[30] At this critical juncture the Consultative Committee took action. As I will discuss below, they found it necessary to take up the matter in the political forum, the General Assembly, in order to pressure DIESA/CSDHA into favourable action.

The issue of human resources was influenced by two other factors. First, we were seeking to transform established institutions into inclusive organizations–teaching elephants to do ballet, so to speak. That fact was not reflected in accounts that simply stated 'four senior women's programme officers including travel to the field'. Such accounts give no hint of the investment toward gender equity that was under way. For example, in the UNECA, of 169 professional staff in 1980, only ten were women.

Second, as I have discussed, we were developing a new specialization–women and development. If existing staff had been prepared intellectually and with practical skills to include women appropriately in their activities, there would have been no need for special SWPOs. The fact is that women were not included, and that special, long-term efforts had to be made by women at senior level to effect those changes. The SWPOs, like ourselves at headquarters, were working at policy, programming and project levels wherever they were assigned. Obviously, not all of their activities had 'project outputs'; rather, they were investments in creating an institutional capacity for change.

From time to time donor governments, like the Americans, the Dutch, the Canadians and the Norwegians, actually saw the need and contributed special resources for temporary posts. These were most appreciated, but short-term solutions. They did not solve the underlying problems for the personnel whose contracts would soon expire; their minds were on their security and future employment, especially when they had children to support, as women so often do.

Given those difficulties–and many others–I must say once again that the women who filled the SWPO posts in the regions, initially Daw Aye at ESCAP, Vivian Mota at ECLAC, Thoraya Obaid at ESCWA and Mary Tadesse at ECA, and the staff who serviced the Fund at headquarters, were not just qualified, they were very special committed people.

A distinctive role for the fund: as catalyst

The second of the three principles that were spelled out for the Fund at the first session of the Consultative Committee related to VFDW's role as catalyst for change. The meaning of 'catalyst' underwent a continual evolution during the first several years of operations as the Fund adopted procedures and practices designed to fulfill its mandate. Periodically reviewing policy while considering project proposals, the Consultative Committee underlined VFDW's distinctive role as catalyst in the UN system, and added that it should have policies and standards of its own that were flexible enough to reach a new target group–low income women.

When the Consultative Committee met for its fourth session in 1980, we summarized the guidelines that were already in place to protect and enhance that role:

○ a limit of up to US$50 000 from the first allocation to the regional commissions would be placed on research other than that which was directly related to the planning or evaluation of particular projects and programmes

○ United Nations inter-organizational meetings should not be supported by the Fund

○ scholarships and fellowships were not to be funded when these already existed and should be made available to women as well as men

○ working capital for small-scale projects could be funded through provision of revolving loan funds

○ a recipient government was expected to make a substantial contribution to a project, in cash or in kind

○ equipment and supplies could be funded when these were an integral input within a project

○ buildings and fixed capital assets were not usually funded.

Further defining VFDW's role as catalyst, the Committee found that VFDW monies were particularly suitable for:

○ innovative or experimental work that might, if successful, later be funded from other sources

○ small projects that might not be acceptable to larger funds, by way of the 'flexible funding' arrangements through headquarters and the regional commissions

○ when it was important to supplement other work with a minimum of delay, without waiting for the negotiations that precede a second phase of an ongoing project.[31]

In reviewing these guidelines, one can trace the enlargement of the Fund's original mandate. Some of the language of the 1980 Consultative Committee statement–for example 'innovative and catalytic' would reappear in 1984 in the General Assembly decision to create the continuing, autonomous Fund that came to be called UNIFEM.

Over time, the meaning of the term catalyst was broadened. In 1981, it was used in the sense of attracting additional financing to projects the Fund initiated. That year, US$4 million was contributed by the UN Sahelian

Fund, the UN Interim Fund for Science and Technology, and a non-government organization, Volunteers in Technical Assistance (VITA). The money went to three of the Fund's ongoing projects in the Sudan and the Sahel that promoted afforestation and fuel conservation through improved-stoves technologies. Shortly after, UNDP committed $500 000 to the Eastern and Southern African Management Institute (ESAMI), which had not only brought the subject of women into the general curriculum but was running the first phase of a management training programme for women under a UNIFEM grant through ECA/ATRCW.

In the following year, the catalytic role of the Fund was extended further: to use monies for projects which, if successful, should become self-reliant or be duplicated or extended by governments or other organizations. That dimension itself was broadened to include 'co-financing' of approved projects by donor countries and efforts to attract the attention of policy-makers.

As a result, during 1982, UNDP integrated the Fund's project on educational materials for a women's extension programme in Bahrain into its own large education project. Co-financing was found for community development in Oman and refugee training in the Philippines. A rural health project, initiated by ECLA in Bolivia, resulted in a new national policy and strategy to the year 2000. Micro-enterprise projects in rural production in Honduras, soya milk production in Nicaragua, rural employment in Thailand, tailoring in Tanzania, sea salt in The Gambia and fuel-saving stoves in Mali and Niger were all co-financed by other funds or adopted by UN, government or voluntary agencies.

In mid-1984 the Fund's role as catalyst was expanded yet again. VFDW's special expertise in the women and development field would increasingly be made available through programming missions to governments, multi- and bilateral agencies; the purpose was to ensure that women were appropriately involved. The institutions receiving that assistance ranged from the World Bank, to regional development banks to non-governmental organizations.

That programming aspect of its work became one of the most effective approaches because it was rooted in the Fund's extensive field experience. Staff from the Fund were welcomed on programming teams because of the expertise they shared and because they were seen as being able to generate financial support for projects. In other words, the Fund was seen as a participant as well as an adviser, and that was the source of its clout. On this subject, I cannot agree with those who would turn UNIFEM into an advisory service or specialized agency and leave the project financing to UNDP and IBRD, or with those who say that UNDP should finance UNIFEM. To have power, UNIFEM must control substantial resources of its own.

UNIFEM's expanded role as catalyst for change became one of the two dominant elements when its mandate from the General Assembly was revised in 1984.[32] (See Annexe 2). 'The resources of the Fund shall be used mainly within two priority areas; first, to serve as a catalyst, with the goal of ensuring the appropriate involvement of women in mainstream development activities, as often as possible at the pre-investment stages.' The second priority was related: 'to support innovative and experimental activities benefiting women in line with national and regional priorities'.

Olubanke King-Akerele summarized the usage of the term catalyst in a document for the Consultative Committee entitled *Innovative and Catalytic Projects: Criteria for Their Selection,* in 1987.[33] On behalf of the Fund secretariat, she described catalytic activities as those 'which open or strengthen women's access to "mainstream" resources and other involvement in shaping the future of their societies'. Her basic premise was that UNIFEM should continue its flexible approach to programming and project selection. At the same time, some criteria were arrived at. Projects should demonstrate:

○ an element of newness in a given location or with a certain target group

○ potential for providing an opening to mainstream activities

○ a scale of activities that encompasses a large or representative segment of the population

○ a potential to influence policy to give necessary consideration to women's conditions and needs

○ potential to enhance the organizational and absorptive capacity of women's groups and associations

○ potential to enhance the self-reliance of women

○ the existence of appropriately oriented leadership and a participatory approach to project design

○ dual impact, i.e., increase productivity while lessening burdens.

In 1988, I asked one of our Junior Professional Officers to review 136 UNIFEM-assisted country and regional projects that had been approved between April 1985 and June 1988, to determine quantitatively the amount of resources leveraged by the Fund. UNIFEM had attracted nearly double its own investment to its projects. US$17 million had been leveraged over the three-year period, and another $5.6 million was expected (and received) within months of the publication of the paper *Initial Findings: UNIFEM's Catalytic Role in Attracting Financing from Other Sources.*[34] The latter contributions included: a Danish donation of $4.2 million to establish a credit scheme for the productive activities of women in Tanzania, UNIFEM's largest-scale project at the time and one that moved it to the new position of financing large-scale projects in its field of competence; a contribution of $1 million from ZONTA International, the women's professional organization, that was the largest non-government contribution ever to be received; and an unprecedented $277 000 from a national committee–the Finnish National Committee for UNIFEM.

The general categories of leveraged support appear in the Table 3.2. Those figures do not include the output of programme and project development missions that the Fund undertook or to which it lent its

Table 3.2: Funds leveraged by UNIFEM: 1985–88*

Contributions received	Millions of US$
Projects which were initiated by UNIFEM and adopted thereafter by UNDP	7.6
Co-financed projects with inputs from other UN agencies	4.1
Earmarked contributions from donor countries	5.7
Earmarked contributions from NGOs	1.6
Contributions from national governments and NGOs involved in the project	<u>4.3</u>
	23.3

*In addition to open-ended contributions from governments and other sources.
Source: UNIFEM/CC22/INFO.12

specialized expertise. There were 18 such missions in 1983, 30 in 1984 and 80 in 1987, as seen in Figure 3:2. Their yield included a $668000 Business Advisory Service for Women in Malawi and a $2.7 million, four-country credit programme, both financed by UNDP.[35]

The chart also excludes the output of the Fund's programming work with Round Table exercises, National Assessment of Technical Co-operation

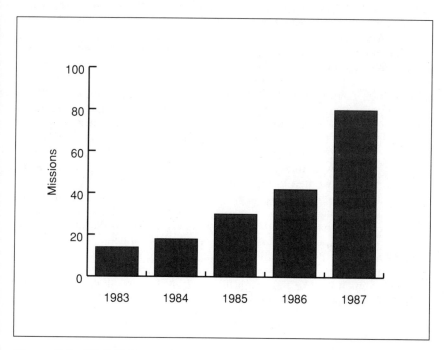

Figure 3.2: *UNIFEM transforms planning missions with governments and donors*

Assistance Programmes (NATCAPs), country programming and national development planning, which became a very important component of UNIFEM work. There is no question that the funds attracted from other sources multiplied the value of UNIFEM's inputs.

Margaret Mwangola, the Director of the Kenya Water for Health Organization (KWAHO), testified to the Fund's catalytic role during our interview in Nairobi in 1993–a decade after UNIFEM assisted her organization with sociological and community training work. 'The UNIFEM funding gave us status in the donor community world and has opened doors for us in numerous places, including other UN agencies', she said.[36] There are, no doubt, innumerable other groups for which UNIFEM performed the 'door-opening' function because it dared to take risks. In the case of KWAHO, we reviewed a somewhat discouraging evaluation of its early work, but then decided to contribute an amount that was relatively large for an NGO–$153 000–that included assistance to sharpen the organization's management skills. That investment proved to be positive.

That UNIFEM was fulfilling its catalytic role was proven on a daily basis during my years as its Director. Our staff worked closely with colleagues in the UNDP regional bureaux and in ILO and FAO, who often became interested in the projects and persuaded their organization to contribute to or adopt them. Other deliberate efforts to exercise the Fund's catalytic role were made when UNDP Resident Representatives (country officers) visited headquarters and sought appointments with us, and whenever Parliamentarians and NGO representatives came as delegates to the General Assembly.

A seldom recognized outcome of UNIFEM's role as catalyst is the placement of its former staff. Our Deputy Director King-Akerele is among the top nine staff at UNIDO. Other former staff and consultants are now employed as country Resident Representatives/Co-ordinators for UNDP. At the time of writing, one-third of that group are former staff or frequent consultants of UNIFEM; however, there are just 12 women among 119 Representatives.[37] Our short-term staff and JPOs have joined other UN and voluntary organizations as well. If UNIFEM was fully budgeted for its mission, one can well imagine that its service as a training ground would bring many more women to high posts in the UN system and elsewhere.

Even at its current, modest size, UNIFEM's unwritten policy of using national and regional experts whenever possible (rather than costly international experts), has paid off handsomely. We followed that policy *as a means to create experts from among the women*, as happens in networks of men. Thus, a very positive side-effect of a women-specific fund, and one that further justifies its existence, is that *its role as a catalyst* allows qualified women to take their rightful place in decision-making positions in large-scale financing organizations.

CHAPTER FOUR

Reaching the Poorest: a Continuing Challenge

Development programmes that fail to pay adequate attention to women's productive activities are not only morally indefensible but economically absurd.

Bradford Morse, Administrator, UNDP

IMAGINE SITTING at a desk at the United Nations headquarters in New York, being assigned to identify, develop and monitor activities that would support women in about 100 countries in their efforts to lift themselves and their families out of poverty. That was my job description.

Three challenges demanded immediate action. First, project cycle systems–procedures for submission, appraisal, selection, monitoring and evaluation–had to be devised and put in place. The fact that there was a fund for women, as well as information on its procedures, had to reach more than a hundred countries. Second was the need to explore ways to increase direct contact with countries and to speed up financial transfers and other supports to projects. Third, we had to reach low-income women where they lived and worked. That would involve reaching out to their community-based voluntary groups as well as to governments. UN development co-operation had no channels to local NGOs as project executing agencies at the time.

Procedures of the project cycle

UNIFEM support was meant to reach women in relation to the needs they themselves identified, and not according to what people at global headquarters thought they needed. Women, however, were not used to articulating their needs in a multi-paged UN project document. I recalled my own painful initiation to UN project-writing at ECA, and wondered how on earth we could expect people with three years or so of schooling to fill out a highly technical UN request form. Two changes were necessary: one in the type of document we used; and the other, in our expectations about written expression.

In March 1979, we published a small pamphlet: *The VFDW: What it is, what it does and how to apply.*[1] It was followed by two others.

A summary of the procedures booklets appears in the box on page 42. We explained that the VFDW forms could be substituted with UNDP's standard forms–an option that was meant to encourage the UNDP officials to assist us, and in particular for use with larger-scale projects.

Speaking of UNIFEM's early publications in 1993, Nancy Hafkin, who had been chief of information at ATRCW/ECA and is now head of ECA's Pan-African Development Information System (PADIS), had this to say:

One of the things which was superb about UNIFEM were the published materials. From the very beginning, it had materials that were easy to

VFDW Procedures Booklets

'Information Booklet 1', published in 1980 contained submissions procedures, criteria, and a flow-chart depicting the procedures for national or regional applications by governments, NGOs, and UN organizations. At the time, proposals could be submitted either through the UNDP country office or the regional commission; they would be reviewed by both in any case.

'Information Booklet 2' of May 1981 guided grant recipients through the process of Project Monitoring, Progress Reports and Project Review and Evaluation. It explained that they should be prepared to submit three types of reports: (i) a Progress Report on both the substantive and financial aspects at six-month intervals; (ii) a Review of the project, or Evaluation Report for a long-term project at least once every two years or upon completion of the project; and (iii) a Completion Report for projects of less than two years' duration.

'Information Booklet 3' contained Sample Projects: National, Regional and Subregional. To assist interested parties, and to make the Fund's work known to potential donors, we published, in quite humble fashion, first a Voluntary Fund Note, starting in November 1979 and later the Development Review. (CSDHA had put out a Decade Note in October 1978 that contained information on both VFDW and INSTRAW).

read, that were attractive, that caught people's attention. I think they were very effective in disseminating the message that UNIFEM was trying to get across.[2]

We had two project cycles annually; thus the procedures shown in Table 4.1 and explained below occurred twice each year.

After 1980, requests for projects could arrive at headquarters from either the regional commissions or UNDP country offices.[3] Of utmost importance were the procedures for appraising requests. UNIFEM was not only new, but it was specifically a women's fund; we could not afford to have many failures. Initial appraisals came from the regional commission or UNDP country office when a project request was forwarded to it. Those appraisals assessed the viability of the overall project and gave special attention to its relevance to the particular national and regional development priorities as well as to the capacities of the proposed executing agency for carrying out the project effectively.

At headquarters we screened the requests, protecting the Fund's unique identity by referring many of them to other funds when we judged them to be inappropriate to VFDW guidelines and especially in order to avoid overlaps. We referred childcare projects to UNICEF; family planning requests went to UNFPA; and refugee concerns to the UN High Commission for Refugees (UNHCR) or to the UN Relief and Works Agency (UNRWA). In the mid-1980s we brought the appraisers together in a

42

Table 4.1: Project-cycle support system

Project-cycle activities	Support system
1. Project Design	UNDP/Field Regional Commission Programming Missions – Regional Commissions – UN Agencies – Technical specialists (usually from region) – Governments
2. Appraisals	UNDP/Field Regional Bureau Regional Commission UN Technical Experts Specialized Agencies Branch for Women
3. Formulation of the Recommendations to Consultative Committee	Secretariat
4. Recommendation by Consultative Committee	
5. Approval	Fund Director
6. Implementation/Reporting	UNDP/Field – Government – NGO – UN Agency Regional Commission
7. Monitoring/Evaluation	Tripartite – Government – Executive Agency – VFDW External (Specialist) In-depth – Regional Commissions – Technical Consultants

more formal system. PACs–project advisory committees–were to discuss the projects and make recommendations to our Fund secretariat. We then set out our proposal to the Committee.

At headquarters, after a project was approved, we started what should have been a simple process, i.e., moving money from UNHQ to a project in a low-income country. That turned out to be an unbelievably bureaucratic, exhausting and inefficient process. Multiple-signed authorizations had to proceed from office to office so that a final authorization (allotment advice) could be issued. But that advice could only be issued to another UN organization, not to a government or a voluntary organization.

Before the year was out I was negotiating to transfer money from the UN to UNDP and thence to field projects. While it was a workable interim solution, it left us saddled with two bureaucracies, each set up for a different purpose. The only long-term solution would be to associate the Fund with a UN organization that was in the business of development and operational activities. For that reason, and to ensure that our funds did not get co-mingled with those of the regular UN budget, the GA finally decided to move the Fund to a new administrative location–UNDP–in 1984. We would have to wait until then to eliminate the UN middleman. Meanwhile, our accounting situation was a bit like having one's feet in two different boats, being unsure whether they could continue in the same direction.

I recalled that one of the reasons for my presence at headquarters was to ensure that financial transfers were moving efficiently to the field. Now we had to take radical action, even at the risk of disturbing some bureaucrats. After the Consultative Committee met with UN finance officials to question an eight-month delay in transfers, Chairperson Rolf Lamerzahl wrote to Assistant Secretary-General Sipila. He urged an early meeting with UNDP on the matter. (See the following section.)

By 1982 we got the financial transfer system down to two to five weeks between my desk and the field office. Efficiency improved even more when

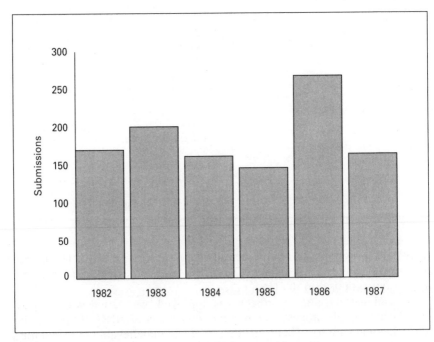

Figure 4.1: *Submissions to UNIFEM for consideration*

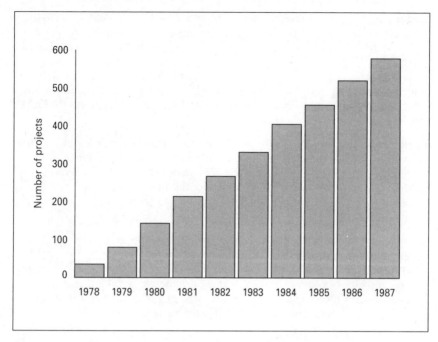

Figure 4.2: *Thirty to six hundred in a decade: UNIFEM's cumulative projects 1978–87*

Akerele and I were given certifying authority to transfer money to projects. The difference between the VFDW and the vast majority of trust funds in the UN was finally dealt with. We no longer heard the disparaging comments of some of our colleagues that the Fund was 'simply a trust fund'; the new directives allowed us to bypass their offices. A glance at the number of projects received and financed over the years provides some understanding of the work that two annual project cycles involved. See Figure 4.1 *Submissions to UNIFEM for consideration*. Figure 4.2 shows the total number of projects funded by UNIFEM from 1978 to 1987.

Some very sticky matters remained in our dealings with the UN finance offices. One was the disposition of so-called 'UN property'. An example was the cloth purchased by the UN to be sewn into shirts during small enterprise training projects. Despite the value added, the completed articles were still identified as UN property and were not to be sold. They could be piled up in a warehouse, however, which they were in Swaziland for some years. Disposing of piglets born of UN-purchased pigs was even tougher.

Towards systematizing the measurement of project results, in the early 1980s Akerele and Janice View, an intern from Princeton University, worked on what we called the Fund's Success Index, that included both cost-benefit analysis and economic analysis of projects. By May 1983 that idea evolved into the Fund's Knowledge Bank which was a method to systematize project-support processes and experiences and to provide a qualitative assessment of the impact of projects, in addition to the usual concern of financing agencies that projects meet their projected, often quantitative, goals.

While retaining the principle of having documents be self-explanatory and not straying too far from the UNDP format, our two consultants, Caroline Pezzullo and Freida Silvert, added unique features to UNIFEM's documents.

○ the expected project results were divided into economic, social, political/policy, information, technological, participatory, and personal. Each of the categories gave examples. For instance, for the economic concerns, the quantitative output would be the increase in income, or savings, or credit/loans given; the qualitative output would be financial awareness and book-keeping skills.

○ to augment the possibility of measuring the impact of a project on a given community (if the project was geographically circumscribed), a community analysis form was provided. This referred to land ownership, crop or other product, type of water and energy supplies, and transport available. Employment, education, housing, health, and the gender division of labour were included in this baseline data.

○ a brief profile of the project participants was included, to get an overview of the age, marital status, size of household, and annual income as a basis for assessing change.

○ *Progress Report* and *Final Report* forms were also revised, to harmonize with the new project document.[4]

Placed in a *UNIFEM Project Manual,* the forms were accompanied by briefs on UNIFEM history, mandates, guidelines, and procedures for project support. Special guidelines were added for three frequently financed types of projects: small-scale enterprise, training, and revolving loan funds. The Knowledge Bank made monitoring and evaluation information accessible through a computerized database.

The UNDP partnership

The regional SWPOs were extremely helpful and I consider them co-founders of UNIFEM. Yet it was evident that the Fund still had inadequate outreach to the least developed, land-locked and island countries, and to the poorest women. By March 1980, when the Committee met for the seventh time, the RCs were asked for input on how the Fund's goals could be better met. Over the next several months it was agreed that the best way would be to involve UNDP's country offices to an even greater extent.

Already mentioned is a second reason for increasing UNDP's role: the Consultative Committee and I were exasperated with the bureaucratic processes of the UN, whose budget systems were naturally geared to salaries, equipment and services at headquarters rather than to the field projects. As an alliance with UNDP would also give us an opportunity to influence that organization, we approached Bradford Morse, the Administrator.

In September of 1980 we reached an agreement in the form of the Memorandum of Understanding between the UN Controller and the UNDP Administrator mentioned earlier. It enabled us to transfer lump sums for specific projects from the UN to UNDP. It also gave UNDP field offices a greater assisting role in the design and supervision of projects.[5] By increasing the involvement of the central funding organization of the entire UN system (UNDP) it became easier to co-ordinate Fund-assisted activities with the wider development effort of the UN and bilateral aid organizations.

A circular from the UNDP Administrator to its more than a hundred field offices instructed such offices on the assistance to be given by UNDP and stressed that the existence of VFDW funds should in no way lessen UNDP's own mandate to support activities of benefit to women.[6]

The agreement took hold rapidly. While in 1980 there were 50 per cent regional and 50 per cent country level projects, by 1981, 77 per cent were country level and by 1983 over 90 per cent of total resources disbursed by the Fund reached women directly in their own countries. In 1987 regional

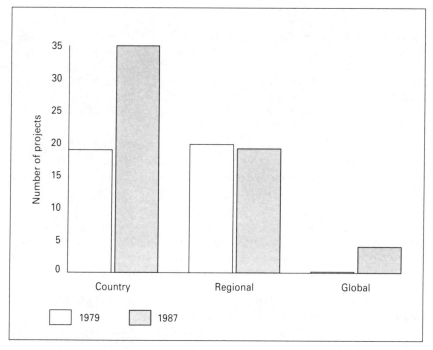

Figure 4.3: *UNIFEM focus on country level: 1979 versus 1987*

47

projects increased, but more than one-third of the projects continued to be country level ones, as seen in Figure 4.3.

There was something of David and Goliath in our strategic position: UNIFEM had only about one-half of one per cent of the resources available to UNDP. And while the Fund was making use of UNDP systems we were also working toward the transformation of United Nations development co-operation processes so that women would gain a more equitable share of resources. In that effort, Dr Ulla Olin of Sweden became our number one partner. She promoted women's interests while serving as a senior UNDP officer.[7]

Olin was a skilled professional and a courageous international civil servant. She was not fearful of finding her organization or the UN system to be less than perfect, nor of saying just that. In 1980 Olin put together an evaluation entitled *Rural Women's Participation in Development*, in which the UN agencies that were working in developing countries concluded that the subject of women was generally overlooked in programmes promoting popular participation in development.

A follow-up Inter-organizational Assessment in Rwanda, Democratic Yemen, Indonesia and Haiti analysed all of the UN support in each country. Its findings were even more discouraging: of $500 million allocated to the four countries, only about 13 per cent was for 'projects designed exclusively for women or designed to include women as well as men'. With characteristic understatement, UNDP found those results 'in some respects disappointing.'[8]

Olin–and the UN Secretary-General–knew of several instances wherein 'projects supportive of women' had been drafted and proposed at country level, but low priority was given them when decisions on the allocation of resources were made. (See Part II: Empowerment in Syria.) Reasons for those circumstances were cited as 'oversight of the economic roles of women, and scarcity of women among planners and decision-makers in aid agencies and governments'.[9] Commenting on that information, the Consultative Committee observed:

> The need for special resources such as those of the Fund to fill gaps, to stimulate change and to demonstrate the value of full involvement of women in development assistance activities thus became clearer.[10]

Our next mutual effort with UNDP was joint programming assistance and it became the subject of another field circular.[11] We sent four programming missions to assess the prospects for reallocating existing project resources that were in projects that UNDP assisted. Vested interests were too strong, however, by the time a project was underway. That less than successful effort became a major influence on VFDW's revised strategy: to send programming missions at pre-investment stages. Such missions became an integral concept of the Fund's expanded mandate in 1984. They were particularly important during UNDP's Fourth Programming Cycle 1987–91 when Africa, where women were the primary food producers, was deep in economic crisis.[12]

The UNDP Governing Council commended UNIFEM's new operational directions, with special reference to its programming approach, and urged the Fund to intensify those approaches to secure mainstream consideration of women.[13] Chapter Ten of this book describes some of the innovative actions taken in response to that mandate.[14]

Olin was replaced in 1987 by Norway's Ingrid Eide, whose approach was more one of advocacy than technical analysis and field action. Upon Bradford Morse's retirement, William Draper II took up the Administrator's post in May 1986 and began to emphasize management over the substantive aspects of programmes. Those two key changes created the need to clarify the distinction between the work of UNIFEM and that of the UNDP's Division for Women in Development. The roles of UNIFEM and the newly created Division of WID (Women in Development) were spelled out by Eide and myself for the UNDP Governing Council. (See box.) In brief:

UNIFEM is operational, as a specialized fund providing financial and technical assistance to developing countries; its catalytic role is with the overall UN system, not just with UNDP.

The Division of WID has mainly management and mobilization functions within UNDP, for reorientating existing resources, including increasing the proportion of women on UNDP staff.

Fortunately, by the time of the changes in personnel at the top of UNDP, co-operation among staff at the operational level (the regional and country offices of UNDP and UNIFEM) was already institutionalized. The Fund had become autonomous, with its own mandate to pursue and its own procedures.

New partners in attacking poverty: non-governmental organizations

Low-income women often work together in mutual aid organizations or solidarity groups in order to meet their personal, family and community needs. They save together in small merry-go-round clubs: they market produce co-operatively; they build roads and schools; and they help each other out in times of need. The trust and management skills they build up over the years in grassroots, self-help groups make them key players in efforts to overcome poverty. Such groups may or may not be formally recognized by governments as NGOs but they are critical to human survival. We had to reach them, either directly or through intermediaries. The latter included traditional women's organizations such as national councils of women, business and professional organizations, associations of university women and others that had international linkages.

UN systems posed certain obstacles to reaching women through their own organizations. UNICEF provides a perfect example. Because of the procedures it established during the 1960s and 1970s, UNICEF's support reached the poorest women mainly through maternal and child health programmes in which women were still perceived as welfare recipients.

49

The Distinct Roles of the Division of WID of UNDP and UNIFEM (4 June 1987)

UNIFEM is operational. As a specialized fund it provides financial and technical assistance to developing countries. UNIFEM's project and programme support is directed to the overall UN system of development co-operation–not just to UNDP.

o UNIFEM's mandate (A/RES/39/125) gives the Fund dual responsibilities to serve as catalyst with the UN overall system of development co-operation (not just UNDP), and to directly support innovative and experimental activities benefiting women, in line with national and regional development priorities.

o UNIFEM as catalyst develops model approaches to the appropriate consideration of women in mainstream activities, on a selective basis. These are shared with other funds and programmes. UNIFEM's financing of innovative programmes and projects makes possible their expansion or replication by others.

The Division of WID, in contrast, has mainly management and mobilization functions within UNDP, for the reorientation of existing resources of UNDP.

o The Division seeks to ensure the systematic consideration of both women and men in the identification, formulation and implementation of programmes/projects funded by UNDP and its associated funds.

o The Division is concerned with increasing the proportion of women among UNDP staff as a whole and their proportion among senior staff; and in training all UNDP staff to consider how that half of populations who are women are addressed within all of its programmes and projects.

In summary, the work of the Division of WID and that of UNIFEM are complementary and mutually supportive.

That perception was very different from UNIFEM's. There was also little relationship between NGOs and any of the development funds or specialized agencies such as UNDP, the World Bank, FAO, and others. The role of NGOs was seen as being 'in consultative status with ECOSOC', rather than as partners in development activities. Local and national NGOs simply didn't exist for most of the UN.

Most UNDP grants went through the UN specialized agencies to the developing countries, although a change had been made to allow direct resource flows to governments as executing agencies. I had long and tedious discussions with UNDP's financial officers in 1979; they said we could not, and I said we must make NGOs executing agencies for projects. After hours and even days of exploring alternative approaches, we adopted the system that UNDP used to finance activities of national governments in developing countries. We extended that system to NGOs, with the proviso that 'government had no objection' to an NGO project. UNDP would now transfer the funds on our behalf.

The impact of that agreement, formalized in the 1980 *Memorandum of Understanding,* was profound. Just 6 per cent of our executing agencies were NGOs in 1979. The figure jumped to 45 per cent in 1983 and 50 per cent in 1985. (See Figure 4.4.) UNIFEM had blazed a trail for the UN system that UNDP, the World Bank and others would follow.

The growing importance of NGOs as a model for the UN system led us to learn more about the effectiveness of their projects. *UNIFEM and Non-Governmental Organizations: a Documentation and Analysis* was a desk study ably undertaken by Sony van Arendonk-Marquez, a consultant from the Philippines. She reviewed the evaluations of 38 projects which had been part of the Fund's Forward Looking Assessment.[15]

The evaluations were scrutinized to find out how effectively NGOs implement projects by comparing them with the performance of other executing agencies. Factors that might account for effectiveness were

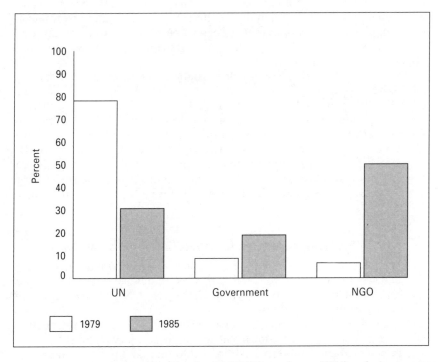

Figure 4.4: *Executing agencies for UNIFEM projects: NGO role increases*

identified. it was determined that 90 per cent of the concerned projects were effective to a good extent. The major reasons for their effectiveness turned out to be participation and leadership.

○ When participants themselves were involved in the formulation of project goals or the design of a project, such a project 'could be expected to be fully effective.'

○ Effective projects showed 'a high incidence of leadership'–a factor just as important as the participation of beneficiaries. Leadership could bring a 96 per cent chance of effectiveness. Male leaders were often important too: 'Where male leaders (who might otherwise oppose a project for traditional reasons) perceive women's contribution to the project as key to overall economic improvement for the community, they will support it'.

○ The inclusion of national or international experts on project staff was associated with effectiveness, whereas projects with only local experts were less effective. (As seen elsewhere in this study, UNIFEM used few international experts.)

The study also found that involving volunteers related to effectiveness, and that the scale of a project (being over or under a grant of US$200000) did not appear to affect efficiency. The largest proportion of effective projects (56 per cent) were NGO-implemented; the next largest (35 per cent), government implemented; and the smallest (9 per cent), joint government–NGO implemented. 'Combining effective and partly effective projects, NGOs scored 95 per cent while governments scored 80 per cent effectiveness.'[16]

UNIFEM continued to keep in close contact with the grassroots through the NGOs because that is where the women are. Some NGOs found UNIFEM 'the only UN organization with a holistic view of women'.[17] The NGO community was also where the fewest external resources were flowing between 1970 and the mid-1980s. Even when other UN organizations, including the World Bank and UNDP, discovered the value of NGOs, innumerable women's organizations did not benefit; instead, resources flowed to organizations that were newly formed, male led and large scale. Part II of this study will describe several NGO projects in detail.

Evolving strategies for operational activities

The challenge of reaching the poorest women was a continuous one and, to that end, UNIFEM had to be flexible in seeking new strategies to enhance its work. That evolution is shown in Table 4.2: UNIFEM strategies for operational activities 1978–91.

As seen in Table 4.2, from its creation through 1979 the Fund sought to strengthen regional and national capacities to assess women's situations and to plan and carry out projects directed to rural and poor urban women. High-level posts were financed for senior regional officers; women leaders

Table 4.2: UNIFEM: Strategies for operational activities 1978–91

	1977–9	1980–84	1984–5	1985–8	1988–91*
1. Thrust	Regional: project approach	National: project approach	Evaluations	Programming approach as framework for operational activities	Sustainability: institution building human development
2. Partners	Regional commissions UN agencies	UNDP Governments & NGOs UN specialized agencies	National & regional experts Governments & NGOs	UN system of organizations governments & NGOs development banks	UN system of organizations Regional development banks economic communities regional centres governments & NGOs
3. Strategies	Regional and sub-regional studies/surveys Identify national institutions, i.e. national machineries/directories Train for project development (sub-regional) Development planning projects	Field projects with specialized agencies Initial projects with national machineries, governments & NGOs Variety of subject areas with economic emphasis	Selection of priority approaches: (1) Influence mainstream (2) Direct support within national & regional priorities (3) Institution building Identification of key substantive areas with universal application Innovative/catalytic	Mainstream pre-investment activities: • Round tables • Country programmes • NATCAPS Regional frameworks: • African investment plan • PAPLAC • APDEV Substantive areas with universal application: (1) Food technologies (2) Credit facility (3) Management systems	Catalytic and innovative support through: • Strengthen *national institutional capacities* of sectoral ministries, national machineries, NGOs including self-help groups: • *Human resource development* through management training, apprenticeships, etc. • *Direct support to projects* within regional frameworks

* See Workplan: Operational Activities for the Biennium 1988–9

53

were trained for programming and project development; and publications on development methodologies were disseminated.

From 1980 to 1984 the Fund action moved more directly to individual countries. Support went to innovative and catalytic projects that were in harmony with national development plans and had the potential to become self-reliant. On request of the Consultative Committee, cross-regional priority needs of women began to be identified: food cycle technologies, energy resources and credit systems were the first. To ensure appropriate technical backstopping for these, economist Marilyn Carr and credit specialist Tekkie Ghebre-Medhin were brought on UNIFEM's staff.

The Forward-looking Assessment that was completed in 1984 and the advice of the Consultative Committee would sharpen the Fund's focus; thereafter it would seek to influence mainstream resources and institutions so that women would both gain from the large-scale funds and have voices in setting priorities at all levels. In addition, direct support continued to go to women through projects they identified; institution-building (government and NGO) was emphasized for the purpose of sustainable development. Those goals and strategies, confirmed in General Assembly Resolution 39/125 of 1984, led us to a programming approach.

The programming approach looked at UNIFEM's work holistically rather than as a collection of 'projects'. As a result, UNIFEM's top priorities combined those expressed in specific regional plans of governments and those of women themselves. The programming approach provided a policy framework for the Fund's investment in a particular region.

The first of the regional priority programmes was the Africa Investment Plan. Adopted in 1984 after consultations with the Africa Regional Co-ordinating Committee and ECA/TRCW, it made Africa's main priority its own–food security–and found its roots in women's contribution of 60–80 per cent of the agricultural work on that continent. AIP was in accordance with the *Lagos Plan of Action for the Economic Development of Africa: 1980–2000*, that had been adopted by heads of state and government through the Organization of African Unity. The *Lagos Plan* had a complete section on women. (AIP is discussed in Chapter 10 of this book.)

The policy framework for Latin America and the Caribbean was designed by outstanding women of the region–Carmen Barroso (Brazil), Magdalena Leon de Leal (Colombia) and Rhoda Reddock (Trinidad and Tobago)–whose approach was to study the extensive literature on women and then discuss priorities and strategies with policymakers in government agencies and NGO leaders in fifteen countries. Their report had four sections: a policy framework based on analysis of the main issues that emerged; a presentation of the interrelationships between government and non-government actions; a programme of action with objectives, priority actions and administrative structure. It also contained a regional profile with basic data on employment, education, health, legislation and the media. The document, entitled *Participatory Action Programme for Latin America and the Caribbean (PAPLAC)* was published in September

1986[18] and was implemented immediately. PAPLAC's priority areas were four:

○ Rural women in agricultural production, fishing and agro-industries

○ Women in the urban informal sector, in particular domestic service, cottage industries and independent or family trade

○ Violence against women, and

○ Communications systems.

The conceptual framework and strategy for Asia was designed at a UNIFEM Think Tank in Chiang Mai, Thailand, early in 1988 and published as the *Asia and Pacific Development Strategy (APDEV)*.[19] The working documents that were considered by the representatives of NGOs, governments and international organizations in the Asia/Pacific region included the Report of the 1984 Tokyo inter-governmental meeting for the World Conference to Review and Appraise the Achievements of

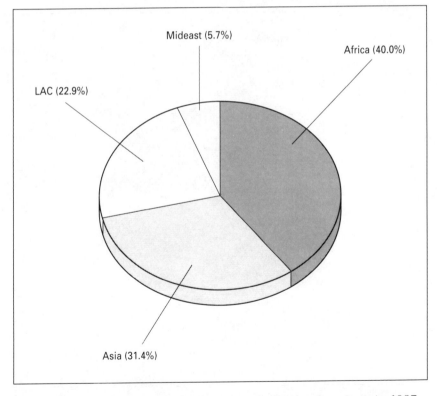

Figure 4.5: *Where UNIFEM funds went: country level projects in 1987*

the UN Decade for Women, and the Policy Statement of ESCAP at its forty-third Session in Bangkok in 1987.

The overarching programme priorities of APDEV were:

○ The human resource development of women

○ The participation of women in development activities, and

○ Women's access to and participation in mainstream economic activities, particularly agriculture, the environment, and industry.

APDEV contains a set of policy-directed approaches and specific measures for implementing the programme.

As seen in Table 4.6, human development and sustainable institutions became UNIFEM's priorities in the work programme approved by the Consultative Committee in 1988. Figure 4.5 shows the distribution of UNIFEM's resources to country projects by region in the same year. It shows the Fund's priority investments in the least developed countries (the majority of them in the Africa region), while still assisting activities in all of the developing regions. Figure 4.6, 'Types of projects supported', shows

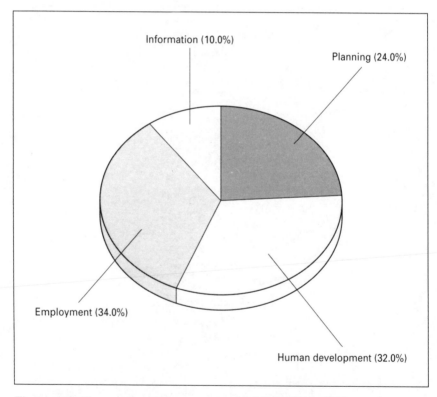

Figure 4.6: *Types of projects supported by UNIFEM, 1988*

employment and human development as the priority demands on the Fund's resources, followed by policy planning, and information activities.

Side by side with that substantive evolution of UNIFEM's strategies was UNIFEM's deep involvement in world politics, to which we turn in the following chapter.

CHAPTER FIVE
Women and World Politics

UNIFEM should be 'a separate and identifiable entity in autonomous association with the UNDP' and 'play an innovative and catalytic role in relation to the UN overall system of development co-operation'.

A/RES/39/125, 1984

ANY FUND EXISTING within the UN inevitably becomes involved in politics, but a very small fund, directed to women, is uniquely vulnerable to politicization. VFDW's priorities were not widely known early in its life, nor was it large enough to carry any weight, in the view of a few delegations. Instead, it was perceived to be a convenient instrument that could be used to advantage in certain problem areas.

Being the politicians that they were, the members of the Consultative Committee understood that, once one special cause was allowed to be mentioned in a VFDW resolution in the General Assembly, the floodgates would open and innumerable demands would take the Fund away from its mandate. Year after year, they would engage in quiet discourse with delegates, sometimes with our secretariat involved, to explain the Fund's procedures in detail and to keep its mandate intact.

Efforts to commit the Fund's resources to issues which already had specific UN trust funds and/or programmes were thwarted by one of the Fund's own guidelines: it was not to duplicate the work of existing funds. Our vigilance paid off. There came a time, however, when UNIFEM was caught up into political entanglements. Such a situation occurred after the Copenhagen Conference when, despite the lack of any evidence to support the charges, UNIFEM was singled out from other funding sources to be the scapegoat in a dispute.

Before describing that period in UNIFEM's history, it is important to note that the political storms we faced were of two different types. There were those that arose from the clash of policies between governments; they were usually based on North–South or East–West differences. One had to be sufficiently astute on political issues to steer the Fund around or through the clashes in order to ride the political waves, so to speak, between a rock and a hard place.

The second type originated in the struggle for control that took place within and between bureaucracies. In that instance, one had to know something about bureaucratic behaviour and the human longing for power, and be able to grasp the complexities added to those in the arena of a multi-national civil service.

The Fund found itself embroiled in three major storms during the early years: an intergovernmental one after Copenhagen; then a combination of

58

both types in what I have come to call 'The Battle of Vienna'; then a bureaucratic one with UNDP, which was politicized.

Guilt by association: the Copenhagen Conference

VFDW was drawn into North–South politics and suffered the most severe and crippling blow to its growth after the 1980 UN mid-Decade Conference, convened at Copenhagen to assess the progress being made in implementing the Mexico City Plan of Action. The Fund had become operational just two years earlier, and the demands on its resources had soared. Expectations for its continued growth were high in developing countries and regions.

The plenary sessions, the corridors, and the press briefings blazed with emotion-laden views at Copenhagen. The United States and three other countries withheld their approval of the Programme of Action for the Second Half of the UN Decade for Women that had been designed by government delegates. One of their stated reasons was that the Programme of Action contained the following: 'The UN organizations, the specialized agencies, UN organs and funds, Governments, international and regional intergovernmental organizations and other groups are called upon to provide assistance in consultation and co-operation with the PLO, the representative of the Palestinian people'. In other words, the intent was that every organization in the world that provided development or charitable assistance should work in collaboration with the PLO. No organization was mentioned specifically, however.[1]

'The Fund got caught up in a classic case of guilt by association', said Carol Leimas, who represented the American Association of University Women at the UN. 'The Programme of Action that came out of Copenhagen contained several sentences that the US could not endorse, sentences that equated Zionism with racism and sanctioned UN support of the PLO. But there was absolutely no connection made between VFDW and the PLO. In separate sections of the Programme, the VFDW was praised for its work with rural and poor urban women'.[2] In the Programme, as in a Conference Resolution, the Fund was urged 'to continue and intensify its efforts to give special support to women most in need and to encourage consideration of women in development planning'.[3] Leimas called VFDW 'one of the brightest spots on the UN horizon. Here is a UN agency which is doing just what the UN is supposed to do–helping poor people from developing countries to pull themselves up by their own bootstraps.'[4]

Thanks to a technicality (a continuing resolution) the US Congress appropriated a million dollars in 1981; the prohibition took hold in 1982.[5] Assistant Secretary of State Elliot Abrams, explaining to a delegation of women that there would be a 50 per cent cut in the US contribution, said that it was in retaliation for the 'politicization' of the Copenhagen conference: 'the Reagan administration intends a strong message to Third World countries and the UN leadership that the US may have to take the abuse in the UN, but we don't have to pay for it'.[6]

An amendment introduced by Congressman William Lehman of Florida

59

caused Congress to refuse to appropriate even the meagre half-million dollars. (In the Senate, however, Charles Percy adroitly made possible a $500 000 contribution to the Fund's projects through USAID and UNDP.) Of note is that, in the same year, proposals for US voluntary contributions to UNDP, UNICEF, FAO and ILO were significantly increased to a total of $329.3 million, including, for the first time, $45 million for the International Fund for Agricultural Development. The Copenhagen Programme of Action had no effect on the US grants to those organizations.

Misunderstandings about the Fund and the issues spread in the US and VFDW became a scapegoat. *MS Magazine,* for example, gave totally incorrect information, stating that at Copenhagen, 'Jewish women watched a Program of Action adopted (by a vote of 94 to 4) . . . that established a UN fund to be spent on Palestinian women in consultation and cooperation with the PLO'.[7] Others claimed that VFDW money had been used to support the Conference. On the contrary, as is clear from all the records, no fund for Palestinian women was created at Copenhagen, and no VFDW resources whatsoever were used for the Conference In fact, members of the Consultative Committee and of our Fund secretariat who were present at Copenhagen resisted–consciously, carefully and successfully–every effort to link VFDW to any issues that were politicized at the Conference.

In 1982, Leimas, Mildred Robbins Leet and I prepared a brochure on the Fund, to be issued by the UN Association of the USA. By 1983, many American women were moving into action. Patricia Hutar, who headed the US delegation to the Mexico City Conference in 1975, mobilized a US National Committee for VFDW, rallying Senator Percy, Congresswoman Lindy Boggs and the actress Jean Stapleton to assume honorary positions. Non-governmental organizations became active as well. They wrote letters to Congressmen to restore the US appropriation for the Fund.[8]

Even when restoration of the Congressional appropriation to VFDW was on the horizon, its opponents still had energy to expend. Explaining his 1983 recommendations to the House of Representatives, Congressman Lehman argued, curiously, that the Foreign Assistance and Related Programs Appropriations Bill for the financial year 1982 'did not represent any weakening of the . . . commitment to programs which assist women in less developed countries.'[9] Like Abrams, Lehman could not identify any connection between the Fund and the phrases in the Programme of Action.[10] The fact is, there was no connection.

Lehman's facts were also wrong about a VFDW contribution to the Copenhagen Conference. He failed to mention the organization that did contribute: the US Agency for International Development (USAID) gave $200000 for the Conference. The contribution by AID was from its Women in Development budget. As voted on by the UN General Assembly, including the US, the major costs of the Conference were borne by the UN regular budget. VFDW made no contribution at all.

The representative of B'nai B'rith to the United Nations, Harris Schoenberg, finally accepted a long-standing invitation to meet with me on 3 January 1983. He spoke of 'the women's programme in the UN' as if

60

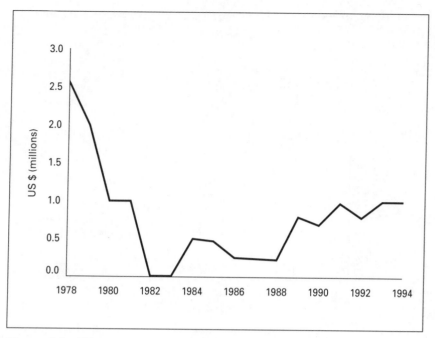

Figure 5.1: *US contributions to UNIFEM: 1978–94*

there were just one in the entire system. He seemed oblivious to the existence of the many and diverse programmes–those of ILO, FAO, Vienna, the Voluntary Fund, etc. He linked VFDW with the Copenhagen Programme of Action but, like others, could not cite any reference. There was none to cite.[11]

It was guilt by association. The developing countries had used their political clout and the US, in retaliation, used its financial clout, but against a mistaken enemy, i.e., the world's poorest women. The leadership and energy of women in and outside of the US Government, like Patricia Hutar, Barbara Good, and Korynne Horbel was weakened. Gradually, with the support of Leimas, Norma Levitt, Hutar, Millie Leet, Carol Capps, Mildred Marcy, Virginia Allan, Peggy Galey, Virginia Hazzard and others, the US grant was restored, but only at the half-million dollar level. (See Figure 5:1.) Fortunately, other countries had stepped in to fill the gap when the US withdrew. Norway, a country of four million persons, contributed $1.4 million–but the momentum of the Fund was shattered.

VFDW found certain ironies in the Copenhagen crisis. One was that the country that was most strongly opposed to 'politicizing' women's issues was the same country that politicized the plight of the poorest women in the world. The other was that the accusing fingers were pointed at a non-contributing Fund by a country whose own government had given significant financial support to the controversial Conference.

Asked to assist in regaining US support for the Fund whose clients were

61

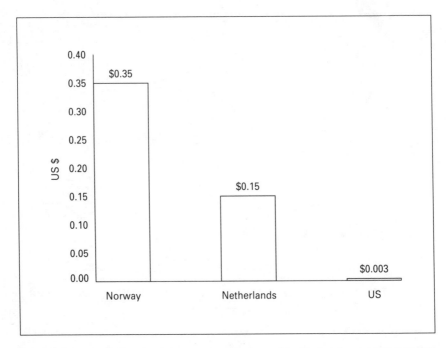

Figure 5.2: *Contribution per person: Norway, Netherlands and US in 1992*

the poorest women, then-US Ambassador to the UN, Jeanne Kirkpatrick, used a bit of casuist language to say: 'My position is to have no position on the matter'.[12]

For some observers, the matter provoked profound sadness. 'The US's deep retaliatory cuts to the Voluntary Fund will not be felt by those deemed to have been hostile to US interests in Copenhagen. It will affect Third World rural and urban poor women, the recipients of small loans and training opportunities'.[13] That judgement was correct, as seen in Figure 5:2: *Contribution per person: Norway, the Netherlands and the US*. The Fund learned a very hard lesson about politics, and we reinforced our convictions about the importance of strong National Committees as educators.

The battle of Vienna

The question of the location of the Fund, whether it should be at UN headquarters in New York, or with the CSDHA in Vienna, contained elements of global and bureaucratic politics. There were two considerations involved. First, CSDHA was mentioned only once in the Fund's enabling resolution (A/RES/31/133; see Annexe 1) *vis-à-vis* fund-raising, not management. The second one was a substantive issue. Was VFDW a fund for development co-operation with low-income women in poor countries, therefore requiring other development co-operation funds for technical and strategic support during its early years? If so, proximity to those other funds–UNICEF, UNDP, UNFPA, UNSO–was essential; they were located in New York, as were representatives of *all* the developing countries with which VFDW would work. (Few such countries had representation in Vienna.)

If, on the contrary, VFDW was a fund for research, policy review and backstopping, the Commission on the Status of Women (CSW), its location with CSDHA in Vienna would be correct. In other words, the Fund's identity was linked to its location. The battle of Vienna became a test of the very nature of the Fund's work.

In 1979, DIESA/CSDHA made an internal administrative decision to have the Fund's secretariat moved to Vienna in 1980. The CSDHA, with its Social Development and its Women's Branches, had been cut off from the Department of International Economic and Social Affairs and relocated to Vienna, where the Austrians had constructed the Vienna International Centre (VIC) as a UN headquarters while Kurt Waldheim (Austria) was UN Secretary-General. Austria lobbied the members of the Consultative Committee to ensure that move. One member of the Committee, however, stated that there were:

> very considerable economies of scale to be gained by administering the Fund in close proximity to other Funds, DIESA and the Budget Office, and it was difficult to see how those could be maintained if the Fund were to be administered outside New York. This had implications for the efficiency of the Fund, including financial efficiency.[14]

At the same time, both the Consultative Committee and the General Assembly expressed the desire to see the activities developed by the Fund continued after the UN Decade for Women came to a close in 1985 (A/RES/34/156). The Committee urged that an outside consultant be invited to review the Fund for considerations on the issue of relocation. Fortunately, we had started collecting data on the Fund in 1978, in order to track activities and trends and to report them to the Consultative Committee and General Assembly in a Forward Looking Assessment. During the period 1978–81, several trends had emerged: there was an increase in requests for projects targeting women living in urban slums and working in large industries; refugee women began to be seen as a population in need of assistance, and projects increasingly focused on co-operative employment, technologies and revolving loan funds.

By 1981, this preliminary analysis of VFDW operations reported that 31 per cent of the projects supported were in the area of employment; 30 per cent were in human development; 24 per cent focused on planning; 9 per cent on energy and 6 per cent on information. (See Figure 5.3.) It also showed an increasing emphasis on country level rather than regional projects (Figure 5.4.) As foreseen, these trends led to increases in the resources going directly to rural and poor urban women.[15]

The consultant selected to review the Fund's work, Dudley Madawela (Sri Lanka), submitted the two papers requested by the Consultative Committee: *The Activities of the VFDW*, and *Administration of the*

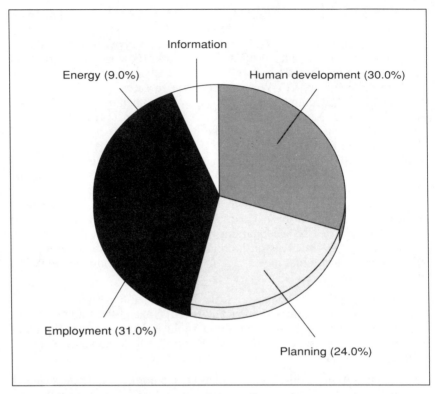

Figure 5.3: *Types of projects supported by UNIFEM in 1981*

VFDW.[16] For the first paper he drew on reports from other UN organizations to the Copenhagen World Conference. It was apparent to him that those agencies had not mobilized an appreciable volume of new resources nor had they reallocated what was available to programmes benefiting women directly, particularly those in low-income rural and urban areas. Madawela concluded that VFDW was very much needed in the UN system.

In his paper on administration, making use of the Forward-Looking Assessment, Madawela noted that the volume of administrative, substantive and managerial activities of a fund was dependent 'not so much on the level of resources as on the number of projects to be serviced'. From that point of view, he said, the VFDW needed more substantive and administrative support within it to discharge its responsibilities effectively and efficiently.

Reviewing the Madawela Report in 1981, members of the Consultative Committee discussed the interrelationships between VFDW and BAW. As a technical assistance fund, VFDW's main function was to 'respond to practical needs within developing countries, whereas BAW had an important advocacy role and responsibilities for monitoring, standard-setting, co-ordination of research, etc.'[17] The Committee then decided that member

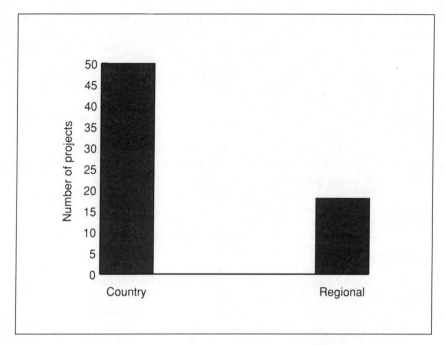

Figure 5.4: *Country versus regional UNIFEM projects funded in 1981*

states should be invited to submit their views on the future of the Fund and its administrative location.

The most controversial issue on the floor of the Third Committee of the General Assembly in the autumn of 1981 was the location of the Fund. East–West tensions were high at the time, and the Austrians sought to establish an identity as a neutral nation by becoming a major UN centre. It was important for them to have the offices at the VIC fully occupied, so they dispatched a special Ambassadorial representative to lobby the Third Committee of the General Assembly, and made their first pledge (US$21 000) to the Fund.

Reporting to the General Assembly on the Future of the Fund, the Secretary-General summarized the views that he had solicited from UN organizations.[18] Twenty of the twenty-two respondents supported the continuation of the Fund after the Decade for Women ended. They stressed in particular four aspects of the fund's work:

o VFDW was catalytic and innovative

o there was the need for a special fund

o the Fund had a co-ordinating and integrating role to play, and

o it assisted women at grassroots level and other low-income women who would not otherwise get access to resources.

On the question of the location of the Fund, the viewpoints of member states were contained in the Annexe to the Secretary-General's Report.[19] Of the twenty-four member States that replied, twelve favoured the NYC UNHQ option, eleven favoured Vienna, and one had no view at all.[20] Unsurprisingly, Secretary-General Waldheim and Assistant Secretary-General of CSDHA in Vienna, Letitia Shahani, supported the position that the Fund should be moved to Vienna, proposing that 'all necessary measures' would be taken to ensure that its work would not be disrupted during the relocation.[21]

In the midst of these General Assembly deliberations, the Austrian Ambassador vanished, apparently recalled to Vienna. A reason given for that disappearance was a trade-off of votes in the Security Council on the subject of Secretary-General Waldheim's proposed third term in office. The Austrians withdrew their pressure to move the Fund to Vienna when another delegation offered them a vote for Waldheim's re-election.[22]

Two competing resolutions were on the floor during the session. A compromise resolution, A/RES/36/129, accepted by consensus late one night in November 1981, did not favour a relocation to Vienna. Sponsored by the Netherlands, New Zealand, the Bahamas, Morocco, Oman, Samoa, Senegal and others, it received oral support from the three sponsors of the first draft, India, Jamaica and Nigeria–all members of the Consultative Committee.

As the Consultative Committee continued its discussions over the following three years, all possible options were explored for the future of the Fund.[23] At the request of delegations, we crafted several matrices, some with comparative information on the legislation and administration of various trust funds; others on the pros and cons of associating UNIFEM with UNDP, UNICEF, CSDHA, DTCD, etc. Delegations found the UNFPA to be the most interesting model. Like VFDW, it began as a small UN trust fund managed by the Controller before it was relocated in association with UNDP; thereafter it gained complete autonomy.[24]

While the debate on the purpose of the Fund and its consequent location continued, the Office of the Under Secretary-General for DIESA, J.J.Ripert, in New York, and CSDHA in Vienna sought to ensure that the staff of the VFDW unit was kept to a minimum, lest delegations be intimidated by the cost of moving the Fund from New York to Vienna. In response, as described in Chapter 3, the Consultative Committee brought the issue of staffing to the political forum, the General Assembly, in order to pressure the secretariats of the CSDHA and the DIESA to review the heavy workload of the staff,[25] and to take any necessary actions to protect the administration of the Fund. The Committee's concern attracted broad backing in the General Assembly and became incorporated into a 1982 General Assembly resolution.[26]

Among the comments on the floor of the General Assembly during the debate were those that related VFDW to its development work at country level. One statement is illustrative:

We could go on indefinitely drafting new international instruments about women. This would provide work for diplomats and bureaucrats–most of whom incidentally are male. But it would not help women. We women already enjoy on paper all the rights we need, in the Universal Declaration of Human Rights, the International Covenants, the Convention on the Elimination of Discrimination Against Women and other international instruments. We do not need more paper rights. We need paper rights confirmed by reality. And, particularly in the developing countries, women need practical assistance.[27]

Before the end of December, 1982, the UN Administrative Management Service and the internal auditors had been mobilized by then USG Shuaib Uthman Yolah (who replaced Ripert). Never have three professionals been so carefully scrutinized.

Under-Secretary Yolah announced his actions on the AMS recommendations to the Consultative Committee: two professional posts would be created as a matter of urgency, and the Unit would have greater authority over the day-to-day management of the Fund than had been the case in the past, when most decisions had to be cleared with Assistant Secretary-General Shahani, in Vienna.[28] The General Assembly expressed its appreciation to the Secretary-General for his timely actions in 1983.

While negotiating with bureaucratic and international political units about the continuation, we were reminded that working to empower the poorest women was threatening to some high-level and powerful people. One reason for that conclusion was that over the weekend of 24 March, 1984, VFDW's offices were unexpectedly moved from one building to another 'in a most disorderly manner, without any warning or preparation that would have permitted adequate packaging of work'.[29] Important documents and cables were scattered along the route of the move; project files were thrown in wastebaskets. There were no phones in the new, inadequate space.

Colleagues from the International Women's Tribune Centre brought us a whimsical hand-crafted sign: 'They can move us, but they can't stop us'. They were right. It was also interesting to observe that the space from which we were so abruptly removed remained vacant for more than a year.

The question of the location of the Fund and its future administrative relationships would continue to be controversial. Beneath the surface, as earlier noted, it was about the primary purpose of the Fund—was it to empower low-income women in developing countries? After my retirement and his, former USG/DIESA, J.J. Ripert stopped me for a long discussion on a streetcorner near the UN. He made very clear his belief that VFDW should have closed down at the end of the Decade for Women, 1985; that was why he had sought to send it off to Vienna. In his view, I was responsible for the Fund's continuation and growth, which he still considered a mistake. That conversation confirmed my earlier belief that some high officials did not support the principle of a special fund for women. Fortunately for the Fund, they were the exception.

A new mandate: hard-won autonomy

By 1984 the *Forward Looking Assessment* was completed by a team of twenty-five external evaluators organized by Deputy Director Akerele, assisted by regional commission officers Vivian Mota, Daw Aye, Thoraya Obaid, and Mary Tadesse, and by UNDP country officials. Forty-two projects–a representative group from each of the four regions–were evaluated in the field and another thirty subjected to desk review at headquarters. Together, these projects reached 63,000 beneficiaries and represented 21 per cent of the value of the Fund's project support at the time. The evaluators examined several aspects of Fund activities and influence, ranging from national policy to household labour allocation, in order to assess the impact of projects directed specifically toward women.

A close look at actual projects revealed that economic needs predominated among requests for support, especially from the poorest communities 'for whom the cash economy is a formidable adversary'.[30] Crucial components of the effective projects included credit, training, and transport. Women's self-reliance and self-confidence were increased by the prospects of earning cash incomes. 'Nonetheless', the Assessment said, 'the importance of personal, non-monetary rewards should not be overlooked; for people, particularly women, living under the worst possible conditions, personal gains are often the first step in involving them in development activities'.[31]

The overall evaluation of the Fund identified three major lessons from the experience of the first several years: 'the Fund must grow; it must accelerate attention to the project cycle; and it must keep pace with and contribute to the resolution of the developmental issues and processes involved in providing technical co-operation'.[32] The important and far-reaching role for the Fund '. . . to fill gaps, to stimulate change, and to demonstrate the value of full involvement of women in development assistance activities' (A/35/523) was also reiterated.[33] The Fund was viewed as a 'special purpose window' within the total UN development co-operation system.

Drawing on those findings, the Consultative Committee made special reference to the Fund's interactive role between women and the larger development effort. Members affirmed two priority areas of action for the future.[34]

o The first emphasized the Fund's catalytic role in highlighting the importance of women's issues for other organizations; it was in a sense a corrective function. Through its specialized expertise the Fund could increase its role in making available technical assistance to governments, multilateral and bilateral agencies, with the goal to insure the appropriate involvement of women in mainstream development activities, as often as possible at pre-investment stages.

o Second, the Consultative Committee recommended that the Fund should give priority to working with women's groups, with special emphasis on

68

non-governmental organizations but also including governmental machineries for women.

The Committee also pointed out some priority areas that had emerged in all four regions over the years, including credit windows, food-cycle technologies and management training. Members suggested that these areas might be 'packaged' into a single strategy. (This was done later, see Chapter 10). It stressed the importance of preserving the unique identity of the Fund, for 'it needed flexibility in order to retain its capacity to innovate. This implied the ability to take risks, and sometimes to fail.' Members were satisfied that, with the expertise it was able to access from UNDP and UNICEF, the Implementation Unit 'guaranteed that a good professional job was being done.' Finally, they stressed that 'strengthening the self-reliance activities of the poorest women demanded the highest levels of expertise; it was more complex and costly than assisting those better off.'[35]

The General Assembly could now take the most important decision on the Fund since its creation in 1976. (See box: 'Decision-making on the future of the Fund after the Decade for Women'.) Nonetheless, delegates requested face-to-face meetings among the concerned parties. Two informal consultations were arranged–one for the Africa Group and the other an open session. Representatives of the UNDP Administrator, the Legal Office and UNIFEM were present. UNFPA also attended, because delegates looked to its history as a model for UNIFEM; it was created as a trust fund in the UN, then associated with UNDP, and finally became a large-scale fund on its own. For most delegations, that was the ideal trajectory; the Fund must be autonomous in its relation to UNDP.[36]

Based on the views of governments, on the FLA and on the records of other UN funds *vis-à-vis* women and development, a draft resolution prepared by the Consultative Committee, co-ordinated by Ragne Lund of Norway was put before the Third Committee. On 14 December 1984, the General Assembly passed resolution A/RES/39/125 entitled *Future arrangements for the management of the Voluntary Fund for the United Nations Decade for Women.* (See Annexe 2.) The resolution established:

> . . . a separate and identifiable entity in autonomous association with the UNDP . . . which will play an innovative and catalytic role in relation to the UN overall system of development co-operation.

The resolution retained but expanded the original mandate of the Fund, resolution 31/133. (See Annexe 1.) As earlier discussed, the priorities of the Fund would be mainly two:

○ to serve as a catalyst, with the goal of ensuring the appropriate involvement of women in mainstream development activities, as often as possible at pre-investment stages, and

○ to support innovative and experimental activities benefiting women in line with national and regional priorities.

69

Decision-making on the future of the Fund after the Decade for Women

As requested in earlier GA resolutions, the VFDW Secretariat prepared three Reports of the S-G for the 1984, thirty-ninth, General Assembly to assist in its decision.

○ A/39/146, *Views of Member States on Continuation of the Activities of the VFDW:* its Annexe and Addendum 1 contained those views. The 24 responses to the Secretary-General's note verbale all found the VFDW to be one of the outstanding successes of the Decade for Women. Praised for its efficiency and professionalism, the Fund was viewed as the main UN mechanism for technical co-operation on behalf of women. Until the long-range goal of development was reached, the Fund should continue as a readily identifiable entity, supporting 'innovative development projects which have women as their primary target, in addition to its catalytic role in regard to mainstream development activities'. Thirteen respondents expressed the view that the Fund should remain in NY and be transferred 'as an autonomous unit to the UNDP'. They stressed that it should 'preserve its own identity and image, and have a degree of flexibility to enable it to continue as a catalytic and innovative agent and maintain a broad outreach to governments, women's organizations, NGOs, the regional commissions and specialized agencies. Some found the existing arrangements cumbersome.' *Only one government favoured relocation of the Fund within the CSDHA in Vienna.*

○ A/39/569, VFDW: *Report of the Secretary-General* summarized the findings of the *Forward-Looking Assessment*, and included the standard annual report of the Secretary-General on the Fund. Addendum 1 to this Report provided information on the senior women's programme officer posts at the regional commissions.

○ A/39/571 was entitled *Possible Future Options for Continuing the Activities of the Fund.* These were:

(1) Under the auspices of the DIESA/CSDHA located in Vienna;

(2) Under the auspices of the Department of Technical Co-operation for Development; or

(3) As a special fund in association with UNDP.

The Secretary-General estimated that the one-time cost of relocating the office of the Fund to Vienna would be $55 000. He cited the Consultative Committee's reference to the key role played by UNDP in administering more than 90 per cent of the resources of the Fund.

Further,

Fund resources should be a supplement to and not a substitute for the mandated responsibilities of other UN development co-operation organizations and agencies, including the UNDP.[37]

To facilitate implementation of the expanded mandate, special new management arrangements between the Fund and UNDP were contained in an extensive Annexe to the resolution. They 'delegated the management of the Fund and its administration, including responsibility for the mobilization of resources, to the Director who had the authority to conduct all matters related to its mandate and was accountable directly to the Administrator'.

At last, the Fund was autonomous, with authority over funds, projects, and staff, and reporting only to the UNDP Administrator. The Consultative Committee also remained independent and able to offset any bureaucratic pressures from UNDP because it derived its authority from the President of the General Assembly.[38] I was told many times in the ensuing years, by others including colleagues in the UN Office of Legal Affairs, that Resolution 39/125 was unique and almost a *coup d'état* in bureaucratic circles. The Resolution gave UNIFEM full authority over its own affairs. Our challenge thereafter would be to gain enough financial strength to exercise that authority to the fullest.

In 1985, on the advice of the Consultative Committee and with a decision by the General Assembly, VFDW was given its new name: the UN Development Fund for Women. Danish JPO Merete Johansson consulted widely about several acronyms under consideration: UNDEPOW, UNADEFF, UNDFEM, UNIFEM, UNIDFEM. The acronym UNIFEM was selected by the Consultative Committee for its pronounceability, and because 'fem' meant woman in the three major languages used in UNIFEM publications: English, French and Spanish. There would be no need to adapt the acronym to another language as was the case with UNDP, which is PNUD in French and Spanish.

After six years of political and bureaucratic controversy, UNIFEM no longer spanned two organizations and two locations. Women had their own, autonomous Fund. The change would become official on 1 July 1985, just in time for celebrations at the Nairobi World Conference on the Decade for Women. That the resolution of the two controversies had a defining impact on contributions to the Fund is clear in Figure 5.5: *World voluntary contributions to UNIFEM 1978 to July 1994.*

With good will evident among all the concerned parties, we looked forward to technical negotiations with UNDP that would transfer the Fund from DIESA/CSDHA of the United Nations. But the first meeting brought astonishing news that crushed our expectations. The Associate Administrator of UNDP, G. Arthur Brown, stated that UNIFEM should be administratively located within UNDP's Bureau for Special Activities–several bureaucratic levels away from the Administrator himself!

Recalling the protracted and intense discussions among government representatives during the course of the Assembly, I questioned the rationale for such an arrangement. The UNDP officials had had opportu-

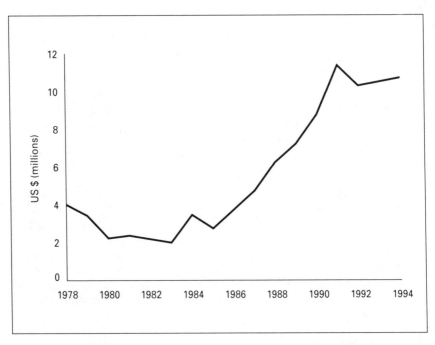

Figure 5.5: *World voluntary contributions to UNIFEM 1978 to July 1994*

nities to express any diverging views at the time of the negotiations. Delegations had made their views very clear: UNIFEM's autonomy must be carefully guarded if it was to be associated with UNDP. Checks and balances were incorporated in the resolution for that purpose. In my considered judgement, therefore, the matter of the Fund's being 'a separate and identifiable entity in autonomous association with UNDP' was a political one, not administrative, and thus outside my jurisdiction.

Finally accepted as a political issue, the question of the administrative location of the Fund was referred to the Consultative Committee, which reiterated the view of the General Assembly:

> The Fund in its future arrangements should be accorded full autonomy in its day to day operations under the Director as defined in the Resolution, in direct association with the Administrator of UNDP, and should be accorded high visibility in the UN system as a separate and distinct Fund for development assistance to women.[39]

The Chair of the Committee, Rose Arungu-Olende, conveyed these views to the UNDP Administrator. Associate Administrator Brown replied, acquiescing 'with some reluctance', but then spoke of a trial period of two years, after which the matter would be reviewed. Members stressed that the arrangements with UNDP should be 'in strict accordance with resolution A/RES/39/125'.[40]

The Administrator himself addressed the Committee's Eighteenth ses-

72

sion in September 1985, and he spoke of the remarkable progress made in establishing the 'very special relationship' between UNDP and the Fund. He reaffirmed the decision of the General Assembly on autonomous association. Even that was not the last word. In March of the following year, when the Consultative Committee met for its nineteenth session, Brown expressed his view that the Administrator could not be accountable for the Fund and yet delegate his authority over management and administration to the Director.[41] Once again Chairperson Arungu-Olende confirmed the validity of the Resolution, 'In the Committee's view, Res. 39/125 was very clear, and members saw no problem with the Administrator's delegation of his authority to the Director of the Fund. UNIFEM was to be autonomous in its operations, and not become a part of UNDP administration.'[42]

Suffice to say that we were all becoming weary in this, the third year of UNDP's efforts to absorb the Fund. But David was not to be easily defeated by Goliath. In September of 1986 the Associate Administrator once again appeared at the Committee, this time declaring that project approval rested with the Administrator himself. He reported that UNDP was undergoing a restructuring exercise and that UNIFEM's administrative location would be considered together with other UNDP-administered funds. He also explained the progress being made in drafting some 'working guidelines' between the Fund and UNDP; they would soon be put before the Committee for its review. Officials of the United Nations Office of Legal Affairs looked at the matter differently. They saw no need for such guidelines, considering the Annexe to Resolution 39/125 to be 'in itself sufficiently comprehensive and clear to cover the relationship between UNDP and UNIFEM'.[43]

The Guidelines seemed to me to represent an alternative approach to gaining control over the Fund after the fact, even though the Consultative Committee and the Director stood adamantly in defence of the General Assembly Resolution giving it autonomy. They contained nothing much new except a few administrative details only implied in A/RES/39/125. In that same year, the Associate Administrator spoke of the UNIFEM Director as 'defensive' about the Fund. I wondered if a man in my position would have been seen differently: as a person of great determination, as courageous.

Despite the bureaucratic furore, we were able to strengthen our work in the field with UNIFEM national/subregional officers stationed in Thailand, Nepal, The Gambia, Senegal, Zimbabwe, Peru, Mexico and Trinidad, to develop and monitor programmes and to advise NGOs and governments. We had sought to build a system, not a bureaucracy, and we had accomplished just that.

CHAPTER SIX

Core Resources and Outreach to Partners

If we help 100 000 women become self-reliant, we help 400 000 children.

UNIFEM Annual Report, 1988

ONE OF THE BIGGEST responsibilities for a Fund manager is resource mobilization. A trust fund–also called a voluntary fund–receives no money from the 'regular budget' of the United Nations. Every penny must be raised from governments, inter-government and non-government organizations and other donors. That calls for building close relationships with representatives of member states, including their parliamentarians, and with the non-government sector. One must also maintain a constant flow of public information materials and activities, in order to educate potential contributors on the work of the Fund.

Effective, carefully evaluated projects have priority of place in any fund-raising strategy. A successful track record is far more influential than pleas for help or a conceptual analysis of women's needs. Therefore, making the effectiveness of activities known became a key element in the earliest days of our fund-raising. We had to counter some gender resistance to a special fund for women. For example, one development co-operation ministry official in a major donor country told me that her superior asked: 'Could any separate women's Fund in practice handle satisfactorily the sort of development projects we have in mind?'[1] Similar questions arose from a concern that the new Fund would draw resources away from vested interests. In response, the Consultative Committee expressed its view that 'the particular appeal of the Fund will attract government pledges as core resources which would not have been available elsewhere in the system.'[2]

By 1986, when 300 new requests had come in for support, I considered fund-raising to be of the greatest importance. UNIFEM was at a possible turning point: if it could mobilize enough resources to meet the multiplying demands it might join the ranks of larger-scale funds and realize the vision of delegations to the General Assembly in 1984, i.e. to continue on its upward path and become a fund like UNFPA. One member of the Consultative Committee proposed a management study. Completed in 1987, it turned out to be beneficial.[3] UNIFEM gained three long-overdue senior posts, with responsibility for each of the developing regions. A structural change in the Fund's financing system was also recommended. It had been designed at my request by Tekkie Ghebre-Medhin, our credit systems specialist, to move us from a 'full-funding' to a 'partial-funding' system, i.e., rather than maintaining a 100 per cent reserve for commitments to projects, we would keep a reasonable emergency reserve.[4] That technical change would allow UNIFEM to make not only more but also longer-term commitments than had been possible earlier. It would also please donors who did not wish to have their contributions lying idle in the bank.

Government pledges

The largest–and most often the only–contributors to UN development funds are national governments. For that reason, the Thirtieth General Assembly of 1975 had decided to convene a special pledging conference to give all governments the chance to announce their voluntary contributions to the two new institutions for women, VFDW and INSTRAW.[5] This first Pledging Conference for the UN Decade for Women took place at UN headquarters in November 1977. Thirty-three countries pledged a total of $3.5 million to VFDW for 1978, of which $2.6 million was from the USA. Adding the unspent IWY money and the interest it earned brought VFDW's early resources to $5.5 million.

After that year, the Secretary-General organized a UN Pledging Conference for Development Activities, that included all of the special funds–UNDP, UNICEF, UNFPA, UNIFEM, INSTRAW and many more. The Consultative Committee regularly appealed for contributions to the Fund through its bi-annual reports. In 1980, for example, members 'noted with regret that commitments from the Fund could not continue at the current rate unless additional resources became available'.[6] From the beginning, the member from the Western European and Others Group (WEOG), Dr Spens of the UK, took two actions at the time of each session of the Committee. She met with WEOG members to brief them on the Fund's activities; then she prepared her own brief report on the Consultative Committee meeting for Permanent Missions in New York to send to capital cities. There is no doubt in my mind that her actions built the credibility of the Fund with those key donors during the crucial first six years.

We were anxious to have a broad range of donor countries, including developing countries themselves whose symbolic pledges of $1000 or more indicated their appreciation of the Fund's work. We celebrated when we reached an interim goal: 100 countries had contributed to the Fund. We were not as successful in getting a regional balance, however. The 'resource-rich' countries, mainly those of OPEC, were slow in joining the donor group, although Sheka Fatima of the United Arab Emirates contributed a very welcome $500 000 at the Nairobi Conference.[7]

As was seen in Figure 5:5, even in economic hard times, when pledges to some of the other funds stagnated or fell, those to UNIFEM continued to gain an average annual increase of 14 per cent; for 1988, just after celebrating the Fund's Tenth Anniversary, the increase was 19 per cent. Against the growing demands on the Fund, however, the question '14 per cent of what?' was realistic, not cynical.

National Committees and an NGO Advisory Committee

In 1980, the Commission on the Status of Women broached the idea that national committees be organized to launch educational campaigns about the Fund. It was an idea which had appealed to me for a long time. I knew how effective UNICEF's national committees were in making its work known to the general public in their respective countries and raising their governments' grants. UNICEF had appealing, innocent children's faces to attract interest. UNIFEM would have women; not just mothers, but extraordinarily hard-working women who were known for their sheer physical labour and for the maintenance and well-being of their families and communities. We needed to get their story out to men and women everywhere, to communicate the true image of the Fund and its work with the poorest women in low-income countries. National committees could do just that.

It was fortuitous that the energetic Helvi Sipila was about to retire from her post of ASG/CSDHA at the end of 1980 and was eager to promote the idea of national committees on the Fund. Sipila had global influence because of her leadership of the Mexico IWY Conference, and before that, as International President of the professional women's organization ZONTA. She formed the Finnish National Committee on UNIFEM in 1981, with 400 individual and 30 organizational members. In Finland also, the United Nations Association, led by Secretary-General Hilkka Pietila, had been an early supporter of VFDW; with the 'One Percent Fund' (working people pledged one per cent of their salaries to development projects in poorer countries), they contributed $20 000 in 1982.

The pioneering Finnish Committee for UNIFEM set an example for others. Membership and contribution cards were placed in post offices. On UN Day, a breakfast was sponsored by a bank. On International Women's Day, a seminar at a University was followed by a concert and an exhibit of UNIFEM projects. During their first year the Committee brought Jacqueline Ki-Zerbo from the Sahel. She travelled throughout the country with President Sipila and supervised a fuel-saving stove construction contest in snowy downtown Helsinki. Items bearing the IWY logo–scarfs, table and cocktail napkins, umbrellas–were sold in the largest department store. Members barraged their parliamentarians with letters urging increased government contributions to UNIFEM. YKNK, as the Committee is called, soon had its own offices.

By 1982, there were four national committees: Finland; the UK/UNA Women's Advisory Committee led by Bertha Bradby; the Danish Committee with banker Birte Roll Brandt as President; and Belgium, with Lily Boeykens. We held the first of what became biannual global meetings in tandem with the CSW meeting in Vienna in October 1984 and met informally again during the 1985 World Conference in Nairobi.[8]

The Second Global Meeting of National Committees was hosted by the Belgian National Committee and Government in Brussels in 1986.[9] To celebrate the Finnish Committee's contribution of $118 445 to the Fund in 1984, the Third Global Meeting took place in that country in 1988.

Chairpersons/Presidents of six national committees attended, some with their alternates.[10] As of 1988, the Finnish National Association had contributed $450 000, and the Finnish UNA $68 279. Sipila had formed the 'Fund for the UN Decade for Women, Inc.' to collect royalties on the commercial use of the IWY and Decade symbol, the dove of equality, development and peace.

The movement was well established now with Australia, France, Germany, Iceland, Japan, New Zealand and Spain in process of setting up committees. Developing countries began to join when the Philippines established a committee. (See Annexe 3: List of national committees on UNIFEM, 1993.)

The financial contributions from the Committees in no way tell the whole story of their work. Most important is their members' influence on their own governments' contributions to UNIFEM. I recall instances of that effectiveness. When the UK contribution to UNIFEM arbitrarily ceased in 1984, a campaign was launched by the fledgling UK Committee to bring its Government back into the donors' fold. While travelling through London that year, I was taken for discussions with The Hon. Timothy Raison, Minister for Overseas Development, who then agreed to restore the pledge to UNIFEM for 1985. As alluded to earlier, following the withdrawal of US support for UNIFEM, US Committee Chair Patricia Hutar testified before the Senate Committee on Foreign Relations, explaining how her Committee, in collaboration with several national women's organizations,[11] had worked to restore support to the Fund. In Finland the Committee's contribution to the Fund caused some embarrassment to Government, which then multiplied its support in 1986 in order to stay ahead of the civil society!

An NGO Committee for the Decade for Women had been formed at UN headquarters to promote the Mexico Plan of Action and women's interests generally, not just at the UN but among their own organizations. In 1983, that Committee contributed $11 000 to the Fund, joining many of its member organizations in becoming a contributor.[12]

ZONTA International's contribution in 1985 was unique in UNIFEM history; members pledged $500 000 for 1986–87 in support of five UNIFEM projects around the world. Two years later, they increased that pledge to one million dollars. Their formula was clever: with an average of 35 members in each of 1000 clubs around the world, a million dollar pledge could be met in just over three years if each member contributed $10 per year. In actual practice, each club usually finds its contribution through group fundraising activities. An unprecedented approach to partnership with UNIFEM! Figure 6.1 shows both governmental and NGO contributions.

Nonagenarian Esther Hymer, a long-term, dedicated and creative representative of the International Federation of Business and Professional Women at the United Nations, had the idea that UNIFEM should have its own NGO Advisory Committee. Thirteen representatives came to a meeting on 9 August 1988. (See Annexe 4.) On the following day they reported on their decision to organize the group to strengthen the relationship with UNIFEM.[13] They selected Claire Fulcher as Convenor, and Doris

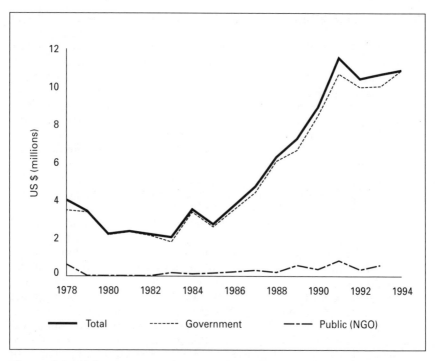

Figure 6.1: *Voluntary contributions to UNIFEM, 1978 to July 1994*

Vaughn and Virginia Hazzard as Secretaries. To add to their legitimacy, their Convenor and Secretaries met with the Fund's Consultative Committee that year. They were introduced as 'NGOs in Consultative Status with UNIFEM'.

The Committee, now consisting of twenty organizational members, represents more than 60 million women and men in at least 170 countries worldwide.[14]

Earmarked contributions

One complication in accepting contributions from the voluntary sector is that the contributing organizations often want to adopt or co-finance specific projects. The reason given is quite a human one: the members of the contributing group want to know their recipients by name and place, and they want periodic reports on the progress of the projects they finance or co-finance. Members sometimes seek to make group or individual visits to the projects as well.

We had no precedent in the UNDP system for NGO adoption of or co-financing projects; UNICEF however had a system of 'noted projects' that were not to be financed from its regular budget but could be 'adopted' by governments or others. In 1981 it was decided on the advice of the

Consultative Committee that government or NGO donors could support specific projects.[15]

Governments also use the earmarking approach in order to satisfy their own constituents–taxpayers. At times, donor governments favour countries or substantive areas that are of strategic or humane interest to their own national policy or to citizen groups. For example, Canada was motivated by a humane concern when it contributed $1.5 million for UNIFEM's food-cycle technologies programme (WAFT) at the time of the African drought.

Public Relations

To keep potential users and supporters informed, and to maintain the Fund's partnership with the international women's movement, we started our public information activities with the three earlier mentioned *Information Notes*. Then came the *Voluntary Fund Notes*, press kits, exhibits and *Development Review*–equally modest productions containing summaries of effective projects around the world. The film *Change*[16] told the story of women micro-entrepreneurs who were making use of credit funds. We commandeered the services of people like John Issac, the UN's prize-winning photographer, and Perdita Huston, the journalist, when they were traveling for other purposes. John Madeley later visited projects for us, published articles in the *Financial Times* and conducted interviews on the BBC.[17]

Farmers, Merchants and Entrepreneurs was distributed at the Nairobi Conference in 1985, together with brochures in various languages and the *Forward Looking Assessment*. As earlier discussed, in accordance with the Fund guidelines, our resources were not spent on events like global conferences. Nonetheless we did have booths, distribute literature, join panel discussions and show films on the Fund at both Copenhagen and Nairobi.

Two years after the Nairobi Conference, when we celebrated the Tenth Anniversary of the Fund at UN headquarters, testimonials came from numerous Prime Ministers, Presidents and other world leaders. (See Annexe 6.) By that time Goodwill Ambassadors were helping to promote the Fund's work: Hon. Phoebe Asiyo, former MP in Kenya (later re-elected), and Marcella Perez de Cuellar, wife of the Secretary-General were the first. (Most recently the actress Julie Andrews was also selected.)

Project and programme publications started with the *Guide to Community Revolving Loan Funds;* it remained popular for more than a decade. Next was a booklet on fish-smoking technology, a subject that is still a high priority for UNIFEM in West Africa. A series of *Food Technology Source Books* was produced with a substantial grant from the Italian Government. Another publications series was the *Occasional Papers*, an informal format for disseminating information about the Fund's project and programme experience.[18]

In a perfect world, a fund manager would dismiss earmarking as causing unnecessary administrative burdens. In the real world, however, money for women is scarce, and a new fund must build confidence. Suffice to say, we went on with earmarking, hoping for the day when it would not be necessary. A larger Fund capacity for information activities could well alleviate the problem, since there would then be a regular flow of descriptive material to satisfy the public relations needs of donors.

Satisfying donor governments' political concerns is another question. A Fund manager must ensure that donors are not dictating the subjects of projects and that host countries are agreeable to the projects' adoption by a donor country.

UNIFEM: from an idea to a durable institution

We saw in Part I of this book that the women and development concept and movement evolved with the momentum created when fifty-four countries became independent after World War II and joined the world community. Disillusionment with modernization (dual economy) theories, that posited that the growth of GNP would trickle down to everyone and in so doing put an end to poverty, then opened the way for putting people first. Women were prepared for that opportunity and their voices began to be heard.

Women working in the UN quickly grasped the revolutionary notion that even the poorest women in the world are central economic actors. Thus the UN, with its global outreach, became the principal advocate and guardian of the women and development movement. Women in turn brought the authority of the UN to the spread of their message, as they built a movement on strong indigenous traditions of leadership in their societies. By 1975, they were aware that existing institutions had failed them and new ones were needed; they created UNIFEM and INSTRAW.

The early history of UNIFEM showed that transforming a bureaucracy like the United Nations is a daunting chore that should at times be circumvented. That was done by moving the Fund from the United Nations to UNDP, gaining the advantage of using its network of country offices and UN system relationships. That move also gave UNIFEM a voice of its own as an autonomous entity, a fund.

UNIFEM became a powerful catalyst for change in several ways. It drew millions of dollars–more than double its own investment–as complementary inputs to projects it initiated. It also assisted the design of projects of other organizations so that they would benefit both men and women. Seeking to meet low-income women most effectively through their own organizations and with their own needs, UNIFEM took innovative actions that would affect the entire UN development co-operation system. First, non-governmental organizations were made executing agencies for projects in a system that relied mostly on its own organizations and was just beginning to finance governments. Second, UNIFEM found a way to provide assistance in the form of a renewable financial resource, the revolving credit fund. Third, it gave institutional support (as distinct from project support) to governments' national machineries and to NGOs.

The UN is by its nature political and demands political acumen of its civil servants who hold positions that relate to the General Assembly. Creating an equilibrium among three parties–diplomats, NGOs and international civil servants–is the recipe for success in the UN. A civil servant heading a fund on her/his own can survive neither the political arena nor the bureaucratic mire. With support from key member states, such as UNIFEM's Consultative Committee members, each of whom represents a whole regional group, and with sisterly support that characterizes NGOs, one may tire but will not lose out. Keeping that tripartite alliance in balance multiplied the outreach and influence of UNIFEM as a catalyst for change.

UNIFEM rode through political storms: the outcome of the Battle of Vienna, that was in fact about the very nature of the Fund, defined its purpose as development co-operation. The battle with UNDP's bureaucrats was also won, and UNIFEM's autonomous status was reinforced because the Fund had a very strong General Assembly resolution (39/125) and a very determined intergovernmental committee appointed by the President of the General Assembly. The Fund would reach all the way from grass-roots to global levels in its search for new development paradigms.

One political storm left UNIFEM scarred. That came in the aftermath of the Copenhagen Conference, when the poor women who were our partners were targeted as scapegoats for decisions made far away from them. Even though other countries came forth to fill the gap the United States left when its contribution was withdrawn, and NGOs launched a successful campaign to restore the US contribution, the momentum for rapid expansion was lost.

Yet UNIFEM grew at an even pace; its contributions increased at an average of 14 per cent annually into the 1990s, even when the global economic crisis led some countries to reduce their contributions to other multilateral funds. Based on women's demands, it developed its own specializations: food-cycle technologies and credit systems, while consulting with regional representatives in order to design conceptual frameworks for priority emphasis in each developing region.

New operational partners were added after the first years during which the regional commissions and UNDP helped the most. They ranged from the local NGOs just mentioned to the regional development banks and subregional economic co-operation associations of governments. Human development and sustainable institutions took priority in the Fund's work as the new century came into view.

Just as low-income women became victims of political vendettas they would also be buffeted by powerful economic forces that are outside their control. Women took risks and succeeded despite such negative forces; how might they have succeeded if the forces were favourable! We shall see those forces operating as we turn to Part II of this book: UNIFEM at Work in the World.

PART TWO

UNIFEM AT WORK IN THE WORLD: CASE STUDIES

We turn our attention now to the previously mentioned factors that interrelate with each other in the struggle to overcome poverty: economic empowerment; social justice; and political participation. Women and men who are poor lack access to the resources necessary for wealth to be produced rather than simply redistributed. They are also denied the well-being that is fostered by good health care and education, and their voices are not heard when decisions are made on the future of their societies.

In the pages that follow I describe UNIFEM's work in the field, including the views of participants, organizers and others. The UNIFEM-assisted 'projects' are grouped according to the principal factor each of them chose to emphasize in order to combat poverty. I start with economic empowerment, which dominated the requests for assistance. In the final chapter, I attempt to analyse whether and how the projects contributed to reducing poverty, empowering participants, creating or strengthening sustainable institutions, and/or had catalytic effects. I also speak to the role of the United Nations as principal advocate and guardian of the women and development movement.

Part Two, Table 7.0: Information on UNIFEM-assisted projects, overleaf, is a reference for the projects discussed. In addition, there is a table with relevant data about each country that is considered.

Table 7.0: Information on UNIFEM-assisted projects discussed in this study

Approach to poverty	Financing Year started	UNIFEM grants* (up to 1989) First project #	Second project #	Total (US $)	Executing agency	Co-operating agencies
Economic Productivity						
China Tailoring	1982	CPR/82/W01	–	203000	NGO	GOV
India Mahila Haat	1984	IND/84/W01	IND/87/W02	85818	NGO	
India Sericulture	1980	IND/80/W05	IND/88/W01	227000	GOV	NGO
Laos Textiles	1983	LAO/82/W01	–	213371	NGO/UN	GOV
Mauritius Arts	1980	MAR/80/W01	MAR/80/W02	92238	NGO	GOV
Philippines San Miguel	1979	PHI/79/06	PHI/81/W03	70300	NGO	
Philippines Rootcrops	1979	PHI/88/W01	–	81000	NGO	GOV
Swaziland Credit	1979	SWA/80/W01	SWA/81/W02	77600	GOV	UN
Social Justice						
Argentina Rural	1987	ARG/87/W01	ARG/87/W02	372079	GOV	INTERGOV
Barbados Food	1984	BAR/84/W01	–	61390	NGO	GOV
Bolivia Pottery	1980	BOL/80/W02	–	165222	UNIDO	
Bolivia Milk	1983	BOL/83/W01	–	186000	NGO	3 GOV
East Africa Management Training	1980	RAF/80/W04	RAF/84/W07	211944	INTERGOV	GOV
Kenya Water	1983	KEN/83/W01	KEN/86/WO3	197775	NGO	GOV
Mexico Welders	1985	MEX/85/W01	Phase II–1989	320000	GOV	
Oman Communities	1979	OMA/80/W01	OMA/81/W02	549000	GOV	
Sahel Stoves	1980	RAF/80/W05	Several	844000	INTERGOV	GOV/NGO
Syria Literacy	1985	SYR/85/W01	–	50000	GOV	NGO/UN
Tanzania Technologies	1987	URT/87/W01	–	251000	GOV	NGO
West Africa Fish Smokers	1984	RAF/84/W02	Several	644532	GOV/NGO	
WAND Caribbean	1978	RLA/78/03	Several	186600	NGO	NGO/GOV
Yemen Biogas	1986	PDY/86/W01	PDY/88/W01	214000	GOV	
Participation in Decision-making						
Kenya Green Belt	1981	KEN/81/W02	–	122700	NGO	
Peru Workers	1982	PER/82/W01	PER/84/W01	119115	NGO	
Peru Kitchens	1986	PER/86/W01	–	18000	NGO	
Peru NGO Network	1988	PER/88/W01	–	100000	NGO	
Peru Technology	1988	PER/88/W02	–	264201	NGO	

* UNIFEM only; excludes co-financing and follow-up financing by governments and other funds.

CHAPTER SEVEN

Economic Empowerment

An alarming number of families survive solely on the woman's earnings.

National Commission on Self-Employed Women, India

AUGMENTING WOMEN'S access to productive resources must be recognized as the central element in anti-poverty strategies. Among the poor, all women work, said the National Commission on Self-Employed Women–an Indian Government Commission inspired by the Self-Employed Women's Association (SEWA). The Commission found that 'an alarming number of families survive solely on the woman's earnings'; the numbers ranged from 20 per cent to 60 per cent in every group that the Commission interviewed. It estimated that one-third of the country's families were female-headed, and in another third of families women provided at least 50 per cent of the family income.[1]

Those figures match my own global estimates. The irony is that, twenty years after the International Women's Year, working women are still thought to 'supplement the family income' earned by male breadwinners rather than being seen as breadwinners themselves.

The vast majority of women in low-income developing countries do not work for government-regulated wages but draw their earnings from the informal sector, as family labour or self-employed persons, often working out of their own homes.[2] Informal sector businesses are typically small scale and labour intensive. They use simple technology, are short on capital, have few or no other employees, and are orientated to local markets. The informal economy is the largest and usually the fastest growing segment in the private sector of national economies. It is estimated that it will have to generate the majority of the 120 000 jobs per day that must be added to the world's employment capacity by the year 2000.[3]

The informal sector is actually the dominant economy because the vast majority of people in developing countries make their living in that arena. Mary Racelis of the Philippines, who has had many years of international experience, had this to say:

The informal sector is marginalized, but it is not marginal. As an Argentine sociologist says, it should be called the popular economy. And the society has to be reckoned in those terms. To the extent that poverty comes from unequal resources, change is possible. Economic development activity must be significantly located in the popular economy and not just in the 20 per cent which is export-orientated, or large scale manufacturing. Of course you have to have a national policy for improving the economy, or you will simply share what few resources there are more equitably. You need community organization, but also you need to expand the economic pie.[4]

Women are in fact flooding the informal sector to eke out small profits to feed the family. This trend is particularly common in areas where there are few wage employment openings and the economy is stagnant or in decline. When governments institute structural adjustment programmes, retrenchment follows and women are often the first to lose their jobs.[5] In the informal economy, women market smoked fish, raise chickens, grow food crops, extract oils, keep bees, make bricks, process salt, brew beer, sew school uniforms, and craft baskets and pots. They learn to make carpets, roll cigarettes, manage inns and restaurants, mine stones and gems, and to do carpentry work. They are domestic servants and they carry headloads. Some sell drugs and others turn to prostitution. Those endeavours and countless other small enterprises are estimated to employ up to 70 per cent of the labour force in the rural and urban areas of developing countries, yet they are only now being recorded by statisticians.

Despite their ingenuity and effort and their being preferred as workers by some transnational corporations, women's earnings in the informal sector and in wage labour are far less than those of men. They have less education and training, fewer assets to use as collateral, and little access to technology. They are frequently tied to home-based production and nearby markets because of family and farm responsibilities and cultural influences. Women endure these difficult conditions because the informal sector represents the only source of income they have to allay their own hunger and that of their dependent children.[6]

India provides an enlightening profile of poor women workers. According to the Commission on Self-Employed Women, only 10 per cent of poor people work in the formal sector. The informal sector includes 108 million women–97 per cent of all female workers. Yet official statistics would have us believe that women produce only 10 per cent to 15 per cent of the national income. India's self-employed women workers average 277 rupees a month; that is half of what men earn. In the formal sector, women average 964 rupees a month.[7]

The Commission explained:

We began to discover the anomalous situation that 89 per cent of the female work-force was in fact invisible; it did not count as part of the labour movement, its contribution to the gross national product was rarely accounted for and the women workers were not even counted by the censuses.[8]

Commission Chairman Ela Bhatt added:

I learned that these women are better fighters against poverty than their men. They have more calculating, stable, forward-looking strategies to deal with their own environment. Yet the women remain poorer.[9]

That same business sense holds true in the Philippines. Mary Racelis spoke of the Secretary of Agriculture, Arturo Taco, who had got into a big rice production programme involving credit and then found that many farmers were defaulting.

When he began to analyse the situation, he finally insisted that women should also sign for the loans. And once they did that, the payback rate jumped significantly.[10]

Racelis also spoke of the scale of activities in the popular economy and of the limited possibilities women have to expand their businesses in order to move into the formal economy:

> The popular economy is just a huge number of small groups. Many women's groups are satisfied at that scale. It provides them with a kind of basic security, a little supplement to their income. But the fact is, if you look into businesses as a whole, out of many only a few will evolve. For example, a woman starts by cooking bananas and selling. When she does it pretty well, she adds cooking fish balls, and pretty soon she is packaging–wrapping them in cellophane. Then she has to hire someone–a relative probably. Over time she will have a restaurant. There is something to be said for keeping a smaller size. Women want to keep their businesses in the family and they don't want to become open stock corporations.[11]

Because UNIFEM asked women what they actually wanted, and because our mandate had strong anti-poverty elements, the largest share of UNIFEM assistance (42 per cent from 1978–83 and 34 per cent in 1988) went to projects in the overall category of employment, mainly in the informal sector–the popular economy–for micro-enterprise development.

The Fund had prerequisites for assessing the potential effectiveness of income-raising projects: a socio-economic study of the situation, condition, and environment of participants; a feasibility study of the economic and technical viability of the project; a marketing strategy; skills training and management development; access to credit through local banking facilities or a revolving credit fund; and systematic monitoring.[12] Guidelines for the feasibility study and for the marketing plan, profiles of the participants, and the community analysis were all contained in the *UNIFEM Project Manual*.

There follow nine case studies on UNIFEM-assisted activities whose primary concern was productive employment. The resources requested were for capital (revolving credit funds), technologies, training and marketing. The Economic Roles of Women project in Swaziland was UNIFEM's pioneer use of a revolving loan fund. The Cartegena Small Enterprise project moved the concept forward by leveraging more money from co-operating banks; I have a short human interest story from that project.

In the Philippines, the success of the credit fund for swine-fattening at San Miguel led to establishment of a risky venture–a medium-scale industry. Another Philippine credit project: Production, Processing and Marketing of Root Crops, thrived despite affliction with endless natural disasters culminating in the eruption of Mt. Pinatubo. The National Commission on the Role of Filipino Women, that was UNIFEM's partner from the beginning, created the Philippine Development Plan for Women to ensure both the existence and the implementation of policies benefiting women.

We shall briefly review three enterprise projects that were factory- or workshop-based: Women's Textile Ateliers in Laos, Tailors in Beijing and Craftswomen in Mauritius. Finally, we move on to India where Increasing Sericulture in Udaipur District and Mahila Haat (Village Markets) illustrate the centrality of market-awareness and policies for broadly-based growth in incomes, i.e., economic democracy. The sericulture project also provides our most vivid example that empowerment calls for more than income in the family.

At the end of this chapter on Economic Empowerment, I make some comparisons of the strengths and weaknesses of the projects in the areas of credit, technology, management and marketing, then comment on the projects' vulnerability to national and international political and economic forces.

Innovation in Swaziland: the first United Nations credit fund

Change comes, maybe much slower than we would like, but it comes.

Christabel Motsa

We have shown people that a bank can lend to women.

Mphaya Simelane

Swaziland is a tiny country in southern Africa, landlocked by South Africa and Mozambique. 69 per cent of the population (estimated in 1995 to be 960,000) lives in rural settings where two-thirds of households depend solely on women, who often find it difficult to make ends meet; 55 per cent of those rural households are poor. When no male is present, women have to add to their own gender-determined agricultural work (planting, weeding, harvesting and storage), the traditional male tasks of land clearing, planting other crops, and caring for cattle. Because they often have to pay school fees and purchase food and clothing for the family, most rural women earn extra cash through crafts, beer-brewing, healing, or trading in the informal sector of the economy. In fact, over 60 per cent of households earn income in this fashion. Letta Dlamini, who joined the Ministry of Agriculture in 1967 with responsibility for food and applied nutrition, spoke about women's responsibilities:

> Swazi men have never stayed home. They always went to the mines in Johannesburg or any other place they could find work. Women have always stayed home–have always headed the homes. Though women are said to be weaker in strength, you will find that about 80 per cent of the children who get an education get it from their competitive mothers, who say 'My child should be as educated as my neighbour's child'.[13]

In Swaziland the Queen Mother shares power with the King, who is currently Mswati III. About 60 per cent of the land is Swazi National

Swaziland

Demographics

Population	0.86 million
% urban	31
% rural	69

Income

GNP per capita	$1090
% in absolute poverty	48
%of rural population	50
% of urban population	45

Health

Life expectancy	Women: 60	Men: 56
Infant mortality	73	per 1000 births
Maternal mortality	107	per 100000 births
Access to safe water (%)	30*	

Education

Illiteracy rate	Women: na	Men: na
Girls as % of boys in secondary school	98	
Girls as % of boys in tertiary school	88	
Girls as % of tertiary science/engineering students	43	

Work

Households headed by women (%)	40
Women as % of labour force	34
Female wages as % of male	73

Representation

Parliamentary seats held by women (%)	4**

Source: See source table in Annexe 7.

*Water data is for 1983–85
**The Times of Swaziland, Oct. 17, 1993

Land used by small-scale producers whose holdings average about three hectares in size and are characterized by low agricultural productivity. The women of those 100 000 small farms that create about 19 per cent of GNP were the subjects of a UNIFEM grant.

The remaining land averages 791 hectares per holding and is owned by foreign companies, government ministers, or a financial trust operated by the Monarchy. It contributes more than 60 per cent to GNP. Economically, at this writing, Swaziland is heavily dependent upon its neighbour, South

Africa, and it is also a member of the relatively new Southern African Development Community (SADC).

Swaziland's economy grew rapidly for two decades until in 1980 the price of its major export, sugar, plummeted on the world market. At the same time, the country was struck first by a severe drought and then by Cyclone Demoina, in 1984. The growth level dropped from 7 per cent to 3 per cent per year, drastically reducing employment possibilities. The unemployment rate, coupled with a population growth rate of 3.2 per cent, has led the government to emphasize ways to generate informal sector employment in both rural and urban areas. The Economic Roles of Women Project provides us with examples of that new informal sector thrust and with the lessons learned from that endeavour.[14]

Origins of the project

My research visit to Swaziland in 1993 came twenty years after I was team leader for the ECA Women's Programme Itinerant Training Workshop in Home Economics and Other Family Oriented Fields that took place at the University of Botswana, Lesotho and Swaziland. The workshop marked an early stage of the women and development movement. UNDP Representative Hugh Greenidge (Barbados) proposed to the international team that we design a more permanent training centre for women. In 1975 the project began; it has endured for two decades and still remains strong as the twenty-first century approaches. The Netherlands Government and the UN Department of Technical Co-operation for Development (through UNDP) gave substantial core support. UNIFEM provided the revolving credit fund; UNICEF a technology component.

Entfonjeni, close to Piggs Peak and about 150 km north of Mbabane, the capital city, was selected as the first location for the project; it was within the Government's Northern Rural Development Area (NRDA) which had a staff of teachers and health workers. The first products of this new small enterprise training centre were very traditional: school uniforms, sweaters and shoes, tie-dye tablecloths, vegetables, poultry and pigs. A number of other potential activities were tried but discarded when competitive products flooded across the border from South Africa. In turn, however, some of the training centre products were sold in South Africa. Early on, they were also sold to urban Swazi women who bought in bulk for resale in the towns.

I asked Christabel Motsa about that focus because it came under heavy criticism from feminist scholars and others for being 'too small' and for teaching 'traditional women's skills'. Motsa replied:

Swaziland is a patriarchal society. And here gender roles are played out very significantly, much more strongly I think than in any other society. So in my view it would have been very difficult to start a women in development project in the first place. But lucky for us, it did start. I think the reason that it was fairly successful was the conscientization, the workshopping that preceded it. By the time it really came in 1975, the society was almost ready to accept that kind of thing. Men were ready to release women to go for long periods of training, for three or four months. The project wasn't threatening by then, because it started slowly.

The things that were really significant, like the brickmaking, the welding, and the revolving loan fund–the non-traditional activities– were added on gradually as time went on. Sometimes that is not the worst thing you can do![15]

Linda Vilakati, the dynamic national director of the Project, spoke bluntly to UN Radio in 1983:

We had to rewrite the project document and put in the needs of women and their families in communities in the rural areas. That made us concentrate on projects which would help women make money.[16]

The project was 'a learning process', said Vilakati, at a time (1976) when there were very few guidelines on assisting rural women with micro-enterprises. Motsa told me that Vilakati's personality helped the project a great deal. Recognizing women's multiple responsibilities to their farms and families, as well as their urgent need to have enough time to earn money, Vilakati added an appropriate technology emphasis, first for household use and later for production. The technologies developed at the centre included cooking stoves that were raised off the ground so as to protect children from being burned. Food-drying methods were taught and huge concrete jars were fabricated to catch the rain from the roof or to store grain. To give mothers the freedom they needed to earn income, communities built their own day-care centres modeled on the one at the Entfonjeni centre.

The community revolving loan fund

After evaluating the project in 1977, the team asked Dumsile Shiba, the extension worker: 'If there was just one thing you could do for the women, what would it be?' She replied without hesitation: 'Give them bank credit so that they can purchase the equipment they need to start up their businesses.' At that time, 96 per cent of Swazi women found it impossible to get bank credit.

We did not know at the time that Vilakati and Shiba's proposal would transform United Nations development co-operation strategies. Until then, the funds that used the UNDP system, interpreted their mandates for technical co-operation in a very narrow way. They could finance experts for specific time periods; they could purchase equipment, and pay for training; but they never thought to replace their practices of giving handouts to communities by revolving credit funds that could be used as renewable financial resources.

If women were to be served in a sustainable way, that system had to change. It was changed, but only after exhaustive debate, followed by an exploration of the new accounting methods that I described earlier in this book. The protests by the accountants brought smiles. How could a responsible accountant depreciate a credit fund as he did a Landrover, or consider the money as an expenditure, like the salary of an expert? We finally found a relatively unused category of expenditure, the grant, as the line item for credit funds. UNDP could agree to that. We then published the *Guide to Community Revolving Loan Funds* as a resource for those who wished to weigh the possibility of such a fund or start to manage one. With that breakthrough women could be treated as financial managers rather than objects of welfare. There followed many requests from UNDP staff and others for UNIFEM assistance in providing RLFs within projects they assisted.

The revolving loan fund for Entfonjeni graduates was inaugurated with a deposit of E1000 (US$333) in the bank in 1978. Five thousand US dollars were contributed by VFDW through UNECA in 1979, and a smaller grant from the US Embassy in Swaziland arrived shortly thereafter. ZONTA II International of Denmark also contributed. Tekkie Ghebre-Medhin, former ECA Women's Programme accountant, joined the project staff in 1979. In 1981, UNIFEM added $32 000 directly to the project, and in 1986, $40 600.

The credit fund became operational in 1980, and by 1983 150 graduates of the training programme had benefited. Women could take out two kinds of loans: one for equipment, and the other for operating capital. The project bought supplies in bulk through its Input Supply Facility which meant considerable savings for the women. The facility eventually had five stores.

'By the time the revolving fund came about', said Christabel Motsa, 'people were ready to say "of course women need this support". But we were forever concerned that the men would not permit women to get loans. If the woman was unable to pay it back, the whole family would be affected as the family resources would have to be used to repay the loan. Now', she added, 'both men and women see the need for this kind of project'.

Vilakati told UN Radio that the credit fund 'made a tremendous impact on the attitudes of men'. Husbands and fathers would help to pay the women's loans and at times even purchase equipment outright.[17]

Between 1980 and 1982, four more training workshops were opened across the country–in Spofaneni, Sithobela, Mahlangatsha and Mahamba-Zombodzie. The number of graduates reached 3000 in 1990. Study tours were arranged for women from Lesotho, Tanzania, Mozambique and Uganda; Namibia later opened its own centre. By 1990 there were 37 on staff, 35 of them provided by the Government. All construction and vehicle maintenance costs were also met by Government which contributed $269 000 that year. Profound change had come about since the early days when Vilakati asked me to join her in visiting various government Ministries to 'speak for the United Nations' in order to leverage government contributions to the Project.

The credit fund worked, thanks to Vilakati and Ghebre-Medhin. In mid-1983, the repayment rate was 80 per cent–a high figure for Swaziland at the time. No interest was charged on the financial loans initially and management obtained income through the sale of equipment. Pre-co-operatives were established, with each group giving itself a business name.

The RLF goals were: to open mainstream financial resources to women; to expand the credit base; and to accustom women to borrowing from banking institutions. Those purposes were the foundation of the project agreement with the Swaziland Development and Savings Bank (SDSB) in 1984. The bank would lend four times the value of the Guarantee cum Risk Fund established with the UNIFEM grant. Under this original agreement the bank charged 10 per cent interest to borrowers, of which 8 per cent was deposited to the Risk Fund and 2 per cent reserved to meet its own costs. Borrowers deposited in the Bank 10 per cent of the value of their loans. In 1986, the repayment rate reached 85 per cent , with a default rate of 2 per cent only.[18]

A 1990 evaluation team interviewed 15 per cent of current trainees and held focus groups with graduates; they surveyed the credit experiences of 90 graduates through homestead visits and group interviews. The team's findings indicated that the broad objective of improving women's integration into economic development was being met in four ways:[19]

o training added a new skill or improved an existing skill to a level that enabled women to begin producing orders in their locality when they completed the course

o the skill enabled women to work at home and thereby improved the balance between their domestic and agricultural responsibilities and their income-earning needs. In fact, several women had given up more remunerative vending or paid labour to learn a home-based skill even though marketing home-based products was more difficult. Demand was lower for non-traditional subjects such as carpentry and leatherwork although there were untapped markets in those fields

o the new skill enabled women to increase their options for income-earning. Most trainees and many graduates came to the center with previous production, selling and/or work experience. Interviews confirmed earlier studies, namely that women practised several income-earning activities

o women who applied their skills, even on a part-time basis, were earning money. Eighty-one per cent of the credit users reported no difficulty in marketing. Reported incomes varied from E50 to E1110 per month, with a concentration in the E200–300 per month range. The average income of graduates compared favourably with the average for the urban informal sector of E237/month.

The evaluation team found, however, that the project objectives were not being fully met. Most of the credit interviewees cited operating capital as their greatest constraint–they could not get it. (That problem would be resolved in negotiations with the SDSB, as discussed below.) The team was critical of the bank's record-keeping, and of its operating procedures with low income producers. They dared to question the bank's commitment to small producers.

The evaluation also found that the 1990s trainees were considerably younger than the original groups. 58 per cent of the new trainees were in the 20–25 age group and were school dropouts; 69 per cent of them were married and nearly 78 per cent had children. All of them had the primary responsibility for supporting their children, and they enrolled in training for that very reason. They continued to fit the UNIFEM criteria, however, because they were very poor.

Economic need was still of overriding importance in the project.
1990 Evaluation

On the recommendation of the team, a special evaluation of the credit component of the project was undertaken in 1993.[20] The evaluator identified such problems as the practice of compounding interest, which caused borrowers to pay up to five times the amount of principle on their loan. That matter was resolved. The evaluator recommended that the bank and the project return to the group-lending approach that was in practice when the project managed the credit fund; that system relied on peer pressure for repayments. Day-to-day management of the fund, including selection of recipients and monitoring repayments, was returned to the project. The centres were closed while project staff had a three and a half month training course.[21] The transformation of staff from a community development to a business orientation was absolutely necessary.

I spoke with Mphaya Simelane, Agriculture Manager, and with Welcome Lomahoza, Rural Credit Officer at the Swazi Development and Savings Bank, about the bank's new experience in lending to women entrepreneurs.[22] They confirmed that previously the bank had only loaned money to small producers in agriculture, almost all of them men. Back then, women had to get their husband's consent and then go through a lot of red tape to take out a loan.

The Project made a breakthrough for women, Lomahoza said, not only because direct access to credit was new to them, but also because no man could borrow money from it. Asked about women and collateral, Simelane explained:

Initially, we relied on the husbands' providing security or collateral for their wives, children, cousins or other relatives. Technically, a woman married in Swazi custom can own property, so she could buy a piece of land and build her own house–but that did not happen often. In the past we relied on cattle as security–cattle that belonged to husbands or fathers. But thanks to the Economic Roles of Women project, women no longer need collateral. We rely on peer pressure, not on cattle.

> The bank has learned from the women and development project that peer pressure works. Now we encourage people to borrow in groups.

'What proportion of your field officers are women?', I asked. 'Zero', Simelane replied, and then reverted to a very traditional explanation. 'We tried, but because women had to travel long distances, they found the job rather strenuous and went back to the office.' He informed me that

SDSB now had one woman manager and that there would be more in the future.

Simelane said that his mother belonged to a solidarity group in which each woman had six tiny plots. They ordered fertilizers on a group basis and had them delivered. The E15 his mother and the others got from each plot after harvest was put in a joint fund to be used for basic needs like sugar and salt. 'If it wasn't for my mother, I would not have gone to school', he said.

The bankers were greatly impressed by women brickmakers and provided them with a number of loans.[23] Construction agencies hired them to make bricks and build houses. Women have added roofing tiles to their skills, so they can provide almost everything one needs for a house. The training came initially from the Women and Development project, Motsa explained.

> The brickmaking is expanded beyond the project now. Women ask their community development officers to teach them the skill. The bricks are very cheap but strong. Unfortunately, a lot of what the women are doing doesn't get counted in the GNP, because it is in the informal sector, and that is where the statistics fail us. We need gender-differentiated data.[24]

I went with Collin Tshabalala, home industry officer of the training programme for the Piggs Peak area, and Mariam Nxumalo, who attended the 1973 ECA workshop, to visit graduate working groups. A workshop at Entfonjeni had eight women and one man working in four departments: cookery, sewing, shoecraft and carpentry. Their average income per month was E70 (US$23).

> My husband provides some supplementary income to my shoemaking work. He sews.   Lydia

Another group had been making large jars for water-harvesting for two years; they are able to make one jar per day. A big jar accommodates about eleven bags of maize and sells for E110 to members and E150 to non-members. The group had built themselves a shed where they planned to market vegetables. They used their own bricks. Another group had 21 members. They grew maize as a cash crop. They planned to add candle-making and fencing to their maize and water-jar businesses. To start up the business, they used the training materials they were given at Entfonjeni graduation. That money from sales kept revolving so that they did not have to take out a bank loan.

Block-moulders were the final group we met. They had built a fine workshop/salesroom, with technical advice from the project. Tshabalala said that he had invited a Co-operative Union to work with them on organization skills, but the Union tried to get them to change their product line to a grocery shop instead. Their president told us:

> We make a type of sisal basket that is much in demand. Here in the shop we sell clothing, brushes, rugs, wall hangings, pottery and basketry. We

House builders win international award

Two women's groups in Swaziland that manufacture building blocks for house construction won the prestigious Habitat International Coalition Award.

The award, worth $1500, went to Takhele Ncheka Building Block-makers and the Tfutfukani Bomake Building Blockmakers.

Takhele Ncheka Blockmakers, a group situated in the south-west of the country, started in 1983 soon after a severe cyclone had struck Swaziland and devastated the traditional type housing. Women affected by the collapse of their homes approached government for help and were given information about soil cement blocks which are cheap and easy to make.

With the help of credit from UNIFEM the women purchased the machine and materials they needed for making the blocks and were soon in business–not only making blocks but houses too!

In the north the Tfutfukani Bomake Building Blockmakers group received a one-month training course in blockmaking skills, and again with the help of credit from UNIFEM, purchased a machine for making the blocks. The group found that the demand for their blocks was endless–and this group too has involved itself in house construction.

The Habitat International Coalition Award is presented to the woman or women's organisation that plays 'an outstanding role in human settlements development'.

John Madeley

took out a loan years ago to buy the moulder for the blocks, paid it back within a year and have not borrowed since. We bank our money as a group; and have E2000 (US$666) saved now. We will buy a sewing machine and some groceries to sell. We meet twice a week, to work together.

The group has helped me with inputs to my farm. I need to earn money for my family.

Lydia

Swaziland as a model

The Swaziland project has exceeded its goals. That is not to say that it is free of problems, nor that it won't continue to have them. But it has transformed attitudes and has made possible a better quality of life for thousands of women and their families. Key evidence of the impact grass-roots activities can have on national policies is the current move in the Swaziland government to create a national women's policy.

Under-secretary in the Ministry of Economic Planning, Isabella Katamzi testified to the catalytic effect of the project:

96

When the Women and Development project started in Piggs Peak, it was such a dynamic programme that we all were aware of it. More women go into businesses of their own, and as long as we have revolving funds, opportunities will be there for the women to be emancipated and to be more a part of development. Swaziland, a very culture- and tradition-bound nation, has been able to integrate old and new without pushing the women backwards.[25]

Further evidence of the catalytic effect of the project comes both from banks and from government:

o The Risk Fund with SDSB releases four times its own value for loans from the Bank to women.

o Financial institutions have been more willing to provide loans to groups of women, because the revolving loan project proved so successful.

o The success of the pilot project at Entfonjeni convinced government to further institutionalize it by expanding training and loan systems in five locations in the country, and to support a staff of 39; more than 3000 women have been trained.

The quest for economic empowerment has largely been successful:

o Evaluation shows that the graduate trainees hold their own in income-earning in comparison with the urban informal sector. The project continues its anti-poverty orientation: trainees are selected for their economic need in rural areas where 50 per cent of the people are poor.

o Project activities are not aimed only at income-generation, but also at lessening women's workload and improving the quality of life through technologies appropriate to water harvesting, grain storage and other tasks.

o Women have been trained for co-operative micro-enterprise and peer-group financial support.

With access to credit, women–not just project trainees but all Swazi women–are able to go into businesses of their own, and they are doing so; even in non-traditional fields like brickmaking, house construction and carpentry. Men not only did not object to the project but began to be supportive of it. Husbands and fathers assisted in loan repayment or purchased equipment. The project stopped being a threat and is now welcome. Motsa concludes that there is now a positive attitude toward women, even within the government.

The women and development activities are as permanent as any institution can be. To achieve this sustainability, the perseverance of donors has been key: the UNDTCD and the Netherlands are still providing assistance, and UNIFEM stayed with the project until 1990. 'Donors were very patient with us', said several interviewees. The importance of that patience among all concerned parties, and their willingness to work together as institution-builders for a long period is an element of development that is too often undervalued.

The UN role as a force supportive of women's capacities to transform development is confirmed by long-time observer Christabel Motsa, who recalls that it took a lot of convincing of government that this was a project worth supporting. 'During that period, the external support was crucial. Without that support, I don't think we would see the kinds of results that we see today. Prevailing development paradigms of the time had worked against the possibility of the project', said Motsa. 'We started at a time when the development thinking was capital projects–big projects. So if you were into some small project the economists would tell you, this is a non-starter, it is non-viable, the economic rate of return is zero, and so forth. We needed that outside support to show women's importance and that starting small is not bad'.

UNIFEM gave the Economic Roles of Women project an award at the Nairobi World Conference on the Decade for Women in 1985. Swazi women of all walks of life rose up and danced in the aisles, proudly in solidarity with those who could not travel so far. They still deserve that honour.

From micro-enterprise to setting policy in the Philippines

New Generation

I am Maria
taught to cook and wash
to be bought
not to remain

He is Pedro
left to play
morning til noon
because he's male
and would lose nothing

So what if I play
and Pedro is taught to cook and wash
please tell me
what would be lost.

Ruby Enario, *Review of Women's Studies*,
University of the Philippines (December 1992)

Half a world away from Swaziland, the women of the Philippines struggle with the burdens that are placed on them by the anonymous forces that control the economic arena in which profit and loss on a global scale determine the survival of a village household. As throughout this book, it is only by putting a human face on the initiatives to overcome poverty that we can begin to grasp the transformation that occurs when women take charge of their own destiny and enter the development scenario.

In this section we will examine case studies of projects UNIFEM assisted with credit funds in several areas of the Philippines. They provide us with

Economic independence in Colombia

When I went to a workshop for the Small Enterprise Project, I learned that there were no women trainees. When I asked why, they answered, 'No women come to our classes. They don't want to learn. They are lazy and not interested.' Can you imagine?

Lola Rocha

One of UNIFEM's earliest projects re-educated the Cartagena Small Enterprise Project to include women's activities in their definition of skills suitable for a micro-enterprise, to hold classes at times and in locations amenable to women, and to give women access to credit. This project was a joint effort with UNICEF and the National Training Service of Colombia (SENA). In the past, SENA had trained men for industrial carpentry and shoemaking jobs, and the Cartagena Project redesigned SENA training to include accounting and personnel management training for women seamstresses, bakers, and cooks. The UNIFEM credit fund served as bank collateral: for every $2 deposited, $17 were loaned. The difference this project made in the lives of poor women of Cartagena is palpable in the story of Concepcion, a baker, which was related by two of her daughters to UNIFEM's Perdita Huston in 1984.

Concepcion was fifty-four and the mother of four when she joined the Small Enterprise Project. The children's father had left her long before, so she was the sole provider for her family. The children had a stepfather, who held a job as a chauffeur; however, he provided moral support rather than financial. He 'is really nice, but he would leave every once in a while. Mother said it was because there was too much confusion in such a small house: four grown children, bread-baking, no space . . . Mother says it is not up to the second husband to feed the first man's children', tells the oldest daughter, age 18. The daughters are not so convinced of that logic, but it is clear that their family is content now that their mother has been able to expand her business on a solid footing. Once Concepcion received training and a loan from the Small Business Project, she was able to feed her children, to expand her house, to buy a refrigerator and a TV. Without the constant stress of space and money, the children's stepfather returned.

'My mother never thought of herself as a businesswoman until she went to the training courses, even though she has been baking since she was a child,' adds her younger daughter. It was the eldest daughter who introduced her mother to the Small Business Project: 'I took her there. I wanted her to see where the training center was. It was important that she meet others to see how it is possible to do something like this.' Concepcion completed the training in accounting and obtained a loan for $1150. 'It was dangerous for her to go alone to classes sometimes, but our father encouraged her and he told my older brother to accompany her.' With the loan she expanded the house by adding a room more than twice the size of the three others. This is the combination kitchen, dining room and bakery, and includes a professional bread oven and a refrigerator. Her youngest son started an ice-cream business once they had the refrigerator.

Concepcion's youngest daughter, aged 16, wants to train as a secretary so that she can help her mother with the finances. 'It is important for women to be able to earn,' she believes. 'So many women are left by their husbands and can't feed their children. All women should be economically independent. I certainly want to be.'

informative examples of the risks and difficulties that always seem to accompany anti-poverty actions with low-income women. Then we will turn our attention to the national policy level and to UNIFEM's work with the National Commission on the Role of Filipino Women (NCRFW) in designing the Development Plan for Women, 1989–92.

Before proceeding, however, it is important to note that women's contribution to the Philippine economy and their able management of household income only came to be widely recognized in the early 1970s. The impetus generated by the preparations for the 1975 IWY Conference led to the acknowledgement of social class differences in the society. The reality for rural and village women was found to be the experience of losing out, of slipping further into poverty.[26]

Something needed to be done. As a start, the government created the Commission mentioned above (NCRFW) in 1975. Innumerable NGOs were then formed to address family poverty issues; their purpose was to make opportunities available for women and men to earn income in the popular economy, the so-called informal sector. Our case studies will show some of the results of those efforts.

The country: culture, governance and economy

The Philippines has endured a series of violent shocks over the past decade. The assassination of the Presidential candidate Benigno Aquino Jr. resulted in political turbulence and the rise of his widow to the Presidency. A prolonged drought was broken only by a severe typhoon which preceded a massive earthquake on the main island of Luzon. As if those disasters weren't enough, Mount Pinatubo erupted after lying dormant and 'agri-culturally friendly' for more than 400 years.

But the most serious calamity in the view of many Filipinos was 'the debt bomb' that struck the country in 1983. The external debt was then US$24 billion, and by 1991 it had shot up to US$32 billion–the equivalent of 70 per cent of the GNP.[27] Fifty-four per cent of the 69 million Filipinos live in absolute poverty–the figure is even higher (64 per cent) in the rural areas.

Even though the Constitution provides that the highest item of national expenditure should be education, in 1990 just 2.9 per cent of GNP was assigned to that category. The shortage of teachers, books and classrooms is still severe. Although in 1989, 4 per cent of gross national product went to health costs, by 1990 that figure had plummeted to just one per cent. The Department of Health calculated that due to the cuts almost 400 000 children would be denied milk and vitamins.[28] The paramount reason for such a low investment in the well-being of the people–including the future labour force–is debt-servicing, which absorbed 36.5 per cent of the national budget in 1990.

Can you really change the World Bank?
Staff of the Women's Resource and Research Centre, Manila.

100

The Philippines

Demographics

Population	69 million
% urban	46
% rural	54

Income

GNP per capita	$770
% in absolute poverty	54
%of rural population	64
% of urban population	40

Health

Life expectancy	Women: 67	Men: 63
Infant mortality	40	per 1000 births
Maternal mortality	100	per 100000 births
Access to safe water (%)	82	

Education

Illiteracy rate (%)	Women: 11	Men: 10
Girls as % of boys in secondary school	99	
Girls as % of boys in tertiary school	143	
Girls as % of tertiary science/engineering students	49	

Work

Households headed by women (%)	11
Women as % of labour force	37
Female wages as % of male	86*

Representation

Parliamentary seats held by women (%)	11

Source: See source table in Annexe 7.

The economic crisis has impacted most severely on women: a pattern that occurs worldwide.[29] Inevitably in such a situation, factories and other workplaces close; hospital and school budgets are cut back; and governments retrench their staffs. What follows is that women assume the burden of society's well-being. Inflation bites into the value of household earnings, exerting further pressure on women to seek two or even three jobs for their family's survival.

Eventually, many people resort to petty trade, household and vacant lot production, and temporary portage and delivery jobs. The informal sector–

the popular economy–swells, mainly with women who are striving to earn an extra peso. Professional as well as poor women are affected; they try to earn enough for their families and the many needy relatives and neighbours who descend upon their households.

Another profound effect of such a crisis is the emigration of people for overseas employment. In the Philippines, men emigrate initially as seamen (a traditional skill) or to other countries such as the Gulf States where they do construction work or unskilled labour. Whenever the economy is stagnant, women also begin to seek their fortunes outside the country. In fact, since 1987, more females than males have left annually in search of temporary employment. Many become victims of maltreatment or rape. Josefa Francisco, Director of the Women's Resource and Research Centre, told me:

> They go as domestic helpers or entertainers, which is a euphemism for prostitutes. Educated women also leave. Some teachers go to Malaysia, Hong Kong and Singapore as domestic workers. Some even reach Italy, Germany and Canada. Prostitutes or entertainers are in Japan, Cambodia, Bali, Greece. The state itself is peddling the people, and there are no minimal protective mechanisms or protective laws.[30]

'As long as the haemorrhage of resources continues, economic recovery is out of the question', said Leonore M. Briones.[31] Those are the conditions under which millions of Filipinos struggle to survive, and UNIFEM has made a very small contribution to assist them by providing resources for productive employment. Revolving credit funds were particularly useful in rural areas and communities such as Porac and San Miguel.

Production, processing and marketing of rootcrops

The children can now ask for money for school needs without so many problems and so many arguments. Arguments came because there was no money.

Patricia Jiminez

Women farmers tried new agricultural productive activities, again by using a revolving loan fund. 'The twenty-six letters in our alphabet are not sufficient to give names to our storms every year', Rufina Ancheta said.[32] Because of the capricious weather, sturdy rootcrops like sweet potato, yam, cassava, taro and arrowroot were being introduced to extend the often low supply of rice in the Philippines. UNIFEM, with ESCAP, had already in the early 1980s successfully demonstrated on a pilot scale the capacity of rural women to produce and process root crops. The Rural Improvement Clubs (RIC), an NGO with a network of 7500 clubs across the country, approached UNIFEM in 1988 to broaden that experience. UNIFEM provided $50 000, including a training component, and a $30 000 revolving credit fund. An additional $31 000 was given when the eruption of Mount Pinatubo devastated many project farms.

Within a three-year time-frame, the project set out to increase 200 family incomes by 30 per cent, create awareness of family nutrition, and enable women to organize and manage small scale agro-industrial activities. It achieved all of its goals to a great extent, including an average 25 per cent income increase–from 2500 pesos ($93) to 3125 pesos ($116), despite a succession of major disasters: an earthquake, typhoons, the volcano eruption and floods. The infestations of pests and diseases that followed all of those made it almost impossible to grow most crops, including rootcrops. The volcanic eruption alone left 50 000 people permanently homeless.

Through the project, members of the RIC clubs in eight pilot *barangays* (villages) in four provinces were trained in rootcrop production technology, processing, income-generation management and marketing, as well as in credit systems, by the staff of the Department of Agriculture, the Agriculture Training Institute and other specialized organizations. Each site had 25 beneficiaries with at least two hectares planted in rootcrops. Most club members also engaged in several income-producing ventures such as hog raising, poultry, goat raising, cattle fattening and handicrafts.

I visited Porac in Pampanga Province with Patricia Jiminez, Provincial Project Co-ordinator, early in 1994. The RIC group there was formed in 1988 and became a co-operative in 1990. Rice and sugarcane cultivation dominate an area that also contains forest lands, swamps and marshlands. Travelling to Pampanga we saw the devastated lands from which people had fled. 'They will be back', said Jiminez, 'They want to live and die on their land'.[33]

'I think that through the rootcrop and other projects Porac family incomes have about doubled', said Jiminez. That would bring monthly income to about 4000 pesos. Men are happy that wives are helping augment the family income', she said. 'The children can now ask for money for school needs without so many problems and so many arguments. Arguments came because there was no money.'[34]

When Mt. Pinatubo's eruption endangered agriculture, the women decided to process the young arrowroot plants into cookies rather than continuing with the production of mature arrowroot that could be lost to the lahar–the mud flows (rivers) that are triggered by heavy rains in the volcanic area. They bought the supplies from other RICs and sometimes made cookies from cassava. Their cookies sold in supermarkets, grocery stores and bakeries, both locally and in Manila, and they set up their own co-operative shop too. They are now negotiating with exporters at the Philippine International Trade Exhibit who are interested in their product, and they hope to do their own exporting after they get enough experience. After successfully using the 85 000 peso UNIFEM credit fund loan for the cookie business, the Club was considered credit-worthy and negotiated a 250 000 peso ($9300) loan from the government's Department of Trade and Industry (DTI).

Co-operative Manager Leonor Popatco, a volunteer, spoke about the variety of businesses in the co-op. 'Monthly we produce about 2000 cannisters of cookies' she said. 'That brings us a net income of P2000 to P3000 ($74 to $111) a month. For the whole project we have an income of P5000 to P6000 ($185 to $222) a month, and that is separate from the individual income of members. Some members also have individual projects, like the swine fattening you have seen, candy-making and macaroni snacks,' she said.[35]

Leonor Nagrampa has been President of the RIC for five years, during which Club membership increased from 25 to 32. 'When members have trouble paying their loans', she said 'we talk to them seriously, and they pay little by little.' They were preparing to buy a new oven with regulated heat, which would enhance the appearance of the cookies.

Like other members, Nagrampa raises pigs at home. She bought five sows with a loan of 30 000 pesos from the RIC, and now has thirteen piglets. 'Pork is always saleable in the Philippines' she said, 'and you can even tie a pig under a tree, fatten it and sell it.' Her pighouse actually had met stringent qualifications and was made from concrete. Asked what she wished for other women, Nagrampa expressed the hope that every woman could be successful in business.[36] Another member, Elvira Estrella Morales has been an RIC member for five years. She joined because it promised a way to help her family–her farmer husband and two children. She buys shoes for her children and groceries for the family with the money earned from the cookies. Her proudest achievement, however was her new cement block home.

Asked about transforming the women's traditionally family-oriented, service mentality to a business one, Jiminez said that, yes, they had difficulty persuading the women to use their cookie-baking skills for sales. Traditionally, women baked cookies to serve for special occasions like weddings. But gradually, when they tried selling, they took to the idea. The Department of Agriculture taught them marketing, pricing, packaging and other agribusiness subjects.

Project effectiveness factors: the rootcrop project as model

The personal development of the beneficiaries can be attributed to the training they had in project management..an intrinsic value that cannot be quantified. According to them it is priceless.

Rootcrop Production, Processing and Marketing, Final Report, July 1988–December 1993, Agriculture Training Institute, Department of Agriculture, Manila.

At the start of the project, the women were afraid to take out loans, but once over that hurdle, they soon found that they needed more money. The DTI and the Land Bank of the Philippines were persuaded to open credit lines to women. Co-operatives were established on every project site and the flexible credit/financing schemes suited the agricultural production cycle and its variability. Jiminez placed great importance on the '*buklod*' system, whereby loans are made to groups of five women and each of them is responsible for repayment. Other credit schemes adopted that approach. Women even got the courage to engage in 'men's work', like buying and selling rice and fattening cattle.

Economic empowerment was evident among the women. Not only did they raise their income by an average of 25 per cent through the project, but they also entered other income-producing enterprises. They adopted new technologies, such as a sweet potato chopper (obtained at 50 per cent discount to members), saving themselves the hours they spent in processing that could be used for household tasks or animal production. However, they were discriminating in their choices and refused some new technologies that they did not consider appropriate.

The success of the rootcrop project activities was attributed by participants both to the ease with which they could be interwoven with other farm-based economic activities and to the strong support of their husbands and children.[37] Local officials in the sites have been so impressed with the project that they have donated water supply systems and allowed the use of vacant lots as processing centres.

> Formerly these women baked cookies just for special occasions. We had a very hard time convincing them to make arrowroot cookies as a business.
> Patricia Jiminez

Jiminez added another success factor that made a very important contribution to the sustainability of the co-operative as an institution. 'I attribute much of their success to the background of the co-op manager. She is dedicated to the project. And all the money is accounted for, entered in the book. Another success factor is the co-operation and credibility of the members. When they say they are going to pay the loan they really do it', she said. Asked what she looked for when starting a new group, Jiminez replied: 'We look for an active organization, that has some experience already with putting up a project.'[38]

Those who evaluated the project for UNIFEM found that 'the project has done an impressive job in developing women's leadership, socialization and organizational skills. In addition to economic benefits the women cited the opportunities for self growth as the project's most positive impact on their lives.'[39] They also looked to the future:

> The rootcrop project offers the opportunity of serving as a development model of how women can be transformed from subsistence rural producers into entrepreneurs. The project's current success at the rural stage should be pushed even further specifically towards the direction of enterprise development.[40]

The early ESCAP-assisted project had been a catalyst for change, and that catalytic effect continued with the larger-scale project as credit systems were opened to women, who then entered new fields of enterprise.

The San Miguel venture: from raising pigs to medium-scale industry

> As long as those pigs are eating properly, so shall we.
> San Miguel participant

In another rural area of the Philippines women would move from backyard swine husbandry to home-based manufacturing and then to centralized workplaces–a sometimes trying transition.

105

I was born in San Miguel, became a teacher here and was a district supervisor of education. Manual Collado, an officer from the local government and community development unit, found that when he called meetings of farmers 75 per cent of those who attended were women. He presented the problem to me and I said: 'Okay, why not organize the women of San Miguel?' We got the chance to start the swine fattening project with 70 women. When I reached compulsory retirement age–65–little changed except that I could give them full time as a volunteer leader.[41]

The speaker, Emma Santa Ana, is 77 now, and still a major decision-maker at San Miguel. She is able to take risks as an experienced business person and general manager of two factories. The San Miguel women's group she fostered began with pig raising and then moved on to making small toys, clothing and sweaters for export; some of them carry the St Michael label of Marks and Spencer in England. There were tough moments as the women transformed their thinking from community development to micro-enterprise and then to medium-scale industry.

Sylvia Ordonez, co-pioneer with Emma Santa Ana, was the student leader selected to represent youth when the National Commission on the Role of Filipino Women (NCRFW) was created in 1975. She took other student leaders to San Miguel Bulacan, fifty miles from Manila, to live with families there and learn about their country's history. San Miguel was a poor rice-farming area that was frequently battered by floods or droughts. Ordonez had always wanted to find a way to thank the women of San Miguel for their generosity with the youth, she told me during an interview.

NCRFW proposed to hold a meeting with rural women in a very expensive hotel in Manila to find out what those women wanted. The meeting would cost 300 000 pesos. I was a bit disturbed, and drove for four hours beyond Manila to La Union. I stopped by the roadside and asked a group of farming women: 'What is it that you want? What needs do you have?' The women were very vocal: 'Do you see where we are?' they asked. 'This is a rice paddy. This irrigation system, if we are given a little money to extend it, can cover more hectares and we will be able to double our current production. All we need is cement and a few other things like steel bars. We will get our own sand and provide the labour'.[42]

'To me, that was the bottom line. I asked what irrigation meant to the women economically, and they said it would double their production', said Ordonez. 'The whole thing would cost just 17 000 pesos. I got some money and in less than a month the women invited us again: They turned on the faucets and the water flowed in. I felt that it was like putting blood into a vein.' She continued:

Back in Manila, I read an article about the *Voluntary Fund for the UN Decade for Women (VFDW)*. There would be money available provided it didn't go to workshops or wasteful things like too much overhead. I liked that statement very much. This time I went to San Miguel, and met

Callado, the man Emma Santa Ana spoke of, who had organized the women with her. Invited to speak at their induction, I said that I was willing to help if the women would go beyond beautification and the traditional roles given to women. I told them of my experience with women in La Union who had become partners with men. The women of San Miguel were willing to pick up the challenge by going into economic activities. I told them I would connect them with the VFDW.[43]

Ordonez' next step was critical and would prove catalytic. She went to the Development Academy of the Philippines for technical help to write up the proposal. In brainstorming sessions the San Miguel women said they wanted to transform their local custom of keeping a couple of pigs in the back yard for subsistence purposes into a business. Then they got an agriculturist, human behaviour specialists, and systems people involved.

'What we turned out was a model programme that has been used for nearly twenty years with other groups because it had very important elements, such as clustering the beneficiaries for mutual support and projecting future incomes. We used a small Canadian grant, $5000, to try a breeding programming. The Voluntary Fund money–$61 000– included a community revolving credit fund for fattening the pigs for sale'. The request was submitted to the Voluntary Fund by the Development Academy of the Philippines and the NCRFW in 1977. It was one of the first projects we approved. Later, in 1981, UNIFEM granted an additional $20 300.

> In San Miguel, when you ask to see the pigs, they will ask: 'Which ones do you want to see? The Canadian pigs or the UN pigs?'
>
> Sylvia Ordonez

Sylvia Ordonez became President of the Foundation for the Advancement of Filipino Women (FAFW), an NGO established in 1978 to improve the economic, social, and cultural status of women. Emma Santa Ana became a member of the Board. It was a time when 'everyone in the world was just beginning to talk about women getting into economic activities' Ordonez observed. Santa Ana added that 'The goal of our group in San Miguel changed: we would expand the family income. Besides Sylvia, Daw Aye of the UN Economic and Social Commission for Asia and the Pacific (ESCAP) supported us.'

> When we first met with the women in San Miguel, the men were outside peeking in, afraid that if the women said the wrong thing, the chance for the pigs would be lost. Years later, the women asked me to help the men with a post-harvest facility. In 1989, the men were inside the classroom and the women were outside watching what their men would say!
>
> Sylvia Ordonez

The women began their work co-operatively. After a four-day, live-in training seminar at the Bulacan Farmers' Training Centre, they met once a month for three years to learn the skills needed for taking care of pigs, such as building pens and using commercial feed and medicines. One of the things that made the project unique was that the women earned while learning. Within a year, participants' incomes increased by 30 per cent.

Going to meetings and being trained away from their homes initially caused a big problem with husbands. 'We made the live-in training one of the conditions for participation. If the women cannot even be allowed by their husbands to go in training away from them for one week, then we would not accept them' said Ordonez. She observed that in time 'that became a non-issue', and the women would joke about it, saying that once they started going outside their homes they began to care how they looked and their husbands noticed that. Soon, husbands, families and communities seemed to respect them more. 'Until then only the man made decisions because he was the only one earning. Now husband and wife decide together, or she decides. The whole family works together. The children fetch water, the husband fixes the pen, the woman feeds the pig. Women's social contacts became wider, they became alert and even emerged as leaders, because we trained them to talk instead of being shy,' Santa Ana explained.

The revolving loan fund we sponsored was the core of the San Miguel project. It provided $48 (P1000) to each woman for the pig pen, feeds, veterinary drugs and six gilts (valued at $13 for a two-month old piglet). Those who sold piglets after weaning made $3.80 to $4.80 each in net income. Fattened pigs sold after four months meant a net gain of $9.50. The estimated household income before the project, $333 per annum, was thus increased by 30 per cent.

A unique feature of the project was that half of the women's earnings had to be saved. Each woman had to open a bank account with a co-signatory from the project and the money was put aside for emergencies; the women were very good at paying it back. The other 50 per cent of their earnings was spent on the children's education, their number one priority. After that, their earnings went toward home improvement and health expenditures.[44]

By 1981 the success of the project led to an overwhelming demand for a chance to participate. From 70 members, the group increased to 150. Four hundred applicants had been turned down because of a lack of resources by the time the Voluntary Fund grant ran out in 1982. A final evaluation study, completed for the VFDW, carried out with a sample of thirty-five participants, showed that the women's incomes had increased by 40 per cent , and in 80 per cent of the cases the members had reached or nearly reached self-sufficiency; they were able to buy piglets and feed with their own savings.[45] The total savings of the groups amounted to nearly one million pesos, half of which would be reinvested in their toy-making project and the rest was used to buy agricultural land and a fifty-seat bus.

In 1985, out of its 154 projects worldwide, UNIFEM selected the San Miguel pig-fattening project and seven others to exemplify the work and potential of low-income women. The project was uniquely effective as an anti-poverty strategy. It grouped women in their own organization, the KBB ('Village Women', in Tagalog), which soon spawned several other activities. In addition, the training programme methodology became a model for over a hundred similar training courses offered in different parts of the country by the Technology and Livelihood Resource Centre (TLRC), a government programme.

The San Miguel group was able to borrow a million pesos from TLRC, but, before they could benefit from it, there was a drought followed by the threat of pig cholera. When the cost of feed then went up, the people began to sell off their pigs at low prices. The women, however, continued to repay their government loan and some continued raising pigs. Many were still raising pigs when I visited in 1994.

The experience of the UNIFEM-assisted project had empowered the women and created group solidarity. They would surprise even themselves as well as others when they later created their own foundation and a medium-scale enterprise. Those giant steps would bring UNIFEM back into their lives seven years after the pig-raising project was completed.

Stuffed toys and garment making

Ordonez was once again the intermediary for the women of San Miguel when she was approached by a businessman who had heard of the San Miguel women and wanted to ask them to accept an order for sewing. In November 1986, the women's community organization, KBB, negotiated with the businessman. On the very same day, thirteen of the women who had sewing machines came together and began the first sewing centre.

'The home-based groups started to multiply all over the place. FAFW loaned them short-term working capital to pay the salaries of the workers until the lot was paid for,' said Ordonez. Four months after the initial agreement, there were 38 home-based sewing centres in San Miguel. Three hundred stuffed-toy makers were earning 200–350 pesos a week, and the highly skilled earned 500 pesos.[46]

The Foundation of San Miguel Women, Kababaihang Barangay Livelihood Foundation (KBBLF), was created in 1987 to handle all of San Miguel's resources, eventually replacing FAFW and bringing the project completely under local control. Members who had been officers of the co-operative KBB group for ten years led the Foundation. In the same year, DAN DEE International, a multinational stuffed toy manufacturer in the USA, ordered 2500 dozen stuffed toys a month. Receiving and distributing raw materials, collecting finished products and maintaining quality became an overwhelming task for KBBLF.

At an Asian regional conference of UNIFEM in 1988 we discovered that Daw Aye, formerly of ESCAP, was working for the women of San Miguel in their new venture. She reported that FAFW sought a grant or loan to assist the San Miguel women's plans for expansion. A year later, UNIFEM approved a request by FAFW for $300 000, including a revolving loan fund for the stuffed-toy production. TLRC would provide both technical and financial support also, and FAFW contributed $95 000. San Miguel Bulacan Toy City Inc. was organized and officially registered as a corporation to manage the project for KBBLF in 1989. The initial goal was to consolidate the scattered home-based production centres into two large ones with 50 high-speed sewing machines.[47]

When global competition in toy production increased, the San Miguel women turned to garment manufacturing on contract with a Manila factory called JR Garments. That change came at the time when the Philippines was seeking to improve its competitiveness on the international market, where it had only 1 per cent of garment market share, and the government believed that the garment sector had the greatest potential of any Philippine manufactures for increasing exports.

I visited Toy City with Emma Santa Ana and some of the women of KBB and its Foundation. We met women who still worked out of their homes, where they knitted 1500 sweaters each week. We spoke with Elisa Geranima, age 23, who was also going to school.

I learned to knit when I was 18, and I make five sweaters each week. I can earn 450 pesos a week, working at home, and I use the money for my three children, age seven, four, and two. My husband is a bus conductor.

Santa Ana explained that when the knitting groups started in 1985, they used needles imported from Taiwan and Thailand. Then a local family invented and was now selling bamboo knitting needles. The preceding year at the factory they had retrained 700 women and men but, 'retraining them is very hard, because once they are skilled, they look for bigger salaries'.[48]

Santa Ana had often been questioned about the hiring of men in a women's project. Her reply was 'What's wrong? These men are the children of our women members. We are not only providing work for the women of the family, but also for the children, for the whole family.'

Working in the factory helps me very much. I can support my family with the money. I use it for my kids allowance and to buy daily needs in our home. And for my needs too. Some of our trainees go to Manila to make more money at another factory. Some just stay here to support their parents' work in the rice fields.

Imelda Mata, factory worker

When my daughter comes home from school, after a period of time she starts knitting. We make eight or nine sweaters a week, and earn 3500 pesos a month. We use the money for school, for food, and for fixing up the house. We have new windows and cement flooring.

Rosalinda Evangelista

Edna Briones had knitted at home until she came to the garment factory. She still knits in the evening to earn money for her small child. The most difficult problems her friends have are financial ones, she said. Some of them work at San Miguel, and others have gone to Manila. One after the other, the women told us the same story: they work to get money to spend on food and clothing for their families, and once in a while for themselves.

Santa Ana told me that about 800 women were now part of the knitting groups in San Miguel–a far cry from the original seventy pig-raisers. Many women found it hard to learn at first. 'A very healthy woman, one of our first seamstresses, came to me crying and saying "I cannot learn". She was ashamed and afraid to tell me. But now she is a sample maker. From such experience we found out that the best way to teach was "each one teach one"'.

The main factory, Toy City, bustled with activity. There were piles of colourful cloth to sew and each person had a bin in front of his/her machine where finished work was collected and inspected. Santa Ana explained that the young workers earn an average income of one hundred pesos a day doing piece-work. May Lizardo, the production manager, said that forty-four workers produced 1500 to 2000 pieces a week. One of her problems sounded very familiar; after workers learned to sew they would seek work elsewhere, where they could get a higher wage.

Leaders at San Miguel

Felicitas de Guzman had been KBB chairman for ten years and she was now the President of KBBLF, the Foundation. She explained that the Foundation sought both funding and projects for the KBB members. Besides the knitting, sewing and pig raising, they had started the *Greening of San Miguel*, a backyard fruit tree planting project to cultivate mangos, papaya, and cashews. I asked de Guzman whether she had thought of running for political office. There would be an election in 1995, she said, and some of the men had encouraged her to run. 'But I said, men first before me. But I don't know, I might . . .'

Teresita de los Santos was in her fifth year as president of the association of women of San Miguel, KBB. She didn't raise pigs because she lived in a residential area. But she produced lanterns and also cooked; she had introduced that kind of work to the group. 'I told them they must learn new things, not just to venture into business, but also for the family.' Teresita took me to visit the homes of members. 'Our husbands are very happy about what we learn and earn,' she said, adding:

> We are poor farmers. We belong to the poverty line, as they say. But we have learned how to earn together. Joining an organization is a sacrifice, but it is good to learn.[49]

The song of the KBB women conveyed that spirit:

> We cannot live alone in this world. We must be together with others. It's our responsibility to help people. God put us together to help one another.[50]

Josefina de Guzman, KBB's swine-breeding co-ordinator, was a living testimony to that philosophy. She told me:

> I joined KBB to learn pig raising. Now I give medicines and advise the women on care of the pigs. My work helps my family, my children's education, and our family income. Aside from that, I have made new friends and learned how to be a leader, and also a good follower.[51]

111

Difficulties arise

The new industrial sewing venture was laden with challenges. The move from home-based work into two large centres soon discouraged many women workers who had family responsibilities. Emma Santa Ana and the women of San Miguel had expressed their preference for retaining home-based production centres so that women could simultaneously take care of family, farm and production responsibilities. That methodology–admittedly traditional–had worked, they felt, although co-ordination and quality control were difficult. FAFW, however, favoured risking a more industrial approach. The compromise was to start with two centres and then, over five years, to organize more.

When the high-speed sewing machines arrived in 1991, 239 workers who had sewn stuffed toys had to be retrained to produce garments. At the end of the training period, however, only 56 workers remained. Many of them had found more lucrative employment elsewhere or had started small production at home with neighborhood women. General managers who were recruited by the contractors did not last long, nor did they find additional contracts for Toy City. Their pay was high and their effectiveness low. With some reluctance, Emma Santa Ana herself took on the management of this medium-scale industrial venture after four other managers had failed.

Santa Ana and Ordonez both identify the major source of the start-up problems at Toy City as the underestimation of the time element involved in training workers up to the point of proficiency. And that meant underestimating the whole cash flow and working capital needs. Ordonez reflected on the first project:

> With the pigs we had no problem, because there were only 70 beneficiaries and because agriculture is different from industry. And with the piggery project we had one week live-in training sessions as one of the conditions.[52]

The 1993 evaluation completed for UNIFEM agreed with that conclusion, citing the groundwork needed to make a medium-scale venture succeed in a traditional rural setting, and adding that more of the local women should have been included in the decision-making about external finance, so that they would be 'passionately involved'.[53] Nonetheless, the evaluators agreed that the skill training goal had been attained.

It is primarily the young and unmarried who now work in the garment industry in San Miguel and outside. Older workers have returned to household and farming activities. The problem of home obligations remains unresolved and consequently the momentum of women's empowerment that the piggery project had triggered had not carried over into the new circumstances.

The evaluators noted that one of the lessons learned is that medium enterprises are 'not necessarily more efficient than small home-based enterprises'. Also, rural women's efficiency is 'not necessarily increased by putting them to work in a professionally managed environment'.[54] Their recommendation suggested sitting down and listening to women who have

112

made activities work and then studying the structure and rationale for that success.

Speaking of the many home-based workers who are under contract in San Miguel, Ordonez said:

> If you interview them you will find that they are the ones that the project trained to sew. We have to learn to allow things to happen naturally and not to control them too much. We were very fortunate in the project to have leaders like Emma and Felicitas and the others who have become something like a council of elders. People ask me: 'Isn't that project finished? When will it finish?' My answer is, it will never finish, because it's a growing thing, and it has now taken its own pace. It's alive. I think it will metamorphose. I think it's time to think of women in a bigger way: they have a bigger role to perform. In San Miguel Bulacan, during the time of President Cory Aquino, and now President Ramos, they dealt directly with our President. You can see that they are very capable of handling big things. I think we have proven that if they are assisted, and if the assistance is well-directed, they can do bigger things–policy things.[55]

Mary Racelis reinforced that view of the empowerment value of women-specific groups. She spoke of a meeting of urban poor women, when some visitors from abroad came in to look at a project. Each participant in this slum area was called to explain what she was doing. Racelis said: 'I remember one woman got up, said her piece and then sat down. She sighed and quite ecstatically said: "I did it! I really did it! I spoke to all of these important people! I actually did it!" I think she could do that because of the women's groups that meet, and the NGOs that help them.'

As long as men are in power, and look at gender issues as very special issues and not as a matter of right, then I think we have further to go. There is need for special attention, special funds for women.

Sylvia Ordonez

San Miguel as a model

When you add up the accomplishments of the women of San Miguel, they are extraordinary. The women empowered themselves economically. To a great extent on their own, they have found their way from seventy women fattening pigs in their back yards, to managing 800 women engaged in home-based industries, to a medium-scale industrial venture and a tree-planting programme. They have emerged from family poverty; now they employ their own sons and daughters. No one knows how many women have started their own ventures or found good salaries after learning skills at San Miguel and then migrating to seek their fortunes in Manila or overseas. In short, they used UNIFEM's first grant as a catalyst for change. All this in seventeen years–years when the national economy plummeted and hurtled thousands of people into poverty.

Critics who cavalierly condemn 'all those little projects' that women engage in and who want more 'large-scale projects' that yet retain a local management and participatory character have much to learn from the women of San Miguel. It is not easy. There are many risks, and the majority of risk-takers who get trained are young and ready to pull up stakes in a personal search for a better life.

Despite all the difficulties, the evaluators gave a positive assessment:

> The Toy City project . . . alters significantly not only the technological mode of production but also the existing social arrangements and value systems which for generations have shaped the lives of the beneficiaries.[56]

Start with small workshops and training sessions; include marketing skills; ensure a supply of raw materials: that was the system that the women of San Miguel developed to accommodate their income needs with their family responsibilities. Staying near home, even though it meant a lower income, was a trade-off some of them were willing to make.

Teaching women to sew or knit is also often criticized, but the women I interviewed counter that criticism. For them, sewing and knitting produced income from work they could do right at home, with one eye on the baby. And they could knit at night. Sewing was only one of a cluster of activities, including swine fattening, many of which brought income and all of which were right for some of them at certain times in their lives.

The women created institutions: KBB and KBBLF. To do this, Santa Ana's shining leadership was matched by that of other women in the community like Felicitas de Guzman. And they in turn benefited from the collegiality of Ordonez, the youth leader who cared and shared her contacts in financial circles and in the power structure of the Philippines. That linkage and solidarity between grassroots women and highly educated city women needs to be seen more often.

President Carme Guerrero Nakpil of FAFW added to that: 'KBB has not only scored a victory for grassroots participation through organizational strengthening, but it has also gained international recognition (the UNIFEM award at Nairobi) which, to my mind, is a milestone in the history of the Filipino women and therefore in that of the entire nation.'[57]

Often overlooked features of development activities are initiative, leadership, and linkages with policy and authority. Daw Aye of ESCAP commended the San Miguel women: 'Through those years, even though you had to rely on some outside assistance, finance and expertise, the core contribution to the growth of the organization came from within yourselves'. Thus through organization do women empower themselves.

With that evidence of women's economic empowerment through credit funds, technology and training in Pampanga and San Miguel and of NCRFW's work at policy level in the Philippines, we now turn briefly to UNIFEM's co-operation in establishing workshop-based production in Laos, China and Mauritius before returning to co-operative production in India. As will be seen, the factory settings offered opportunities to make use of technology in different ways.

A Philippine development plan for women

Women and development is not just women's issues but concerns that affect women, men and children as well as the country's prospects for growth and social development.

Remedios I. Rikken, Executive Director NCRFW

The National Commission on the Role of Filipino Women (NCRFW) created in 1975, was an initiator of the first economic enterprise activity in San Miguel that we discussed above, one of UNIFEM's earliest partners in the Philippines. The Commission was created 'to work towards the full integration of women for social, economic, political and cultural development at national, regional and international levels on a basis of equality with men.' Executive Director Remedios I. Rikken credits NCRFW's former Chairperson, and the first Chairperson of UNIFEM's Consultative Committee, Senator Letitia Ramos Shahani with the idea of the PDPW.

In 1987 UNIFEM gave the NCRFW a boost by financing its four-day national planning conference to prepare the Philippine Development Plan for Women (PDPW). The Conference reviewed the Philippine Development Plan: 1987–92, reviewed major departmental programmes of government, and consulted NGOs on the situation in various sectors. It then made concrete policy recommendations in agriculture, industry, trade, science and technology, housing, social welfare, education, health, population, tourism, arts and culture. Subsequently, UNIFEM financed a Filipina principal officer, Dr Rosa Linda Tidalgo-Miranda (later a UNIFEM staff member) to assist in the design of the PDPW. The Fund has continued to assist strengthening of the institutional mechanisms in government to implement the plan.

The PDPW follows the basic outline of the government's Development Plan, by dividing its contents into Economic Sectors and Social Sectors. Special sectoral concerns were added: women and migration, prostitution, violence against women, media, and arts and culture. The PDPW then defined the infrastructure and technology support that would be needed, and proposed an implementation strategy. UNIFEM now gives supplementary financial assistance to the institutional mechanisms in government that are charged with implementing the Plan. A successor to the 1986–92 Plan is on the drawing board.

Factory-based production in Laos, China and Mauritius

The productive activities of San Miguel evolved over more than a decade, from backyard swine husbandry to factory-based garment production. We now consider a Laotian model that combines home and factory production, then wage employment at a factory in China, and a workshop in Mauritius.

Laos	
Demographics	
Population	4.9 million
% urban	22
% rural	78
Income	
GNP per capita	$250
% in absolute poverty	na
%of rural population	85
% of urban population	na
Health	
Life expectancy	Women: 53 Men: 50
Infant mortality	97 per 1000 births
Maternal mortality	300 per 100000 births
Access to safe water (%)	28*
Education	
Illiteracy rate	Women: na Men: na
Girls as % of boys in secondary school	66
Girls as % of boys in tertiary school	48
Girls as % of tertiary science/engineering students	36
Work	
Households headed by women (%)	na
Women as % of labour force	na
Female wages as % of male	na
Representation	
Parliamentary seats held by women (%)	9

Source: See source table in Annexe 7.

* Data is for 1988–90

Laos was severely bombed during the twenty-five year Indochina war, and the infrastructure has not yet been rebuilt in many of the rural areas, where 80 per cent of Laotian people live (most in absolute poverty). Only 11 per cent of the population has access to safe drinking water and the rate of maternal mortality is among the highest in the world at 300 deaths per 100 000 births. Even when the weather is dry, communication is difficult since Laos has one of the smallest ratios of paved roads to people in the world, and there is only one telephone for every 500 people.[58]

In the early 1980s Daw Aye, Senior Women's Programme Officer at ESCAP, met with the leaders of the Association of Laotian Patriotic Women (ALPW) to discuss their priorities and to design a support package. Not surprisingly, the need for incomes dominated their concerns, and they spoke of wanting to use their weaving skills more efficiently. Returning to Bangkok, Daw Aye organized a Mission financed by UNIFEM.

The preparatory mission was fielded by the International Labour Organization and the Food and Agriculture Organization, and the members went to Laos for consultations with the Government and with the Women's Association. At that time the Government of Laos wanted to reduce the trade deficit and increase foreign exchange. One area of concern was the textile industry: Laos was importing eight million metres of cloth and produced only two million domestically, and much of that was woven from the 250 tons of cotton yarn imported each year. The irony for Laos was that the dependence on foreign textiles had developed in a country where weaving is a traditional art practised by most of its women who weave the family clothing at home.

Mission members submitted a detailed technical proposal to UNIFEM to fund improvements in quality and in the productivity of the home weavers. UNIFEM allocated $213 371 to implement a pilot training project which also investigated the possibilities for producing yarn from raw cotton within the country rather than relying on imports. The project was executed by the ILO, working closely with the Government and with the ALPW.[59]

In the first phase, a hundred women received technical training in Vientiane Province. The workshops covered improved spinning, dyeing and weaving techniques (including pattern reading), as well as quality control, equipment maintenance, design, management, and budget control. A co-ordinating committee, chaired by an ALPW representative was established to oversee the project.

UNIFEM acted successfully as the catalyst for a much larger project when UNDP financed an 18-month expansion of the programme in 1984; by 1989 UNDP financing had risen to $1.9 million. The UN Capital Development Fund (UNCDF) also provided $800 000 for 225 looms and dyeing equipment for weavers, as well as tools and chemicals for spinning and dyeing the yarn. Sweden, Australia, and Belgium soon assisted. Each weaver paid a portion of her earnings into a revolving fund to finance distribution of the improved looms to other home weavers.[60]

With the expanded financial support, the project grew into two components. First, the Laotian Women's Pilot Textile Centre in Vientiane produced yarn from raw cotton in eight separate production units that employ sophisticated technology but few workers. Secondly, women trained at the Centre received improved looms so that they could produce the cotton cloth in their homes; they are the vast majority of workers. Weaving supervisors from the Centre brought yarn to the women once a month and then picked up the finished cloth. Back at the Centre, the cloth was, and still is, marketed domestically. The training includes annual trips to neighboring countries to see how other textile enterprises are managed.

The project could ultimately support 500 weavers, with an output of one million metres of cloth per year, i.e., about 4 per cent of domestic demand. The Centre had achieved self-sufficiency in yarn production by 1988 and expected to produce 24 per cent of the domestic demand for cotton yarn. It has transformed the national textile industry. With the increases in productivity and quality, a Laotian woman weaver working at home could earn $15–$30 per month in 1988, or $180 to $360 per year. Such an income is enough to significantly raise a family's standard of living in a country where the average per capita income was only $250 in 1995. [61]

The factories in China that we shall now discuss had no rural outreach.

Women tailors in Beijing, China: success that did not last

The view of the ordinary Chinese man has changed a lot since 1949. Before 1949, men looked down on us. Women were mostly home-bound, not involved in the economic sector. This situation has improved. The constitution of China and its laws strongly advocate female equality . . . [but] research has shown that in their hearts, Chinese men still view women traditionally.

Professor Wei Zhangling, Chinese Academy of Social Sciences.

Chinese women state that women's situation has improved substantially since 1949, but wide disparities remain between the opportunities available to women in comparison to men. For example, the illiteracy rate of women, 38 per cent, is more than twice as much as the illiteracy among men, 16 per cent. The major reason is that adult women have on average only 3.8 years of education, whereas the typical Chinese man spends 6.3 years in school.[62] In the last few years, the All China Women's Federation (ACWF) that was established in 1949 to relieve women's poverty and fight discrimination against them, has intensified its campaign to increase women's access to education in order to improve their chances for employment.

The lack of opportunities for women reached a crisis point in 1979; the immediate cause was a change in China's agricultural policy. Previously, the collective effort of rural workers had been compensated without regard to gender, but after the change individual effort was rewarded. As a result, men's greater physical strength became of value on the farm while women were considered a burden. As explained by the Beijing Municipal Women's Federation: 'If we carry out the responsibility system [compensation for individual rather than collective effort], some women will have nothing to do. Men are stronger and there is not enough work on the farms for both.'[63]

That policy change stimulated the migration of unemployed rural women to the cities looking for a better future; unless they had university education, however, there was little work for women in the cities. Women from rural areas had received at most a secondary education, and many had attended only primary school; their marketable skills were limited. Why do

China

Demographics

Population	1238 million
% urban	30
% rural	70

Income

GNP per capita	$470
% in absolute poverty	9
%of rural population	13
% of urban population	na

Health

Life expectancy	Women: 73 Men: 69
Infant mortality	27 per 1000 births
Maternal mortality	95 per 100000 births
Access to safe water (%)	71*

Education

Illiteracy rate (%)	Women: 38 Men: 16
Girls as % of boys in secondary school	73
Girls as % of boys in tertiary school	50
Girls as % of tertiary science/engineering students	na

Work

Households headed by women (%)	na
Women as % of labour force	44**
Female wages as % of male	na

Representation

Parliamentary seats held by women (%)	21

Source: See source table in Annexe 7.

* Water data is for 1988–90
** China labour force data covers population over 15 years old.

women lag behind? Poor families will educate boys rather than girls . . . Women's illiteracy is still high in China and the cause of poverty.[64]

With very few opportunities in either the countryside or the city, many women lived in harsh conditions. In their struggle to survive once they arrived in the cities, some women established micro-enterprises despite the traditional Chinese view that women belong in the home. For example, in 1973, ten housewives pooled their labour together to make ends meet by sewing and washing. They called the micro-enterprise the Yang Hong Yun

Shirt Factory; the business was precarious, however, and the women continued to live in poverty.

Their fortunes changed when the ACWF and the Beijing Municipal Women's Federation mobilized their resources to provide job security and a decent wage to unemployed women in Beijing. In 1982, these organizations received UNIFEM funding in the amount of $200 000 to establish three Tailoring-Knitting-Weaving factories for women; $100 000 came in the form of a revolving loan fund which was later recycled for additional micro-enterprises in Beijing's poorest counties. At the same time, the Chinese government provided in-kind and monetary contributions valued at $900 000.

$60 000 of the UNIFEM grant went to the women at the Yang Hong Yun Shirt Factory in 1983; it enabled them to acquire 60 high-speed sewing machines and train workers to use them. Productivity increased and the factory expanded by hiring an additional 100 people. 92 per cent of the employees were women and 30 per cent of them had a disability. The factory produced 150,000 garments per year which the women sold to rural Chinese people at the affordable price of $2 per shirt. Two additional factories would be financed by the end of the 1980s.

By 1986, the women of Yang Hong Yun finally began to earn decent wages for the first time in their lives: 160 yuan or US$43 per month. The factory purchased sixty more sewing machines and employment rose to 233. The jobs included benefits such as pension plans, health coverage, and day care; equally important, the women's work was appreciated. Managers were promoted from within and sewing machine operators also designed the patterns for blouses and dresses.[65] 'Though modest, the factory's workrooms are clean and well-lit. In winter, a small pot-bellied stove warms the chill Beijing air.'[66]

Unfortunately, this modest success was not to last. The entire operation had collapsed by 1990. Hong Yun remained open, but only twenty women remained employed. The women with a disability paid the highest personal price in the lay-offs. The Beijing Women's Municipal Federation reported that many of the women found similar employment elsewhere or set up their own family sewing operations, but the disabled women remained unemployed. Once repaid, however, the credit fund did assist micro-entrepreneurs in the fringe areas of Beijing.

What happened between 1987 and 1990? When UNIFEM asked in 1993, the management had already dispersed and it was difficult to identify the precise cause of the initial success and then equally rapid demise of the project. What is clear from our interviews is that there are two primary factors to consider: the internal costs and management of the factories, and the external changes in the global economy and Chinese society.

Within the business the cost of benefits rose as women reached retirement age. The Hong Yun factory had substantial benefit obligations by 1990, with pensions to eighty retired employees and medical insurance since 1973. It could not cope.[67] Furthermore, the escalation of benefit costs occurred as the factory was coming under the direction of a new and inexperienced manager. 'We were told that the role of the director was pivotal in the early performance, but he left for another factory and took the most skilled personnel with him. He was replaced by a woman in 1990. She was very dedicated and tried hard, but was not as competent as the previous director'.[68] Further, ACWF did not have the technical support system that ALPW had in Laos.

Externally, there were significant changes in China's role in the global economy. The price paid by the domestic market for some garments was substantially lower than the price paid by the foreign market. China became one of the major low-cost producers of garments for the industrialized world. The two other garment factories supported by UNIFEM turned to exclusive production for the Japanese market in 1987. The Japanese customer financed the equipment and guaranteed to purchase the entire output. While this relationship may have eliminated independent business decision-making from the ACWF projects, it did provide some security in the increasingly competitive market.

It is interesting to examine the actions that a later (1988) UNIFEM-assisted garment factory in the rural Jiuzhai area of China[69] took to protect its independence under similar market conditions. The Jiuzhai enterprise began as a small sewing operation that relied on one large industrial mill for fabric and for selling the completed garments domestically as well as abroad. To create economic independence, the women decided to capture the whole production chain. They used UNIFEM funds to produce their own fabric rather than purchasing it from the mill. They also hired a marketing staff to link their garment output to the demand in the local market. (It will be seen that this strategy differs from one advised for *Mahila Haat* in India.) Unfortunately, the Hong Yun factory in Beijing did not take similar measures when competition intensified; perhaps that was because, in the largest city in China, opportunities arose for the managers and most of the workers to leave the firm for others that were better situated. Of the four factories assisted by UNIFEM, Hong Yun is the one that met serious difficulty.

Besides the down-turn in the economy, there is yet another external force working against women's employment: the growing sentiment in Chinese society that women should return to the home, leaving industrial jobs to the men. A representative of ACWF told us: 'Under economic reforms the employment pressure has led some male policy makers to think that women should return to their kitchens. Women have fiercely opposed this view . . . As China becomes more market orientated and enterprises profit-driven, discrimination against women in the labour markets is increasing. This is a special problem for young women.'[70]

China's national machinery, the ACWF, worked to have government establish an official Committee on Women and Children in 1990. Specifically to combat the discrimination against women at the level of both education and jobs, in 1992 the Committee succeeded in getting government to pass the *Law of the People's Republic of China on the Protection of Rights and Interests of Women*. Many of the women we interviewed expressed hope that the provisions of the law would make a difference. One such provision is: 'Where parents or guardians fail to send female school-

121

age children or adolescents to school, the local people's governments shall admonish and criticize them . . .' Another asserts the following: 'In such aspects as promotion in post or in rank, evaluation and determination of professional and technological titles, the principle of equality between men and women shall be upheld . . .'[71]

With the experience of both entrepreneurial failure *and* success behind it, and with a strong new legal basis for its actions, ACWF has intensified its work during the last five years. Its accomplishments are staggering: over a hundred million women received literacy and/or skill training; ten million women have benefited from credit schemes. As we saw, UNIFEM's experiences in China and Laos had fully different starting points. Strong government backing, marketing assistance and investments by other UN and bilateral funds made an important national industry in Laos, that has wide employment outreach and secure markets. For ACWF, the initial failed experience led to a factory that had backward and forward linkages to raw materials and markets at the Jiuzhai enterprise. Mauritius provides yet another model.

Dynamic craftswomen in Mauritius

The second stage of industrialization consists precisely in creating our own models, our own designs . . . beyond the need to modernize our methods of production, it is necessary also to create. [72]

For over twenty-five years, unleashing women's creativity has been the cornerstone of one Mauritian development organization's strategy for involving women in development. The two founders of the Societé pour la Promotion des Entreprises Specialisées (SPES), Helena Langlois and Francis Rey, provided capable technical guidance and unflagging faith in the human spirit of Mauritian artisans. They created SPES in 1967 during a period of economic stagnation and unemployment in this island nation located in the Indian Ocean off the coast of East Africa.

At that time, the most rapidly expanding sector of the economy was tourism, so SPES trained local artists to produce craftswork for that market as well as for Mauritians. Since 90 per cent of the trainees were women, they wrote to UNIFEM in 1980 requesting financial assistance for silk-screening machinery, arguing persuasively that 'SPES already has the building, pilot activity assures a market, and management [is] in experienced hands.'[73] UNIFEM allocated $51 538 for a silkscreen printer and a camera, and SPES provided creative jobs for thirty rural women. In 1993, fourteen of the original workers were still designing and training new employees; others had become entrepreneurs in their own right.

A guiding principle of SPES has been to use Mauritian materials in the artwork. '[Before SPES] the fabrics, the raw materials, the designs–all were imported.'[74] SPES decided to use local clay to produce pottery in 1980. '[No-one had yet] carried out scientific experiments with local clays and so Mauritian potters use solely imported clays and commercial glazes.'[75] SPES undertook research for two years to determine which local soils would be optimum. UNIFEM then allocated $40 700 to

Mauritius		
Demographics		
Population	1.1 million	
% urban	41	
% rural	59	
Income		
GNP per capita	$2700	
% in absolute poverty	8	
%of rural population	12	
% of urban population	na	
Health		
Life expectancy	Women: 73	Men: 67
Infant mortality	21	per 1000 births
Maternal mortality	108	per 100000 births
Access to safe water (%)	100	
Education		
Illiteracy rate	Women: na	Men: na
Girls as % of boys in secondary school	97	
Girls as % of boys in tertiary school	52	
Girls as % of tertiary science/engineering students	20	
Work		
Households headed by women (%)	na	
Women as % of labour force	35	
Female wages as % of male	na	
Representation		
Parliamentary seats held by women (%)	3	

Source: See source table in Annexe 7.

purchase the additives necessary to improve the clay, one kiln and a pottery wheel, plus some funds to rebuild the workshop that was destroyed by a cyclone. Thirteen years later, Langlois wrote: 'We still have one potter from the initial 1980 group, now considered a Master Craftswoman. She trains potters, and also creates designer pottery. From the rest of the original group, one started her own enterprise, and two women are working in other potteries.'[76]

To expand the creative possibilities of clay artwork, SPES hired a ceramic mosaic expert to train the staff when the Mauritian Commercial Bank commissioned a large, colourful mural and the intense colours they developed for glazes can be seen in later SPES work. In 1992, SPES potters developed an entirely new material for ceramics by combining the Mauritian clays with local basalt rock and sugar-cane bagasse fibre. This material is particularly suited for Raku quick-firing. The artisans were trained by an English potter to make appropriate kilns from old drums lined with the ceramic fibre developed by NASA for spaceships. It was only a year later that a top European jeweller asked SPES to develop Raku jewellery after seeing a SPES miniature Raku fish in a Portuguese exhibit.

The Society managed to compete on the global market and to succeed while continuing to value the creativity of Mauritian women. In fact, the directors of SPES, Langlois and Rey, credit the programme's international marketing success precisely to the development of local talent: 'If you are only a simple manufacturer, a cut of fifty cents off the price can mean failure. The success of [SPES] knitwear is due in part to the fact that we have developed our own designs for which it is possible to get prices which are a lot more interesting.'[77]

SPES also kept up with the latest crafts technology. 'SPES was able, with UNIFEM project equipment funding, to start a type of CAD/CAM system of graphics for printing on paper and textile', attaching the software to the computer-controlled silkscreen camera and press which UNIFEM had funded. SPES used the technology to combine silkscreening activities with ceramics, printing logos for firms and hotels and their own folkloric designs on ceramic pottery. Today, the CAD/CAM process is integrated with electronic knitting machines connected to dialogue computers suitable for cottage work. In 1990, SPES' computerized upholstery design project was called a model project for the UNESCO Decade of Culture (1990–99).

SPES has a quarter century of providing income to Mauritians and has proven institutional strength. Its most unique features, when compared with the factories in China and Laos may be its level of technological sophistication, combined with a nurturing of creativity. The Laos ateliers, however, were able to offer far broader employment opportunities in the battle to overcome poverty. The Jiuzhai enterprise in China is still young, but also promising. SPES hires wage workers, many of whom stay for years. It is a prototype that calls for thoughtful consideration.

Because SPES is a micro-industry, it is difficult to compare it with the larger-scale projects that we have reviewed. Nonetheless, common threads are woven through projects like Udaipur, San Miguel and SPES. Three commonalities come to mind: sustained leadership, long-term external assistance and excellent technical support.

As will be seen in the following section, UNIFEM assistance in India has also had a broad outreach.

More than economics: UNIFEM in India

I am leading the kind of life that my mother could only dream of.
Andu Bai, Sericulturist

India

Demographics

Population	931 million
% urban	27
% rural	73

Income

GNP per capita	$310
% in absolute poverty	40
%of rural population	42
% of urban population	33

Health

Life expectancy	Women: 61	Men: 60
Infant mortality	88	per 1000 births
Maternal mortality	250	per 100000 births
Access to safe water (%)	73%	

Education

Illiteracy rate (%)	Women: 66	Men: 38
Girls as % of boys in secondary school	52	
Girls as % of boys in tertiary school	42	
Girls as % of tertiary science/engineering students	24	

Work

Households headed by women (%)	na
Women as % of labour force	29
Female wages as % of male	na

Representation

Parliamentary seats held by women (%)	7

Source: See source table in Annexe 7.

In India the popular economy is enormous. As we have seen, it includes 108 million women–97 per cent of all female workers. Self-employment is often home-based garment or cigarette production; petty trade or vending; services such as laundry; agriculture, construction, carpentry, and the like. As was noted earlier in this book, only 10 per cent of India's poor work in the formal sector. And two of every five of India's 931 million people live in 'absolute poverty'. The average annual income per person is $310. Women are at the lower end of every income spectrum: 80 per cent of India's self-employed women earn less than 500 rupees ($16) a month.

Indian women leaders by no means simply accept that *status quo*. They are strong believers in working together to achieve better lives. Well-organized women's groups pressured the Government of India to appoint a National Committee on the Status of Women as early as 1971. In 1977 the Planning Commission established a Working Group on the Employment of Women. Additional commissions and working groups were set up throughout the 1970s on women's access to science and technology, adult education, women's studies, village-level organizations of rural women and women in agriculture.

The effectiveness of government policies has been a matter of great concern to women leaders. For that reason, the Centre for Women's Development Studies submitted a proposal to UNIFEM in 1983 to finance a study on the role of public specialized agencies working in production/distribution, credit/finance, rural development, health, education and social welfare. The extent to which those organizations translated national policies about women into practices was analysed, and then discussed in a series of workshops with government officials. Training modules were prepared for the Administrative Service programmes with public agency employees.[78]

Women leaders managed to get 30 per cent of the Integrated Rural Development Programme resources allocated for women in the national plan for 1984–5. But evaluations in 1987 determined that those allocations were of little benefit. I was told by Madhu Bala Nath, UNIFEM representative in India, that 'In some states the amount actually committed to women was as low as 7 per cent. Nonetheless, the allocations are a very good lever for women to be able to access funds, once they are empowered', Nath added.[79]

The most recent National Commission, and a powerful one, was on Self-Employed Women and Women in the Informal Sector, mentioned earlier in this text; it has awakened the country to the enormous size of the informal sector of the economy, and the near hopelessness of many who work within it. 'Many women told of earning abysmally low wages–as low as one or two rupees a day. There was widespread night-blindness from malnutrition, harassment by officials–from physical abuse by forest guards to collecting bribes–and abuse by police in market places', the Commission found.[80]
As the Commission observed:

> After having to spend twenty-three years breaking stones and head-loading in a Rajasthan mine, or peeling and beating coir for eighteen years, or being born into a migrant road crew, or carrying toxic sulphur powder for seven years–all for a fraction of the legal minimum wage–what reason is there to think that their families' lives will change?[81]

The Government's seven National Development Plans have been key targets for women seeking change. Gradually but surely, the content of the Plans as regards women evolved from a welfare orientation to education, and then to economic empowerment–the subject of the Seventh Plan. That Plan also made the much-criticized dowry system illegal and called for strengthening the village women's organizations, the Mahila Mandals.

UNIFEM's Nath has herself changed the government's way of looking at working women. She told us how that came about because she sought to add a question to the national census that would express the reality of women's contributions to the national economy. 'The Registrar General said to me: "Mrs Nath, you are asking me for the moon. Do you know what the census operation is like in India? We have 1.6 million enumerators, and do you think we can train them to capture more information relating to women?"' Not easily discouraged, and armed with the findings of the National Commission on Self-Employed Women, Nath pursued her point until a new clause was added to the census question 'What work do you do?' The new words were 'including unpaid work on farm and family enterprise'. The result in the 1991 census was a 44.4 per cent increase in the economic participation rates of women, just by that one intervention, said Nath.[82]

Despite some positive policy measures and the innumerable initiatives of government, NGOs and UN organizations, India, not unlike other countries, has a long way to go. Attitudes die hard, and attitudes toward women call for a long and tedious social revolution. Just one example illustrates that point: Of 8000 abortions in Bombay after parents learned the sex of the foetus through amniocentesis, only one would have been a boy.[83] A 1994 law passed by Parliament provides severe punishment for sex-determining pre-natal tests; ending a pregnancy because a fetus is female is now outlawed. But Madhu Kishwar, editor of the women's journal, *Manushi*, warns that previous statewide bans in Rajasthan and elsewhere have failed, and 'laws have had little effect on changing behaviour'.[84]

Economist R. Sundarshan points to economic planning as an area that women must influence even more intensely. The concern about women has been overtaken, he says. 'There isn't much attention to valuing women's contributions in the non-monetary economy now. The latest fashion is the environment.'[85] Because India is frequently cited as one of Asia's fast-growing economies, soon to become another 'Asian Tiger', there is an urgent need to trace the direct linkage between macro-economic policy and mass poverty as a preparation for changes in economic policy. Two of UNIFEM's assisted projects that I shall describe illustrate that linkage in a very vivid way. The sericulture project assisted by UNIFEM in Udaipur is one of those. After eleven years of operation it has become a model for other organizations, including the World Bank. After reviewing its history, we will then examine Mahila Haat, a federation of village market women.

Sericulture in Udaipur

Rajasthan State on India's northwest border is home for the Bhil tribal people whose area in the Aravalli hills in Udaipur District is severely drought-prone. The Bhils depend on low-yield agriculture from their small holdings of rocky and dry land where they live in isolated stone houses. A few bushels of wheat or maize is all they can grow. Because the soil is too barren to grow vegetables, the nutrition levels of the Bhil people are low, and to add to the deficiency, a source of food and fuel was lost when the forests were progressively and illegally cut down. While nearly a quarter of India's total population is considered undernourished, the state of tribal people like the Bhils is even worse.

Deep indebtedness to money lenders became a way of life for the Bhils. At times debts would have to be paid by unremunerated labour over several generations. To supplement a sparse income from agriculture, men seek wage labour on construction sites and road repair. Women work hard, giving ten to twelve hours a day to economic activity such as collecting fuel and fodder, carrying water, working with men in agriculture–the kind of work that was completely overlooked in earlier censuses. Like men, they also find employment in construction and roadwork, but earn only 40 to 60 per cent of men's wages. There was little hope for better-paying employment for either men or women because the overall literacy rate in Rajasthan is 17 percent, and female rural literacy is only 5 per cent.[86]

Seeking ways to enhance women's incomes, the Rajasthan government commissioned a study by the Agriculture Department of the University of Udaipur which indicated that sericulture would be appropriate for the area because it was agro-based, labour-intensive, and needed a minimal initial investment. It also suited families who traditionally eked out a living together from forest products and agriculture. Furthermore, there was thought to be an insatiable market for silk in India. In 1979 the Rajasthan Government asked UNIFEM (then VFDW) to assist its project entitled Increasing Sericulture in Udaipur District.[87]

The project was a four-year activity to generate additional and direct employment for 300 tribal women. To be qualified for the project, a woman's family had to hold 0.1 hectare of land for mulberry production and have access to water. It was understood that both men and women would grow mulberry, but the silkworm rearing and silk reeling would be women's responsibility. That division of labour suited the local culture.[88]

The UNIFEM input of $127 635 covered technical training for mulberry cultivation, silkworm rearing, equipment and a van, compensation for loss of crops and a revolving credit fund for purchasing cocoons from the cultivators. The fund would be reimbursed upon sale of the silk yarn. Government contributed the equivalent of $169 000 for technical staff, buildings and vehicles. Rajasthan's Tribal Area Development Department (TADD) was assigned as executing agency for the project. Its extension staff–almost all men–were to train women in the technical aspects of sericulture.

At UNIFEM headquarters, as we followed the periodic reports on the project, questions arose as to whether it benefited women to the extent intended. As told elsewhere in this book, our experience with a pottery project in Bolivia alerted us to situations where men might take over when technologies were introduced to women and income resulted. An evaluation at Udaipur in 1987 confirmed that more attention needed to be given to women's participation and benefits. It also showed that income targets had been met: $100–three times the earnings from traditional crops–could be earned from just 0.1 hectare of mulberry. A classic development situation had crept in however–*cash crops had displaced food crops*. Food shortages resulted in poor diets and malnutrition. In addition, children's education had not improved and alcoholism had increased dramatically among both men and women.

The productive activities of what was intended to be a women's project had been co-opted by men, who were rearing the worms *and* deciding how to use the income. Women were burdened with the portage of 'massive amounts of mulberry leaves'. In short, the development targets of the project were not yet achieved. People were not better off.

A second phase of the project was based on the findings of that evaluation; it drew $99 000 from UNIFEM and $80 770 from government. This time the project was more specifically directed to development goals: 'to empower the tribal woman and raise the quality of life of her family'.[89] It would involve an additional 200 women, bringing the total to 500, and it would encourage them to organize grassroots groups through the Mahila Mandal ('village organization') movement. By organizing, the women would become 'the focal points of development activities in their villages'.[90] Besides sericulture, other income-earning projects would be planned once the village groups were formed. Such groups were seen as sustainable institutions and they would be the basis for future activity.

To empower the women even more, there would be health and nutrition activities for them and their children, and school-going would be encouraged, as would habits of saving money. Two other UN agencies joined the project's co-sponsors to strengthen its activities. The World Food Programme (WFP) offered food-for-work for mulberry cultivation and participation in the Integrated Child Development Service centres; the UN Fund for Population Activities (UNFPA) assisted health and family welfare activities.[91]

Most importantly, a local non-governmental organization called Aastha– meaning 'faith in the people'–was brought in to assist in mobilization and to raise the awareness of the women in the Mahila Mandals. The techniques of women staff members included field trips to meet SEWA members, health and nutrition education, poultry farming, vegetable raising and discussion of community issues through the use of plays and puppetry. Women who wanted to start a Mahila Mandal in their village would choose five women to be trained by Aastha as leaders for their monthly meetings. The members could still produce silk independently but then process and sell it as a co-operative. That community and family leadership training complemented TADD's training of the groups in the technology of silk production. The economic activities of the project were thus complemented by empowering ones.

In its second phase, the project has been very effective. Incomes have continued to rise; the average family income has gone from US$32 to $226 a year, and some women earn as much as US$700.[92] An advantage women find in sericulture over agriculture is that the former gives them work and income all year round.

Incomes in relation to the number of crops harvested annually are shown in Table 7.1:

Besides that income from sericulture, some women get extra money by crafting bamboo trays and montages, adding up to US$310 to their yearly incomes. The value of their productive and family responsibilities has been enhanced and they have been given the gift of time to choose what work to

129

Table 7.1: Annual incomes from sericulture

No. of crops per year	Gross annual income (US$)
1 crop: Rs3–4000 per crop	115 to 153
75% raise 2 crops a year	230 to 306
20% raise 3 crops a year	345 to 459
5–10% raise 4 crops a year	460 to 612

Source: L. Creevey, (ed.) 1994 *Changing Women's Lives and Work.* UNIFEM, New York.

do, thanks to the eighty-one wells that were dug to counter drought conditions. Andu, a participant, spoke of what the project meant to her: 'I am leading the kind of life that my mother could only dream of. And I no longer need to work long, backbreaking hours in the fields'. Andu Bai added, 'Now I don't have to do road labour like I did before. And now we have fresh vegetables all the time. Our family income has increased five times over.'[93]

Now that family decisions are made jointly, women use their new income for food and other family needs, for renovating their homes or for building new ones. Interestingly, many of them refused to take loans from the project's revolving loan fund to construct their rearing huts for the silkworms. 'They had spent a lifetime in a state of indebtedness to local moneylenders, so they managed to save enough to finance their own huts without taking any credit', according to Madhu Bala Nath.[94] Like women in Swaziland, they rejoiced in being free from money lenders; they had reached a self-reliant status.

For Hira Bai and her family, 1993 was like any other year. The family had suffered from malaria, but recovered. Crops had not been good due to drought: only about two sacks of corn had been produced. The family earned only Rs1000 from the sale of corn. The other sources of income were sericulture, which brought in Rs1800, and work as labourers.

Hira Bai was appreciative of the sericulture programme since it enabled the family to earn at home. It also brought in cash to meet the family's essential needs without having to mortgage the family's silver (jewelery). The children could be sent to school with the money earned.

Source: UNIFEM *Case Studies,* 1992–1993

TADD recently began to hand over to the women's co-operatives some of the more technologically sophisticated processes of silk production. A woman-owned co-operative society at Pai village set up a reeling plant to process the silk. The co-operative purchases cocoons from five nearby villages and makes thread; workers in the small factory earn forty rupees a day. The same co-operative society is learning to make a type of chapati for sale in Udaipur city.

Sericulturist Brij Mohan Dixit of TADD explained that sericulture is a highly labour-intensive industry and eighty to ninety per cent of the work is done by women. 'We find that the efficiency of the women workers is much greater than that of men: reeling, cleaning the cocoon, feeding the mulberry leaves', he said.

Because decisions on the degree of mechanization to adopt in the sericulture industry will determine the future incomes of the producers, I asked Dixit about TADD's views on that issue. He replied:

> Our basic object is to generate more and more employment, isn't it? So at every step we take due care that mechanization won't replace labour. For example, in reeling, if you use power-operated machines together with manual labour, we welcome the mechanization. Wherever the product quality increases and efficiency of labour also increases, mechanization is adopted. Where the quality is the same, and the work can be done manually, we reject mechanization.[95]

That explanation did not answer the need to increase productivity in order to maintain income under the pressure of competition from silk producers in other parts of India or overseas. When others mechanize, can the women remain competitive and still make a good income? Or is there a way to maintain the price of silk by making the Udaipur silk cloth unique as a handcrafted material? Those questions were made more urgent by two decisions taken far away from Udaipur, in Delhi and overseas.

When the Indian Government lowered tariffs on imported silk in 1993, a flood of silk came in from China and Korea where the industry is mechanized. Because of fewer labour inputs, the imported products are cheaper and the quality is more consistent. The sale price of silk yarn in India dropped from Rs 1600 a kilo to Rs 700 a kilo that year (It rose to Rs 1000 in 1994). Caught in that competition, yet not wanting to lose income, the government sold Udaipur silk very late but still at a fair price that year.

A related issue was the World Bank's entry into sericulture in India. The Bank hoped to bring 2000 acres of land under mulberry over a five-year period; it already had seventeen project areas. A cocoon market would be opened, reeling would be taken over by private entrepreneurs, and the mulberry species would be improved. In contrast, UNIFEM had just 140 acres under mulberry. UNIFEM's Nath met with the World Bank Mission in Udaipur in 1991. She expressed her concerns about the Bank's approach to promoting the 'sericulture industry' in the national economy. For Nath, 'if the two projects were not well co-ordinated, the richer farmers in the area would commit a great deal of their land to mulberry at the expense of food cultivation.' From its own Phase I experience, UNIFEM was aware that such a situation has negative effects on family food security. It would also tend to widen the gulf within the tribal community. 'The rich will get richer', she said.

I asked Parfulla Nagar of TADD whether the women were insured against another market crisis, noting particularly the World Bank's competitive sericulture projects. He said that in his view the import problem

131

was a temporary setback. His main concern was that the World Bank methodology was commercial, with no consideration for 'human inputs', such as organizing women to improve family well-being. The Bank was 'target and technology oriented,' Nagar said. Despite that commercial orientation, workers on the Bank schemes produced only enough cocoons to earn money to feed themselves: they did not reach the Bank's commercial target. Apparently they were unwilling to produce for the sake of producing, as the Bank wanted. The UNIFEM approach, in contrast, was linked with concrete improvements in women's lives and created a high level of motivation among them. Nagar explained that approach:

> Once the beneficiaries receive their annual income through sericulture, they are armed to take on other programmes. Then we offer additional economic programmes, as well as education, health and hygiene, and horticulture. That is the benefit of this system of UNIFEM.[96]

Aastha staffer Fommu Shrivastava was blunt about the Bank approach. 'Bank projects typically stress getting as much land as possible under cash crop cultivation. We heard officials on one project say proudly: "This land used to be in corn, and now it's mulberry". There's a kind of ruthlessness, of not thinking about the family and the rural condition as a single unit. It's quite a contrast with the holistic approach of the UNIFEM assistance'.[97]

> The World Bank is primarily interested in generating a surplus in silk production. UNIFEM is primarily interested in generating income for women.
>
> TADD meeting, 1994

Some agreements were reached between the Bank and UNIFEM, including the Bank's sharing its crop research with TADD. Aware of the need to motivate farmers and of women's influence on the community, the Bank would send some women from its projects for leadership and awareness training by Aastha. An issue of great concern at the time was the proposed cocoon market in Udaipur. The women were experienced as petty traders in their communities but that was not the same as being prepared for a highly competitive silk auction. In UNIFEM's view, once an open cocoon market was operational, the women would be handicapped and there would be opportunity for middlemen to come in and exploit the farmers. The bankers thought otherwise: that a competitive market would stimulate growth in the industry. With the decision made for a cocoon market, UNIFEM had to ensure 'an intensive programme of organizing women's groups so that they could participate effectively in the growth,' said Nath, adding, 'we must prepare our women's groups to face a competitive silk industry which may come in over the next five years of the IBRD project period.'[98]

UNIFEM's approach actually influenced the Bank, Nath reported three years later.

> The successful features of the [UNIFEM] project, namely a very effective outreach to women through the involvement of an NGO,

132

the focus on women for the development of communities, and the intercropping of mulberry with vegetables, are now being dovetailed into the World Bank's National Sericulture Project that is operating in 17 States of the country, with a potential of impacting about 70000 rural women.[99]

The human dimension of Udaipur

In Pai Village, discussions in the Mahila Mandal had been wide-ranging for some time. Issues included child marriage, health, income, preschool and school education, forest protection, road building, drought and scarcity of water. The group took proposals on some of those topics to District officials and one result was a new road; its construction also provided employment. Two Mandal members had been trained and were running *balwadies* (crèches) and others were now trained in traditional medicine. Javeri and Amri Bai said 'We were unable to speak in front of people earlier, but we now feel confident to pass on knowledge to other women'.[100]

Mira Bai, the President of the Mahila Mandal of 150 women at Pai, excitedly told her group about her meetings with the President and Vice President of India in Delhi on Republic Day, 27 January. She spoke of the work of her organization and its needs. They had drinking water, but still had problems with wells. They purchased and distributed fertilizer and good quality seeds, but they wanted technology to free up their time for cash-crop production without sacrificing their home responsibilities. Solar cookers and an electric grinder were their priorities and the co-operative planned to get a loan for the grinder. They had calculated the cost of electricity, the quantity of wheat that could be made into flour in a day, and how much they would charge per kilo for grinding.

'This group sees itself as looking after social problems as well as sericulture and other economic activities, such as flour mills. They take creative collective decisions to help the women in their area solve problems', Shrivastava explained. One group of women refused to vote for a village leader who had become corrupt. The Aastha representative commented: 'There is a kind of maturity in this group; they analyse problems, find solutions and then act'.[101]

The positive impact of the project on the quality of life was confirmed by a recent survey of forty-three participants. The survey found that family diets were more nutritious, decision-making was shared in the family, and women's opinions were sought by husbands and other family members. Women have more authority than previously. Overall, the participants were more self-confident, and 88 per cent of them had no objection to having sericulture take up their leisure time. Several participants said that because of the project they were able to stop their husbands from drinking and from beating them. Four out of five husbands found the project helpful to the family because it added to family income.[102]

Women who were Mahila Mandal members felt empowered to 'speak out on issues of concern and act collectively to bring about changes in their lives'.[103] Nath observed that some people felt threatened by women's new

133

ability to question and demand explanation for activities that impacted on their lives.[104]

The value of reformulating the activities, after Part I of the project ended, became clear. Not only had incomes continued to rise, but women's status and the well-being of families were significantly improved and consumer habits were profoundly changed during Phase II. Women were empowering themselves not only in the Aastha-assisted Mahila Mandal groups but also in the group of 2500 women who received technical training from the TADD officers who had adopted the 'UNIFEM system'. Yet the Mahila Mandal women clearly differed from the others in their degree of self-confidence and their capacity for community action.[105]

> We have been able to pay off our debts and to build a new brick and cement house.
>
> Punki, a participant

Udaipur sericulture as a model

Of the many unique features of the Udaipur project, two interrelated ones stand out. One is the way the training programme was phased in, with the productive activities that generate income starting first, followed by the empowering ones. The other is the way in which, despite their great diversity, government and an NGO worked together. A good deal of intersectoral planning and patience contributed to that success. The flexibility of all parties, including the donors, is also mentioned by observers as a key factor in the effectiveness of the project.

How does the Udaipur sericulture project stand up to our three variables for the reversal of poverty trends?[106]

○ Economic empowerment has been experienced and poverty has been reduced by women's access to productive resources. Incomes have tripled in comparison with those earned from traditional agriculture; malnutrition is down; houses are improved. There has been a multiplier effect, with 2500 women, rather than the early target group of 500, now engaged in sericulture. Wage employment has been created to distribute fertilizers and saplings and to purchase cocoons. The co-operative employs women and some men in processing. Interestingly, individuals have successfully initiated enterprises, such as poultry rearing, that failed as group businesses.

The question still persists, however, as to whether the women are ready to hold their own in a 'free market' in order to earn a maximum amount for their work. The issue of the degree to which mechanization should be introduced into sericulture production also remains unresolved in the view of this writer, yet the need to do so is multiplied by the competition of World Bank projects and imported silk. It appears that there will have to be an up-front investment in technological innovation at Udaipur if incomes are to remain stable in the face of plunging prices per kilo of silk, compounded by inflation. The search for appropriate mechanization may concentrate on production per hectare in order not to sacrifice the human development, social and motivational dimensions of the project. Alternatively, perhaps the lesser-grade Udaipur silk can be seen to have some special features that add to its market value, just as the 'bleeding colours' of Madras cotton added value to fabric some decades ago.

Nagar felt that the project was now almost ready to be autonomous. It takes at least five years of training and awareness, he said, to make a project viable. But an additional phase of the project was needed to give women technical support, including how to market their silk.

○ Sustainable institutions are being created in the villages. The Mahila Mandal co-operatives are support systems for productive activities, community action and mutual assistance during family crises. The ten women's groups assisted by the NGO Aastha are said to have almost completely stopped anti-social customs like alcoholism and polygamy. They have lobbied several agencies to get health centres opened, hand-pumps repaired, roads constructed. They run their own nursery centres for members, and have increased the school enrolment of boys and girls.

○ The project has been a catalyst for change far beyond any expectation. The seventeen World Bank sericulture projects affect some 70 000 people, and the project led the Bank to adopt anti-malnutrition practices such as intercropping, and to focus on women and the development of communities.

○ Women themselves have been empowered–self-reliant and self-confident. From their organizational base they demand explanations for activities that impact on them, thus holding government staff accountable for their actions. Many have been trained to run crèches, raise poultry, and to engage in businesses other than sericulture. A number of them have received leadership training. They have become self-sufficient in food, thanks in part to the WFP assistance.

Nath makes a very salient point. 'The normally accepted view is that literacy is the stepping stone for development. However, the project has proved that although literacy is important, it is awareness-education appropriate to the lives of the people that makes a critical difference to the development process.'[107] She adds that, with the World Bank now in the picture, 'the UNIFEM project has another dimension, that of creating competitive entrepreneurs to exist and survive in an industry that will change and grow very fast. It is a new challenge and a new demand'.[108]

Mahila Haat: the village market

As a facilitation centre for poor women producer groups, Mahila Haat is to strengthen the groups' market linkages and organize them into a federation to get the policy changes they need.

Project Document

Mahila Haat ('village market') has a more halting story to tell about economic empowerment of women. It is an organization that was created in 1984 to reach out to Indian women working in the popular economy–the informal sector. They are home-based, self-employed women workers who 'compete with an increasingly commercialized and competitive environment and face many impediments to getting credit, raw materials and marketing outlets. Many of them are bound in exploitative relationships with contractors. Many are held hostage by suppliers who control their raw materials, or by middlemen who control their access to the market.[109]

As a facilitation centre for poor women producer groups, Mahila Haat was meant to strengthen the groups' market linkages and organize them into a federation that would give them a voice to get the policy changes they needed. That concept was one with which UNIFEM could agree, and initial financial assistance of $14 541 was offered in 1984.[110] An additional $71 277 was granted in 1987[111] and a third grant was given in 1989 by UNIFEM.

Mahila Haat is the brainchild of Devaki Jain, the Director of the Institute of Social Studies Trust (ISST) in Delhi. ISST, a thirty-year old organization established to do social science research, became a studies and resource centre for the women's movement in India in the 1970s. Its primary activities are research, documentation and counselling. It also engages in networking, advocacy and activism, and in institution building. As one of ISST's institutionalizing activities, Mahila Haat is scheduled to become a fully autonomous organization.[112]

During its first phase, Mahila Haat completed a directory of women's micro-producer groups in several states of India, and held two workshops with fifty-three of those groups. Endorsing the need for the proposed support structure, the participants observed that facilitation was required at two levels, the sophisticated urban market and the rural markets. They advised that over the long term, Mahila Haat should strengthen women's income-earning capacities and create solidarity so that women could articulate their problems to the Government with a strong voice. A registered federation of producer groups from all over India should be set up, the workshop participants added. An evaluation of the project found that the first phase had achieved its set of objectives.

Those activities formed the basis for the second, operational phase. Its organizers proposed that it should focus on design and product development, marketing, and procurement of raw materials. Over a five-year period it was to create strong regional centres and information networks on issues relating to production processes, technological choices and development policies. It would also formulate policies and set up pilot rural marketing outlets in four states.[113]

A 1987 evaluation considered the proposed Phase II activities to be 'extremely ambitious', and suggested that Mahila Haat concentrate on just three or four sectors of the economy that were already dominated by women producers and marketers, such as the dairy, silk and food processing industries.[114] Those proposals were not adopted at the time, although

ISST management did decide to work mainly in one state, Uttar Pradesh, while giving some assistance to marketing and networking in other states.

For example, from 1992–3 Mahila Haat trained 380 women of the Kumaon Hills in Uttar Pradesh state in skills for the wool industry, such as dyeing, carding, spinning, and carpet weaving, knitting and wool processing. Another 138 women entered training in 1994. Two training-cum-production centres were set up for carpet weaving and a retail outlet was opened in Almora. Quality and design were emphasized in all of the programmes, along with ways to market their products. A wool bank run by an NGO had 320 members for whom raw materials were purchased in bulk. Assistance for such activities came from the Governments of India and Norway.

> Women were not interested in health, education and childcare training. But when I started an income-generating programme, they were very interested. Now that they have income, they want those other subjects too.
>
> Krishna Bisht, Director, Mahila Haat

During my recent visit, discussions about women's production inevitably returned to market issues. They revealed the dilemmas faced during efforts to raise the incomes of the poor. Tara Sharma Apachu, a former director of Mahila Haat, posed some questions: 'Is it feasible just to depend on a local market? Are we aiming at something without knowing whether it is possible to stand on our own feet? Do women have enough managerial skills?'[115]

Nath responded that many marketing issues were beyond the control of women producers. She drew on the Udaipur experience where silk yarn was sold at 1600 rupees a kilo until a new macro-economic policy of the Indian Government allowed a flood of imports of machine-made yarn from China and Korea. Weavers had also lost out because the raw material they needed was being exported, so they had nothing for their looms. The driving force is our macro-policy, governed not just by our own policy-makers but by policy makers sitting in other parts of the world' she said.[116]

The immediate question for Mahila Haat was about the use of wool. Village women knew that artificial yarn made from nylon would sell more quickly than the coarse wool they were knitting. The colours of the nylon yarn were more brilliant, it was easier to knit, and it was available. Further, virgin wool products cost three times what nylon yarn products cost so they only appealed to the upper level of the market, like Delhi, not to the average village market.

Referring to a macro-study she had done on the wool industry, Nath said that large-scale industry would pay women the price they demanded if they set aside knitting and specialized in a single process of the wool cycle, like carding. By monopolizing a particular process they would be in a better bargaining position. Apachu countered that women were very proud of the creativity they put into carpets and sweaters. They did not want to do something as mechanical as carding; they wanted to use their traditional skill. Nath's comment on that point seemed inevitable: 'There may be a tradeoff. They decrease their creativity, but they earn more, and they are catering to village markets.' Nath pointed out that catering to a village market with its limited purchasing power involved an awareness of people's need for day-to-day items like food and other basics; that's where the money flowed.[117] That kind of information about marketing options is what Mahila Haat was originally intended to bring to village market women.

The reader will note that there was a dramatically different approach to similar issues in Mauritius, where the project directors argue that creativity is the key to development, and furthermore the foundation of financial security. Creativity enabled the Mauritian craftswomen to retain their market niche despite global price fluctuations. However, the Mauritians failed to establish a foothold in the local market that Mahila Haat hopes to serve in India.

The future of Mahila Haat   Mahila Haat is progressing in its work with women producers, giving them training and marketing outlets. But is its original, innovative concept intact? Nath observed:

> The innovation of Mahila Haat initially lay in its proposed ability to create a critical mass of women micro-producer groups who would be in a bargaining position by the strength of their numbers. Mahila Haat could send out information on macro-economic debates in Delhi to the 89 per cent of India's working women who are self-employed. In that way it could become an 'industry-watch' and take advantage of economic forces in the markets.[118]

That is how Mahila Haat had originally been envisioned when it had a business person with an MBA to assist in its design. When she left and management employed community development field workers, the vision of transforming development from welfare into business opportunities for women was, however, never realized. Mahila Haat settled into the 'traditional' income-generating approach that took hold in the world in the 1970s when the women and development movement was young.

That approach also influenced the type of research that supported the project. Research was conducted mainly at the micro, self-contained level, for example, on the wool producers of a given village. The findings consequently related to getting raw materials, enhancing design, and marketing locally. The larger national policies that impacted invisibly on the lives of village women were not researched. A macro approach would have identified national and international market forces that indicate where market demand is and where it is likely to go in the near future. As an example, Nath mentioned a macro-study UNIFEM had sponsored in one village that showed 'the demand in the larger market was not for the kind of wool those women were producing'.[119]

Mahila Haat experienced an additional problem that is common to

138

externally assisted projects: the short-term grant. For reasons of their own budgetary cycles, multilateral and/or bilateral donors often contribute for a two- or three-year period. Such grants are not conducive to attracting people with specialized management and marketing skills, much less to retaining them. The combination of a strong professional staff with technical knowledge and continuous leadership such as the sericulturists had could have made a major difference at Mahila Haat. Meanwhile, the needs that were so clearly articulated remain unfulfilled.

How does Mahila Haat stand up to our three variables for the reversal of poverty trends?

Mahila Haat served several hundred women with its training–mainly to upgrade the quality of their wool products. While no exact income figures are available, sales are known to be brisk. Yet the women are still subject to policy changes by government and the function of forming a critical mass of microproducer groups, to be in a bargaining position with government has not been realized.

Instead, Mahila Haat has served a few hundred women, making backward and forward linkages for their products (the wool bank and marketing sweaters and carpets, for example). The intended institution is still fragile and has strengthened only relatively few producer groups. The catalytic effect is still missing.

Although Mahila Haat is in some ways successful, it is not the innovative, powerful and empowering organization that its designers envisioned. I asked why it had turned out that way. The thrust of the project was marketing, but there has been no marketing specialist in charge, so there was a major gap. In addition, the organization needed strong, continuous leadership which never materialized.[120]

A post-script on economic empowerment

Like those in the Philippines, the activities assisted by UNIFEM in India were co-operative enterprises at some stage of the productive cycle. The China factory hired workers, while in Laos there was a combination of hired atelier workers and home-based workers who were spread throughout the countryside.

SPES in Mauritius had several unique features when compared with the activities in India, Swaziland and the Philippines. In addition to the fundamental focus on creativity, SPES incorporated new technological developments whenever possible. In contrast, others' technology threatened the incomes of the sericulturists in India. SPES has a private enterprise image and management style combined with a non-profit status: that is a prototype that calls for consideration. In so doing, one must of course bear in mind its small scale, a feature that supports innovation.

Domestic market sensitivity was strong in Laos and in the Philippine rootcrop projects, whereas San Miguel and SPES were export orientated. In nearly all of the projects, credit systems and management leadership were keys to effectiveness.

The projects that set out to raise incomes did so, as will be reviewed in detail in the final chapter of this book. A word of caution arises most clearly from the sericulture experience: that raising family income may not improve the quality of life of family members. Women must personally be empowered and strongly influence the control of earned income. That lesson will arise again when we speak of political participation in the coming chapter.

The sericulture, the Mahila Haat and the China factory projects clearly indicate how macro-economic decisions and influences, both national and international, reach all the way down to the small producer and trader. UNDP Economist R. Sundarshan said that, while the impact of structural adjustment programmes is yet to be fully felt in large parts of the economy, 'the worrying thing is what happens to the informal sector. That is where the majority of women work'. He is convinced that to avoid the further impoverishment of families, women must be present at the policymaking level and must be well prepared to exercise influence there:[21]

> The investment has got to be in empowering women to seize political and decision-making roles in the administration in development planning and in local and national authorities. That's the only way you will get sensitivity to change.

Social justice is the second aspect of poverty alleviation; we consider it next.

CHAPTER 8
Social Justice

If you are working for the improvement of women and I am working to overcome poverty, it's the same thing. We can work together. Fighting poverty by working with women all over the country is a very slow job. It is not as easy as making a treaty or constructing a 100–storey building.

Eduardo Ishi Ito, Peru

IN THE INTRODUCTION to this book, I spoke of the three aspects of poverty–economic, social and political–that were identified following the Fund's consultations with grassroots women who articulated their needs. As reported in the previous section of this book the economic aspect involved access to resources and opportunities to enhance productivity. Projects of that kind, such as sericulture in India and rootcrops in the Philippines, had as their principal objective raising family incomes through economic growth; their first inputs were technology, credit, technical advice and the like.

As we found, however, if they are to succeed in reaching the long-range goal of development–people's well-being–projects aimed at economic empowerment must inevitably interrelate with elements of social justice and political participation. Key factors in developmental effectiveness were grassroots empowering organizations: co-operatives or women's organizations in the civil society.

We now turn to a group of UNIFEM-assisted projects that have social justice as their primary concern. Their principal aspect is access to the basic amenities necessary to a dignified existence, often called social or basic needs. As we describe them, they are of two kinds: those that foster human development, such as education, training, health and employment, and those of a community service nature such as provision of water and fuel, afforestation and sanitation. They often involve non-governmental organizations: co-operatives, credit unions, farmers and women's organizations, and community development programmes. Like the economic projects, they aim to increase people's capacity to live self-reliant lives–in other words, to empower them.

The denial or neglect of social justice in the pursuit of economic growth has dire consequences for people. As Vivian Mota, senior social development officer at ECLAC explained: 'Priority has to be put on both the creation of wealth and the quality of life'.[1] Cuts in governments' provision of health and education during the global economic crisis of the 1980s and 1990s had devastating effects on social justice in low-income countries; experience proves that women and girls bear the greatest burdens of those cuts. It is they, rather than all citizens, who subsidize their national economies, stepping in and filling the education and health gaps for their

141

families and communities.[2] It is they to whom most of the social debt is owed.

Attempts to compensate for the withdrawal of social services by providing 'safety nets' for the most vulnerable people, such as the Social Investment Fund in Bolivia and the programme of actions to mitigate the social costs of adjustments (PAMSCAD) in Ghana, have had innumerable shortcomings. The World Bank's own report on Ghana says:

> The difficulty in targeting assistance to the poor stems from two factors. First, the poor are not concentrated in any particular area. Second, their consumption pattern does not differ distinctly from the pattern for the non-poor.[3]

In other words, the poor also need food, clothing and shelter.

The Bank goes on to explain that attempts to avoid the shortcomings of similar programmes elsewhere had only generated new problems for PAMSCAD. Further, administrative procedures were cumbersome and the rate of response from the poor was 'less than expected.'[4] Despite these insights, and those that were quoted earlier in this text that 'the social sectors are in crisis' in Tanzania, Ghana and Tanzania are praised as models of successful structural adjustment.

The experience of a UNIFEM-assisted project in Senegal also illustrates a failure of justice to women and, in addition, the difference in the impact of economic recovery policies on women. Senegal put structural adjustment programmes (PAS) in place starting in 1985. These overlapped the country's seventh economic and social development plan, 1985–9, which identified projects that became the subject of a UNIFEM-financed study on the integration of women in development plans and programmes (later called mainstreaming) completed by the Ministries of Planning, Social Development and Agriculture in 1988.[5]

The researchers summed up that 'there was a nearly total absence of consideration of women, except in the social sector.'[6] They recommended the improvement of the data and statistical base for projects and heightening the sensitivity of policymakers. The report went on to say that, for the sake of expediting development, more women, together with their families, had to be involved in, and benefit from, projects; the tensions in the social relations between women and men had to be eased and there was a need for greater solidarity among women's groups. Finally, government commitment to women had to be reinforced.

Two of the researchers, Aboubacry Demba Lom and Sira Soma Sy Seck, explained during our discussions in Dakar that the study was not followed up because national attention at that time turned to special structural adjustment activities. The irony was that the special programmes recommended to lessen the impact of structural adjustments were women-specific ones; pressure to include an equitable share for women in large-scale projects such as those reviewed in the study had subsided. Justice eluded women.[7]

We turn now to some examples of activities that place a high priority on the social dimension of poverty in order to achieve social justice through the empowerment of women. We look first at the Caribbean, then Bolivia, Western Asia, with a focus on Oman, Syria and Yemen, and finally Kenya, Mexico and Argentina. In the Caribbean case, the movement was a gradual one as concepts of women and development matured. In Bolivia the positive effects of women's access to technology contrast with the effects of denial to that access. In Western Asia, cultural considerations called for starting with women's work in the home and with education. In Kenya, the project set out immediately to strengthen community capacities to provide basic needs for water and sanitation.

Toward a new development paradigm: WAND in the Caribbean

Market-oriented economic growth . . . is leading us away from meeting people's needs.

Peggy Antrobus

Evidence that economic reform and structural adjustment programmes exacerbate the existing conditions of poverty comes from the Caribbean. As Alfredo Jefferson of UNDP Barbados told me: 'The structural adjustment programmes hit in the areas where it hurts most, the poorest. And that is the crux of the whole matter . . . If girls had options for vocational education at secondary level they could get out there and make a living. A lot of women who head households would be better able to provide today. So I say, open up the whole stream and forget tradition'.[8]

The majority of the Caribbean people face problems of unemployment, poverty, inadequate services, malnutrition and illiteracy. Women are worse off than men, however, because they are often the sole or major providers for children, and their access to resources such as land, credit, training and technologies is severely constrained.[9]

Flora Pascal typifies many women who say 'I am just a housewife'. Asked what she does, Pascal replied:

○ plant four acres of bananas
○ sing in the choir
○ decorate the church
○ look after six children
○ take care of the house
○ sell home-made baked goods outside the home
○ grow anthuriums for sale
○ get up at 3:00 am to walk one and a half hours to my farm and back
○ additional chores like washing, ironing

Nesha Z. Haniff, 1988. *Blaze a Fire: Significant contributions of Caribbean Women*, Sister Vision, Toronto.

143

A university partnership in the Caribbean

The history of the partnership between the Women and Development Unit (WAND) of the University of the West Indies (UWI) and UNIFEM is in many ways a story of the evolution of the women and development movement itself over its first one and a half decades. Within just a few years WAND's goal would change from 'integrating women in development' to 'empowering women for social change'.

WAND was established within the Extra-Mural Department of UWI at the Barbados campus in August 1978 (just after UNIFEM became operational) at the recommendation of a seminar co-sponsored by the Jamaica Women's Bureau and the University. WAND's Plan of Action included 'promotion and support for programmes and projects to improve the social and economic status of women; raising the level of consciousness and awareness of the reality of women's lives; and identifying skills and programmes in the region to facilitate regional technical co-operation'.[10] The methodologies adopted by WAND were technical assistance, training and communications.

Even before being officially established, WAND sought support from UNIFEM (then VFDW) for expanding income generation projects for women engaged in crafts and agro-industrial production. Those women had little access to technologies or any credit to purchase raw materials. The project that UNIFEM agreed to finance with $36 000 included a survey of entrepreneurs and a seminar. That workshop was followed by a series of sub-regional ones, all of which examined management and marketing concerns.

In 1980 an additional $53 600 underwrote a sub-regional communications and information programme that gave WAND its first communications officer, who initiated what would be a long-lasting endeavour; it included publication of a Caribbean resource kit for women's groups, feature articles and a newsletter. The grant was for just a year, but attracted other donors–USAID and the Carnegie Corporation.[11]

WAND became not only an executor of UNIFEM-financed projects but also the technical adviser to other groups that UNIFEM assisted; the 1980 UNIFEM/ECLAC regional workshop on development planning and programme planning is an example. WAND hosted the training workshop and served as adviser.

Perhaps most appreciated was the third grant of $97000 for institution-building for WAND itself (RLA/83/W03). Entitled *Strengthening programmes for women in development* the project included technical assistance to agencies and programme participants, training of trainers and extension workers, and advocacy for women's issues through communication with key individuals and organizations. WAND focused in particular on training local leaders at the community level to improve their own communities. The budget items were sufficiently broad to allow for a great deal of flexibility. Although WAND had put together a mosaic of donor agencies, they needed institutional support for overall management as well as for field activities.

Peggy Antrobus spoke about that grant: 'The most significant thing about

144

UNIFEM's assistance to WAND was that it was the first agency to recognize the importance of supporting programmes and institutions as distinct from projects.'[12] She also found UNIFEM unique among funding agencies because it provided NGOs with a link to the rest of the UN system. Our view from within the UN system was that the importance of institutional support to NGOs was grossly neglected at that time; donors often resisted broad grants, preferring project grants whose impact could be measured in bushels of beans or numbers of trainees. The burden of managing projects is great and, in addition, when grants are tied to projects, management has little flexibility to try innovative activities that are often high risk. To this day, programme funding is a much overlooked method for strengthening institutional capacities.

A technical assistance outreach: Grenada

Grenada was an early recipient of WAND's technical assistance through the Inter-American Commission of Women (CIM) and UNIFEM assisted project, *Women's Apprentice Motor Mechanic Scheme* of 1983. Seventeen women were selected for an intensive two-year training to learn to repair light vehicles, jumbo trucks and tractors, but they also needed, and received, additional training. As journalist Meryl James-Brian put it: 'they also learned about self-pride, self-control . . . communications skills, budgeting, health management and group cohesiveness and support'.[13]

WAND provided tutorial assistance to the professional development workshops for personal and group empowerment that were an integral part of the training. Mechanic Glenda Pascal told James-Brian how she was empowered by the training:

Now I can stand up in the presence of people and speak and explain something. Before I used to laugh and run and hide like a little child. A big woman like me! Now I can earn a living on my own. I am more independent.[14]

Building a community: St Vincent

Of all of its technical assistance programmes, the one in the small rural community of Rose Hall, at the foot of an active volcano on the tiny island of St. Vincent, remains the star in WAND's crown. The farmers of Rose Hall produce most of St. Vincent's carrots, and in addition they grow yams, ginger, sweet potatoes and other vegetables and fruits. In 1981, WAND invited the women of the village to participate in a pilot programme to increase their self-confidence, skills and access to resources. A farmer and mother of four named Chaddis Stapleton, who became the group's facilitator, says that the project changed her life. She told the guests at UNIFEM's tenth anniversary celebration that she was so shy that she was unable to speak during the first three days of the initial training course.

145

After a three-week training programme in participatory approaches to needs assessment, programme planning and evaluation, the Rose Hall Working Group was formed. In addition, a farmer's group was created and 40 per cent of them were women; then an adult education programme began. Sewing, fruit preservation and candy-making were promoted to raise incomes. A farm supply shop was opened and a pre-school was started. A special bonus: 'relations between men and women are richer and stronger', said Stapleton.[15]

Asked what were the biggest obstacles the Rose Hall project faced, Chaddis Stapleton said that, at the very beginning, there was opposition from men who thought that the women wanted to take over the village. Then a workshop was organized on the role of men, and that was the turning point. The men realized, she said 'that it was not so. There had to be better male-female relationships. To be successful, we needed men to work alongside the women'. [16] A second obstacle was financial, seed money for the pre-school and the bakery; but thanks to WAND, donors appeared to assist.

Did other women in the community experience empowerment as Chaddis Stapleton did? 'Yes,' she said, 'there are lots of women who were very shy and didn't know how to talk to people. They have gained a kind of confidence. If the Queen of Sheba came right now, they would go up and talk to her.'[17]

Chaddis Stapleton accepted UNIFEM's award to WAND on the occasion of the Fund's Tenth Anniversary. There, in the solemn ECOSOC Chamber at the United Nations headquarters, Stapleton invited the Secretary-General, the President of the General Assembly, numerous Ambassadors and other guests to join hands and sing the Song of the Rose Hall Working Group (by happy coincidence, the tune is O Tannenbaum–Oh Christmas Tree–and the General Assembly President was German):

> The time has come when we must share
> And to assist in any way
> So let us join in unity
> To build up our community
> Oh what a village this will be
> With benefits for you and me
> With time and talents we will give
> To build up our community.

Such a community-style celebration had not happened in ECOSOC before in recent memory.

An impact evaluation of the Rose Hall project in 1991 concluded: 'There is compelling evidence that individuals, women and men, especially those who have been involved in the working group, have become empowered. There are many indicators of this empowerment both at the individual and collective level.[18]

I asked Chaddis Stapleton what she would do for other women–if she could. She responded: 'I would help them to realize their potential, and to know that they can make it once the willingness is there, once the readiness is there; they can make it.'[19]

Micro-enterprise in Barbados	
Barbados	
Demographics:	
Population	0.26 million
% urban	48
% rural	52
Income:	
GNP per capita	$6,540
% in absolute poverty	15
% of rural population	23
% of urban population	na
Health:	
Life expectancy	Women: 78 Men: 73
Infant mortality	10 per 1000 births
Maternal mortality	27 per 100000 births
Access to safe water (%)	100
Education:	
Illiteracy rate	Women: na Men: na
Girls as % of boys in secondary school	88
Girls as % of boys in tertiary school	148
Girls as % of tertiary science/engineering students	49
Work:	
Households headed by women (%)	45*
Women as % of labour force	42*
Female wages as % of male	na
Representation:	
Parliamentary seats held by women (%)	14

Source: See source table in Annexe 7.
*Marva Alleyne, 'The Barbadian Family, with specific reference to the woman as head of household.' Bureau of Women's Affairs, Barbados, 1993.

Barbados data is revealing of the region. An island nation of just 166 square miles, its population is 257 300, with 20 per cent under fifteen years old. More boys than girls are enrolled in primary and secondary schools, but what is interesting is that more women than men attend University and 90 per cent of adult education students are women. Women bear heavy economic responsibility for the family: 45 per cent of households are female-headed. Women were 42 per cent of the labour force in 1993–down from 46 per cent in 1992, a reduction considered by

147

government to be a direct result of the economic crisis and the structural adjustment measures it adopted.[20]

The National Organization of Women (NOW) *Training for Food Preservation* project also benefited from WAND's technical support. NOW President, and currently a Senator of Barbados, Carmeta Fraser designed the project to train women for commercial activities, particularly in food preservation, that would contribute to national development through import substitution and provision of a package of services to small-scale entrepreneurs. UNIFEM approved a contribution of $61 000 to the project in 1984, with forty women to be trained initially. By the end of the grant, that number had risen to four hundred women.

Senator Fraser, who is now Food Promotion Director for the Barbados Marketing Corporation, still uses the equipment provided in the original UNIFEM grant as she works with unemployed women, youth, and farmers (both men and women) in food preservation. At the training-cum-production centre, 3000 gallons of syrups are made annually from local fruits like passion, tamarind and bitter cherry; 600 gallons of pepper sauce are also turned out. Other products are pickles, ketchup, vinegar, guava jelly, chocolates and other candies.

Fraser first heard of VFDW through Dennis MacIntosh and Trevor Gordon Sommers at the UNDP office in Barbados. She obtained a Government commitment to fund the building where the training would take place, thanks to the intervention of the Bureau of Women's Affairs. Some of the early courses were of two or three weeks duration while others lasted three months. Fraser remembers vividly that all of those early courses were immediately oversubscribed; some women wanted to use their skills for the benefit of the family, but most also sought incomes. By the time of my visit in 1993, Fraser had trained literally thousands of women and some men too.

The original project collaborators were the Ministry of Agriculture, the Institute of Management and Productivity (BIMAP) and the Industrial Development Corporation. The entrepreneurs benefited from specialist teachers in marketing and accounting, agronomy, and microbiology among other subjects.[21]

The UNIFEM grant–the first assistance given to the training project–was catalytic in that it opened a veritable flood of support from other sources. Assistance came through the National Development Foundation (which Fraser now chairs) from the Organization of American States, FAO, the European Community, the Inter-American Development Bank and the Agriculture Guarantee Trust, and locally from the Rotary Club (a total of more than $725 000). The IDB grant provides credit to entrepreneurs, including both individual and peer-group systems.

The training and micro-enterprise that followed have had a tremendous impact on Barbados. Fraser explained:

What it has done is to bring a lot of women out of their shells who had talents they did not realize they had. They did not know that they could work and not have to depend on a man for money; that they could make

148

sweets and pepper sauce and sell crops. The women found that there was somebody who cared about helping them to get training, and to create markets where there weren't any. We put them on television and had them written up in the newspapers. We brought them to the forefront.[22]

Senator Fraser, like other recipients of UNIFEM support, has learned how UNIFEM works as a catalyst for change by identifying and trusting in women's grassroots activities.

Dennis McIntosh of UNDP had observed the food preservation training from the start. What has been achieved? I asked. He replied: 'We are developing a group of women entrepreneurs in Barbados. Many of them would not have moved ahead as successfully as they have without the training. The project brought them together, mobilized them and helped them to look at common problems they were facing.' Were there weaknesses? McIntosh cited two. 'The follow-up was not very good, because, you see, we are finite. We help them get moving, but then they must pick up their own momentum. Also, in many projects expectations were raised by government commitments. But often the government did not come through, and it was a disincentive for those women. That is where the weaknesses were.'[23]

Evaluations of WAND

As part of its contribution to women and development concepts, programmes and projects in the Caribbean region, WAND established a documentation centre and assisted in the creation of UWI's Women and Development Studies. WAND's major themes–health, youth and rural development–have been retained while others have been added, such as violence, the environment, economic policy and the media.[24]

Work with intermediary organizations in pursuit of the goal of empowering communities has begun to replace direct community work, such as that done in Rose Hall. This strategy recognizes both the long-term nature of the process of transforming communities and the importance of people who are very knowledgeable in an area effecting that transformation.[25]

Peggy Antrobus uses 1984 as a marker for a radical change in WAND's development strategies. Up until that year, WAND, with UNIFEM and other support, helped 'to put women on the agenda' as Antrobus expressed it.[26] 'You could see very clearly that government sectoral policies and macro-economic development planning took women into account. It was not only the women's desks, women's bureaux, it was the ministries of agriculture, ministries of community development and ministries of education. The sensitivity to women translated into improvements', she explained. But gradually, WAND realized that the CARICOM (Caribbean Community) women's desk was the more appropriate agency for dealing with governments' sectoral policies.

Other factors also influenced WAND's transformation. 'After 1984, everything changed.' said Antrobus, 'Caribbean governments bought into the ideology of structural adjustment full sail, without any criticism. And its impact began to be felt'.[27] The same year, Antrobus attended a meeting

149

in Bangkok that would give birth to a new organization, DAWN, Development Alternatives with Women for a New Era.[28] At that meeting, Latin American women spoke about structural adjustment and women. Antrobus listened carefully and later, at a Caribbean regional meeting in Barbados to prepare for the Nairobi Conference, she introduced the first critique of economic adjustment policies. It became *The Bridgetown Statement of 1985*. Soon the Commonwealth Secretariat and other organizations joined the critics.

WAND had shifted from a largely professional/technical approach to an increasingly political and feminist one, which sought 'to empower women to promote changes in the system'.[29] This shift perceived the existing system as exploitative of women's labour for the benefit of men in their own households, for local élites and for the interests of international capital. It also recognized that women's interests have not been received sympathetically in political structures.

In 1990, WAND's Tutor/Coordinator and Founder, Peggy Antrobus, was appointed Secretary General of DAWN. This association between WAND and DAWN led WAND to place even greater emphasis on macro-issues like trade, the global economy and economic reform measures. By 1993 WAND and its fourteen staff had adopted a new, social-justice oriented goal:

> to seek to make a contribution toward building the human and institutional capacity for a model of development which is integrative, equitable, self-reliant and sustainable. In pursuing this goal WAND will focus on building on its earlier work by strengthening regional networks of groups working in the areas of community development, health and the young, and using these experiences to point a path toward an alternative model of development.[30]

Even with its new goal, WAND is seen as a training institution focusing on women's development. It has earned 'tremendous respect' from people in the region because of its pioneering efforts in introducing participatory methods for training, planning and research; and its support of fund-raising for other groups.[31]

The 1993 Evaluation paid a great tribute to UNIFEM's intermediary organization in the Caribbean: 'The thousands of people reached directly or indirectly by WAND, if they are not yet persuaded of the need for change, have surely questioned their assumptions about themselves and about their social environment'.[32]

'Ten years ago we were seeking integration. Now we are seeking transformation', Antrobus says. She makes another very perceptive point: 'We are at different paradigms now. One is market-oriented economic growth, with privatization and structural adjustment. That's where governments are. But we realize that is leading us away from poverty alleviation, away from meeting people's needs, and that more and more women are going to be left behind.'[33]

Transferring technology: UNIFEM in Bolivia

Under the control of women rather than men, commercial milk production is more sustainable over the long term, as men tend to seek to
maximize herd size, while women tend to maximize output in more
moderate size herds, seeking a more diversified livelihood strategy.

UNIFEM's Milk Project, An Evaluation (1992)

Bolivia	
Demographics:	
Population	8.1 million
% urban	54
% rural	46
Income:	
GNP per capita	$680
% in absolute poverty	60
% of rural population	86
% of urban population	30
Health:	
Life expectancy	Women: 64 Men: 59
Infant mortality	85 per 1000 births
Maternal mortality	600 per 100000 births
Access to safe water (%)	53
Education:	
Illiteracy rate (%)	Women: 29 Men: 15
Girls as % of boys in secondary school	85
Girls as % of boys in tertiary school	na
Girls as % of tertiary science/engineering students	na
Work:	
Households headed by women (%)	na
Women as % of labour force	42%
Female wages as % of male	na
Representation:	
Parliamentary seats held by women (%)	0

Source: See source table in Annexe 7.

Social justice is also a concern in the vast Andean region, where climate is
not kind to most of landlocked Bolivia's 8.1 million people (1992). Sixty
per cent of them live in absolute poverty. The barren and windswept
altiplano, the high plateau between the Andes mountain ranges, is 12,000
feet above sea level and has been the centre of the Aymara and Quechua
Indian cultures for centuries. It contrasts sharply with the fertile, lush
tropical rain forests of the east. Between these two regions lies a third,

151

the mild valleys where one-third of the people live. Two and a half million peasants own their land in the countryside. 'Land ownership is a right hard won by the Bolivian *campesinos* in the 1953 revolution' and the 1967 Constitution prevents the division or transfer of that land.[34] Yet 86 per cent of rural dwellers survive under the cruel poverty conditions that have forced many of them into the rapidly growing cities; 59 per cent of the people lived in the countryside in 1970, but only 46 per cent do so in 1995.

As will be seen in the description of milk production activities in the Altiplano, women maintain the subsistence economy through agricultural production, including tending the animals. Although two of every three Bolivian women are illiterate, their entrepreneurial skills are visible indeed in the informal sector of La Paz where, since 1983, seven out of ten hawkers have been female. (See box.) In Cochabamba 65 per cent of women are employed in the informal sector. Women's productive work has begun to be recognized in official statistics: they were said to comprise only 21 per cent of the active labour force in 1970 (World Bank) but 42 per cent in 1995 (WISTAT). Informal sector income is less than half of that in wage employment.[35]

Hawkers in La Paz

As a result of the worsening of the economic crisis in the 1980s there was a significant increase in the participation of women in economic activity in Bolivia. In the city of La Paz the proportion of women involved in economic activity, mainly in independent businesses, rose from 28% to 44% (virtually one out of every two women). . . . It is estimated that from 1976 to 1983 the number of micro-traders increased by 70% with the most striking feature being the significant increase (83%) in the number of women. In 1983, 71% of the 41 615 hawkers in the city of La Paz were women. These micro-traders sell items that make up the basic family shopping basket, especially foodstuffs. The heavy competition in the sector as a result of the increase in the number of hawkers, and the gradual decline in demand tends to depress earnings, which in turn results in permanent instability and insecurity.

Women in Latin America and the Caribbean: the Challenge of Changing Production Patterns with Social Equity, CEPAL, Santiago 1991.

Bolivian income per capita was $650 in 1991, but like levels of income in earlier years, its value was seriously offset by the global economic crisis that began in the early 1980s, with an average rate of inflation between 1980 and 1992–the UNIFEM projects years–of 221 per cent ; it fell to 9.3 per cent in 1993. To counteract these trends, government adopted a structural adjustment programme in 1985 and then created a National Emergency Social Welfare Fund to mitigate the harsh impacts of the adjustment on the social sector of the society.

A starting point: health and nutrition

The health and nutrition field was a culturally acceptable entry point for working with women in 1979, when Bolivia became one of the first countries to be assisted by UNIFEM in the Latin American region. The project Warami Wawantin: a commitment to life (Aymara language) began with technical support from the UN Economic Commission for Latin America and the Caribbean (ECLAC). Its objective was to improve the health situation of rural families in six densely populated departments of Bolivia by imparting appropriate information on health and environmental sanitation. But instead of using the time-worn approach of having extension workers give lessons to groups of women, the project introduced a participatory methodology. The villagers would themselves be the agents of change. To this end, a few trainers from the Maternal and Child Division of the Ministry of Public Health were sent to Chile for initial education on how to train women from rural communities to serve as health extension aides. A second phase of the project brought UNIFEM's input to $224 000, complemented by a $1.2 million government input. The outreach was to more than fifty communities.

Bolivia's Council of Ministers officially adopted the participatory methodology for use between the years 1982–2000. The methodology was also introduced shortly thereafter in Brazil, where UNIFEM assisted a community study that designed a university-based participatory health system that was one of the first in Latin America to introduce the idea that health is a community issue, not just a medical, scientific issue; the project had a 'very very big impact' at the policy level, said Mariam Krawczyk of ECLA.[36]

In 1982, UNIFEM provided technical assistance to a project jointly undertaken by the Government, the World Food Programme and the National Confederation of Mothers Clubs. The recipients of that assistance were the Mothers Clubs that had been organized by the Ministry of Public Health in the 1960s. Originally set up for the diffusion of public health and nutrition information, they would now be converted into self-sufficient, self-managed productive units. Activities were centred in the departments of La Paz, Cochabamba and Santa Cruz, including the locale of UNIFEM's earlier project, Wawami. The World Food Programme donated food–wheat flour, vegetable oil, canned fish and meat, powdered milk, and rice–to be sold by the clubs at subsidized prices to nursing and pregnant women with children under the age of 14.

'We were organized to be given food, now we are organizing ourselves to produce it!' said the women of El Alto and Rio Seco, poor districts on the outskirts of La Paz. By the end of 1983 there were 30 000 women in 117 Mothers Clubs. They had built greenhouses and bakeries, organized day-care centres, and furnished community wash-houses and showers with solar heating in the peri-urban areas. In the countryside they planted potatoes, cereals, fruits, vegetables, and coffee. The National Confederation of Mothers Clubs served as a conduit for the groups' ideas and problems and sent out technical assistance in return.

The Mothers Clubs were appropriate development institutions in a country where revolutions had caused abrupt changes of government

153

nearly 200 times in 160 years, leaving the civil society to hone its own survival techniques. The food-for-work system of the World Food Programme kept starvation away, but it also risked creating dependency on free food; UNIFEM became aware of this when it began to assist a new project, Milk Production in the Altiplano, in 1985. The milk production and a pottery project in Huayculi both were designed to introduce training and technologies as vehicles to enhance women's and family well-being and productive work; the results of each were profoundly different.

Milk production in the altiplano

Here we did not have much in the way of income. But when the women started to organize, our situation started to improve.

Amale, farmer

The Tiawanaku zone sits high on the drought-prone northern altiplano in the Department of La Paz. Its population of 4000 persons in six communities was among the poorest in Bolivia in 1982. Until the revolution of 1953 brought land reform and small peasant holdings, the altiplano was an area of large haciendas. Even after the revolution, however, it retained its traditional combination of livestock production with subsistence crops. Livestock provided the raw materials for women to produce wool and cheese to sell when cash was needed. The cattle manure was used for cooking fuel because the area was now almost completely deforested.

For decades there had been attempts to improve livestock development in this area of the country where sheep, llamas and alpaca are predominant but cattle are used for ploughing and represent the peoples' savings. When markets for milk opened up, the cattle population increased. The amount of milk produced in a given year varies with the climate, but cattle can survive years of drought even when few crops are grown. The agrarian system in the altiplano uses such little technology that the whole family has to work in order to sustain productivity; staple foods are potatoes, beans and barley.[37]

In the altiplano it is women who maintain the household economy. Because they speak the Aymara language almost exclusively, however, they depend on men who can speak Spanish and Quechua for linkage with the outside world. The strong community-based culture of the Aymara is evidenced in the associations that are run by male heads of household. Gender differentiation is clearly defined and in the early 1980s women still exercised very little authority, seldom participating in public organizations. Their social position was 'very low' in a situation lacking basic services of health, education and social protection for women and children.[38]

Not only because women do not speak Spanish, but also because the market pays male labour about double what it pays females, it is men who migrate in search of wage employment. They usually return for planting and harvesting only, leaving the women to care for the family, the crops and the animals. When the time comes, however, it is the men who market the livestock, control the cash, and give to their wives only as much as they judge is appropriate. Rural extension workers (men) are aware that women are the principal agents in the economy: 'She manages the family, she does everything', they say, then add: 'but men do the hard work'.

Origins of the project

In the early 1980s, while the National Community Development Service (SNDC: Servicio Nacional de Desarrollo de la Comunidad) was active in Tiawanaku, the Bolivian Committee of Co-operation (BCC) promoted the formation of women's groups for milk production in that area. The dairy plants had been built during the mid 1970s when human protein deficiency became a worldwide concern. BCC was an affiliate of the Interamerican Commission of Women (CIM) whose concern was that most projects directed to women failed to employ the advanced technology that would have been offered to men. The Bolivian President of CIM, Gabriela Touchard, submitted a request to UNIFEM 'to increase dairy production in rural areas and increase incomes of families involved in the industry.' The project was approved by UNIFEM for $186 000, with a CIM contribution of $10 400 and technical support from the Corporation for Development of La Paz (CORDEPAZ).[39]

The project was to generate new employment opportunities by training women to use new milk production technologies and by teaching them administrative and marketing techniques for small enterprise development. It would also enable women's ranching co-operatives to obtain credit. By improving the animal stock the intention was to increase milk production from three to six litres per day per cow, and to conserve the environment by reducing the number of animals per hectare. Initially, 150 families in five communities would benefit: 24 cows and one bull would be provided to 25 groups, each consisting of six families. Most importantly, the merit of the project was that 'for the first time in Bolivian history women were taken into account in an agriculture and rural development project . . . Previously, extension services were given only to men and there were no female extension workers'.[40] The project opened opportunities for human development to women.

Partners in the project were the dairy development plant in La Paz, PIL, which would collect and purchase the milk, and its Fomento Lechero (FL) Division of Milk Production that would give technical assistance; both were to be assisted by the UN's World Food Programme. SNDC would assist the community development dimensions of the project while the Bolivian Institute of Agricultural Technology, IBTA, would advise on technical matters such as nutrition supplements to the forage and the number of cattle that could be supported per hectare with and without improved forage.[41] Like the majority of UNIFEM assistance at the time, a budget item of 66 per cent of UNIFEM's contribution was to be used for in-kind credit for cattle (on the hoof). It would be repaid in kind as well, although the 10 per cent interest levied was to be paid in cash to cover administrative costs. Recipients would build their own simple stables and the project would acquire improved seed and provide animal health care.[42]

An NGO with strong qualifications in managing projects involving women, called Appropriate Technology for Rural Women (SETAM), was selected to co-ordinate the project as its executing agency. Under the administration of Yara Carafa, the overall goal of the project was restated: to give greater value to the role of the peasant woman by achieving her formal and recognized participation in the productive system of the country.[43] SETAM not only anticipated obstacles but then encountered a major one almost immediately; the Mothers Clubs in the communities had a welfare rather that a production mentality. They were used to receiving free food or clothing rather than being given access to the productive means for raising their own incomes. SETAM resolved that dilemma by selecting only those communities that did not request free food for participation in the project, and then completed UNIFEM's situation analysis by visiting community leaders and farm homes to explain the project and encourage participation.[44]

The community development group, SNDC, organized 112 women with the approval of their husbands. In anticipation of the benefits they would gain, the women built 150 stables with straw roofs and adobe walls. The work was completely self-financed, although, when the project finally started, UNIFEM loaned money for materials that the women needed to further improve the stables. With the family providing the labour, it was possible to construct a stable valued at $800 for just $120. CORDEPAZ then paid for a full-time artificial insemination technician and the community of Achaca was selected as the AI centre for outreach to other communities. Despite some resistance to accepting new technologies, eighteen residents, five of them women, trained as artificial inseminators.

In 1985 the project began with 284 beneficiaries: 120 men and 164 women. Integrating men in the project was in keeping with the Aymara orientation toward community. More than that, it helped men to understand women's economic contributions. As one male farmer said: 'Here we did not have much in the way of income. But when the women started to organize, our situation started to improve.' Carafa added that she had often heard men say, 'I want my wife to study, to learn.'[45] Yet because the women were monolingual and often illiterate, language remained a major impediment for the project since most male technical providers, including those of CORDEPAZ, spoke no Aymara.

Participants received an identification number for selling their milk so that payments would be properly made and they would have access to credit from Fomento Lechero. They could also select the technologies from the package offered by the project. That system, intended in part to ensure that women would benefit directly from the sale of milk, was only partially effective.[46]

At times, the low level of competence in some of the co-operating agencies caused unnecessary problems. The semen initially produced at the new centre was poorly handled and consequently ineffective. That led many participants to reject artificial insemination; instead, they opted to improve their skills in herd management, which in fact resulted in significant increases in milk production and income. PIL's credit system also provoked suspicion when its records of transactions were poorly kept. For example, deductions continued even after a community had repaid its loan, and high levels of butterfat in the milk were recorded as 'average' by PIL, which 'saw such irregularities as small glitches in bookkeeping'.[47]

As already seen, it was the women of the area who were faulted for not knowing a second language; extension agents were not expected to learn to speak the language of their clients. Further, the providers of technical assistance from the co-operating agencies frequently felt that reaching men was sufficient; they expected men to pass on the information to women, but that did not happen automatically. The latter misjudgement is not unique to Bolivia; what has been called the 'trickle-*over*' philosophy is commonly practised by extension workers who do not grasp the importance of women as productive agents.[48]

> The official peasant promotion entities, including the PIL, were not convinced of the necessity of separate and focussed outreach to women . . .
>
> Evaluation 1992

There were 574 participants in the project by 1989. About 78 per cent of them were women; whereas in most areas that PIL serviced, 75 per cent would be men. Associations of Milk Producers were formed by men and women together after SETAM had tried to form separate women's organizations. Again, the community culture of the Aymara proved to be the more effective. A mid-term evaluation in 1989 triggered a number of changes. Literacy classes and training sessions were offered both to women and men in each community. In addition, the project was more closely linked to FAO in Bolivia. The regional FAO sent trainers to train women to become leaders in dairy production, processing techniques and cheesemaking. Unfortunately, the FAO programme ended abruptly when an international donor inexplicably withdrew its aid.[49]

Quantified results of the project A quantitative evaluation of the results of the project in 1992 produced the following:[50]

○ between 1985–91, 151 hectares of improved forages were planted; 55 of them were planted in alfalfa which, having a far higher protein content that barley and oats, contributes to increased milk production–628 improved animals were born between 1986 and 1990;

○ some 227 farmers received credit for food concentrates during the first half of 1989 only; that appears to imply their widespread use over the years;

○ based on farmers' adoption of improved practices (artificial insemination; hectarage planted to alfalfa, etc.) the annual increase of income per family for 400 families was estimated to be $24, an amount that is impressive when one considers that the increase was gradual in the early years while participants were acquiring assets and skills, and that many additional benefits could be expected after the formal conclusion of the project.

The value of the infrastructure generated by the project is as follows:

Table 8.1: Bolivia: Value of infrastructure generated by UNIFEM Milk Project

Infrastructure Type	No.	Proj. Cont.	Comm. Cont.	Total-US$
Hay sheds (galpon)	25	$ 2652	$ 9473	$ 12125
Stables	210	$11911	$ 81075	$ 92986
Milk pickup centres (Cebtros de Acopio)	14	$ 4479	$ 9072	$ 13551
Roads, Irrigation		$ 3435	$ 8789	$ 12224
AI Centres	2	$ 3655	$ 3638	$ 7293
Dairy training centre	1	$27463	$ 20749	$ 48212
TOTALS		$53595	$132796	$186391

Source: UNIFEM Women's Milk Project, 1992

Table 8.1, Value of infrastructure generated, shows that the project contribution for infrastructure was less than half of that of the communities. UNIFEM contributed $53 595, and the community $133 696, for a total value of $186 391. The evaluators noted in addition that the infrastructure may well have had a demonstrable effect on farmers who did not participate in the programme; that effect could not be quantified.

Calculation of the increase in family incomes during the life of the project has some revealing dimensions. In the project zone, Tiawanaku, 78 per cent of the producers selling milk were women, whereas in other zones only 25 per cent were women. These percentages have a strong influence on the amount of income that is put to family use. From in-depth interviews undertaken by SETAM, it was estimated that 25 per cent of the cash received by men was spent neither on the family nor on the farm ('on drink, fiestas, clothing or perhaps a mistress'). In sharp contrast, women spent 100 per cent of their income on the household. On that basis, US$37 was 'saved' per family per year by the 192 families who sold milk regularly; over the life of the project, that amounted to $31 000.[51]

The profit derived from the shift from cheesemaking to milk production was also calculated, since liquid milk fetches 20 per cent more than cheese. That brought a 20 per cent increase in incomes during the project. (In addition, women saved about four hours a week that would have been spent on making cheese: clearly an immense benefit but it was difficult to quantify in monetary terms, so it was not added into overall profit.) The benefit to families from the switch to milk totalled $38 000 or about $45 per year per family during the four years of milk sales from the project.

The total cost to UNIFEM over a four-year period (this amount includes post-1989 funding; 1989, it will be recalled, is the cut-off point for most of our study), $424 100, is the figure used by the evaluators for a cost-benefit analysis; the results appear in Table 8.2.

Table 8.2 indicates that the costs of the project to UNIFEM exceeded the

Table 8.2: Bolivia: Quantifiable monetary costs and benefits of UNIFEM Milk Project

Benefit or cost	Estimated value
Benefits:	(U.S. $)
Increased net income from increase in milk and meat production ($9761×4.5 years)	$43925
Infrastructure built with assistance from UNIFEM project	$186000
Added income to family as result of women receiving income from milk (4½ years)	$31000
Profits realized from shifting from sale of cheese to raw milk (4½ years)	$38000
Total quantifiable monetary benefits	$298925
Costs:	
UNIFEM grant (1985–91)	$424100
Benefits + Costs	−$125175

Source: UNIFEM Women's Milk Project, 1992

quantifiable benefits to participants by $125 000. The net cost is thus no more than $125 000 and perhaps considerably less if one includes the indirect effects of the project, such as improved cattle stock, infrastructure, etc. which last beyond the life of the project.[52]

The participating women said that the project was enormously valuable to them. 'After training in leadership and group skills we are now part of the real business of our community. We are not afraid to speak up in meetings. And we have incomes of our own'. For the women, the combination of the leadership skills and new sources of income gave them the greatest gift of all: 'Our husbands respect us more'.[53] The project's primary aspect of social justice was accompanied by economic empowerment.

A type of income for Bolivia which cannot yet be captured quantitatively is the conservation of the environment. The UNIFEM-assisted project demonstrated an environmentally sound method of cattle raising.

The impact of the men's milk production strategy of short-term profit maximization can be seen in southern parts of the altiplano, such as San Jose de Llangas . . . where increased desertification is associated with the increase in cattle. Sheep, llamas, and alpaca, the traditional animals of the altiplano, while complementary to cattle in their feeding patterns, do much less physical damage to the soil and ground cover with their hooves.[54]

Why the difference in the herd size? As we have already seen, in the altiplano it is women who maintain the economy. It would thus be in their interest to have fewer but more productive cows, and to increase the production per hectare plus the nutritional value of forage. Men on the other hand relate their personal wealth to the number of cattle they have accumulated.

Sustainability

The potential for the project's sustainability has been reduced by macro-economic factors in Bolivia: in particular by policy decisions on the privatization of government-owned para-statal industries such as PIL. The cost of milk collections from the Tiawanaku area is high and cannot be expected to bring the profits a private corporation would seek.

It will be recalled that the dairy plants–PIL–were created in the mid-1970s when the government policy for 1971–91 made them key instruments of development. They were obliged to offer technical assistance and set up credit systems; but in 1985, during the initial phase of structural adjustment, government policy changed. Operation of the dairy plants was transferred to the regional development corporations which did not take an active interest in them, and when the Privatisation Act of 1992 prohibited investment in them, maintenance declined and equipment decayed. Producers in Tiawanaku, like Luisa Osco and Martha Quisepe, were told such things as, 'the car broke down somewhere and another car would have to come to collect milk'. Poor management meant that producers got paid only every three or four weeks; in the winter, when milk production was lower, collectors would not come at all.[55]

The evaluators suggest that a cause of the decline in service and the delayed payments lay in the remoteness of Tiawanaku from La Paz, where the milk is processed. Many producers reverted to making cheese, and after 1988 the quantity of milk sold decreased by 25 per cent and the number of suppliers also decreased. (In 1994 the producers requested technical assistance for cheese-making.) Many participants, however, adopted the technologies introduced by the project: artificial insemination, improved pasture and food supplements, upgrading barns, hay sheds, irrigation, roads and other infrastructure. Incomes did not double as the project had hoped, but they did increase. And the project's immediate goal, to give greater visibility and recognition to women's economic activity, was realized.

Sustainable institutions and empowerment

Women from the project area remain active in the Associations of Milk Producers even though the project ended in 1991. Osco and Quisepe reported in 1993 that every community has its own association, affiliated with others in Tiawanaku. The organizations appear to be sustainable over the long term, but the women are disappointed that they no longer have training courses, and that an extension worker 'drops by but goes away', leaving them without assistance.[56]

The women continue to prefer mixed gender economic organizations to separate, women-specific ones. This may be because the former are production-orientated while the latter, in Bolivia, have tended toward welfare. Nonetheless, separate training groups for women have been maintained in the mixed groups. That training, including literacy, has brought women to a readiness for broader participation and they are now willing to insist on having their own incomes.

SETAM integrated the technology and resources of the co-operating groups into the project, 'but there was not the reciprocity needed among the co-operating organizations to adapt the excellent techniques of the project that could enhance their own work. Unfortunately, when Fomento Lechero had the chance to work closely with the Project staff, they did not, viewing the project and its staff more as nuisances than as allies'.[57] Others say that the dairy workers 'did not want to get mixed up with the conditions that UNIFEM expects'.[58] Gender was not seen as important to the success of rural development programmes. The project demonstrated vividly that conscious measures must be taken so that women are included and acknowledged as agents of development, and that greater visibility must be accorded the quantitative results of projects.

SETAM is preparing a third, amplified phase of the project to be financed by a national institution, the Social Investment Fund. Carafa observed that when the UNIFEM/SETAM project began, it was innovative because it veered away from the weaknesses of most projects that were supposed to benefit women, those that used 'appropriate technology and a little money'. Now she wants to build on and expand the experience of the dairy project to the entire industry, to a whole sector rather than just 'a project'. She found that women were being selected to represent the entire community in the Tiwanaku area–but not in other areas.

The catalytic effect of the whole endeavour seems not yet to have been maximized within the UN family of organizations. In Chile, UNDP was quick to pass on UNIFEM's experience with micro-enterprise in slum areas. However, despite the obvious achievements of the Milk Project in terms of environment, income and quality of life, the UN's World Food Programme has no female extension workers. As the WFP representative expressed it: 'When I came to this country two years ago I noted that usually men work only with men. I have the same problem that Carafa had eight years ago'.[59] When I asked why WFP was taking no action in that regard, and whether WFP was investing in studies about soil, forage and other aspects of dairy development in the area of the altiplano which their project covered, the representative replied that WFP is not implementing the project; it is only financing it.

The importance of women's access to employment is not yet reflected in the employment policies of the government's new Emergency Social Welfare Fund (FSE), which was established in 1986 to decrease the human cost of the 1985 economic adjustment programmes.[60] Between 1988 and 1990, FSE accounted for 50 per cent of the total public investment in health, education, basic services, urban development, housing and multi-service systems. It financed more schools, miles of roadways, sewer and drainage systems, housing units and other facilities than did the relevant Government Ministries. However, the projects did not incorporate gender guidelines. In fact, the country's household survey and another research project found that 90 per cent of those who were given employment were men, apparently because they were identified as 'heads of household'. Many of the new jobs were in construction. On inspection of a number of project sites, men were nowhere to be seen, but large numbers of women and even children were found working. 'They are "unpaid family members", and the "heads of household" are at other jobs or simply not working', the researchers were told.[61]

Fortunately, the project has been a catalyst for change in the attitudes of men who were directly exposed to it. Farmers interviewed at a milk collection point in Tiawanaku said: 'the women are actively participating, especially in decision-making.' They might not be the manager or president, but they are active. Extension worker Fernanco Endos added: We see that the woman is the principal agent in the economy, in the *campesino* economy. She manages all the income. She does everything. Usually she delivers the milk, too, although sometimes the men or the children help with that'.[62] As pragmatists men also recognize that women have a vote in electing presidents of associations; SETAM is trying to understand how that reality influences the community and the family.

Future generations in Bolivia, as in other countries, will pay dearly for the neglect of women in economic productivity projects. We saw how women can expand milk production through qualitative rather than quantitative increases, thus helping to save the environment. We also saw their readiness to adopt innovations and the re-investment they put into the family from their new income. All of those achievements came despite the co-operating agencies' reluctance to make women farmers a target group. Milk Producers' Association member Quisepe summed up the value of the project to her family and country:

> Before the project, I had between two and three litres of milk in summertime. Now I have thirty litres, mainly because of improved forage. We began to use alfalfa when the credit fund for seeds was introduced.[63]

That happened in the poorest region of Bolivia. UNIFEM's Nora Galor assessed the project: 'It leveraged technical assistance from the dairy development organization, and that has made a great difference.' For the participants themselves, the most important part of the project was 'the leadership and group skills that, combined with new sources of income, made their husbands respect them more.'[64]

The potters of Cochabamba: where are the women?

Nearly 20 aid and development organizations working in the province direct virtually all of their efforts to men.
Women of Misque: the Heart of Household Survival

The introduction of productivity enhancing technologies and training is not always as effective as it was with the altiplano milk producers. I include the following case study because it illustrates the beliefs and blindnesses that too often paralyse the good intentions of mainstream development co-operation organizations to support women. It illustrates the failure of social justice.

162

In 1979, UNIFEM agreed to finance a project to upgrade the technologies of women potters in Cochabamba in the valley region of Bolivia between the altiplano of the Andes to the West and the humid Amazon region to the East. In this region many men are away for six months out of every year, so that 55 per cent of the households are actually run by women half of the time. The province is filled with spring-green patches of farmland.[65]

The pottery project at Huayculi near Cochabamba was one of UNIFEM's very first projects and since it was to be executed by the UN Industrial Development Organization (UNIDO), we were pleased to be channelling mainstream expertise toward women.[66] That enthusiasm did not last, because UNIDO never understood what was meant by a project directed to women despite the explicit terminology in its project document: 'upgrading traditional technologies through extension services linked with a co-operative scheme for women'. In fact, UNIDO practised the traditional 'trickle-down' approach: by training men, the women would surely benefit. Our requests that women be hired in all the upgrading processes met with some weak efforts: one local woman potter was trained together with a man. Because such half-hearted efforts did not incorporate women in the fundamental way that was originally intended, and we had many more promising possibilities for investment, we terminated our funding in 1983.

When planning my field visit to Bolivia in 1993 I was informed that thanks to a series of German grants the project still existed. That made it appropriate for my research to determine the status of activities assisted by UNIFEM a decade or more ago. During my visit I interviewed a group of male workers at the attractive central workshop that is equipped with pottery wheels, electric kilns and a gas-fueled kiln; the centre also provides the tools for collecting and purifying clay. Then I went to the nursery school across the road to meet with a group of women, the intended beneficiaries of the project. The result of the trickle-down approach was still painfully clear. I was told that 'the artisan should learn, practise and produce at the central project workshop. And he should help his wife to learn at home, where the family workshop will become a micro-enterprise, with the man as the manager'.[67]

The fact is that women were excluded from the skills they needed and from the management and marketing training that should accompany the establishment of a micro-enterprise. They were also excluded from co-operative membership. Women's isolation increased; not only did they continue to work at home, but now men were encouraged to relocate their work to the new central workshop where the equipment was. Women at home simply worked clay with their bare hands. In fact, those 'family workshops' are basically a space inside each woman's home where she moulds clay into small figurines and fires them in a traditional kiln. There is no purification of the clay, no potter's wheel, no gas kiln for firing.

The men I interviewed explained that women were being trained at the workshop to paint and glaze the pottery pieces. That was true in part, but what I learned from the women was that only seven teenagers, out of a potential workforce of 350 women, go for the training. To all intents and purposes, the Center *is* 'the project'. Both those who run it and the co-operative members are men, with the exception of three widows who have taken the place of their husbands. The Center management includes two Assistant Artisans, an Administrator, and groups organized for weekly training sessions and practice at the pottery wheel.

How do the unintended beneficiaries and technical assistants legitimize the situation?

'We are not training women to shape the clay and prepare the raw material because of the resistance men have to women participating in that work. Since our objective is to train for the family workshops, we must respect their way of production. We do not try to change that', I was told by Eduardo Baudoin, the technical adviser appointed by UNIDO in 1990.

Given that Baudoin's statement means the women must work by hand without potters wheels or other technology it is ironic that the men of Huayculi expressed the strong view that mechanized production is superior to production by hand. At every opportunity during my interview with them, the men spoke clearly of their need for improved machinery. Co-operative President Jacinto Vargas gave an explanation at an Evaluation and Continuation meeting sponsored by UNIDO in July 1993:

> Huayculi can survive without machinery, for these men are accustomed to producing by hand. However [producing by hand] entails a very high social cost. It is a crime for artisans to spend hours to bring the clay, wet it, knead it, transfer it in a little pail from one side to the other to extract the impurities. That is time which could be much better spent at the wheel . . . [68]

Indeed it is a crime. As a result of the women's lack of access to even the equipment currently installed at the Center, the clay figurines handmade in moulds do take an inordinately long time to produce:

> The whole process takes at least fifteen to twenty days: to get the material, to prepare the little pottery, to buy the paint. Then it takes six hours to fire the pottery . . . and the problem is that our kilns at home do not always work. If we could get an electric kiln for all of the Mothers Club, it would be better. [69]

The women also spoke of their need for a credit fund to purchase their paints. But what they really need for firing the figurines is a large, modern kiln like the one which the men use for second firings at the Center.

No-one seems to have given any thought to the fact that the women have other work to do. Their traditional responsibilities in the home have not changed at all: 'We live the same lifestyles as our mothers and grand-mothers. They tell us that when they were young, they did the very same things we do: cooking, washing, taking care of the house, husband, and children–besides the pottery work. Life is hard for women . . .'[70] By leaving the individual workshops in each woman's home and removing all male labour, the project has simply added to her workload. There is talk

164

of modernizing the family workshops by providing them with gas or kilns, but that day never seems to come.[71]

What do the women of Huayculi think?

When they first spoke to us, the women of Huayculi were not critical of the project, but as the interview wore on they opened up. First, they contradicted the men's statement that women were not excluded from the Center's resources but just from certain tasks. That arrangement suggested a gendered division of labour in which the men collected and shaped the clay and women decorated and glazed the pottery, whereas in reality only 2 per cent of the women work inside the Center.

In their own words the women said, 'There is some kind of problem here, because as we work at home and men work at the project, we feel we are being bypassed. We would like to have our own business, managed by all of us, separate from the men. We have a Mothers Club house, and we would like to have [a workshop] like the one the men have.' Nobody helps the Mothers Club, they said. Pottery is the only way for them to get incomes since they live in town and do not engage in agriculture.

The UNIDO project is, regrettably, far from unique. A research report on the neighboring town of Mizque stated that the nearly twenty aid and development organizations working in the province direct virtually all of their efforts to men: technical education for farmers, new seeds, animals and fertilizers, loans and scholarships. They ignore women farmers in an area where a high percentage of women run households and farms for much of the year. It is only when aid is directed through the Mothers Clubs that it actually reaches women.[72]

What seems really unjust is that the women do not even earn much money from their pottery work. This is due not only to the fact that they have to labour long hours to produce work of dubious market value and without the advanced tools that should be made available to them, but also to the lack of training in marketing for their work. Only men receive the training in management, and only men attend the planning meetings; there was not one woman at the Evaluation and Continuation meeting attended by the members of the co-operative, technical advisers and government representatives.

Although they are not incorporated in the project, the women do sell to a middleman the hand-made clay figurines they produce. 'We go and sell to a person who buys all the things we produce. But we sell at a low price, and the person sells at higher prices. He receives more than we do.'[73]

I asked why the project does not work with women 'to upgrade traditional technologies . . . linked with a co-operative scheme for the integration of women in the development process', as stated in the original UNIFEM/UNIDO agreement of 1979. The reply was that the subject is a delicate one because men want their wives to stay at home. Are there not profound contradictions between the original project purpose and these warnings about questioning men's views? It is well-known that in low-income communities, men's resistance to women's economic participation

165

dissolves quickly when benefits begin to accrue to the family; we saw that in the altiplano.

A myth persists in the face of a reality which contradicts: it: the myth that men do the hard work. It appears fairly obvious from this vantage point that it is harder to make a clay pot without a wheel than with one.

Reflections on technology transfer: UNIFEM's work in Bolivia
UNIFEM's two major interventions in Bolivia–Milk Production in the altiplano, and Upgrading of Technologies in Huayculi–had profoundly diverse effects on women and on their communities. In the altiplano, women were offered technologies in the form of training, improved seeds, and artificial insemination for the cattle; they adopted those improvements with ease and profitability. In Huayculi, despite the stated purpose of the project, the actual participants are men, and women have been almost totally denied access. The latter is indeed not an uncommon eventuality when technologies and/or incomes are involved, as we saw earlier in this book in relation to Phase I of India's sericulture project.

The power of myth can be overcome when women have access to resources. In the altiplano project there was no expression of fear that the gendered division of labour would be altered and the culture conse-quently disturbed when women's economic activity was assisted; nor an attempt to hide the real division of labour. In Huayculi, women spoke of their need for income and of their dependence on their pottery as a source of cash, but their only organization was the Mothers Club that continued to maintain its welfare orientation. The organizers of the project did not hear them.

Women in the altiplano were able to increase their incomes significantly, which helped to reduce the poverty in that area. As members of Associa-tions of Milk Producers, the altiplano women work side by side with men to sustain those organizations. Recall that the women said that the most important part of their training was 'the leadership and group skills that, combined with new sources of income, made our husbands respect us more.'[74]

The difference between the two projects is vivid. The most influential factor turns out to be the executing agency and the co-operating agencies that handled the projects. In the altiplano the main creator of the idea for the project was the women's organization, CIM, and the executing agency was a women's technical agency, SETAM. Both were locally based and managed. Beyond those two there were several other co-operating agen-cies, but although some of them cannot be said to have understood the centrality of women to the local and national economy, any harm they might have done was limited because they did not have decision-making power over the project and its budget.

In Huayculi the executing agency, UNIDO, was an external international organization rather than one indigenous to Bolivia; it had almost no women as professional staff and no experience in design or management of projects directed to women in the 1970s. There may have been an honest belief that benefits to men would automatically enhance the lives of women in poor situations, but even that expectation should not have allowed for the complete abandonment of the specific objectives of the project. The experience in India is relevant here. When TADD executed the sericulture project, only technical productive knowledge was communicated and all of the extension agents were men. When the NGO, Aastha, was brought into the project during its second phase, the women silk-raisers gained self-confidence; they were empowered both as producers and in their family lives. (Aastha had both men and women workers.) In Bolivia, the milk producers were empowered but the women pottery-makers, with no NGO involved, were left without either technological knowledge or personal confidence.

Argentina provides another model for involvement of rural women through mobilization of whole communities, including their many non-governmental organizations. There, UNIFEM and other agencies transformed their approach from a troubling to an empowering one in an impressive move toward social justice. (See the box.)

Western Asia, too, has focused on social justice–assisting women and communities by training and community development, as we shall see in the following section of this chapter.

Argentina

All the organizations involved in rural development were involved in this project. It exploded!

Pilar Campana

The Cachi agricultural project in Northeast Argentina reached 4800 families. This 1987 development project was the first ever to incorporate rural women in Argentina, and it was destined to have a profound impact on national policies. The major sponsors of the project were the International Fund for Agricultural Development (IFAD) and the Inter-American Development Bank (IDB); the total value of the project was $29 million. UNIFEM input in 1987 was targeted to facilitate women's access to the project's credit and technical support facilities.

One development worker, Pilar Campana, calls the Cachi project the most important influence on her life; but she adds, 'I want to be sincere. That Cachi project had some problems. There was no specialist in training rural women in Argentina, and that was the type of person we needed. But nonetheless, the project demonstrated how to work with rural women.'

The next project was for an entire province, the Sixth Province of Argentina, where over 60 per cent of the 53,000 subsistence farm families live below the poverty line. Many of the households are temporarily or permanently headed by women. This project was sponsored by the Interamerican Institute for Agricultural Co-operation (IICA) and by the Instituto Nacional de Tecnologia Agricola (INTA) as well as by UNIFEM. It was this second project that significantly influenced government policy.

'Government institutions, NGOs, peasant organizations, the Church– all the people involved in rural development were involved in this project. It exploded,' recalled Campana. The plan was to involve women within a national policy initiative for rural development in order to influence future policy and programme formulation at both the national and provincial level. Where the Cachi project had been problem-ridden, this one was a dramatic success. This time, the three trainers and the four regional promoters had experience. Furthermore, by pooling together all the people involved in rural development, the project got more action, more money, and a better deal for women.

The project co-ordinators targeted two groups of women: the first group consisted of professional women who worked at the national and provincial level on rural development programs. The goal was to increase their capability to incorporate the needs of rural women in the design and implementation of productive and social projects. Three intensive fifteen-day training seminars were held during the first year of the two-year project to discuss the organization of women, their participation in planning, and alternative types of income-generation. The trainees then collected and anlysed information on the situation of rural women, which national planners used to formulate policies that impacted on the women's lives.

The second target group was the rural women themselves. They were typically the mothers of six children and lived in peasant households where they bore the double burden of domestic chores and subsistence/ cash crop cultivation. Despite their economic activity, these women did not take part in the decisions of family or communal life. The project included a revolving loan fund that made small investments in income-generating activities and social changes. 'To this moment, positive action continues in that area,' Campana said. 'The women's groups are still closely linked with INTA, getting technical support. The project was very catalytic in Argentina. It raised consciousness and taught development people how to work with rural women.'

Development amidst sudden wealth and civil wars: UNIFEM in Western Asia

Poverty is a serious issue, especially in many of the countries that are not oil producers.

Thoraya Obaid

In situations of war and civil unrest and of an abrupt change to non-traditional values such as those that accompanied the sudden acquisition of oil wealth in the Gulf region, and produced 'the petro-dollar culture', people tend to adopt extreme positions as a way of insulating themselves against violence and disruption. In Western Asia such forces have compelled many people to choose either materialism or fundamentalism, either modernization or a conservative type of Islam. 'That is the crisis we are living', said Thoraya Obaid of the UN Economic and Social Commission for Western Asia (ESCWA). Eventually, the interaction of forces will come to a middle way–will accommodate the positive Islamic concepts and the positive modern concepts. It is a rebirth process.'[75]

Obaid illustrated the dilemma for women in a recent radio interview with an Algerian woman who was asked:

> 'Are you with the Islamic political party, or are you with the Government?' She replied 'I am with neither. If I go with the Government, they will take my son into the army and he will have to fight and die. If I go with the Islamic party, they will "clean" the girls–bury them alive–because they are girls. So I will either lose my son or I will lose my daughter'.

Amidst the political upheavals in the region–the endless conflict with Israel, the Iraq-Iran war, the Gulf War–women are asked how they can dare to request rights for themselves, Obaid said.[76]

And, in addition, economic forces have had major impacts on women's situation in the region:

> Economically women are worse off than a decade ago, because men are also worse off. And there is a vacuum created by the absence or failure of political parties, that had to be filled. People went back to fundamentalist thinking. Islam can be a positive factor for women, but it is being used in its most negative sense. Fundamentalists interpret it as if the only problem Islam has is women. There are no problems of poverty, no problems of unemployment, only problems of women. In that sense, the backlash is very strong. [77]

Cultural conservatism also affects young women's participation in the active labour force. Among youth aged 20–24, women represent less than a third of the number of men in wage employment, and they are especially poorly represented in some Gulf countries. According to ESCWA, young Arab women are generally still economically subordinate to men.[78] Some Arab scholars identify the reason for that conservatism as the fact that young educated Arab women have been socialized in communities that remain traditional and where marriage is the only meaningful goal.[79] Obaid described prevailing priorities:

> A comfortable quality of life, in the material sense, remains the dominant dream of the average woman in the region. Poverty, especially in many of the countries that are not oil producing countries, is a serious issue. Feeding the children is really a serious issue. But still, the overall dream is to have a house and some of the consumer items, a television. . . . This is the remains of the 'petrol dollar culture' that we have in the region.[80]

While the region's overall economic performance had improved significantly by 1992, the impact of the Gulf crisis and war devastated some countries. The UN trade embargo against Iraq cost Jordan $1.5 billion in lost trade and aid in 1990 and $3.6 billion in 1991. By 1995 some 16 per cent of Jordanians live in poverty. In Iraq the mortality rate for children under 5 leaped to 380 per cent above the pre-crisis level, and 29 per cent of the country's children were malnourished.[81] Almost all of the region is still recovering from the social impacts of the Gulf War.

The ESCWA Report summed the situation up: 'rapid political, economic and social development has led to the deterioration of the middle class and an increase in the gap between the rich and poor in some countries'. Further, 'the majority of the poor and rural population continue to be deprived and marginalized in most countries of the region.'[82]

At the end of 1993 Obaid saw some signs of change. 'A group of qualified women all of a sudden appeared in key posts that are non-traditional ones for women,' she said. In Jordan a woman was appointed Minister of Industry; in Egypt, one became a Minister of Scientific Research. In Islamic countries there are women Prime Ministers in both Turkey and Pakistan. Obaid herself was appointed to the highest position ever held by a woman in the UN in the region: Deputy Executive Secretary of ESCWA.

A first for women in Oman

The project became a national community development programme.

Thoraya Obaid

The astonishing leap into the 'modern' world made by some countries of the Western Asia region is exemplified by Oman, where, in 1970, just 1 per cent of primary school age girls were at school, but by 1991, 96 per cent were enrolled, as were 53 per cent of those of secondary school age. At the third level, women's enrolment was 81 per cent of the men's. Yet, at the same time, military expenditures are 293 per cent of combined education and health expenditures.[83]

In 1976, when nine of every ten Omanis lived in rural areas, government reached out to them for the first time through a community development project comprised of training and rural extension activities. After four years, with UNDP assistance, there were eight Omani men and three women trained to manage, administer and to train others at the central level in Muscat; there were also 40 male social workers and 12 health workers at the field level.

In 1979 UNIFEM added an innovative component of $109 000 to the project to ensure that village women were reached. Because Omani women faced culturally based objections to their working in the countryside, eight Sudanese and Egyptian women were hired with the UNIFEM grant as extension workers; they would gradually be replaced by Omani women. The women taught family and child health, literacy, and income-generating skills. The Omani Women Association was reactivated and soon published *Al Omaniya* (The Omani Woman), the first woman's magazine in the country.

The women's activities were re-financed twice, to a total value of $549 000, and as integral to the larger project that reached some 20 000 people in 88 villages. Clean drinking water, roads, public baths, small dams

170

Oman

Demographics:	
Population	1.8 million
% urban	13
% rural	87

Income:	
GNP per capita	$6,480
% in absolute poverty	na
% of rural population	6
% of urban population	na

Health:	
Life expectancy	Women: 72 Men: 68
Infant mortality	30 per 1000 births
Maternal mortality	23 per 100000 births
Access to safe water (%)	62

Education:	
Illiteracy rate	Women: na Men: na
Girls as % of boys in secondary school	88
Girls as % of boys in tertiary school	96
Girls as % of tertiary science/engineering students	44

Work:	
Households headed by women (%)	na
Women as % of labour force	na
Female wages as % of male	na

Representation:	
Parliamentary seats held by women	No parliament

Source: See source table in Annexe 7.

and garbage collection, as well as health services, were components of the overall project. The activities attracted UNICEF, which invested about $1 million.

An evaluation by Dr. Huda Badran (Egypt) in 1983 estimated the rise in family incomes due to the UNIFEM project at 15 per cent, with a range of 720 to 1700 Omani rials per year. By 1985, the programme was extended to 135 villages and 54 settlements. Achievements directed to women included:

○ 42 women's centres established

○ 14 Omani women community development workers and two specialists trained

○ 47 women leaders trained

○ 805 women trained in handicrafts and sewing, and 816 in home economics

- 107 literacy classes conducted

- 509 women trained in national dress embroidery and producing for the market

- US$10 560 dollars worth of wool products sold during 1984

- 86 immunization campaigns conducted and 2561 children vaccinated

- 33 public baths established for women

Obaid stressed the importance of using a culturally acceptable approach to work with women. 'In the Gulf region, training and acquisition of skills are welcomed because education is valued. When you are seen to fit within the culture, any resentment will be lowered, and then you can raise issues regarding women going out of their homes and participating in community activities', she said.

Thoraya Obaid's point was clear:

> Get women out of their homes, even to learn sewing. If they can take the first step of going out of their homes on their own, not chaperoned, they are doing something for themselves. They then realize that this is something for them, it's not for the husband, it's not for the children. The important thing is to find a socially acceptable reason to get them out of the house.[84]

That strategy worked. When Obaid first spoke of training Omani women to cook and sew, I was hesitant, fearful that we would simply reinforce their familiar activities rather than opening new opportunities. But she was from Saudi Arabia and I was not; she knew her region and its people well. Yet my concerns persisted when, two years after the project began, I made a monitoring visit to Oman with Obaid. We attended the opening of a community centre and found ourselves to be the only women present amidst a large crowd. But change was imminent; after another year or so, women not only attended such community functions but spoke at the microphones!

Obaid recalled the beginning of the project more than a decade earlier. 'People were very skeptical, saying that community development was *passé*, that it was an old-fashioned idea. In fact, the project became a national programme of community development and now [1994] there's a whole Directory in the Ministry of Social Affairs, and it covers half the country, men and women. The UNIFEM "women's component" really affected national policy'.[85] It had been catalytic and influenced the creation of a sustainable government institution, in addition to empowering women.

There were other innovative projects in the ESCWA region in the early years of UNIFEM; they ranged from grassroots to policy actions. In Lebanon, projects co-sponsored with UNICEF trained much-needed child care educators. There was also a radio series on health. Regional and national workshops were conducted in the Gulf States to teach women methodologies for data collection and the formulation of national planning models. The most non-traditional training for women in the region prepared them to repair electrical appliances. (See box.) In Syria, however, a more conventional approach was employed, as we shall now discuss.

Working miracles in Jordan

A thoroughly non-traditional, experimental project trained women to maintain and repair electrical appliances in Jordan. Twelve women were enrolled annually in a specialized, career-oriented eleven-month course; another fifteen completed a three-month course on electrical maintenance and safety in the home. An added bonus was the reduction in household expenses through extending the life-span of equipment. The programme was so successful that the Ministries of Social Development and Education took it on the road: they repeated the course and trained an additional forty-five women in several areas of the country.

When the electricity failed in an entire peri-urban area near Amman and a student was able to fix it, a very skeptical community that had witnessed what seemed like a miracle joined in full support of the training. A 1983 evaluation said: 'The project can be considered a great achievement. It relocated women in a traditional society from a hesitant situation in dealing with improved technology to a self-confident one, through mastering of the technology.' (from UNIFEM's *Forward Looking Assessment*, 1984.)

In'am Mufti, now Adviser to Queen Noor, said that her concern as Minister of Social Development in the 1980s was to promote women's involvement in the economy of the country and the income of the families. 'I believed that women need not enter only traditional occupations like sewing and embroidery, as is most often the output of training courses in Western Asia. When we got encouragement and funding from UNIFEM for the electrical training I selected a girls' secondary school as the training site. In that school where "vocational training" was beauty culture and sewing, I wanted the young girls to see that women could enter non-traditional fields.' (Interview, Amman, February 1994).

Mufti believes that the 1960s and the founding of the national university were a turning point for Jordanian women. Girls became the majority of students, because they had higher secondary school grades than boys. They went into medicine, engineering and the sciences. Thus the economic boom of the 1970s and early 1980s found women ready to be employed when men went off to the Gulf to earn high salaries. 'The highest authorities in government, starting with the King himself, supported that transformation', Mufti added. By 1991 there were more girls than boys in secondary school and 118 women to every 100 men in tertiary level education.

When Mufti left the Ministry the training programme was discontinued, but she was able to create another one at a centre at Aqabah when she set up a development foundation for Queen Noor. She said that men in the town 'couldn't believe' what she was doing.

Empowerment through traditional approaches in Syria

If you understand only 50 per cent of the persons responsible for development–the men–you will end up with 50 per cent of development. To understand development you must understand women.

Abdallah Dardar, national programme officer, UNDP Syria.

Syria	
Demographics:	
Population	15 million
% urban	52
% rural	48
Income:	
GNP per capita	$1,170*
% in absolute poverty	na
% of rural population	54
% of urban population	na
Health:	
Life expectancy	Women: 69 Men: 65
Infant mortality	39 per 1000 births
Maternal mortality	140 per 100000 births
Access to safe water (%)	79**
Education:	
Illiteracy rate (%)	Women: 49 Men: 22
Girls as % of boys in secondary school	71
Girls as % of boys in tertiary school	68
Girls as % of tertiary science/engineering students	33
Work:	
Households headed by women	na
Women as % of labour force	15
Female wages as % of male	na
Representation:	
Parliamentary seats held by women (%)	8

Source: See source table in Annexe 7.
* GNP figure is for 1991 from UNDP Human Development Report 1994.
** Water data is for 1986–87.

Modern Syria, a land that interweaves ancient cultures, borders on Lebanon, Turkey, Iraq, Jordan, Israel and the Mediterranean Sea, About half of its fifteen million people are rural-based and 54 per cent of those agriculturalists are poor; in 1987 21 per cent had no access to clean water, and rural medical services were sparse. As elsewhere in Western Asia, the greatest promise for women is education. Women were profoundly and positively affected when primary school attendance became compulsory in the mid-1960s. In 1970, only 21 per cent of Syrian girls passed through the doors of secondary schools; today 44 per cent do so. At the third level there are 68 women for every 100 men.[86] Still 49 per cent of Syrian women are illiterate. Yet 13 per cent of gross domestic product went to military spending; that figure constitutes 373 per cent of the combined health and education expenditures.[87]

It was in 1981 that the Government first asked UNDP to finance two pilot centres for illiterate rural women. That request languished without priority until 1985 when it reached UNIFEM. Our initial appraisal raised serious questions about the adult learning dimensions of the project design: literacy teachers were to be trained too quickly and thousands of women were expected to become literate in six months' time. That was too ambitious.

We invited the International Adult Education Association to identify an Arabic-speaking woman to reformulate the proposal and then we set about negotiating with UNDP. UNIFEM would commit $50 000, we said, if UNDP would pay the rest–$259 000. Government and the General Union of Syrian Women (GUSW) in turn offered $150 000 in kind for premises and administrative support, and an additional $85 000 in cash to pay national project personnel. AGFUND–the Arab Gulf Fund for development–joined an evaluation team when the project was underway, and later committed $263 000 through UNDP.

The project, entitled 'Two pilot centres for literacy and vocational training for rural women,' aimed to establish centres in Bosra and Rastan, and so to 'confirm women's active participation in the political, cultural, economic and social life of the country'. The centres would train 139 women as vocational and literacy instructors and would serve women from 23 neighbouring villages. The literacy course cycles would be of nine months duration; four training manuals would be produced and published, and some supplementary materials would be recorded on video cassettes.

Two unique features characterized the project from the UN perspective. First, it was the very first UN project to be executed by the Government of Syria (UN organizations were responsible for all the others). Second, the co-operating agencies–government, NGO (the GUSW) and international (UNDP, UNIFEM)–created a very effective partnership. 'That is something that doesn't often happen', said the UNDP representative, Kyaw Lwin Hla.[88]

The project began in February 1989, and was the subject of a bipartite review a year later. That review concluded that 'modest progress' had been made. The usual delays had been experienced in hiring staff, but most materials and equipment were already in place or expected soon. One issue had serious implications: the lack of adequate incentives for the literacy teachers, who were adding three hours daily to their existing full-time teaching load at primary schools. They said: 'Look, if we must sacrifice our family life in the evenings, we need to have adequate remuneration'.

The UNDP refused to use its budget or to recommend UNIFEM's for the necessary compensation. Its representative posed the question: How will activities continue after UN support is completed in just three years? He was persistent and emphatic. For the UN to pay salaries was not in the long-term interest of Syria; the project would collapse, he said. It was a question of the sustainability and effectiveness of the literacy programme on a nationwide scale once the two pilot activities were expanded.[89] To retain the teachers, an additional S£2000 a month was needed as an incentive. It took three months to get that approved by Government, but the approval made possible the continuation of the literacy programme to this day.

At the end of the project, a three-person evaluation team reported that the outputs had been achieved as planned. The tripartite co-operation among international and national agencies had 'contributed immensely' to that success. The team judged that the programme had a positive impact on the Bosra and Rastan communities; it had introduced new perceptions of the roles of women and the benefits they would receive from education. Further, the women trainees were empowered; they had become aware of the political, social, economic and environmental issues that touched their lives. The government's first-ever execution of a project was pronounced to be technically, administratively and financially satisfactory, with the Ministry of Culture and GUSW facilitating smooth implementation. The project was judged to be sustainable.

Two thousand and sixty-four women had been trained in the two centres in literacy, sewing and knitting; Al Rastan had a program on fruit processing, and Bosra on dairy processing. However, as regards questions of marketing, the evaluators stated very courteously that 'the benefit of the market survey conducted by ILO was not significant'.[90] An effective market survey could have made a great difference. 'The economy is a market-demand economy whether it is in Syria or anywhere in the world', the UNDP representative noted. 'Creating opportunities without ensuring marketability–cost-effectiveness–and competitiveness with other products that are already on the market' is risky. UNIFEM's project, 'Strengthening institutions for enterprise development for Syrian women', begun in 1993, can be expected to fill that gap.

The evaluators also proposed that twelve months, rather than nine, be the minimum for achieving lasting literacy, and that all of the students be offered courses in fruit and dairy processing, and machine sewing and knitting as well as literacy. Further, the budget item for international consultancies had no significant cost–benefit relationship; those monies could well have been diverted to teacher-training at the local level. Although the special methodologies of adult learning had not been fully employed in the teacher-training (and that should be corrected in the future), a start had been made and the Ministries of Education and of Culture could co-operate in institutionalizing such training. It was also suggested that a revolving credit fund be set up for graduates to purchase the equipment and supplies they needed. In summary, the recommendations of the mission indicated their satisfaction with the project; it was then proposed that 'this successful experience be replicated in other areas'.

My visit to Syria came two years after the project was officially

176

completed (i.e., the UN grants had expired). There was every evidence, and it was confirmed by my UN colleagues in Damascus, that Government continues its support to the activities. I visited Rastan and Bosra with Ghada Aljabi of the Ministry of Culture, and Wedad Reda of the GUSW Executive Committee. Aljabi explained that the Syrian Women's Union had established a training centre at Homs in 1975, International Women's Year. There were women in the Peasants Union and the Workers Union, she said, but they did not include housewives. The Syrian Women's Union was formed for so-called 'non-working' women, most of whom, however, were very much engaged in agricultural activities.

The Women's Union often worked with other organizations. For example, when the number of children needing nurseries and kindergartens outpaced the availability of those facilities, the Union pressed to have every factory, ministry and other organization establish their own nurseries for women workers. The GUSW had some 1400 village, factory and other women's units in the fourteen provinces of the country. In addition, Syria had women Ministers, professors at the University and directors of factories, Aljabi said.

The site of the first centre was the agricultural district called Rastan in Homs Province. After a courtesy call on the governate officials, we proceeded to the Rastan Centre where three subjects were being taught: literacy, sewing/knitting by machine, and fruit preservation; there had also been courses in health. People came to the centre or to an outlet in the town to purchase the sewn/knitted products. The GUSW also had a marketing outlet at the Damascus international airport and exhibited women's products at an annual fair in the capital.

A child's sweater with leggings could be machine-knit in one hour once the producer was well trained. The finished product was sold for about S£150 (US $3.60), a low selling price because the GWSU wanted to meet the needs of low-income families, Aljabi informed us. The producer group was also contracted to do piece-work, sewing workers' uniforms. Cutting was done at Homs, and sewing at Rastan; those women who owned machines worked from their homes. The GUSW assisted in the purchase of machines through an agreement with banks and the women could repay in instalments–about S£700 ($17) a month for 36 months.

The enthusiasm of the literacy students was infectious. An older woman, Sultana, said that she could no longer be cheated because she could read. Latifah said that she was delighted because, 'I no longer need anyone to read the number on the bus or the label on the medicine bottle. I don't need anyone to help me sew a dress. Our health class also helped me to take care of my family'. Other literacy students said they could now write letters to members of their family who no longer lived nearby, but the most frequently cited reason for becoming literate was to help the children with their schooling.

Some of the sewing groups met in homes because the Women's Union had no space for production in the outlying villages and, perhaps more importantly, because it was culturally acceptable for a woman to go to another woman's house. Mustafah Saloum, who lived with her parents and

177

her son after her divorce, taught such a group daily for two hours. Each sweater they made brought 75 dinars of net income to the women.

Fatuma Muhamed had three boys and four girls; one of her sons was at university. Like all women in the area, Fatuma worked in agriculture as well as in the house. Now she had two sewing machines and had taught her daughters to sew; they all make dresses for themselves and for others. Clearly, the project had got her out of her house, as Obaid had advised. She told us:

> Now, if we need to go to the doctor, it is not difficult to do that. We can understand the medicine we are given. We can share in the children's studying. In the past those things were not possible because we were illiterate.[91]

UNDP representative Hla placed a high value on literacy for women. 'Women's literacy has a tremendous impact on the children. Women have a lot of influence on the children of the family because men are aloof. A mother will make sure that the sons and daughters have at least a basic education, if not more.' Hla was well impressed with the sustainability of the activities. 'Why?' he asked. 'Because there is a commitment, enthusiasm from the recipients, the government's Ministry of Social Affairs, and the Women's Union.'

> Once a woman, a mother knows the value of literacy by becoming literate herself, then she will make sure that her daughter is also literate.
> Kyaw Lwin Hla, UNDP, Damascus

Syrian women would soon be further empowered. Hla's conviction about the centrality of women to development had led him to discussions with government about a large programme that would be financed by the UN agency, IFAD with $2.5 million. He repeated to me what he had said to government officials. 'You are talking about extension to improve the productivity of small farmers, I said to them. On what basis? Teaching the men? No. Who are the people working in the fields? They are the women.' Hla requested and got an Arabic-speaking Algerian woman to redesign the project 'so that women were put into it across the board, not artificially,' he said. 'Now we are going to have it: a women-oriented agriculture extension programme,' he added with a good deal of pride.[92]

It was a privilege to work with a UN representative like Hla, whose concept of the UN's role is clear and practised. On the one hand, he knows that financial contributions alone are not enough. 'Political will and commitment are the most essential investment', he said. 'Our UN efforts should be directed to policies and strategies. We should dialogue with high-level government decision-makers to convince them of the increasing roles that women play in the development process–in the family, the community, industry.'

Hla also understands how international attention and support can build confidence and enthusiasm in the development process. 'Our [UN] input may be small, but there is a spirit that it conveys.' I agree with him. That is one reason why the UN has been the leading forum and vehicle for advancing the women and development concept and movement.

Yemeni women determined to get technology and training

People are ready to participate; they are ready to pay. But they need technical assistance and organization.

Mohamed Saleh, ESCWA

Yemen (from 1990)	
Demographics:	
Population	14 million
% urban	34
% rural	66
Income:	
GNP per capita	$520*
% in absolute poverty	na
% of rural population	30
% of urban population	na
Health:	
Life expectancy	Women: 53 Men: 52
Infant mortality	106 per 1000 births
Maternal mortality	1,000 per 100000 births
Access to safe water (%)	59
Education:	
Illiteracy rate*** (%)	Women: 74 Men: 47
Girls as % of boys in secondary school	19
Girls as % of boys in tertiary school	13**
Girls as % of tertiary science/engineering students	32**
Work:	
Households headed by women (%)	na
Women as % of labour force	4
Female wages as % of male	na
Representation:	
Parliamentary seats held by women	1

Source: See source table in Annexe 7.
* GNP figure is for 1991 from UNDP Human Development Report 1994.
** Tertiary school data is for 1980, and does not include former Democratic Yemen.
*** Illiteracy for Yemen prior to 1990; figures for former Democratic Yemen are similar.

Most of Yemen's fourteen million people live in rural areas with little access to safe water, health services, or education. Sixty-six per cent of the people live outside the urban areas. Fully 41 per cent have no access to safe water, and groundwater resources are an acute source of concern for

179

Yemen, where the annual consumption from aquifers is twice as high as the rate at which groundwater accumulates. Most of the land area is desert, and of the arable land only one-fifth is irrigated; farmers rely on uncertain rain for their crops and livestock. For those reasons the basic needs elements of social justice had high priority for ESCWA and UNIFEM.

But the human development aspects are also critical. The situation of Yemeni women is substantially worse than that of Yemeni men. Whereas only 53 per cent of men are literate, women's literacy is lower by half, at 26 per cent. While men receive only 1.5 years of education on average, women receive almost none: usually an average of two to three months of education. In the initial survey of the rural village of Mansoura where this UNIFEM project took place, 82 per cent of the women were illiterate. At an average age of 34, the typical woman had already had six pregnancies, with four or five children living. Infant mortality for Yemen is high at 106 deaths per 1000 live births, and maternal mortality is among the worst in the world, at 1000 deaths per 100 000 live births.[93]

Between 1986 and 1991, UNIFEM collaborated with ESCWA and the Government of Southern Yemen in an effort to improve the lives of these women and their families by bringing biogas technology to Mansoura, a village of seventy families in an agricultural area about sixty kilometres from Aden. Biogas technology transforms human waste and animal manure into (a) gas for cooking and lighting, and (b) fertilizer which is odourless and also free of the microbes which can cause disease. Not only does this make for a cleaner and healthier home, but the fertilizer can in turn create a green garden, something prized highly in this country where only 0.4 per cent of the land is suitable for cultivation[94]: 'In Yemen, usually the plants you see are not purely green. They are more yellow green. But because this fertilizer is very good, about six months after the introduction of the biogas units, you start to see green gardens around the houses.'[95]

The project in Yemen was not only technically strong, it was also empowering. By replacing the firewood with biogas, it freed the women from the task of collecting wood, which required walks of from five to ten kilometres each day. To make the project a success, the women had to influence decisions in the home; some of them 'committed themselves to providing their share in the cost of constructing the digester when the husband had taken a negative position'.[96] The men's initial support was critical for success, as Mahmoud Saleh, an engineer who acted as Regional Adviser to the project, points out: 'The men in the village at the beginning were very reluctant. But after constructing the first three demonstration plants, and after seeing some of the benefits, some of them co-operated.'[97]

Because the biogas units would create some free time for women, the project also opened up extension training services to increase women's literacy and to provide training on sewing machines. Traditionally, Yemeni women stay in the home where 'giving birth is considered a woman's main job . . .'[98] Saleh reports that 'The men in the village didn't want the women to go to the extension work. They didn't want the women to mix with other people . . .'[99] But the women were determined to take advantage of the extension opportunities to learn to read and write and to get some marketable job training: 'they pressured their male heads of households to allow them to attend the extension programmes.'[100] The results were tangible: women's illiteracy rate dropped from 82 per cent before the project to 75 per cent afterwards, but it still remained higher than the 32 per cent rate among the village men.[101] Yet even such a small improvement had a significant impact on village life, as Saleh notes: Gradually, after a great deal of convincing, and after seeing the benefits of such extension courses, the men became very enthusiastic. And there came to be more co-operation between women and men; you could feel the change in the social structure in the village itself.'[102]

UNIFEM played a key role in the success of the project as well as in the promotion of the women's extension programme. Originally, in 1984,[103] the proposal was simply to build some biogas units in a Yemeni village, but UNIFEM suggested instead that the architects of the project incorporate a social approach to the transition by asking the General Union of Yemeni Women to conduct a survey of the needs of women in Mansoura[104]. UNIFEM also encouraged the engineers to build a small pilot project to demonstrate concretely the improved quality of life which the biogas unit would provide. The Netherlands funded that pilot project as well as a seminar to explain the technology and its benefits to government officials.[105] Only after the revisions incorporating social issues, and after the demonstration units were found effective did UNIFEM support the larger plan of building twenty-four biogas units in one village.[106]

As it turned out, that approach was critical to the project's success. Technically, the study revealed that the most appropriate biogas unit for Yemen would be one that required little or no water. This led to the adoption of a Chinese prototype, adapted by the Egyptians, which relied entirely on human and animal urine as the liquid inputs to create the biogas from manure. Socially, the villagers were much more enthusiastic about the project once they saw the tangible benefits from the functioning biogas units at the pilot homes.

First, the pile of manure at the edge of the house disappeared, and with it the flies that were spreading eye disease. Second, the ponds of polluted stagnant water disappeared completely from around the house since all wastewater was transferred via pipes from the household directly into the biogas unit. Third, cooking over the stove no longer produced the clouds of smoke that had been giving women respiratory diseases, and the ovens for baking bread were no longer surrounded by unpredictable flames, so burning accidents were reduced. Fourth, about six months after the unit was installed, green vegetation began to surround the pilot homes since the wastewater treatment plants created water for irrigating gardens, and the sludge from the gas unit was transformed into odourless, dry fertilizer which was safe and easy for women to apply to their gardens.[107]

A fifth and invisible improvement was the end to the contamination of groundwater supplies which had forced the village to close its well and to rely on extremely expensive water piped in by the government. The cost of these units was 200 Yemeni dinars ($50), which is the average monthly income of a village family. A regular septic tank costs about 150 dinars, so,

181

'For 50 dinars more than the cost of a septic tank, you get fuel for your stove and a garden.'[108]

With these benefits clearly demonstrated, it is not surprising that twenty-eight families participated in the adaptation of the technology to the village. Every family was required to provide the labour for installation and money to cover a portion of the cost, which is one reason that some of the seventy families did not participate. And when one biogas unit served several families, a lack of co-operation could cause the unit to fall into disrepair. Another second obstacle was the need for a minimum of two cows to provide the inputs to the system.[109] However, once paid for, it took only two days to install the unit, then two months to get the biogas produced in an adequate quantity to fuel the stove. The engineer estimates that within three years the community was able to run and repair the twenty-four units with minimal assistance from experts in the capital.

The women and the local male technicians in Mansoura were able to keep nineteen of the biogas units in good working condition despite the project being interrupted by the Gulf War, and despite the relocation of the technical people from Aden to Sanaa (i.e., from a distance of 60km to 400km) when North and South Yemen were unified. Because of their consistent effort, the technology transformed their health and the local landscape. According to the ESCWA, 'by the end of the project, Yemeni labourers and engineers were able to design, construct, and operate a complete system independently and successfully without the intervention of experts.'[110]

Another problem was that women's role in the community organizational structure was eliminated early on. The village established a committee to work with the extension workers on implementing the project; initially there were two women on the committee, but one did not attend and the other did not speak. 'This may be attributed to the fact that being a member of a village committee with men constituted a new and difficult experience for the women in this village . . .'[111]

Regrettably, the extension classes which the women had fought to attend were no longer held after 1990. The extension workers needed some means of transportation to reach the village, which was twenty miles from the regional capital of Lahaj where the training centre was located. The project had only one car and that was needed primarily to transport engineers from Aden. ESCWA did in fact order a second car for the extension workers through UNDP Kuwait. While Kuwait was generally considered by Yemenis as the most reliable source for a car on short notice, the Gulf War intervened and the car shipped from Kuwait in 1991 never arrived.

Finally, a cow plague struck the town's livestock during the project, eliminating the inputs to the biogas unit for several of the participating families. Many responded by collecting dung from neighbours and that has kept the units functioning. The project would have liked to establish a revolving fund to enable participants to purchase livestock. This would not only have replaced the animals lost to disease, but it could have enabled families without livestock to purchase the two 'cow equivalents' necessary for a biogas unit. If the entire village had used the biogas units, perhaps the local well could have been reopened.

Despite these setbacks, it is clear that the women of Mansoura benefited from the reduced incidence of eye disease and respiratory problems following the elimination of manure heaps and smoky fires from their homes. These women also managed to break free of the tradition that kept women in the home, when they participated in the extension classes. For the first time, each woman worked collectively with other women from the village and some learned to read and write. The executing agency's representatives also learned to work with women in the process; in the engineer's words, 'Before, I worked in a research institute where 50 per cent of my staff were women, but working as a supervisor is different than just working with people. A supervisor gives orders and people listen, but working in the village, you cannot give orders. You should discuss with them, and deal with them differently. For me, it was a very good experience.'[112]

Today, the project is having a catalytic effect. ESCWA has already established a similar project in Damascus and is currently experimenting with a second in Jordan. Back in Yemen, the University of Aden now offers engineering courses on renewable energy, with the emphasis on biogas. Dr. Saleh is hopeful that the Yemen government will extend the project to a second village: 'People are ready to pay. People are ready to participate. But they need technical assistance and organization. With some effort from the government and from the NGOs in Yemen, this could be replicated with very minor funding from outside.'[113]

Kenyan women put down their heavy load

'I have a personal feeling about women fetching water: I can't stand it. When you first put the twenty kilos of water on your head, I give you five minutes before the pain is down your spine. And the pain stays with you all the way home, all of those miles, all of those hours . . . And when the woman reaches her home, she's too tired even to wash herself.'
Margaret Mwangola, Executive Director of KWAHO.[114]

A woman in rural Kenya works fourteen or fifteen hours every day, and three of those hours may be devoted to fetching water from a source miles from her home.[115] It was to alleviate that workload, and to eliminate the unsafe water that caused many children to die at an early age, that the United Nations launched the International Drinking Water Supply and Sanitation Decade in 1980.[116] Kenya expanded its longstanding efforts to provide access to water through World Bank funding in the early 1980s; this enabled the hiring of engineers, geologists, and public health specialists for a major water-pump development project targeted to the predominantly Muslim South Coast, starting with the District of Kwale. At the same time, UNICEF was mobilizing NGO funding for the Kenya Water For Health Project (KWAHO) of the National Council of Women of Kenya to disseminate low-cost pumps at the village level.

Kenya

Demographics:	
Population	28 million
% urban	28
% rural	72

Income:	
GNP per capita	$310
% in absolute poverty	52
% of rural population	55
% of urban population	10

Health:	
Life expectancy	Women: 61 Men: 57
Infant mortality	66 per 1000 births
Maternal mortality	100 per 100000 births
Access to safe water (%)	28*

Education:	
Illiteracy rate (%)	Women: 42 Men: 20
Girls as % of boys in secondary school	69
Girls as % of boys in tertiary school	45
Girls as % of tertiary science/engineering students	15

Work:	
Households headed by women (%)	22
Women as % of labour force	na
Female wages as % of male	91

Representation:	
Parliamentary seats held by women (%)	3

Source: See source table in Annexe 7.
* Water data is for 1983–85.

By 1981, both projects had come across obstacles. Political conflicts in Nairobi were eroding the momentum of the KWAHO project, and the World Bank's engineers found that they could not persuade the women in the Muslim communities of Kwale to support the major water supply programme at the village level. The solution to the latter problem was to be found in the revitalization of KWAHO.

One woman in the Kenyan civil service, Margaret Mwangola, was asked by the National Council of Women to take over the leadership of KWAHO. Although she did have extensive experience in the civil service, Mwangola had never held sole responsibility for an organization. 'I did not think it would work,' she wrote later.[117] 'The first co-ordinator had been over-whelmed and UNICEF was threatening to pull out . . . To me, a leader was somebody recognized through awards and public acclaim and I had none. After I accepted I wept. The future was terrifying.' Virginia Hazzard of

184

UNICEF remembers Margaret Mwangola in those days: 'When Margaret began, she wasn't like the way she is now. She'd say, "My God! What are we going to do about that?" Now she'd say, "This is what we're going to do about it." You learn all these things as you tramp through the mud.' Hazzard adds, 'If there was any guiding influence on us, it was the United Nations Decade for Women that began in 1975. I guess there must have been at least 5000 fires that got lit around the world.'[118]

Mwangola had a personality that could not be stopped by the first obstacle to cross her path, and her years of experience in the Kenyan civil service provided her with the personal contacts to smooth KWAHO's way. When UNICEF withdrew funding support in 1981, the government stood behind KWAHO: 'UNICEF was a tough agency to defy, but the Ministries were beginning to like the things we were doing. We were busy with the kinds of things the Government would not have time for: hand-pump projects, spring protection, the things that villagers can do on their own without much technology.'[119] She incorporated KWAHO as an NGO in its own right, and applied for and received helpful grants from the US-based Private Agencies Collaborating Together (PACT) and London's WaterAid.

At this point, the World Bank engineers on the South Coast were completely unable to mobilize support in the villages of Kwale District. Drilling boreholes and installing the latest hand-pump technology was not enough to ensure success. With time the hand-pumps would breakdown, and it was critical that the women using the pump be instructed in the technology for its use, and for day-to-day repairs. However, two previous pump projects had already failed in the area, and one had deprived the people of access to even the old village wells by cementing them shut. The communities were not enthusiastic about the arrival of a third project. The fact that all of the engineers were men exacerbated the problem of co-ordinating their actions with the end-users of the product, since Muslim women tend not to interact with strangers who are men.

The African Medical Research Foundation (AMREF) examined the situation in Kwale and recommended that the engineers hire a partner skilled in community organization for self-help. The engineers then called on KWAHO which, in turn, applied to UNIFEM and received $111000 (and later an additional $42000) to train Muslim women in the maintenance of low-cost hand-pump technology.[120] UNDP's Prowess would assist.

Mwangola recalls:

Acting on our analysis was a risk. We had ventured into a delicate social area . . . UNIFEM shared the risk, and that was most unusual for a UN agency. UNIFEM backed KWAHO at a crucial point in our formation. Before KWAHO came in, the learned opinion was that there was no way a water project involving Muslim women was going to work in the Kwale villages.[121]

KWAHO sent in three technicians and two sociologists, Rose Mulama and a man named Munguti. Their goal was to mobilize and train local women to serve as extension workers, who in turn would train village women volunteers. The team would spread ideas on health education, organize the community's finances for pump repairs, and train individuals to maintain the pump technology. After talking with the community, the sociologists wrote that the goal was attainable.[122]

Bibi Hamisi was one of the local women trained to be an extension worker by the KWAHO staff. She was called a WAHA, or Water for Health Assistant. 'Before this water project started, we used to have a cholera epidemic every year,' she told a UN audience.[123] She and her colleagues made sure that the new water project would work. KWAHO made contact with the village elders, conducted surveys, and then called the community meeting that led to the people's request to have a borehole drilled. They organized the community to provide water to the engineers during the drilling process, and then trained twenty-four village women to assemble and disassemble the pumps, as well as to collect from the communities the funds necessary to finance emergency repairs.

The WAHAs wore veils like the other local women, and that enhanced their participation. Halima Hamisi was 23 years old when she became a pump care-taker; later she wrote about her motivation. 'If men are trained, they don't worry so much about the pump, because it is always a woman who fetches water–it is her problem, so a woman will repair a pump more quickly than a man, because otherwise she will have to walk far.'[124] Margaret Mwangola added:

When the women got to the pump, they took off their veils and worked right along with the male engineers, testing, commenting, learning how to use and maintain the pump. The project did a lot for Muslim women. Those women learned the names and functions of all of the pump parts. A doubtful project turned out to be a showcase for the Muslim community.

The new lines of communication improved the project technically as well as socially. The engineers had developed the AFRIDEV pump, the first hand water-pump manufactured in Kenya and had refined it to compete technically with models developed in Scandinavia, Germany, Holland, Italy, and Great Britain. Now, with KWAHO in the field, the engineers were able to get the women's input. Mwangola wrote:

Was the handle too long, its upward arc too high for the women? Shorten it. Should there be a cross bar at the end of the handle so that two women could pump? Try it. Would two women pump together? Ask them. One European pump had a big wheel that made women stretch too much. This was not just an engineering concern, but a sociological matter.[125]

The local health centre in Kwale reported a 58 per cent decline in diarrhoea and a 71 per cent decline in skin diseases two years after installation was complete.[126] Along with the improvement in the water supply has come an improvement in health and hygiene. Mwangola has recorded some of the results. 'It would have been ridiculous to preach about basic hygiene before a village had plentiful clean water'. Family planning, too, 'was ridiculous to consider before, when so many children died of preventable diseases'. Now it is possible to clean dishes, scrub tables, and to wash hands

186

repeatedly and thoroughly with fresh water. 'You see the school-children–cleaner, with brighter, cleaner clothes. Scabies gone, dull look gone. Their teeth look better. Their parents are cleaner. The total outlook of the whole location has changed.'[127]

Such success led the Kenyan government to expand the project to a wider area in 1984 while still maintaining the crucial link between engineers and sociologists–hardware and software. The Swedish International Development Agency (SIDA) has provided continued support to KWAHO to accompany the government's expansion of technical support. SIDA has also contributed to the Kenya Water Institute where the Kenyan Ministry of Water Development trains engineers. As the project expanded, men as well as women were incorporated into the training programmes but as of today women continue to chair many of the village water committees; they are almost always the treasurers.

Back in the Kwale District where the first project took off, there are now 500 water pumps that bring up cool, clean water from wells that go 150 feet deep to tap the runoff that ultimately comes from Mount Kilimanjaro.[128] By 1988, the South Coast water supply project had expanded, from a target area of 300 square kilometers and 25 000 people, to cover 8250 square kilometers and 100 000 people.[129] By 1992, KWAHO employed 140 people and 40 per cent of them are the WAHAs, the women who know how to mobilize and train other women in Kenya's villages on how to get the water pumps that can free their lives from the heavy burden of the daily trek for water.

Margaret Mwangola credits UNIFEM with early and crucial support: 'Our sociological and training work was funded by UNIFEM and it was an eye-opener for both of us. That experience was the basis for our program of sociological survey and guidance for WAHAs.'[130] She added, 'UNIFEM funding gave us status in the donor world and has opened the door for us in numerous places, including UN agencies.' The key point KWAHO emphasizes in working with communities is that,

> The people we are helping, particularly the women, know best what they need and what they want. We can help them discover needs they have buried for a long time, but we cannot go in there and tell them what we will do for them and expect them to accept it.[131]

That most fundamental of all of nature's provision, water, is also the subject of UNIFEM's search for social justice through assistance to women in Mexico, to which we now turn.

Mexican women stop waiting for clean water

We have a saying around here. 'God gave us water, but he didn't put it in pipelines.'

Berta Rivera, Manager of the Tempoal Hand-pump factory.[132]

187

Mexico	

Demographics:	
Population	94 million
% urban	75
% rural	25

Income:	
GNP per capita	$3,470
% in absolute poverty	30
% of rural population	51
% of urban population	23

Health:	
Life expectancy	Women: 74 Men: 67
Infant mortality	35 per 1000 births
Maternal mortality	60 per 100000 births
Access to safe water*	84

Education:	
Illiteracy rate (%)	Women: 15 Men: 11
Girls as % of boys in secondary school	99
Girls as % of boys in tertiary school	75
Girls as % of tertiary science/engineering students	34

Work:	
Households headed by women	na
Women as % of labour force	23
Female wages as % of male	na

Representation:	
Parliamentary seats held by women (%)	7

Source: See source table in Annexe 7.

In Mexico, 51 per cent of the people live in rural areas and 32 per cent of them do not have access to safe water.[133] In 1988 the women of rural Tempoal decided to weld hand-pumps and market them locally. That project and the self-confidence of the women who run it, however, did not develop overnight.

Tempoal is an isolated farming community on the East Coast of Mexico. Women make up a disproportionate number of the adult inhabitants because many of their husbands and brothers have left in search of work in Mexico City or the US. The women usually work eighteen-hour days, including three hours to fetch water, two hours to search for firewood, and more time grinding food grains.

Back in 1910, the men of Tempoal won the right to cultivate their lands as they saw fit. It was understood that the *ejidos* of land could not be sold or transferred to others so that they would always provide a livelihood for small farmers. However, it was not until the agrarian reform of 1973 that women were included in the *ejido* rights. In that year, the wives and daughters of the men who had land rights were organized into collective women's unions of agricultural workers, called Unidades Agro-Industriales para la Mujer (UAIMs). Each *unidade* was granted collective control over an *ejido*, although not always over the most fertile piece of land. The goal was to improve the income-generating capacity of low-income women in rural areas by introducing or upgrading traditional farm production: poultry and pig raising, sewing, mechanization of maize grinding.

Ten years later, out of the original 2000 *unidades*, only 600 remained operational. At that point, the Under-Secretary of Agrarian Reform asked UNIFEM to fund a national survey to ask women's groups what went wrong and then to provide administrative support and training to 150 of the remaining UAIMs across the country. We agreed to assist this second step in the government's action plan to mobilize rural women.[134]

The women of nine *unidades* of Tempoal came together in an umbrella organization called AMCHAC (Asociacion de Mujeres de la Huasteca), with a total of 143 members. AMCHAC participated in empowerment training sessions sponsored by FAO and the Mexican Government, and then generated eleven small projects with capital funding and revolving funds from the World Campaign Against Hunger, PINMUDE, and from the Dutch. These included health centres, maize mills, poultry farms, citrus orchards and a sugar cane project. The women also purchased a car with the external funds: another step toward independence through increased mobility. However, triple-digit inflation caused the purchasing power of the revolving loan fund to erode by 50 per cent despite the careful repayment of the loans.[135]

The women watched the capital disappear and then decided that they needed a project that would make them financially independent from external donations. UNIFEM's regional representative, Klaus Bethke, suggested that the women manufacture water-pumps of a type he had seen in Colombia. The project would create both a product needed by rural women and the profitability AMCHAC needed in order to generate a line of credit for other rural projects. In 1988, the women of AMCHAC submitted a proposal to UNIFEM to build the factory and train themselves in metal work. UNIFEM granted $320000 in 1989.

This slow and uneven development was more than just an economic matter; rather, the entire process of taking financial control of their livelihoods transformed the women participants. They gained 'an ability to express themselves . . . [which] has given them, both individually and as a group, a sense of self-esteem and determination . . .'[136] These women were not going to be stopped, even though 'their activities have been interpreted as defiant' and have generated 'a series of delicate situations' in their homes.[137] The men felt threatened by the possibility of being overtaken in knowledge and earnings by women. Without a doubt, the mechanical design of water-pumps, the welding, the use of metal lathes–all these were not the traditional skills of Tempoal women!

'First we went through training,' noted one operative, Inez Lara.[138] What she didn't report was that when trainees left for Colombia to learn the manufacturing techniques needed to build the pumps, 'several of them left

. . . with black eyes and bruises.'[139] Nonetheless, ten women made the trip and returned to train the rest. The men's attitude seemed to change in 1988 when the women financed a men's fish project in Tempoal with the first income from water-pump sales. The men repaid the loan within six months.

The 400 hand-pumps produced in the first year are evidence of the women's success at mastering the manufacturing technology. The ease with which they install the pump in less than one hour is also impressive. However, the problem that remains unsolved is marketing. 'Most people don't know the pump exists,' says Ms. Rivera.[140] Their clientele need the pumps because only 57 per cent of rural Mexicans have access to safe water, but they are also the poorest people (51 per cent of rural Mexicans live in absolute poverty).[141] The pump is purposely designed for people with no money to spare, so the AMCHAC women must become public relations experts. To that end, the Mexican Government allocated $20 000 in 1992 to send a strategic marketing consultant to work with AMCHAC. The women of Tempoal are printing a brochure with sales charts alongside photographs of the group installing the pumps in villages around Tempoal. The main selling points are the low cost, easy installation and maintenance, and that they are manufactured locally.

Marketing, however, requires that the women move even further from their traditional roles. While most pump users are women, men usually make the spending decisions, so the women of Tempoal are learning ways to convince men to purchase pumps. They are also considering ways to make sales trips beyond the nearest villages while they continue to raise their children and manage the land. In eight years, the rural women of AMCHAC have already acquired the skills of accounting, management, and metalwork; now they are refining the art of customer service and becoming publicity experts.

A summary note

Social justice has to do with building up human capacity and, as seen at the beginning of this chapter, it is interrelated with economic empowerment and political participation in overcoming poverty. The case studies just reviewed had social justice as their principal objective and opportunities for education and training led not only to people's well-being but also to incomes and increased participation in their societies; notable examples are Bolivian milk production, Barbados food preservation, Omani community development and Syrian literacy and skills training. The Kenya water project brought about an immediate betterment of personal health, and the Mexican pumps may be expected to do the same. The lessons from Senegal and Argentina are vivid and not at all uncommon: that women, whose income is inevitably re-invested in the family, are highly unlikely to be appropriately considered at all when there is no specialized financial and technical input, such as UNIFEM can give.

We will now discuss UNIFEM assistance that had political participation as its primary aspect. I shall include SEWA–the Self Employed Women's Association–in this group, not as a recipient of UNIFEM support, but as an extraordinary prototype.

CHAPTER 9
Political Participation

Participatory action means that people themselves take part in the definition of their needs, priorities and strategies at both the micro and macro levels.
Participatory Action Plan for Latin America and the Caribbean
[PAPLAC]   UNIFEM, 1987

There has been a remarkable growth of women's groups, organizations and movements during the past two decades as women have sought to support their families and to take control over their own lives by co-operating together. From grassroots to government to transnational government levels, these women are mobilizing to strengthen their capacities for self-reliance. Theirs is a democratic, participatory process that recalls the community development and popular participation themes and activities of the international community in the 1960s and 1970s, although the movements we speak of today are self-generated. Informed by communications on what solidarity can do, and with leaders who represent the first generation of mass education of women, they have set out to get things done. Taken together, their efforts represent a worldwide movement to overcome poverty through political activity. In their capacity as citizens, women work to change the local, national and global agendas by winning the right to participate in decision-making. Ela Bhatt tells us why:

> If we accept that women's problems are not going to be solved in the course of the current type of development, then we are looking for a political solution–a method of giving additional priority in state policies to measures for helping these women. As past experience has shown, there is little chance of even existing facilities like education, primary health services or access to capital ever reaching women at sufficient and sustainable levels unless they build up an organized pressure.[1]

When women set out to change the national agenda, the goal of political participation becomes synonymous with the 'mainstreaming' that has been a popular approach during the past decade. As discussed earlier in this book, mainstreaming involves ways of getting women's voices heard in formulating agendas for development as well as the means to assure that a fair share of available resources gets into their hands.

Over the past quarter century, a key approach to changing the national agenda in a sustainable way has been to institutionalize women's presence at government policy level. For that purpose, the first thrust was to access and influence governments' national development planning processes. Then, commissions on women and development and women's bureaux were created to compile data and other information, and to act as intermediaries and advocates, linking grassroots and other women's groups with the highest authorities.

This chapter discusses UNIFEM's support of such political actions. It speaks of UNIFEM's deep commitment to, and long record of work in, national development planning; strengthening regional and national institutions; and women's mobilization in the civil society. Case studies of organizations in the civil society come from Chile, Zambia, India, Kenya and Peru.

National development planning

The national planning process was a prime target for women at a very early stage in the women and development movement. As Marva Alleyne, head of the Women's Bureau of Barbados put it:

> The elimination of poverty . . . is very directly related to national policies. And if countries can develop policies that can recognize the economic and productive use of their human resources, of which women form a significant proportion, it is very likely that countries could achieve the goal of the elimination of poverty.[2]

Meeting at regional levels, women asked their UN economic commissions to take action and they often did so with UNIFEM's help. The national development planning activities of the UN Economic Commission for Latin America and the Caribbean were carried out both by the Commission itself and by its regional training institute for planners, ILPES. Thelma Galvez, currently deputy director of the Chilean National Statistical Institute, evaluated those activities within her report on UNIFEM's contribution to ECLAC.[3] She explained that the objective of the Women and Social Development Planning project[4] was to promote the training at ILPES of men and women planners who would integrate subjects relating to women into development plans and programmes. A conceptual framework and tools for analysis were developed and used to modify the ILPES curricula. Fifteen fellowships were granted for women to join the training courses.

An inter-institutional seminar considered how and at what point the status of women ties into the planning process. Its conclusion was that planners would have to take not only economic but also socio-cultural and political factors into account in their analyses. Thus, as regards the training at ILPES, 'the problem was described as being not only one of training more women, but also of shaping a new approach to the issue.' Galvez concluded that, while many of the goals of the project were reached, a much higher investment would be necessary to effect and sustain change in the planning structures and machinery of governments (the project value was $133 700).

In 1993, Vivian Mota spoke of what a challenge it had been for ECLAC to attempt to transform 'a very huge and important governmental process and structure in Latin America, the planning process'.[5] After the Galvez evaluation, she said, ECLAC switched its strategy to the study of national budgets of Caribbean countries in order to determine the actual distribution of goods and social services to women through the national budget.[6] That study led to research and diagnostic analyses of the living conditions of the poor urban women of the region. Galvez herself judged that the new project made 'a substantial contribution to existing knowledge about participatory research in the region' and urged the dissemination of its findings, as had been done in the book *Five Studies on the Situation of Women in Latin America*.[7] Mota informed me in 1993 that the methodology established in that project was still used in the region, and not just with women.

ECLAC also trained women from governments and NGOs to design and execute projects directed to women within overall national planning priorities. Two workshops were held, one in the Caribbean with WAND assistance, and the other in Mexico for Central Americans.[8] The topic, *Training on Project–Programme–Planning Skills*, was given an extended life through the best-selling UN publication mentioned early in this book, *Women and Development Planning: Guidelines for Programme and Project Planning*.[9]

That same methodology, to promote women's participation at the macro-planning level by financing a series of development planning projects, was used in Western Asia and Asia/Pacific countries. In Western Asia in 1978, ESCWA began that process with an expert group meeting on national planning that brought government and NGO representatives together at a training workshop. That event was followed up on with technical assistance being granted to national planners on strategies and methodologies to incorporate women in planning.[10] Thoraya Obaid explained: 'We had quite a few workshops on development planning . . . to train people who were working in the planning area to integrate the issues of women, the needs of women, the concerns of women in the overall policies of the government.'[11]

In the Asia/Pacific region, actions began with a series of case studies on the impact of change on the social and economic status of women, followed by technical assistance to planners. Finally the design for methodologies to strengthen the planning process was shared in the projects executed by the Asia/Pacific Centre for Women in Development (APCWD) and ESCAP.[12] The development planning approach was an early sign of the Fund's ability to adjust its strategy from a project-specific to a broader programmatic one. In the Pacific area, for example, VFDW initiated a series of activities in the field of planning and programme/project development through ESCAP in 1978.[13]

In 1986, an assessment mission was led by Elizabeth Reid to three countries in that sub-region. The final report concluded that 'without strengthening the national machinery for women and the indigenous women's organizations, both aid donors and national governments will continue to make arbitrary decisions about what women of the Pacific want, while women will continue to be increasingly marginalized.'[14]

A second mission confirmed those same findings in other countries and proposed that governments and women's NGOs be consulted in the drafting of an extensive plan of assistance from the UN system. UNIFEM persuaded UNDP and UNFPA to join, and the consultations were undertaken in 1988 by a team of four. Included were two planning economists (one of them financed by the Government of Australia), a demographer/statistician from the Pacific region, a representative of the South Pacific Commission and another from Australia.

The team found that in the ten countries visited, national planning was often dominated by the demands of the donor community. There was an absence of concern for women in all of the offices except in the education and social welfare sectors. Government offices for extension services to women had 'neither the status nor the capacity to influence the planning process'. In the civil society, where National Councils of Women did exist, they lacked the necessary management and communications skills to influence policy.[15]

That mission proposed that a team of four, with experts in human resource planning, management, communications and training, should prepare case studies on the relationships between women and national/sectoral planning and then give technical assistance to four countries. Once again the purpose was to sensitize and train officials from planning offices, line ministries, women's bureaux, and women leaders to meet the need for incorporating women in development planning on an ongoing basis. Strengthening women's offices and aiding in the compilation of statistics and the analysis of laws pertaining to women were among the activities. In other words, the project was to 'mainstream women'. Funding assistance came from Australia, UNDP and UNIFEM.

An external evaluation of the project five years later recommended continuation of the activities by institutionalizing the ongoing ones and adding additional South Pacific countries.[16] The major lesson from the evaluation is applicable to all development assistance: 'Mainstreaming women in development planning is a vital but . . . complex objective that is unlikely to be attained in a short period of time. It demands institutional development to ensure that processes will continue . . .'[17]

Both the Latin American and the Pacific regional planning programmes testify to a fundamental principle: institutional strength underlies the sustainability of incorporating women's concerns in development planning. That principle holds at national level as well, and for that reason UNIFEM invested in 'national machineries', i.e., women's commissions, ministries and bureaux, and federations of women's organizations, which could influence government policies and programmes.

Institution building

UNIFEM sought to strengthen three types of institutions: national machineries, regional women's programmes, and NGOs.

National machineries

During the 1960s, the move to establish governmental commissions and offices at the top levels gathered energy in the UN Commission on the Status of Women. The goal was to develop national capacities to sustain the concern for women at policy and strategy level. In 1971, specific requests for such 'national machineries' were made by delegates attending the African regional conference of women in Rabat, and UNECA began a series of programmes for advocacy and technical support to member states.[18]

In 1974, an Interregional Seminar on National Machinery to Accelerate the Integration of Women in Development and to Eliminate Discrimination on Grounds of Sex took place in Ottawa, sponsored by the UN Centre for Social Development and Humanitarian Affairs. Mayumi Moriyama, Director-General of the Japanese Women's and Minors' Bureau of Japan, served as resource consultant. She stressed the national machinery's crucial and very difficult task of establishing 'effective co-ordination and communication between the various government departments dealing with questions relating to women.'[19] In 1993, Moriyama spoke with pride about how her Women's Bureau had persuaded the Ministry of Foreign Affairs, in the late 1960s, to sponsor what became an annual seminar for women from the Asia region for professional training in administering national programmes for women.[20] Women from other areas also attended.

The creation of 'interdisciplinary and multi-sectoral machinery within government, such as national commissions, women's bureaux and other bodies, and with adequate staff and budget, can be an effective transitional measure for accelerating the achievement of equal opportunity for women and their full integration in national life', said the World Plan of Action of IWY, Mexico City 1975. That suggestion had been made in the earlier regional plans of action for Asia/Pacific and Africa.

Marva Alleyne has a pragmatic reason for the existence of national machineries:

> Countries must not feel that because they have changed legislation, or because they have oriented certain persons to the need for equity and even adjusted policy and legislation, that those activities are going to ensure equity . . . There is always counter-action going on, passed on from people to people through generations ('We did it this way before') and through organizational social history. I see the wisdom of women in establishing monitoring mechanisms [Women's Bureaux] to ensure that there is not what I call slippage.[21]

With its mandate to assist the implementation of the IWY Plan of Action, the Fund had soon responded to fifteen requests for assistance for infrastructural strengthening, technical co-operation and the operational activities of the newly arising national machineries. By 1986, $1.7 million had been allocated for those purposes (75 per cent of it to national projects) and to regional projects (4 per cent) directly related to them.[22] The first UNIFEM assistance went to one of the earliest women's bureaux in Africa–that of Kenya[23]–to develop a research base on its rural programmes.

Terry Kantai, the first Bureau Director, told us in 1992 that the project helped her 'to articulate the priorities in Kenya for women and development'. Current Director Ruth Oeri reported that the Bureau's mandate is now sharply focused on policy formulation and popularization, data collection, analysis and development; training women's groups; and developing training materials. Operational activities are left to other sectoral offices, such as education and agriculture. Oeri has no regrets about the Bureau's structural evolution: 'You don't have a baby today and expect that baby to walk' she said. 'You must undergo a struggle of growing up, with a lot of problems to overcome.'[24]

The National Council on Women and Development of Ghana was founded in 1975.[25] Justice Annie Jiaggie explained that 'Ghana became suddenly awake and wanted to show something at the IWY Conference in Mexico City; women took the advantage and pressured once again for the establishment of a Council at the highest government level'. Current Bureau Director Rebecca Adotey told me that, 'The objectives have remained the same–the mainstreaming of women in government policy so that women's voices should be heard at every level. But the focus has shifted from implementing projects to monitoring the implementation of policy. Our main thrust is education and legal literacy', she added.[26]

A project grant to the Gambia Women's Bureau for food processing technologies was accompanied by another that fortified the Bureau itself with staff and publications.[27] UNIFEM was soon invited to join a mission with the World Bank, the African Development Bank, and UNDP to establish a multi-million dollar project for rural Gambian women. It was the first time that the World Bank approved a women in development project.[28]

The analysis of UNIFEM's Assistance to National Machineries is set out in UNIFEM Occasional Paper No. 2, by F. Joka-Bangura. The recommendations it contains carry the clear message that many if not most of the machineries established by governments were very short on technical and administrative capacities and on financial resources. Dame Nita Barrow was right when she observed that, all too often, the bureaux are 'still a token. They put in a woman and a desk, maybe give her a secretary, maybe not, and call her the women's bureau.'[29]

Bangura observed, however, that 'in the case of not-so-competent national machineries, one gets the feeling that if they had not taken up the question of projects for women, no one else would have.' In her report, she advised that UNIFEM continue to provide consultancy services, training and research services, as well as financial assistance for physical, infrastructural needs and personnel services to the bureaux. Bangura also noted that great care should be taken in making the bureaux into executing agencies for field projects. In short, the new thrust of UNIFEM assistance 'should have as its objective the enhancement of the capacity of these national machineries to influence decisions in respect to women's issues and help them to gain political power and authority.'[30]

UNIFEM did continue to assist the national machineries, as can be seen elsewhere in this text; funds were allocated to the National Council on the Role of Filipino Women, the All China Women's Federation, the General Union of Syrian Women and others. My interviews in 1993–4 with bureau leaders bear witness to the increasing maturity of those offices. Today, national machineries are no longer expected to do everything for women, but they *are* expected to be very effective in a clearly defined way. For example, in Uganda the first priority of the Ministry is a very basic one: women's ownership of land, as told us by the Permanent Secretary of the Ministry of Women in Development, Culture and Youth, Opika Opoka. For Alleyne of Barbados, a bureau is 'a bridging link between women's organizations and the government, and an advocate for the organizations so that women may increase their participation at decision-making level'.[31]

Regional women's programmes

Within the context of the political dimension of poverty that is being reviewed in this section, it is important to re-emphasize the critical role played by UNIFEM in the UN's regional outreach institutions, i.e., in the economic and social commissions. As reported in Part I of this book, the Fund helped to establish sustainable institutions at the regional level by supporting women's units and programmes directed at eliminating the causes and effects of poverty.

For over seven years, 38 per cent of ECLAC staffing for its women's programme came from the Fund. That support takes on even greater qualitative importance in view of the fact that it enabled the work of two sub-regional co-ordinators (based in Mexico and the Caribbean) and a project officer at ECLAC headquarters in Chile.[32] By 1984, UNIFEM had assisted 100 projects in the Latin American/Caribbean region at a value of $5.6 million; 27 of those were executed by ECLAC and several others were planned and executed with that Commission's assistance.

The Fund played a vital role in the development of the ECLAC's Women's Unit in its early years and is still of great importance, said evaluator Galvez. But she went on to say that, 'Although the relative contribution of the Fund was significant, the joint effort of the Fund and ECLAC fell short in terms of personnel strength, continuity and capitalizing on staff experience'. The influence could have been more determining if UNIFEM's resource base had been as large as, for example, that of UNFPA.[33]

ESCAP received ninety person-months worth of senior women's programme officer support from UNIFEM over the seven years. Daw Aye said that 'the main resources for ESCAP to carry out its WID mandate came from the Voluntary Fund, both financially as well as in the form of political support, especially during the early years 1977 to 1983'.[34] She explained the continuous political support as the advocacy that was exercised at the UN General Assembly which transformed the Women's Unit within the Social Development Division into a permanent unit within the Commission Secretariat.

The Fund also served as a catalyst for ESCAP. As Aye observes: 'The initial contribution from the Fund set the Women's Programme on a credible basis, later to attract more funds from donor governments– Australia, the Netherlands, Japan, Norway–and it reinforced implementation of the Commission's mandate to promote popular participation.' Yet another asset was that UNIFEM contributions enabled the Commission to furnish leadership in interagency co-operation and within ESCAP itself.

Daw Aye found UNIFEM's assistance unique in the UN family of organizations because it targeted 'not only the immediate relief of families but the development of human resources for self-reliance. The Fund's assistance generally led to a firm base for self-reliance that could withstand political changes', she said.[35] For Thoraya Obaid, who says that she 'grew up with UNIFEM', the important part that UNIFEM played was 'that it focused attention on women, not in the conceptual aspects (i.e., in plans of action or otherwise on paper) but *operationally*. By having projects in the field, UNIFEM made governments more conscious of the needs of women. Another important role it plays is in attaching women's components to large projects. Eventually those components became the greatest parts of those projects'.[36]

Non-governmental organizations

What is of great importance is that UNIFEM, through ESCWA in Western Asia, made the region conscious of NGOs. Obaid elaborated on that:

> When we started working with UNIFEM it was only natural that the NGOs would be a vehicle for development and for change, particularly in our region, because women's organizations are socially acceptable institutions. NGOs are the natural vehicle for mobilizing women and for change. Remember that the UN used to tell us 'you can't deal with NGOs unless they are endorsed by ministers of social affairs'. That was a big block because not all Ministries would accept that NGOs be involved in their work.[37]

Obaid reminded me of the time we spent promoting NGOs, before the UN development system had 'discovered' them; now NGOs are part and parcel of the UN activities, which is good. 'NGOs are the real people with the real ideas' in Obaid's view.[38]

Karetsa Adegala is one who sees women's groups as conservers of democracy:

> During the times when democracy was not happening, particularly at the national level . . . the women groups in their micro way, kept democracy going. They would have their elections, they would elect their people, sit and democratically decide what they wanted to do. The participation was there. They would agree: if you miss a meeting there's a penalty. They would put their money together and share it equally. I think that, at that small scale, they kept an alternative development perspective. They kept democracy going.[39]

Mary Racelis added the importance of organization to empowerment in the civil society.

> It is by working together that people empower themselves. Through community organizing the ordinary people–farmers, the urban poor– get together, sit together, work together, thinking through issues that really bother them. Through an organizing approach, groups come together to confront those in power. Individuals, when they are poor, don't dare do that, because the stakes are too high. But when you are many, you have force'.[40]

To illustrate how that force can be used, we now profile two NGOs; Isis International in Chile, and the NGO Co-ordinating Committee in Zambia. The former is a regional network for exchange of information, and the latter a national umbrella group that brings thousands of women into co-operation.

Information for participation: Isis in Chile

Isis International (named for the Egyptian mother goddess) has as its purpose to disseminate information on critical issues related to women. From its base in Santiago, Chile, Isis reaches out widely through its network to share information across the continent and around the world. Among their projects is one called Violence Against Women: Information and Policy, funded by UNIFEM in 1988.

Soledad Weinstein of Isis explained that the project originated as a response to the many requests received by Isis's documentation centre for information on violence against women–which was considered a private matter at the time. 'But through the years, under pressure from women's groups, it has become a public matter. Governments are beginning to realize that they have to have policies and give women assistance on this issue. Parliaments have considered domestic violence in Puerto Rico, Brazil, Argentina, Venezuela, Chile and Colombia', she said.[41] Isis's specialized database includes a bibliography and a reference list of individuals and organizations working on the subject, and about 20 per cent of Isis's own work centres on the issue of violence.

The other programmes of Isis are the co-ordination of the Latin American and Caribbean Women's Health Network,[42] publications, and communications. Amparo Claro, co-ordinator of the health network, explained that the idea of a health network came up at a meeting in Colombia in 1984. Isis acted on it and now publishes the *Women's Health Journal* in both Spanish and English. The staff are in contact with some 2000 Spanish-speaking and 800 English-speaking groups, associations, universities, and libraries in the Network, and have established links with the World Health Organization (WHO). The ISIS women were looking forward to the International Conference on Population and Development in Cairo in 1994, which many Latin American and Caribbean women would be attending. (As is now known, that Conference expressed very strong concerns for women.)

The UNIFEM grant to Isis's health network in 1985 was indeed catalytic; grants from the Ford and MacArthur Foundations soon followed.

The NGO Co-ordinating Committee in Zambia engaged in a different type of information activity–person-to-person in towns and villages. Their story follows.

Women mobilize in Zambia

Another example of the mobilization of women comes from Zambia. 'One experience taught us that when we come together we become a force to be reckoned with' said Susan Jere, Chairperson of the NGO Co-ordinating Committee. 'Each women's organization was struggling on its own, in isolation, until we joined forces to support the enactment of the law of inheritance, so that widows and children would not be left beggars when a man dies–when even their home would be taken from them.' Jere said that the women of Zambia finally declared: 'We have had enough. This custom is affecting our marriages. How can you live happily with a man, and how do you work together as a family when you know that upon his death you become a beggar and you lose everything?'[43]

Women's organizations came together, united under the leadership of the NGO Co-ordinating Committee, to lobby government. Even though they got a law passed in 1989 problems still existed: they then went across the countryside educating specially targeted groups: local court justices, chiefs, the police and women themselves. There was a good deal of resistance, Jere said. 'First, they reacted violently against the law. They said "that is tradition; it must continue". So we said to them: All right, it is also African tradition to knock out four teeth of a woman as a sign of beauty. Would you like your daughters to have four teeth knocked out? "Oh, no," they said, "that is different". And we said "it is not different." ' That approach worked: 'Eventually they agree with you. They come around', she said.[44]

Women in Zambia have just begun to act on their agenda. They want women's concerns to be institutionalized at the highest level through a national machinery with Cabinet status. 'Unless you have a machinery, you can't get to government. And what we want most is to have a say in which women represent women . . . Men choose a woman who is not gender sensitive, a mediocre type of a woman, and put her at the top. They pick some unknown woman who will sit there like a statue or a monument and do nothing. And when you complain, they say: "What are you talking about? We have a woman!" Not only do we want the machinery, we want the power', says Jere.[45]

The explosion of women's groups and organizations is worldwide. We saw that in Kenya there are 24 000 women's groups; there are thousands more in India.[46] The most effective NGOs, in the view of Vivian Mota of CEPAL, are 'NGOs which mediate and are channels between people at the grassroots level and the state and other institutions of society . . . My top priority, if I were a funder, would be to strengthen women's organizations . . . I see it as institution-building . . . so women can have access to all the resources they need.'[47]

An exceptional NGO prototype for participation of the most absolutely poor women in determining their futures is SEWA in India, which we shall now discuss.

Empowering the poor: the Self Employed Women's Association

Organizing is the answer to those who are weak economically or socially.

Ela Bhatt

200

'The majority of women in India are poor, are rural, are illiterate and are economically very active. It is these women who should be playing a leading role in the women movements of India'. That succinct description and the words of support were spoken by Ela Bhatt during our interview. Bhatt herself has gained valuable experience as Chair of the Self Employed Women's Association (SEWA) and as Chair of the Board of Women's World Banking. With that kind of background, her words of advice are worth following:

> Organizing is the answer for those who are weak economically, or socially. They have to come together and work and struggle together to achieve a better life. Once you are organized you are not finished, for it is a process, an ongoing process. After twenty years' experience I would put the emphasis on organizing on the basis of economics. In India we have many political rights, but because the poor are still dependent on others for their livelihood, they cannot exercise those rights. I put emphasis on economic organizations–peoples' own economic organizations and particularly women's economic organizations. I think we should work on that for the coming twenty years. We should not copy men, but have certain social values–peace and social justice.[48]

Bhatt went on to identify two of the positive results of women's organizing efforts. The first is the growth in women's self-esteem that occurs when they become aware of their contribution to the national income. Another outcome she pointed to is that differences between women (relative to caste, religion and language) begin to dissolve. In India, women 'have integrated as workers and as producers,' Bhatt reported. 'And of course, they also raise their income levels and now own some assets of their own.'[49]

SEWA has many activities on behalf of self-employed women who would otherwise have absolutely no security in employment, health, or retirement: the Trade Union, registered in 1972; individual co-operatives of artisans, dairy workers, traders, vendors and others; and support services such as the SEWA Bank, health care, child care, legal aid, housing, affiliation to international labour federations and capacity building.

A vital institutional element of the cluster of support services is the bank owned by SEWA members, who are almost all illiterate women. Manager Jayshree Vyas told me that they organized the bank in 1974 with 4000 members; by 1994 there were almost 40 000 depositors who have saved 70 million rupees ($2.3 million). The average loan is 5000 rupees ($162)–a figure that evolved from 500 rupees ($16) originally. 'Initially they were taking a loan either for repaying their old debts or for a little bit of working capital. Thereafter, when their economic situation improved, they bought trade equipment like a small handcart or a sewing machine, and then they improved their living conditions by repairing or extending their houses, or buying a new house,' Byas reported.[50]

> Ultimately the purpose of the bank is to help women increase their income, increase their assets by buying land, paying the mortgage or purchasing equipment.
>
> Jayshree Vyas, Manager, SEWA Bank

'We definitely encourage productive purpose loans, but if a member's past performance is good, we will on occasion loan in case of marriage or sickness in the family', Vyas explained. She gave an example of loans related to land ownership:

> We did a study of a village in a nearby district, and found that nearly 85 per cent of the families had mortgaged their land because of droughts or family problems that caused them to borrow through mortgaging. The land was the only productive asset they had, so they became virtually landless. And the mortgage was in lump sum; it cost them 20 000 to borrow 500 rupees and then they had to pay another 5000 rupees in lump sum to get the land back. But as landless labourers they couldn't make the repayment. The land was in the name of the husband, or in many cases the father or grandfather. So we put a condition when we started helping those women–that the woman's name be added to the ownership'.[51]

The agenda of the meeting of the Board of Directors of the SEWA Bank that I attended had two new items. First, women with really good records in terms of savings and repayments were to be given a VIP card, a 'gold card', that allowed them to get special service; they would be given loans immediately, as well as a 10 per cent discount at SEWA shops. Then there was a discussion on the work security insurance scheme that took effect in 1992, and also on a life assurance plan. Members who deposited 500 rupees would have an automatic deduction of 50 rupees from that earned interest as insurance against sickness and injury, loss by fire or riots, or death of the husband. 'That's a social security, and in the informal sector so far, women have never been insured.' There was a further proposal introduced at the Bank Board meeting to set up a housing services trust.

> In the desert areas, where we have our largest programme, women's income is 70 per cent to 80 per cent of the family income.
>
> Ela Bhatt

I then interviewed some members of the Board of the SEWA Bank, starting with Laxmiben Kota, who represents the bidi workers who roll cigarettes. They range from 18 to 60 years of age and there are 10 000 of them in SEWA, she told me. The workers organized through SEWA because they were exploited by getting paid only two rupees for rolling 1000 bidi. 'Now we are getting twenty rupees for rolling 1000. Before we got organized we were not even recognized as workers. Government people said that there were no bidi workers in our State! We still need to struggle', Kota added.

202

'We need to get houses, better health care, scholarships for the children, a dispensary. Some of us have got those assets. Now all of us should get them.'

Sarashaawhbay Chimairen, president of the cane and bamboo workers co-operative and also a director of the SEWA Bank, had joined in 1979. Her co-operative was organized in 1982 to purchase raw materials as a group, thus getting them more cheaply and thereby increasing their profits. Recently the cane and bamboo workers were having trouble getting raw materials because the forest department was using those products to build a dam. They took their concerns to the government minister and they still continue to pressure the Government to regain access to the cane and bamboo.

Chimairen cited an example of the learning process she had experienced. She took out a loan and gave it to her son for his business, but he mismanaged the money and she had to repay it. 'So I started keeping the money with me, and now when I give to my son he returns it with interest. I am teaching my colleagues how to do their own financial management rather than depending on someone else,' Chimairen said, adding that some of the women were getting alternative jobs, like cooking. 'They save, get loans and do financial planning, which should help, because these days are not good', she added.

> The women are earning more, and have better living conditions. So the future is hopeful, more hopeful than it was.
> Somiben Bharmalji, carpenter and junksmith

Somiben Bharmalji is a carpenter and junksmith. She buys junk then recycles it into drums and storage bins. Even 10 to 11 year old girls are in this business. Before coming to SEWA Bank, Bharmalji and others borrowed working capital at very high rates of interest. Now they are earning more, repaying their loans, and they have savings. SEWA has changed their lives.

When women come for the first time to our workers' education class, they have to introduce themselves, to say their own name, their work and the name of their village. They are not able to speak their own name clearly, they feel so afraid and shy. There is nothing inside like their own identity. It is so painful for them and for us to make them speak their own names. But now those women go to the police station, to a government office, or to meet a Government Minister. They face the world.[52]

The Bank's social insurance scheme was explained at the Executive Committee meeting of SEWA, which then turned to discussing what they wanted for their daughters. What could SEWA do for them? One member, a vegetable vendor, suggested that daughters be enabled to enter training such as radio repairing or electricity. At present, she said, the fees for that kind of training were far too high to be affordable. Perhaps SEWA could arrange similar classes with lower fees. Others spoke of the need to learn business skills.

Another member summed up what women wanted for their daughters in these words:

> They should be able to earn, but besides that, to make decisions, represent their case, talk about justice and know what is good and bad. They should fight injustice and should learn karate for their own protection. They should also learn to be good cooks and independent voters. 'We should prepare our daughters to be good leaders'.[53]

SEWA casts its eyes beyond its immediate environment, to national and international concerns. Besides having conceived and then chaired the National Commission on Self-Employed Women and Women in the Informal Sector, it has a long-standing concern for the legal situation of home-based workers in India and the whole world. In SEWA the home-based workers are members of a trade union, but SEWA also organizes them through their own co-operatives.

> Home based workers are the least paid of all workers, and the most invisible. When you want to organize them the first thing that is said is 'Oh, these are just housewives doing something in their spare time'.
>
> Renana Jhabvala, SEWA

Renana Jhabvala, Secretary of SEWA, explained their fight for a law called the Home Based Workers Protection Act. As a member of international trade federations, SEWA discovered that home-based worker problems are similar all over the world; not only are the workers mostly women but their numbers are multiplying. So, along with running SEWA's national campaign, the members are part of a global campaign to get the International Labour Organization (ILO) to establish a Convention to be signed by all countries of the world. Now the international trade union movement is also interested in such an effort. 'After about eight years of campaigning, the ILO is taking the first step toward passing a Convention in 1995', Jhabvala told me.[54]

Bhatt speaks modestly of all the SEWA work with women in India. 'It hasn't made a very drastic change in their conditions. They are still poor but they generally have sufficient to eat, they do not starve. Also, they have come out of the clutches of private moneylenders, of contractors, middlemen. And SEWA has spread so that there are now autonomous SEWAs in six other Indian states, with a total membership of some 120 000'.[55]

Bhatt says the most important thing for women is to have some productive assets. 'The assets can be a bank balance or a sewing machine; a home so that she doesn't have to pay rent, or even an identity card; a shareholding in a co-operative, or of course land.' In most cases a woman's home is also her work place, and when she does not have to pay rent it is a productive asset that helps the fight against inflation.'

> Women are the leaders for social change. It is the women who have been able to recover the mortgaged land for their families.
>
> Ela Bhatt

What SEWA women have achieved

SEWA keeps close to the policy sectors of government, says Bhatt: 'Whatever experience we have at the grassroot, good or bad, we invariably try to translate it and cover it at the policy level. From the beginning of SEWA we have tried to keep this two-way flow'.[56] Actually, SEWA responds in an exceptional way to the social, economic and political dimensions of poverty that provide the framework for analysis in this book.

Members of SEWA build self-esteem and empowerment, and they overcome differences of class, caste and religion through working together as

---

Two SEWA Stories

Jyotiben lives in Raikhad on the river bank. She sells fish for a living. When the water-level of the river rose, her home was flooded. The fish stored there for sale spoiled and she lost her fishing net too. If she borrowed money for those damages how could she ever repay and feed her family? Being a member of the SEWA insurance scheme, she obtained a loan, after the damage to her home and goods was assessed. First of all she bought a new fishing net. She said 'With my net, at last I can breathe in peace. I can earn and rebuild again.'

Annual Report, SEWA 1993

Hansaben is an executive committee member of Raipur village's dairy co-operative in Gandhinagar district. Her co-operative's milk was of the best quality, grade A, and had been so for years. Some time ago it was suddenly judged to be grade B and the women started getting a lower price per litre for it.

Hansaben looked into the matter and found no error in the sales figures. What went wrong? To find out, one day at 7:30 in the evening she hid in a field when the truck from the dairy came to collect her co-operative's milk. She caught the contractor red-handed adding water to the co-operative's milk, thus lowering its quality.

The next day Hansaben lodged a complaint with the dairy. The contractor was forced to admit to diluting the milk. She managed to obtain the price for grade A milk for as many days as she and her colleagues had been cheated. Extra income of Rs15000 thus came to the co-operative, which Hansaben had saved from ruin.

Annual Report, SEWA 1993

---

trade unionists. Knowing that they can do together what none could do alone, illiterate women proceeded to establish a bank. Bhatt tells how she herself was hesitant to open a bank, 'because we are so poor'. A fellow member of SEWA responded 'yes, but we are so many'. Those SEWA members who were too shy to speak their own names now call on government ministers and other officials.

As catalyst-for-change, SEWA has influenced policy time and again, most successfully through the National Commission on Self-Employed Women and Women in the Informal Sector that was created by government on SEWA's request, and chaired by Bhatt. They are working toward a Home-Based Workers Protection Act in India and, together with other organizations, are near to achieving an international Convention on Home-Based Workers.

SEWA members have increased their access to productive resources and to incomes; they are economically empowered. They have obtained both productive and personal assets, among them carpentry tools, sewing machines, bank balances, houses and land. They have built a unique financial institution that can save for and lend to the poor without taking a loss. They have a social insurance system that guards against a reversal to the depths of poverty by protecting against sickness, injury, loss by fire, riots, or the death of a husband, and a life assurance scheme that protects family survivors should the woman worker herself die.

SEWA has metamorphosed from being part of a trade union to becoming a trade union itself. It has created a bank and a social security scheme. These sustainable institutions have been a major factor for women's empowerment and for influencing national and international policy. SEWA has also spawned other, autonomous 'sister' SEWAs in India.

A most impressive feature of SEWA provides a shining example for the international women's movement: its leadership team–consisting of a handful of educated and committed women in partnership with the workers' leaders who come from situations of poverty. They alternately learn from and lead one another; the educated use their knowledge and contacts to link the movement with national policymakers; the workers in turn teach the educated about poverty and ways to overcome it.

With that enriching story of the trade union, SEWA, that battles poverty, we now turn to participation of a different kind–in defence of the environment in Africa.

A Kenyan woman stands firm

I am a member of the Green Belt Movement. I am a tree planter. It is for me. It is for my children. It is for my country.

Professor Wangari Maathai tells the story of a large wild fig tree that grew near her home.[57] Her mother told her that it would never be cut down and that she must not even break off its twigs. As a child, Professor Maathai collected water from the spring near the tree, 'fascinated by the way the cool, clean water pushed its way through the soft red clay, so gently that

206

even the individual grains of soil were left undisturbed.' Tragically, the tree was cut down to create space for a tea plantation; the spring promptly dried up; the soil began to erode. Food in the area is now scarce, and women search for hours to collect the firewood they need.

These are some of the problems women face throughout rural Kenya and 'they are not acts of God, but of humans,' wrote Professor Maathai in 1988.[58] She noted that although 300 000 billion litres of rainwater fall each year, two-thirds of the Kenya landscape is arid, semi-arid, or desert.[59] While it is often the major proportions of desertification that are discussed in the news, 'the Sahara will not come pouring over us. It is being created a little bit at a time by each household'. Her message is that people can also heal the earth by acting in their own communities: 'We must fight desertification at the family level.'[60]

To reverse the trend, the National Council of Women of Kenya decided to promote reforestation in 1977. A major goal was to re-introduce trees indigenous to Kenya. Kenyan farmers had shifted to the use of imported trees, such as eucalyptus and evergreens, because they provide a quick economic return. However, trees indigenous to Kenya have adapted over thousands of years to its climate and soil; it is those indigenous trees, such as the fig, the croton, and acacias, that can withstand drought–and prevent it. The roots of trees help the soil to absorb rainwater; without the roots, the water simply rolls elsewhere,–taking the fertile topsoil with it.

The Kenyan Department of Forestry promised to supply the National Council of Women's project with seedlings at no charge–a pledge it was forced to amend down to a subsidy because the public response was overwhelming. By 1990, over ten million trees had been planted. To supply seedlings, the National Council of Women asked rural women to staff tree nurseries. With the help of the Department of Forestry, rural women made seed beds and transplanted the seedlings into plastic bags to distribute in their communities; but most of the trees took three to five years to grow.

'At first it was very difficult to convince people to keep caring for them,' Professor Maathai notes. The Council enlisted the help of school children by planting belts of a thousand trees to act as windbreaks around their schoolyards. These were known as the Green Belts and the project took on that name and became the Green Belt Movement. The children took the message of reforestation home to their parents and people in the country-side began to plant trees.

In 1981, the Green Belt Movement wrote to UNIFEM to ask for financial support so that the reforestation could go hand in hand with the elimination of the unemployment status of rural women. 'Unemployment renders people helpless, makes them easy victims of exploitation and injustice,' Professor Maathai writes. UNIFEM responded with an allocation of $122 700. Professor Maathai credits UNIFEM with making it possible for the National Council of Women to demonstrate what was meant by community participation in reforestation.[61] With that money the Green Belt Movement paid rural women a small amount for every seedling that survived for three months; it was the only cash income for many of them. By 1988, there were 600 nurseries[62] and by 1990, more than twice as many.[63] Additionally, the Movement has hired rural women to visit the local people who are planting the trees in order to ensure that the seedlings receive the proper care during the first years that are so crucial for success. For every monthly report submitted, the Green Belt Movement pays these rural women advisers a stipend.

'While it is easier to do things for other people, it does not empower people or encourage them to be masters of their own destiny. Instead, it disarms them, making them dependent and apathetic. They easily place their fate in the hands of experts . . .' The Green Belt Movement has grown because the women of Kenya have spread the ideas along with the seedlings. 'Through the Movement, the women of Kenya have been able to feel and to demonstrate their positive creativity and their ability to be assertive and effective leaders,' wrote Professor Maathai.[64]

Promoting the concept of 'Development by the people, rather than for the people' the Green Belt Movement noted that 'few, if any, people will work for nothing so that others benefit.' Although the majority of Kenya's farmers are women, it is ironic that women do not have ownership rights to land. 'Although women work on the land, and even accept that it is their responsibility to do so, they do not own it.'[65] It was not always so; plots of land used to belong to the entire family or community, but Kenya followed British law and transferred titles to male heads of household. Despite this perverse legal rule, the women in the Green Belt Movement found that 'the men were very eager to plant trees. The men own the land, so for them to plant a tree is to improve their land. The women produce the seedlings, and the men are very keen to plant.'[66] As a result, 'The Green Belt Movement is the first project initiated by women which has become the project of everybody.'[67]

By 1988 the Green Belt Movement had a headquarters in Nairobi, a staff of 800 in the field, and more than 50 000 members throughout Kenya. However, the entire project was thrown into jeopardy when the Kenyan government announced plans to transform the one public green space in downtown Nairobi, Uhuru Park, into the grounds of a sixty-story building for the ruling KANU party. 'If I didn't react to their interfering with this central park, I may as well not plant another tree,' said Professor Maathai in 1989. 'I cannot condone that kind of activity and call myself an environmentalist.'[68] She led the community's opposition to the construction and several members of the Kenyan government sent her unflattering letters which she turned over to the Kenyan press. The public responded with an outcry of indignation. Maathai then appealed to the courts with an environmental impact suit; she lost, and was expelled from membership of the ruling party.[69] In early 1990, one Member of Parliament, Wilberforce Kisiero, increased her political isolation by forbidding her from visiting his constituency because of her 'disrespect' for the ruling party.[70]

Professor Maathai's deepest concerns were for the fate of the Green Belt Movement. The lease of Green Belt headquarters in a government building was canceled with twenty-four hours notice, and no other landlord would rent space to the Movement which was now designated as 'subversive.'

'The majority of the people in the Movement are poor. They hear that the Movement is subversive and they are scared. They don't want to be seen as against the Government. That can get you into a lot of trouble. And the politicians know that is the way the people feel,' she said in late 1989.[71] It was in order to protect the grassroots membership that Professor Maathai told one reporter in 1990 that she 'considered the complex battle a closed chapter and was now keen to resume her movement's activities of improving the environment through tree planting.'[72]

However, the success of the Green Belt women at the grassroots level had by this time won the respect of the global environmental movement. Professor Maathai had received a UN Environmental Programme Global 500 Award and a 'Woman of the World' citation from the Princess of Wales. The international community was concerned about the people's opposition to Kenyan President Daniel Arap Moi's planned skyscraper in the park and re-examined their plans to loan him the $200 million for construction. 'The ruling party wants a monument to itself. Moi's statue will be four storeys tall,' wrote *The Economist*.[73] The Government still maintained the building would be 'good for the environment'[74], but then quietly put the skyscraper's development on the backburner.

The Green Belt Movement was not to be left in peace, however. When asked why the government was continuing to label her as a subversive, Professor Maathai responded: 'I am honest, frank, and dedicated to my work. I think the Green Belt Movement appears threatening because it is organizing ordinary people, poor people, and it is telling them that they can cause positive change to their environment, and that they can do it on their own.'[75]

In January of 1992, Professor Maathai was arrested by police who besieged her home and charged her with 'rumour-mongering'. She was then released. Three months later she went back to the Uhuru Park to support a group of women who had initiated a hunger strike to protest the imprisonment of their sons. On March 3, 1992 riot police tear-gassed the park, and clubbed the women, knocking four unconscious,–including Professor Maathai.[76] Throughout these dangerous times, the international environmental movement's support has been critical for protecting Professor Maathai and the Green Belt Movement from obliteration.[77] She was recognized as Africa's leading environmentalist when the global NGO community selected her to address governments on their behalf at the UN Conference on Environment and Development at Rio de Janeiro in 1992. During his term in the Senate, Vice-President of the United States Al Gore planted one of the Green Belt trees while on a visit to Kenya and, when Maathai was imprisoned in 1992, he and seven other members of the US Senate called on the Kenyan Government to release her.[78]

'All that support saved my life. I know that I am doing this work for all who cherish freedom and justice, and without such ideals, we cannot save this planet,' wrote Maathai after she regained her freedom.

Maathai continues to advocate sustainable development as she did in 1988 when she wrote: 'For many decision-makers, development means

209

extensive farming of cash-crops for foreign exchange . . . If asked, the people would probably prefer a different type of development, sustainable development. Sustainable development is the utilization of national resources by the present generation in such rational manners as would not put the future generations in jeopardy.'[79]

Today, she speaks with more anger at those who stand against the wishes of the global grassroots movement she worked to create.

Is it possible for the rich and powerful to promote co-operation and solidarity rather than domination and exploitation? For example, can they believe in equity and justice for all? Or in tolerance and non-violence to other humans and to all other forms of life? Can there be enough motivating factors to encourage the people of the world to work together for common goals?[80]

For Kenyan women, the answer is, 'Yes.' They told researcher Njoki Njehu:[81]

Everyone was saying, 'stop soil erosion, stop the land from becoming a desert, stop environmental destruction.' Stop this and stop that. But no-one was showing us how. The Green Belt Movement showed how and why!

I can see a difference in our area since we started planting trees. It is greener, there are more fruits available for the children, and I even have leftovers to sell.

The women of Kenya continue to plant one tree at a time, and as of 1994 there are 20 million new indigenous trees greening Kenya.

We now move across the world to Peru, where grassroots groups have kept children's nutrition strong during economic and political crises, and women trade unionists changed national policy.

Grassroots women's organizations in Peru—
empowered, autonomous, massive

What is development? It is being able to face the world, to feel better as a person, to have a place in your family, and to be able to earn one's own living.

Maria Fevres, Peru Mujer Organization

Over the past twenty-five years, streams of people have migrated from the Peruvian Andes into the cities, initiating a period of social upheaval. In 1960, 54 per cent of Peruvians lived in rural areas–many of them in indigenous communities where Quechua or Aymara was the first language. Today, 72 per cent of the population is urban, with eight million of the country's twenty-four million inhabitants living in Lima alone. Underlying this migration was a change in the economy from land-based to industrial. But as the world slid into economic crisis in the 1980s, Peru's industrializing economy spun into the worst economic collapse in over five

210

Peru

Demographics

Population	24 million
% urban	72
% rural	28

Income

GNP per capita	$950
% in absolute poverty	32
% of rural population	75
% of urban population	13

Health

Life expectancy	Women: 67 Men: 63
Infant mortality	76 per 1000 births
Maternal mortality	240 per 100000 births
Access to safe water (%)	53

Education

Illiteracy rate (%)	Women: 21 Men: 9
Girls as % of boys in secondary school	88
Girls as % of boys in tertiary school	na
Girls as % of tertiary science/engineering students	na

Work

Households headed by women (%)	17
Women as % of labour force	39
Female wages as % of male	na

Representation

Parliamentary seats held by women (%)	6

Source: See source table in Annexe 7.

hundred years. The migrants from the Andes in Lima were particularly hard hit because their livelihoods were not yet secure.

A typical shanty town on the outskirts of Peru was described as follows in *The Economist*, December 1987:

Founded in 1971, Villa El Salvador has more than 300 000 inhabitants and has won legal recognition as a municipal district. Four-fifths of the houses–the older ones of brick and cement, the new of inflammable rush-matting–are hooked up to electricity and water, which flows erratically . . . The residents have done almost all of it themselves. Of the thirty-four schools, they have built thirty-two.

When inflation reached 30 per cent to 40 per cent *per month* in 1989 and 1990, the people who were already poor were pushed to the brink of starvation. In response to the extreme economic inequality, violent political rebellion increased; the most significant took the form of the Sendero Luminoso (Shining Path). According to the Peruvian human rights group, Coordinadora Nacional de Derechos Humanos, 29 000 people were killed between 1980 and 1993–either by the Government or by Sendero.

Alberto Fujimori was elected president to combat the hyperinflation and the expanding wave of political violence. The new government responded by promoting a programme of economic liberalization, particularly encouraging production for export. However, in the early 1990s, negative effects were felt when domestic factories shut down because of cheaper imported goods. Massive layoffs were exacerbated by the passage of legislation limiting employers' obligations to employees.

Women, who formed 39 per cent of the non-farm labour force in the 1980s, have been expelled from the industrial sector, and they now constitute well over half of the informal sector labour force. At the same time, they are the breadwinners in 29 per cent of the families. That may explain the results of a survey of young persons conducted in 1993 that found that 40 per cent wanted to leave Peru. Some of the women go to Japan where they are able to find work, although they earn only 50 per cent of men's salaries. Others emigrate to Bolivia, Venezuela and the United States.[82]

In 1992, the Government imprisoned the leaders of Sendero Luminoso so that the threat of political violence no longer hangs over the streets of Lima or the countryside. As this book goes to press, inflation is under control and middle-class Peruvians now find that for the first time in their lives they can save money without having its value disappear. But the economic policies have not alleviated the grinding poverty in the shanty towns that surround Lima. There, unemployment remains high so people have to create their own jobs in the popular economy in order to survive from day to day.

One of the most significant and hopeful developments of the 1980s was the blossoming of the women's movement in the shanty towns. Women came together because the situation was desperate. '[By 1989–90] people's goals were set on survival, actually eating every day. And it was only the creation and maintenance of these [women's] organizations which allowed a fairly large proportion of the Peruvian population to stay alive.'[83] Their interdependence was their strength.

UNIFEM was one of the first institutions that identified their tremendous potential. We began to assist by sponsoring a workshop for volunteers in 1986.[84] Women, however, were asking for more than simple survival. Working with professional women's organizations like Flora Tristan, they petitioned Congress for laws against sexual harassment and violence in the home, for protection at work from toxic poisons, for representation in the labour unions. The campaign resulted in unprecedented legislation that made the employer liable for sexual harassment in the workplace.[85]

Nora Galor, Former UNIFEM subregional officer, spoke of the growth of women's organizations: 'I believe that Peru is absolutely unique in terms of grassroots women's organizations . . . in no other country of the

[Latin American] region do you find those grassroots organizations as empowered, and autonomous, and massive.'[86]

Not only were women becoming vocal, but they were starting to speak out precisely at the time when it was most dangerous to do so, that is, when the economic crisis and the political violence were about to peak. By 1993, two women who did speak out had been murdered by Sendero Luminoso. (See box).

Flora Tristan: empowering women workers

When the economy goes down, women have even more work, because they have to support their husbands who are not working.

Women Workers, 1993.

Peruvian women assassinated for their leadership

Peruvian women's organizations have deep roots amongst the people. They are committed to democratic values and critical of political violence. They work to create new forms of everyday life in order to counter the adverse conditions of the country.

In September 1991, the violent political movement, Sendero Luminoso (Shining Path) shot and killed Juana Lopez, coordinator of the Glass-of-Milk programme in the Carmen de la Legua district of Lima. Thirty thousand people protested in the streets following her murder.

In October 1991, Sendero threatened and then shot Emma Hilario, President of the National Federation of People's Kitchens. Maraculously, Emma Hilario survived, but she was forced into exile by this assassination attempt.

Simultaneously, Sendero threatened to kill Maria Elena Moyano, Vice-Mayor of Villa El Salvador, the settlement of 300000 built by the poor themselves on the outskirts of Lima. She was also the President of FEPOMOVES, the Federation of Popular Women of El Salvador. In October 1991, Sendero bombed the FEPOMOVES food storage centre for the community kitchens. In November, the threats against Maria Elena Moyano intensified. Her friends and colleagues convinced her to leave the country. However, she returned to Peru ten days later, and told them that she would rather lose her life than die of anguish and powerlessness away from the country. On February 15, 1992, Sendero shot her and dynamited her body in front of her two young children.

Her friend and colleague, Gina Vargas, wrote:

I do not wish, in this homage to Maria Elena, to stress her grandeur as leader—which was immense. I wish, rather, to refer to her grandeur as a woman, to the qualities of emotion and friendship that she was capable of communicating . . . She gave so much: her love, her friendship, her confidence, her secrets, her smile, her fear, her disappointments and hopes. She gave what she was.

Peruvian women have some of the finest organizations in the world. Flora Tristan is a women's centre founded in 1979. Because Flora Tristan is committed to bettering the lives of poor women and their families and to achieving a 'balance of power' between men and women, UNIFEM has assisted three of its activities. In 1982, UNIFEM financed a study of female workers in the electronics industry. Out of that grew the second project, in 1984, which empowered women as labour union leaders: a tremendously successful project for working women in Lima's shanty towns. In 1988 UNIFEM helped Flora Tristan assist rural women with La Red Mujer Rural (Rural Women's Network), which publishes a magazine that facilitates communication between NGOs working with women in the countryside of Peru.[87]

Knowing that the number of women in the industrial labour force had been growing since the 1960s, the Centre met with some of them to learn more about their working conditions. They reported that management exercised 'greater physical and hierarchical control' over women than over men.[88] In the 1982 study, with UNIFEM's support of $20 000, Flora Tristan interviewed women in the electronics industry and initiated workshops where 15–20 women would come together to speak from the heart about the dangers, hopes, crises, and successes of their lives.

The impact of the workshops comes through in the words of Ana Robles Godoy, an electronics worker with 20 years experience:

I was just married when I applied for a job [in this electronics factory in Lima]. That was the first problem: they didn't want to hire married women. Unfair isn't it? The truth is that I had to lie; it was uncomfortable . . . I really wanted to tell everyone. [The second problem:] During my first pregnancy . . . I was working in the battery section and it was very toxic, you know. Now other workers and I know that we have legal rights and that we can complain to protect our health and our children's health.[89]

The second project, to train women for union leadership, was funded in 1984 with $99 115 from UNIFEM. The target group was composed of women in the following industries: textile, chemical, canning, and electronics. The idea was to train forty-five women to fight for occupational health and family issues, as well as to increase and strengthen women's participation in Peruvian labour unions generally. To this end, Flora Tristan organized day-long workshops in the countryside where women union leaders and members of different industries and their families met for the first time. Later on, a hundred women and men met weekly at Flora Tristan headquarters. At a time when the union movement itself was unable to form federations across trade lines, the women made personal connections. The results were fantastic.

Women began to engage in national campaigns to change labour legislation and to improve women's rights. The project was then widened to include domestic workers, service sector workers, telephone and bank workers and university students. A Commission was formed, consisting of fifteen women labour leaders from different industries who met with

Congressional and media representatives to set out their grievances and proposals for change. A few men agreed to discuss the campaign put together by the women to make sexual harassment illegal. Changes were effected in two areas: occupational health, and social security for women. The members of the 1985 Commission soon became leaders in their trade unions, where they imparted a new dynamic by using negotiation as a methodology for working with management, and by creating channels of communication between union leadership and members.

With the participation of men, the Commission's agenda was extended from 'women's issues' to 'gender issues'. The men began to discuss the responsibilities weighing on them to support the family in the difficult economic situation; they also talked about freedom of choice in sexual matters and abortion.

> We have to make our male counterparts understand how different our own situation is from theirs. They should help us to get the same opportunities they have. We are working on this now.
> Rosa Dominguea, 33 years old, eight years' experience in the textile industry.

By 1991 a lot of Peruvians were out of work; economic incentives had been offered so that people would leave their jobs. Times were difficult indeed for women, who had to take *any* job, with *any* payment, for the family to survive. The community kitchens helped make family meals possible. 'Men will still wait for a good job', I was told. 'They will say 'Oh, my wife is working, so I can stay at home,' or, 'Instead of a textile worker, I will be a taxi driver, but I won't work at a lesser job.' In summary, 'When the economy goes down, women have even more work because they have to support their husbands who are not working.'[90]

Late in 1993, I met with seven women who had participated in Flora Tristan's workers' projects in the 1980s. These workers were universally grateful to Flora Tristan for the years of meetings and outings. A few of them, such as Zaila Zarazu who worked in the medical industry, had received financial support in times of personal crises. For most of the workers, however, it was Flora Tristan's moral support and the education about their rights as workers that had mattered most. Three of them were now leaders in the International Union of Food Workers (UITA, in Spanish). Others had become leaders in Peruvian trade unions and in their communities.

Some of the workers told me how they were empowered by the Flora Tristan group. Rosa Olea Sandoval and Maria Suarez Gurman explained:

For years, I was the victim of sexual harassment, but I was ashamed to talk about it with other women. Now I feel as if I were dreaming. It is really astonishing how we have improved. When we began to work with

215

Flora Tristan on this matter, I never thought that we were going to have a social debate (Olea).

When I began to work, my children were really small . . . they used to stay with my mother while I was working, but she was old and ill. She was not able to walk, so she used to look after them from her bed, and it was dangerous for the children and tiring for her. That is why, even during working hours, I was thinking of them. I became extremely depressed until I came to the services here in Flora Tristan. Talking with a psychologist has not only relaxed me, but it has also helped me to think carefully about solutions . . . Now we are trying to establish a nursery in the factory so that other married workers with children will not have to experience what I have (Suarez).

Cecelia Roero said she could confront any situation now without fear. As a seamstress, she earned only $2.50 a week in the garment industry until she and her fellow workers went on strike. Now wages are $12 a week; the strikers also received back pay at that rate from 1991. Cecilia was still concerned about the health problems of the workers, especially pregnant women. Her company was starting to change, and as a leader of workers she will persevere in pressing for greater change. Another garment worker reported that if any garments were missing, the workers, mostly single mothers, would have to strip to prove that they hadn't stolen them. Flora Tristan had helped her to regain self-respect and to become a leader among the workers of the industry.

Delia Pascual, who has a very high position in the union, said that many of the people who were laid off were the family breadwinners. All job security was now lost; food workers were hired on a weekly basis, and benefits were being taken away. The workers were negotiating with management over these issues. Luckily, food workers were a bit better off than others, because they had something to eat.

The workers feel that Flora Tristan still has a very important role to play in giving moral support to workers who want to contest government policies. The unions had fought for an eight-hour day; now people are working ten to twelve hours a day in order to keep their jobs, although there is little or no work for women in the formal sector. The newspapers advertise jobs but they are mainly for young men under age 30. Rosa Verastegui said that some people make only a dollar a week, so they have to moonlight and hold down two or even three jobs.

The sharp decline in women's participation in wage employment has led Flora Tristan to revise its mission with workers, shifting some of its energies to alternative employment possibilities in the 'people's econ-omy' – the informal sector. Cecilia Olea, a member of the Advisory Committee, and Patricia Sandoval, Co-ordinator of the women and work team, explained that Flora Tristan is also investigating contemporary markets and industries in the formal sector to see where future jobs will be created.[91] In addition, they are studying the regulations pertaining to women that accompany intergovernmental treaties, such as NAFTA.

A network of rural women's organizations

In the late 1980s, Flora Tristan set out to create a 'complex organizational network, that would contribute to the democratization of the social and political spheres within the country.'[92] They had already worked with the community kitchens and glass-of-milk groups and with women trade unionists. It was time to establish linkages among those and other grass-roots organizations, and to reach beyond the shanty towns of Lima.

Small organizations of women were spread across the country in every village and hamlet but they had little access to resources of any kind. UNIFEM agreed to become a partner again. $100 000 was committed over a three-year period to create networks, train women leaders, establish a documentation centre and to publish a magazine three times a year as a means of communication. Today Flora Tristan has a network of some eighty NGOs that work directly with rural women. Blanca Fernandez described some of the results:

> The promoters have gained strength, and they have the necessary information in their hands to discuss possible activities with the women. Women working a long way from Lima, who were not accustomed to writing in a magazine, now influence local government policy.

UNIFEM's support has been a catalyst for change, and other contributions have been made to ensure that the network activities will continue, Nora Galor told me.

> '[The network] has grown in an incredible way. UNIFEM was able to identify activities and to invest strategic resources when others were eager to get involved but had no idea how to do so. UNIFEM had an *avant garde* role and still has. I would build up UNIFEM presence at country level–it has the expertise'.[93]

Flora Tristan became involved in development when Patricia Porto Carrero did some academic research on the politics of development. At that time, the organization's main focus was on violence against women. As Olea and Sandoval explained, that interface of politics and violence provoked Flora Tristan's interest in the whole area of women and development as the turning point from the meaningful to the possible.

Among Flora Tristan's contemporary programmes, violence against women still takes an important place. There are now special police stations for abused women, and Peruvian women join other Latin Americans in celebrating Stop Violence Against Women Day, on 25 November each year.[94]

Food-cycle technologies

> Most of the women's groups we are working with . . . are very very consolidated organizations.
>
> Andrew Maskrey, ITDG

The poorest regions of Peru include both rural areas and the shanty towns surrounding Lima. UNIFEM gave three different grants to assist women in these areas who were already participating leaders in community life to become financially and nutritionally self-sufficient. In 1985, we allocated $184 000 for Food Production Modules in rural areas and shanty towns. In 1986, we put $18 000 into a workshop on the community kitchens (*comedores populares*); they had been established by Lima women to survive the impact of the global recession and the government's financial policies in the 1980s. The third, and more ambitious, project was allotted $264 000 to develop food processing technologies that would enable small farmers to continue to sell their products well beyond harvest time–and hence at higher prices.

The 1985 food module funding was disbursed through the Peruvian National Office for Food Support to Mothers Clubs, which were grassroots organizations of long standing. The project locations were in three mountain towns (Cuzco, Ancash, and Cajamarca), as well as in some of Lima's shanty towns. Specifically, the project aimed to empower the Mothers Clubs to reach collective solutions to the main problems their members faced. To that end, funding was provided for three guinea pig farms, twenty vegetable gardens, twenty biogas units and for training in accounts management. By 1987, agricultural equipment and tools had been acquired and cultivation was taking place in the Andes. In Lima, transportation proved difficult, so UNIFEM provided additional funding for motorcycles. The endeavor of one Mothers Club in a Lima shanty town is described below; it includes some of the setbacks of their first attempt.

[At] the headquarters of a Mothers Club in dusty Villa El Salvador, 40 women are trying to get a jam business going. Mrs. Trio, President of the Club, has only four children so far, and thus has more energy for the struggle than most of her colleagues who have twice as many. Last January they raised a loan of 10 000 inti ($240) from a United Nations agency [UNIFEM], and have already repaid it. They bought equipment and organized their work, paying women 120 inti a day. On a good day, they can make up to 30 kilos of jam.

The first stove broke down after one day, and a new one cost them 9000 inti. They do not really know how to sell jam outside their neighbourhood, and few people there can afford such a luxury. They have not yet got the right jars, and jam was probably not the best product in the first place. But they are keeping simple books, dealing commercially with educated outsiders, buying better stoves.[95]

The second UNIFEM-assisted project was the workshop on the *comedores populares*–popular kitchens. The first of these appeared around 1978 and they continued to mushroom in the shanty towns of Lima throughout the 1980s. They and the glass-of-milk groups were means of survival for the families who had left the rural areas of Peru in search of better opportunities for themselves and the children. Whereas food was the one thing that agricultural producers have access to in some form or another, people now living in the city found that they could not eat unless they had the means to purchase food. But jobs were scarce, and when they did exist the pay was

218

often only $40 per month. With the hyperinflation, even that small amount lost its purchasing power.

> The community kitchens appear as a collective answer to the food supply problem. They are organized around 15 to 50 families, which saves time in duties that were formerly assumed by each family, and that are now developed in turns. The wholesale purchase of food supplies reduces costs. Some women look after all the children, and they cook so that others may work. Thus, women have time for activities outside their homes. It is only by pooling their resources that they could afford food; only by supporting each other that they could get through hard life.[96]

While the *comedores* were set up, essentially to ensure that people survived, the new arrangement had a surprising result. Cooking at home had always kept women isolated from the larger society but, when that task was performed in a communal kitchen, the women overcame their isolation and were able to build relationships with their neighbours. That new experience became one of the stepping stones for women's involvement in the political activities that Flora Tristan undertook.[97] Nora Galor explained:

> Right now there are may be 6000 *comedores* in Lima. Most of them have existed for at least five years. Those we talked about at that workshop still exist. They provide, each of them, between 70 and 100 meals that cost 20 cents. UNIFEM was one of the first institutions that identified the network of *comedores* as having enormous potential. In UNICEF, right now, we are working with the *comedores*. Everybody is, you see.[98]

The third UNIFEM-funded activity was carried out by the Intermediate Technology Development Group (ITDG) to solve a problem faced by many poor farming communities in Peru, i.e., when the harvest is abundant, prices are low and the surplus spoils. A food processing technology project (one of UNIFEM's Women and Food Technology–WAFT– projects described in Chapter 10) was designed to eliminate the problem by enabling women to store food products so that they could be used or sold at a later date, and/or distributed to wider markets.

This project was distinct from others in that the executing agency was technically proficient in food processing rather than being business orientated or trained to empower women, even though it recognized that an increasing number of women cultivate the farms because men have migrated to cities.[99] I include it here to illustrate the principle of balancing economic productivity and empowerment aspects of projects, even though as a relatively recent one it does not fit my duration criteria.

The project is located in three cities. Huancayo (population 200 000) is high up in the Andes and is a major source of the food sold in Lima. Farmers have about two acres each for potatoes and grains. The project introduced peelers, driers, pasta and toasting techniques for processing cereals, tubers, legumes, vegetables, herbs, meats, and other food crops. ITDG links up with local NGOs on all its projects, and in Huancayo the

219

NGOs were SEPAR[100] and CESCA.[101] One of the goals was to re-introduce traditional Andean grains on to the local markets.

> A lot of the products from the Huancayo area are Andean grain stocks–foodstuffs which have started to disappear from the market-place. So these groups started putting back on to the market products which just have not been available.
>
> Andrew Maskrey, ITDG

Huacho (population 40 000) is on the coast, two hours from Lima, and surrounded by arid desert in what is otherwise the most urbanized region of Peru. Men work as labourers on large commercial farms that grow corn, sugar, and cotton. The women maintain household vegetable gardens and tend sheep, goats, and chickens. The project introduced technologies to process marmalades and fruit wines made from oranges, strawberries, prickly pears, soursop, apples and peaches.

On the other side of the Andes is Pucallpa (population 120 000) in the Amazon region. Most families follow indigenous traditions and practise subsistence agriculture. There is a lack of protein in the diet which contributes to the low life-expectancy. The project focused on a fish preservation technology that was appropriate to the humid conditions.

ITDG disseminated improved methods for smoking fish and drying them with salt, and developed a solar system to dry maize, cassava, beans, and rice. The project also planned to develop milling and toasting machinery to manufacture flour from yucca, maize, and beans. ITDG introduced the technological processes used in other developing countries and improved the processes indigenous to Peru; a total of 32 technologies were introduced.

> With traditional technologies, the conservation lasts no more than twenty days. With the improved technology, the people of Pucallpa can save the food for three or four months.
>
> Daniel Rodriguez, ITDG

In Huacho, the UNIFEM grant helped a Mothers Club that had been founded in 1978 to receive food aid. Later, the women also organized community kitchens and become involved in the glass-of-milk programme. However, by 1990, they wanted to eliminate their dependence on aid by establishing an income-generating project. ITDG's assistance was very important to the group because with it they learned how to produce vinegars and to preserve jams. The women organize their time by taking care of household needs in the mornings and then processing and marketing the products in the afternoons. A member of the Huacho group said:

> This group is now a formal micro-enterprise, and it is one of the best in terms of the region because they have all the legal aspects completely solved now. The neighbour groups all recognize this group as one of the leaders.

The enterprise cannot yet generate the main income but it augments the family's total income. Even that small amount can be critical because the husband's salary is on average $40 per month, which is often not adequate to support the family.

Technical needs and marketing are only two aspects of the project; in addition, the women faced increasing terrorism from Sendero Luminoso. The ITDG Country Director Maskrey explained:

> 'The first difficulty came because we deliberately chose for the project three regions of Peru which were peaceful in 1988 but by the time the project started in 1989, they had turned into three of the areas of the country with the greatest political violence . . . Within six months of the project starting, nearly all the local NGOs had shut down, some of their leaders had been killed . . . the project became limited to a smaller number of groups around the main urban centres.'[102]

Sendero Luminoso attacked the project in Huacho, and the other project sites in Huancayo and Pucallpa received threats. Some women who were undergoing training were pressured not to accept food aid, which led to the splintering of group cohesion. In addition to the outright attacks and threats, the potential for terrorism simply forced the project to keep a low profile. This meant that many women who would otherwise have been trained in the new technologies never learned of the project's existence.[103]

> 'The second problem was the project coincided with the worst economic crisis of the century. When we started in 1988, the Peruvian economy was still reasonably strong; 1989 and 1990 were years of hyper-inflation,' said Maskrey.

It became impossible to realize the goal of raising women's income, because inflation was eroding real income at an extremely fast pace.[104] Any delay in the sale of the products resulted in insufficient revenue to purchase inputs for the next cycle of production. Furthermore, the purchasing power of the customers fell dramatically, causing the market to contract at precisely the moment when the project was introducing new products into the market. ITDG's exclusive focus on production technologies exacerbated the crisis because training in marketing was weak.

As if these factors were not enough to cope with, the executing agency, ITDG, was also handicapped by its unfamiliarity with training women. ITDG worked with local NGOs and expected them to provide the mobilization and personal empowerment inputs. That strategy worked in Huancayo, but in the Huacho and Pucallpa locations the project faced difficulties that were reminiscent of the early years of the India sericulture project.

The problem was brought to UNIFEM's attention when Maria Spada, a UNIFEM officer, submitted a report in 1989. She pointed out that the staff of two of the local NGOs were not trained to work with rural women or to deal specifically with women's economic roles. UNIFEM responded quickly to the report by asking ITDG to call in its staff and that of the NGOs for two days of sensitivity training by the staff of Flora Tristan Centre. There was a certain reluctance on the part of the ongoing project staff to devote their time and money to this training, but once completed, the training did improve their ability to empower rural women.

At Huancayo, ITDG worked with SEPAR, a local NGO that was already sensitized to women's issues. In that location, the project had a substantial impact on changing women's lives; in fact, they see themselves as dynamic agents.

> The women in the production units are very proud of what they are doing, and eager to improve and expand their work. They recognize the lack of defined marketing strategy, but they hope to overcome such obstacles. The training they have given to other women in their community has been very valuable . . . Some have gone on to purchase the tools for food processing enterprises which they plan to set up in the future.[105]

In addition, the project enabled Huancayo women to handle their own finances more skillfully, to 'not be so timid,' and to improve their relationship with their husbands.[106] Was this due to the sensitivity of SEPAR to women's conditions? Or was it due to the traditional strength of women's organizations in Huancayo? Or both? It is hard to tell. Andrew Maskrey observed that 'most of the women's groups we are working with, and I would say particularly the ones in the Sierra, the Huancayo area, are very, very consolidated organizations . . .'[107]

Despite the external and internal obstacles, ITDG notes that the project succeeded in several crucial ways. Maskrey summed up the accomplishments:

> We managed to work with fourteen different women's groups in these areas, in quite difficult conditions in terms of security. And despite the economic situation, the groups managed to produce, they managed to sell in the market, and all the groups are still going.[108]

Now that the project staff is more experienced at training and empowering rural women, ITDG hopes to run a five-year programme of food-processing training courses all over Peru. UNIFEM funding has proved catalytic once again; the British Government has already committed 50 per cent of the funding for the next, expanded phase and the European Union will probably fund the remainder.

Clearly, UNIFEM has played an important role and will continue to do so. The experience in Peru proves the same point made in India; monitoring is crucial to ensure that the appropriate balance is kept between productivity-enhancement and empowerment inputs. The case for UNIFEM's having a staffperson present in a country is once again affirmed and reinforced.

With the Flora Tristan Centre, on the other hand, UNIFEM's role was to extend the influence and strength of a grassroots movement which had already proven itself capable and committed to assisting poor working women. What it needed was additional funding to reach the broadest group of women possible, so that the Centre would make a real impact on the social arena.

The UNDP representative in Peru, Pierre den Baas, sees another role for UNIFEM as well, that of being a partner in efforts to influence funding organizations such as the World Bank, the Inter-American Development Bank, and bilateral aid organizations.

If UNIFEM gets more money, it can play an important role. The critical thing is the availability of resources–you have to have a certain level of resources for people to take you seriously. Staff have to be really knowledgeable, have ideas, know the local situation, so that UNIFEM can make a contribution which people from government, bilateral organizations and development banks think is sufficiently interesting that they will incorporate the ideas into larger projects, for the sake of social development and poverty alleviation.[109]

When UNIFEM is fully funded, it will be ready for the challenge of playing such a role.

> UNIFEM must have enough money to have enough clout to influence policy.
>
> UNDP Representative Pierre den Baas, Lima

A final note

Organization on the basis of employment brought many successes to SEWA and Flora Tristan trade unionists; family food security and a healthy environment were the motives for organizing the Peruvian community kitchens and the Kenyan Green Belt Movement. The committed, long-term leadership of those groups and the partnerships between poor and privileged women that characterized them enhanced women's chances to have their voices heard.

To support women's participation in decision-making, UNIFEM shifted its strategy from training individual women as planners to strengthening organizations that could forge linkages between citizens and their government and put continuing pressure on the national planning process.

Today there is an explosion of women's groups in the civil society. The experience of political participation by the organizations discussed here tells us that those groups have the potential to build economic democracy that overcomes poverty. They can transform economic and social life if we are wise enough to give them the modicum of support and access to resources that they need.

Up to this point in Part II of this book we have discussed organizations, programmes and 'projects' assisted by UNIFEM. In the chapter that follows we shall see how that approach evolved to become a 'programming' one, as UNIFEM centred its investments on the priority subjects of policy and action that were identified by regional intergovernmental bodies and by women themselves.

CHAPTER TEN
The Africa Investment Plan

The first thing is to work with people on their own needs and priorities. Consider them a source of information and knowledge. Listen to them, to know what they know, and build on that. Then take into account their economic capacity. There is no use in introducing a technology which costs money when there is no money to buy it.

Jacqueline Ki-Zerbo

AS UNIFEM'S WORK MATURED and was analysed it became possible to define it as a holistic programme rather than as a collection of 'projects'. We now turn to the Africa Investment Plan (AIP) which was the Fund's first effort to do just that. Adopted by the Fund in 1984 on the advice of African women and planning by Olubanke King-Akerele, the AIP made mainstream Africa's top priority its own–food and agriculture. It was in accordance with the continent's Lagos Plan of Action for the Economic Development of Africa, 1980–2000 that contained a complete section on women, thanks to the efforts of the African Training and Research Centre for Women of ECA.[1] AIP was the precursor of similar programmes in Latin America and the Caribbean (PAPLAC) and Asia/Pacific (APDEV), as we saw in Chapter 4 of this book.

The Africa Investment Plan provided the policy framework for UNIFEM's interventions in line with women's own priorities as well as those of their countries and region. It included food policy; the dissemination of tested technologies and development of prototypes; energy conservation; credit support systems; linkages to major development programmes; and management support to governments and non-governmental organizations. Some examples of AIP investments by UNIFEM illustrate the holistic character of the programmes.

Food policy and food-cycle technologies

In Africa, national self-sufficiency in food production has always depended heavily on women who produce, process, store, prepare and market some 80 per cent of the continent's domestic food supply. From time to time, many countries tried massive investments in large-scale agricultural programmes but found them wanting. UNIFEM, on the other hand, had successfully assisted the transfer of food-cycle technologies such as fish-smokers, solar extraction of salt, palm oil presses, and improved fuel-saving stoves over its first operational years. As seen in Table 10.1, by 1988, 69 food technology or food-related projects, of which 40 were in Africa, were completed or ongoing. The time had come to disseminate those technologies and related supports more systematically.

224

Table 10.1: Food technologies projects

Region	National	Regional	Total
Africa	34	6	40
Asia/Pacific	6	7	13
Latin America/Caribbean	8	2	10
Western Asia	3	–	3
Global	–	–	3
Total	51	15	69

Source: UNIFEM Report, 1988

In 1985, therefore, UNIFEM invested $250 000 of its own resources to initiate a five-year project, Women and Food Technologies (WAFT), to assist countries in implementing their food self-sufficiency strategies, and to demonstrate the importance of emphasizing women in food policy. Two offices, one in Senegal and the other in Zimbabwe, would serve as resource centres for projects throughout Africa. That investment soon attracted other funding. In 1986 the Canadian Minister for External Relations announced her Government's commitment of C$25 million to projects giving specific priority to women within its Operation Africa 2000 programme.[2] Two million dollars (US $1.5m) of that total would go to UNIFEM's WAFT project. Monique Vézina, the Minister for External Relations said:

> The message of the UN Decade for Women is clear. The success of development depends to a great extent on improving the lot of women, not simply because they are half the world's population, but also because of their multiple roles as food producers . . . .[3]

The Governments of the Netherlands and Italy also contributed to the project ($800 000 and $200 000 respectively), for a series of Source Books produced by UNIFEM in collaboration with the Intermediate Technology Development Group (ITDG), and with United Nations and other specialized and technical organizations.[4] The source book topics were oil extraction, fruit and vegetable processing, cereal processing, rootcrops, fish processing, packaging, drying and storage. By 1994, there were eleven such books and over 15,000 copies had been distributed in three languages.

The early focus of UNIFEM's Women and Food Technologies (WAFT) project was on the nine Southern Africa Development Co-ordination Conference (SADCC) countries that range from Tanzania to the independent countries neighbouring or within the Republic of South Africa.[5] The strategy for the sub-region was designed to respond to the priorities of the member states themselves as regards food security by concentrating on women's activities in food production, processing, preservation and preparation, and through small enterprise development. The method chosen was to give women greater access to the technologies and techniques they

225

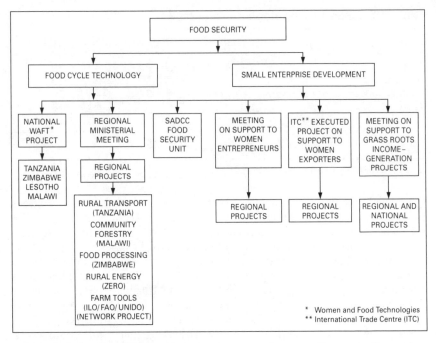

```
                        ┌──────────────────┐
                        │  FOOD SECURITY   │
                        └──────────────────┘
              ┌──────────────────────┴──────────────────────┐
   ┌──────────────────────┐              ┌──────────────────────────────┐
   │ FOOD CYCLE TECHNOLOGY │              │ SMALL ENTERPRISE DEVELOPMENT │
   └──────────────────────┘              └──────────────────────────────┘
```

| NATIONAL WAFT* PROJECT | REGIONAL MINISTERIAL MEETING | SADCC FOOD SECURITY UNIT | MEETING ON SUPPORT TO WOMEN ENTREPRENEURS | ITC** EXECUTED PROJECT ON SUPPORT TO WOMEN EXPORTERS | MEETING ON SUPPORT TO GRASS ROOTS INCOME- GENERATION PROJECTS |

| TANZANIA ZIMBABWE LESOTHO MALAWI | REGIONAL PROJECTS | | REGIONAL PROJECTS | REGIONAL PROJECTS | REGIONAL AND NATIONAL PROJECTS |

RURAL TRANSPORT (TANZANIA)
COMMUNITY FORESTRY (MALAWI)
FOOD PROCESSING (ZIMBABWE)
RURAL ENERGY (ZERO)
FARM TOOLS (ILO/FAO/UNIDO) (NETWORK PROJECT)

* Women and Food Technologies
** International Trade Centre (ITC)

Figure 10.1: UNIFEM's SADCC initiative. (Source: 'Progress Report', Marilyn Carr, October 1988)

needed to increase productivity and reduce wastage. See Figure 10.1, UNIFEM's SADCC initiative.

The first large scale food technology project was launched in Tanzania, where 87 per cent of women live in rural areas. There were already over 7500 organized women's economic groups by 1979, and the incidence of female heads of household was multiplying. The 1980s saw another 'amazing increase in the numbers and visibility of women's groups, far outnumbering other organized local initiatives', and the 'rapid entry and increased participation of African women in the market economy as self-employed or casual workers in the informal sector'.[6]

Tanzania was the only country in the SADCC region where food output's annual growth exceeded the growth of agriculture as a whole in the years between 1966 and 1981–a major reason for introducing the technologies project there.[7] The Women and Appropriate Food Technology project, executed by the Ministry of Community Development, Youth and Sports, initially received $251 000 from UNIFEM;[8] UNICEF and the UN Volunteers gave smaller amounts, as did the Government. Umoja wa Wanawake wa Tanzania (UWT), the national women's organization, co-operated through its village groups which became the locations for the projects.[9]

Toward its goal of improving women's socio-economic status while contributing to the national goal of food self-sufficiency, the project adopted a participatory methodology that involved the village women in the decision-making process, beginning with the baseline research right

Tanzania

Demographics:	
Population	31 million
% urban	24
% rural	76

Income:	
GNP per capita	$110
% in absolute poverty	58
% of rural population	60
% of urban population	10

Health:	
Life expectancy	Women: 52 Men: 49
Infant mortality	102 per 1000 births
Maternal mortality	340 per 100000 births
Access to safe water (%)	49

Education:	
Illiteracy rate	Women: na Men: na
Girls as % of boys in secondary school	74
Girls as % of boys in tertiary school	15
Girls as % of tertiary science/engineering students	8

Work:	
Households headed by women (%)	19
Women as % of labour force	na
Female wages as % of male	92

Representation:	
Parliamentary seats held by women (%)	11

Source: See source table in Annexe 7.

through to the implementation of the projects. The Government's Community Development Assistants were to facilitate that process after they underwent two weeks of training. The groups selected a variety of activities including gardening, pottery, poultry, milling, and cattle raising.[10] An evaluation in 1993 found a 'significant level of success in line with [the project's] initial objectives', with milling and gardening projects having the highest rates of success.[11] I had visited Kiwangwa Village in 1989, when its impressive women's group was calculating its investment and the credit that would be needed to purchase a grain mill. They had received a loan earlier from the Co-operative and Rural Development Bank (CRDB) for raising pineapples which were then purchased by a university professor cum entrepreneur, for sale in Dar es Salaam.

Welcoming us to the village, Chairperson Fatuma noted my previous position with UNIFEM and said: 'You are playing your part. We pledge to play our part'. They did so. The group knew that they would have to raise money for the mill out of their own pockets; initially the 25 members

Table 10.2: Milling machine income/expenditure in Kiwangwa, Tanzania

Component	1991 in Tanzanian Shillings			1991 in US Dollars*			1992 in US Dollars**		
	Income	Expenses	Balance	Income	Expenses	Balance	Income	Expenses	Balance
Services Sold***	Shs 998300			$2218			$4208		
Oil, diesel, grease		368900			820				
Allowance miller		84400			188				
Allowance office		3300			9				
Travelling expenses		59100			131				
Spare parts		54700			122				
Other equipment		18000			40				
Maintenance & Repairs		25900			58				
Hospitality		11800			26				
Other expenses		20200			45				
Subtotal, expenses			646300			1436		———	$2855
Balance			Shs 352000			$782			$1353
Income per participant (per annum)	Shs 13950			$31			$54		

* The 1991 exchange rate was 450 Tanzanian Shillings per US Dollar.

** 1992 data not available in itemized form.

*** Milling Price: 5 Tanzanian Shillings per kilogram.

Source: Lucy Creevey, Changing Women's Lives and Work, 1993.

would each contribute TSh 250/ ($1.70 in 1989) and then a total of TSh 750/ each. Next, they would then take out a loan of TSh 832 000/ with 14 per cent interest, for a total of Shs 948 763/ ($6325 in 1989) which would come due in three years time. The mill would be available to six nearby villages with a population of 6000, and they expected to realize about Shs 550 000/ ($3666) income per year.[12] The Kiwangwa group received the loan at the end of 1989 and had repaid it completely by December 1992. The income per participant was $31 in 1991 and $54 in 1992. For village women whose normal capital seldom rises above $50, the purchase and management of the mill was a significant achievement. The group accounts are shown in Table 10.2.

What would the women do with their profits? 'Build a better house for my family' said one. 'Hire a tractor for tilling more land' said another. My companion on that visit, Marja-Lisa Swantz, who had known the village for a decade, observed: 'The women are not out to get the money for themselves, but for their families and communities. That is impressive'.[13]

The 1993 evaluation of the overall project concluded that:

Evaluations and reports submitted to WAFT and UNIFEM have shown a high degree of enthusiasm and interest in the project in the villages, although the women are not getting the incomes they had hoped for when they joined at the outset . . . In a situation where little has been possible for Tanzanian village women to change or improve their lives, WAFT has opened a new set of alternatives which has great promise.[14]

As could be expected, all was not well in every village. Some of the poultry were diseased; the promised electricity was not brought into the village; tractor projects were not viable. Although there were women who were very disappointed, the vast majority were 'happy' or 'proud', and were empowered by their work. 'Other women in the village look at us as fortunate fellows!' said one. 'I feel superior . . . because I operate and service the machine in front of other women', another said.[15]

The project faced the same dilemma encountered by so many other projects for women during the past two decades: untrained and inexperienced in business, the extension workers suddenly had to become advisers to enterprises with technical, management, marketing and credit dimensions. Even with the strong training components built into the project, that was a difficult transition. Despite great good will, the community development assistants' two-week training in participatory methods had not offset their traditional, more authoritarian training. The project's objective, to simultaneously increase productive rewards while decreasing drudgery, remained an elusive one. As in several projects discussed in this book, the workload of the women increased, but they did not mind as long as they were earning incomes. What is also of interest in this project is the women's choice of technology. They were not satisfied with 'intermediate' types of machines if more advanced ones could be obtained, such as those using electricity. But despite the merits of the participatory approach, the odds against women's success continued to be high because of situations which remained beyond their control.[16] We turn to those now.

The power brokers enter

It is instructive to note that in its 1994 Report, Adjustment in Africa: Lessons from Country Case Studies, the World Bank assessed the Economic Recovery Programme (ERP) of stabilization and structural adjustment that had been adopted with pressure from the World Bank, the IMF, and donor countries and which, whatever its merits, gave total precedence to economic efficiency and productivity growth over social equity. The Bank found that the ERP had 'dramatically turned around economic performance in Tanzania' in all major sectors, but the cost of that 'success' was cruel. In the Bank's own words:

○ poverty continues to be widespread: about half of the population is still below the poverty line.

○ primary health care and education have deteriorated.

○ poverty is pervasive in rural areas: 59 per cent of village households are poor and 90 per cent of Tanzania's hardcore poverty is in rural areas.

○ . . . agriculture services and infrastructure for poor farmers have not improved.

○ rural roads continue to be deplorable.

○ . . . the rate at which Tanzanian students make the transition to secondary school is still one of the lowest in the world.[17]

The Bank summed all that up by saying: 'The social sectors are in crisis'. It is under such deplorable policies and circumstances that women begin to mobilize to gain incomes even while they and their national leaders are being held hostage to a global economic power system that neglects the potential productivity of the poor.

Lesotho community development: year-round water and food

Of the fifty households in Maputo village, two-thirds are headed by women. Rainfall is scarce and soil productivity limited. Over five years, a UNIFEM food-cycle technology project resulted in construction of water catchment areas with small dams, fruit tree planting, bridge construction, training in management, organization of mobile clinics, and soil conservation activities. A revolving-loan fund assisted the distribution of seeds and fertilizer. All this was done with the help of a UN Volunteer, until a Peace Corps volunteer also joined. Food production and cash income have both increased.

Alice Mefi, UNIFEM, Harare
Global Assembly of Women and the Environment 1991

Food policy

UNIFEM's action on food-cycle technologies was not confined to the field level. Like other Fund interventions, it respected the importance of government policies relating to the process of enhancing women's productive activities and reducing their labour and time-consuming burdens. One such effort to mainstream women's centrality to food security took the form of a high-level meeting in May 1988. UNIFEM provided the Government of Tanzania with sufficient funds to host the SADCC Regional Ministerial Conference on Women and Food Technology. The Conference responded to the decision of the Council of Ministers of SADCC that women should be integrated in all SADCC programmes and to UNIFEM's mandate to ensure the involvement of women in mainstream activities.

Delegations from the nine SADCC member states (Angola, Botswana, Lesotho, Malawi, Mozambique, Swaziland, Tanzania, Zambia and Zimbabwe) were led by Government Ministers and included heads of national machineries on women and development, together with representatives of SADCC units, technology centres and NGOs. Five priority areas for regional projects to benefit women were defined: production and distribution of farm implements; food processing; low-cost transport devices; rural energy conservation; and community forestry.[18]

UNIFEM established a permanent presence in the area by locating its own office for Southern Africa in Harare where SADCC's Food Security Technical and Administrative Unit had been placed. That office, headed by economist Marilyn Carr, Senior Adviser on Technology and Small Enterprise Development, provided technical monitoring to UNIFEM-assisted projects and joined SADCC programming missions requested by the sub-region's governments. Women engineers, food technologists, specialists in

---

From labour-intensive pounding to technology development: Zimbabwe

'They say we cannot do it. We are going to do it' five women in Simbamukaka in Zimbabwe told me in 1989. Well, they did it. A local financial institution, the Small Enterprises Development Corporation (SEDCO) extended credit and trained them in business management. ENDA Zimbabwe trained them to operate and maintain the grinding mill that they got in 1990. The diesel mill cost $30 000 including initial spares. They take in $150 a day gross, of which $100 is profit.

The group of 10 women had started in 1983 planting maize and sorghum. Each contributed $60 to join and $4 a month toward buying the mill. They had made 20 000 bricks when we met. A new road was going in; the mill would be placed near it. Said UNIFEM-assisted ENDA staffperson Tsitsi Dzumbira: 'Things exist for women, but they don't know about them until we have a technology demonstration in the area'.

Interview 1989, and ENDA Newsletter 1991

---

gender analysis, and other experts were made available to regional and national institutions and assistance was provided for the design of credit schemes.

Immediately after the Conference, UNIFEM financed a staff member specialized in food cycle technologies, to be recruited from the region and stationed at SADCC's own Food Security Unit in Zimbabwe. UNIFEM also co-operated with SADCC's Industry and Trade Unit in sponsoring a small enterprise meeting in Harare in 1989, and intensified its specialized assistance to countries.

Energy conservation: fuel-saving stoves and fish smokers

'The large scale dissemination and utilization of improved stoves lies in the hands of Sahelian women. Here at least, they will have the final word.'

Jacqueline Ki-Zerbo, 1977

After food policy and the dissemination of tested technologies, energy conservation is a key element of UNIFEM's Africa Investment Plan. Already in 1979 the Consultative Committee to UNIFEM had proposed that the Fund 'identify itself with meeting one or two very specific development needs which were relevant to women in a wide range of countries.'[19] One suggestion related to the growing problem that women in many countries had in obtaining fuel for cooking. The Committee thought that 'a real thrust towards the provision of wood-lots and alternative sources of energy might be a major concern for the Fund'.[20]

In response to this request, we prepared a 'state of the art' paper on *Women and Fuel in Rural Areas*. The paper described how the majority of women used the traditional three-stone, open-fire cooking method, whereby only ten to fifteen per cent of the heat is actually used and the rest is dispersed into the atmosphere. To counter that heat loss, engineers had been working on fuel-saving stoves, but many of the models failed to be culturally acceptable to women. The fabled Ghana stove comes to mind. Because the newly designed stove demanded that one stand up to cook, and women coming from a day's work in the fields preferred sitting, the stoves found a use as cupboards only, and women continued cooking over an open fire.

The paper concluded that the problem of fuel for rural and poor areas was 'urgent, significant and complex'. Wood-lots and cookstoves offered the best potential for project development for the Fund. In addition to conserving the environment, they would alleviate women's workload and effect considerable savings for the family budget.[21]

At that time, CILSS (the Permanent Interstate Committee for Drought Control in the Sahel), an eight-country group, was setting a strategy to limit deforestation and to combat the desertification due to the great drought of 1968–73. CILLS initiated three categories of actions: reforestation, efficient utilization of firewood (the primary energy source for 90 per cent of Sahelian households), and the development of alternative energy sources.

Aware that we had assisted in the testing and demonstration of improved wood-burning stoves in Senegal, CILSS requested UNIFEM to finance a sociologist, preferably a woman, who would work with an engineer to design and promote stoves that were acceptable to women. Jacqueline Ki-Zerbo of Burkina Faso (then Upper Volta) had proposed a number of specific actions that such a co-ordinator/sociologist would take.

That was the beginning; over time the Fund would commit $844 000 to CILSS to support the Co-ordinator, to design and disseminate efficient wood-burning stoves, to train craftspersons to build them, and to train women in their most efficient use.[22]

Ki-Zerbo's first partners were the ministries of environment and forestry; her second were the women who dealt with the fuel supply problem every day; and her third partner was the mass media.[23] She organized national and regional workshops to convince policy makers that the project should be a priority and to involve foresters, vocational trainers and women's organizations in project activities. Stove builders, both men and women, were also trained.

Stoves that would bring heat efficiency up to 40 per cent from a mere 10 per cent were first introduced in places where people gathered: schools, hospitals, community centres. Radio, TV and newspapers were brought in and a newsletter, *Flamme,* was published. The project was catalytic: soon the UN Sahelian Fund (UNSO), the UN Fund for Science and Technology for Development (UNFSTD) and the World Bank co-operated in supporting the stove project with CILSS and UNIFEM.

By 1981–82 nearly 15,000 stoves had been built in six countries. In 1983, Ki-Zerbo assisted the UN Secretary-General in opening a stoves exhibit at UN headquarters. She told the UN Radio audience how village women were trained to build stoves on which pots could fit tightly so that heat would not escape.

After a five-day training, two women who were already skilled in pottery, went back to their villages and trained many other women. Together, they built about 100 stoves in a few months. This was a money-generating activity for some of them.[24]

In 1984, the fourth in a series of CILSS regional workshops brought together Government policy makers, funding agencies, researchers and NGOs. It was decided that, to make a lasting impact on the problem they were addressing, literally millions of stoves would have to be disseminated. The types of stoves identified by the seminar for widespread dissemination were the fixed, 'improved three stones' that closed the spaces between stones in order to retain the heat, the portable metallic, and the clay stove. It was also decided that greater emphasis should be placed on women as craftspersons for the stoves.

In Ouagadougou in 1993, Ki-Zerbo spoke about her work with CILSS and the impact of the stoves project:

First of all, the idea that a humble cooking stove was an object of study by scientists, an object that required the attention of government, and

Burkina Faso	
Demographics:	
Population	10.4 million
% urban	20
% rural	80

Income:	
GNP per capita	$300
% in absolute poverty	na
% of rural population	90
% of urban population	na

Health:	
Life expectancy	Women: 50 Men: 47
Infant mortality	118 per 1000 births
Maternal mortality	610 per 100000 births
Access to safe water (%)	67*

Education:	
Illiteracy rate	Women: 91 Men: 72
Girls as % of boys in secondary school	48
Girls as % of boys in tertiary school	30
Girls as % of tertiary science/engineering students	18

Work:	
Households headed by women (%)	10
Women as % of labour force	49
Female wages as % of male	na

Representation:	
Parliamentary seat held by women (%)	6

Source: See source table in Annexe 7.
*Water data is for 1988–1990.

was equipment in which donors could invest, was something very new. The stoves came out of the kitchen to become a public concern. Second, ordinary women suddenly became a source of knowledge. We had stove technicians and researchers interviewing them to learn from them. Women were filmed cooking on the improved three stone and other new stoves. They became experts. That was very important. Third, UNIFEM really accomplished its mission to be a catalyst. Other donors, like the Science and Technology Fund, the Sahelian Fund and later the World Bank, joined activities on a large scale. That fulfilled our mission.[25]

Processing fish the Chorkor way

The significance of fish-processing technologies to UNIFEM lies both with the gender division of labour in the artisanal fisheries sector, and with the Fund's energy-conservation policies of the AIP. Women are active in the fishing industry all over the world; in some parts of West Africa men harvest the fish but 95 per cent of those who engage in processing and trading are women. Women buy the fish–often from their husbands–and preserve them by smoke, salt or sun-drying. Once preserved, the fish are marketed over long distances through complex and highly organized distribution systems.

Around 1970, FAO and the Ghana Food Research Institute worked with the women of a village called Chorkor, in Ghana, to design a rectangular clay-brick oven which is about twice as long as it is wide, with two stoke holes in the front. It is inexpensive and simple to make and can process up to 180 kilos of fish at a time. Smoke drying for ten to eighteen hours at low temperatures preserves the fish for up to nine months in a tropical climate. With periodic rotation of the trays, an evenly smoked, high-quality product can be achieved with a minimum of fuel. The Chorkor would become a centrepiece of our technology transfer activities.

UNIFEM's work in the artisanal fishery sector began in Benin in 1981. On a stopover at FAO in Rome, I had visited the fisheries officers and found, not surprisingly, that they were equipping men to increase their fish catch, but not assisting women who take over once the catch is landed. We developed a project entitled Co-operatives for Commercial Fish Marketing that was an input into a larger project executed by FAO; it would transfer the Chorkor technology.[26] We had to remain alert, however, lest our FAO colleagues integrate the project resources rather than the fisherwomen into the project.

Local women were organized in five co-operatives to process and market fish, then they were provided with training to manage the improved technologies, including wood-fuelled smoking ovens, and with a credit fund to purchase the fish. It took nearly two years for the women to develop the mutual trust they needed to work and manage money co-operatively, because in that area of Benin men married women from outside the community who had neither blood nor neighbourhood ties with one-another.

The women managed their credit fund so well that they were able to diversify their productive activities to include co-operative pig raising, palm oil extraction and consumer goods stores. The rate of repayment of loans was very high. The women earned between CFA 4000 and 6000 a month ($17 to $25 in 1993) for working two days per week during the fishing season, in a country where the average salary was 8000 CFA a month.[27]

Olubanke King-Akerele spelled out the impact of that first fishery project on women participants in Benin:

> In addition to the improved working conditions, these women, for the first time, were recognized and dealt with collectively as a production group and were involved in a major development project.[28]

The problems to resolve have not all been of a technical nature. In Guinea Conakry, for example, the post-Sekou Toure Government took over and wanted to have a first-ever, visible, symbolic 'women's project'. Fish processing technology appealed to them because of the country's 300km maritime facade and the harvest of about 25000 tonnes of fish for preservation annually. Before the UNIFEM technology specialists' discussions with government could be completed, however, enthusiasm spilled over and there was a great deal of radio publicity that gave women the impression that there would be salaried work available for them. Once it was clarified that self- or co-operative employment was the objective, the project could proceed as a demonstration one. The Chorkor now appears in

236

the national development programme in Guinea for both ocean and lake fishing.

The history of the Guinea project runs contrary to one evaluator's theory that the assumptions informing the project were feminist, that it 'grouped together women from different classes and creeds . . . in a large co-operative'.[29] On the contrary, the assumptions that informed the project were both pragmatic and political: the importance of improved fuel-saving technology for preserving fish and the strategy of a proud new (male) government to make a favourable impression on its female citizens by recognizing their economic activities. UNIFEM's technologies officer for the West Africa subregion, Ruby Sandhu, has a very pragmatic reason for strengthening national capacities for fish processing: 'Tuna are fished off the coast by the French, who send it to France where it is packaged and sent back and sold locally'.[30]

The technology was introduced in Gabon, Guinea-Bissau and Togo in the 1980s, and to Cameroon and São Tomé and Príncipe in the 1990s. It has begun to 'sell itself'–to be copied by private entrepreneurs, for example in Gabon and Cameroon. Fisherwomen in all the countries have learned to adapt the design to their needs. When the catch is small, the design of the oven enables them to use just three or four trays, covering the top one to retain heat. One of the success factors of the project's technology transfer is study tours; women fish-processors travel to Ghana to use the Chorkor with their counterparts for a week or two before they build their own. *A Practical Guide to Fish Smoking in West Africa* (in English and French) written and illustrated by UNIFEM consultant Bill Brownell and FAO staff member Jocelyn Lopez, explains how to construct the stove.

The greatest obstacle to promotion of the Chorkor smoker is beyond women's control: the supply of fish in the ocean is shrinking. West African coastal fishing areas have been over-exploited since the mid-1980s, mostly by industrial fleets from outside the region, many of them contracted by regional governments.[31] That leaves the artisanal fisherman with a much reduced supply, the women with fewer fish to process and sell, and everyone with a lot less protein. Governments seem not to have assessed the importance of artisanal fishing to their national economies; industrial fishing by overseas fleets is a more visible money-earner.

Sandhu, who travels often in West Africa, explained that besides the availability of fish, management is also a difficult problem for women. For that reason, co-operative work, marketing and reinvesting in the business are among UNIFEM's subjects of training.[32]

Each of the several UNIFEM fishery projects also includes a revolving loan fund. Sandhu explained that larger credit funds are now needed so that the fisherwomen can go beyond purchasing fish to making contracts with fishermen, or to buying boats. She summed up UNIFEM's perspective:

We do have a very very large experience in this domain, which is why it is important that we shouldn't leave it aside and say 'Okay, let's go on to something else'. We should bank on that experience, seeing how we can link micro experience with the macro policy level.[33]

237

UNIFEM/West Africa is doing just that–building on its technology experience in framing future action programmes. Two commodities have been chosen for emphasis: fish and cassava–the latter because of its value as a 'drought crop'. The commodity approach is a comprehensive one, ranging from production through marketing.

A water carrier: the *pousse pousse*

Technologies for water supply relieve the time and transport restraints on women's productivity. As already seen herein, time spent on wood portage can be reduced with the introduction of fuel-efficient stoves. The same objective relative to water portage has also been the focus of technological concern. The '*pousse pousse*', introduced in 1985, was still in use in 1993 when we visited the village of Yandegin in Burkina Faso. The *pousse pousse* is a wheelbarrow with four or six large metal rings to hold water jugs or pails; it is built in Burkina at an agricultural equipment workshop. The village had used six *pousse pousse* for about six years; they were able to transport water in pails but preferred inflatable wheels so that their clay pots would not break when traversing the rough terrain.

Eighty women (only five of whom were literate) and 30 men and boys gathered in Yandegin to meet us on a Sunday morning in the shade of their local church. Chairperson Rose Compaore explained that every member of her group paid ten francs to use the *pousse pousse*. The rental fee, plus 500 francs paid by each member, had made it possible for them to keep the pousse pousse in repair and to purchase a grain mill. They paid cash for the mill, with an advance of 250 000 francs, and charged 25 francs for each grain measure–an enamel bowl called a yoruba because of its Nigerian origins. Two young men were trained as millers because no women volunteered when the mill manufacturer offered free training; one of the young men left for Ivory Coast. Because they had to go to Ouagadougou for repairs, and spare parts were not readily available, the mill had been idle for two years.

The women met to exchange ideas after church on Sundays and they also get ideas from radio programmes. They had selected three men to advise their group because women may not decide anything on their own without referring to men. Besides a new mill, they needed a borehole or dam. Campaore summed up: 'All these problems are not just women's problems, they are development problems of the whole community.'

Management support: the case of ESAMI

I think it's important to build a critical mass of women in the management field or any other field. When there is a critical mass of women in a course (to me that is over the one-third point) the whole discussion and

238

orientation changes. Women are more vocal and more open. This changes the whole process.

Misrak Elias, Co-ordinator, ESAMI

How does one describe a typical eastern and southern African woman manager ?

She is middle age, 40–49 years old and highly educated, with a university degree or post-graduate qualifications. She is married and has only one or two children in contrast to the family she grew up in, where an average of 7.4 children was the norm. She is to be found at the highest levels of public sector organizations and private sector corporations, although she is the lone woman to reach such heights of management in the particular organization she works for. The hallmarks of her career success are hard work and skillful management of the work–home interface. She is competent, forward looking and fully committed to her organization's and nation's development goals.[34]

That description comes from an Institute that is well acquainted with women managers–the Eastern and Southern African Management Institute (ESAMI), Women in Management (WID/WIM) programme. ESAMI, located in Arusha, Tanzania, is *the* management training centre for the 17 countries of the sub-region. It trains some 3000 people annually, from ministerial level down, in short or long courses. Before 1980, less than one per cent of ESAMI's students were women; today more than 30 per cent are.

In 1980, with a small seed grant from the Carnegie Corporation, and then a much larger one from UNIFEM ($190 444), ECA/ATRCW and the Population Council joined with ESAMI to bring women into mainstream development planning and management. Misrak Elias was appointed Co-ordinator of the project and was the first woman professional there. 'John Okumo, the Director, was open and supportive, and he was a risk-taker, willing to experiment, and that made all the difference for me', Elias said. She added that very few of her ESAMI colleagues understood the need for such a programme. 'They thought initially it was just something very exotic. Very unnecessary', she explained.[35]

The first course, called Development Planning, Management and Women was launched in 1981, following a year of consultations with governments in the member countries about their priority training needs for planners. Its thrust was to strengthen the awareness of development planners and practitioners about women and development concerns, and then to give them the skills to analyse situations and formulate plans for change. Elias explained:

The course was a milestone in many ways. It was the first African management training programme geared to raise women and development issues. It was also ESAMI's first women and development programme. And it was the first time women came to the Institute as participants and as professional resource persons.[36]

UNIFEM and Elias soon persuaded colleagues at UNDP to invest $500 000 in the programme, and she gained support from the Commonwealth Secretariat and Canadian CIDA.

Many other courses were built around that first one, and in time WID/ WIM was working in three areas. First, there was a workshop on influencing senior policymakers, such as Permanent Secretaries. The second focused on equipping women managers with the analytic and organizational skills to move into strategic positions. The third area was directed at development managers (the officers who worked at implementation level) to sensitize them to gender issues while enhancing their skills.[37] The programme later added training for women entrepreneurs.

'Governments sent women to our Women and Management courses and men to the mainstream courses' Elias said. 'But we wanted to expose the key decision-makers, mostly men, to women's courses also'.[38] As an inducement they offered two fellowships per country–one for a man and the other for a woman; if governments didn't send men to be trained in the Women and Development courses they didn't get any fellowship. They also devised a strategy for increasing the number of women in mainstream management courses. 'We used the common marketing strategy of "buy one and get one free",' said Elias. Any organization that was willing to sponsor a female staff member to any of the ESAMI Institute courses could send a second woman free. Quite a few organizations took them up on that offer, for which the Ford Foundation gave scholarships.

> Influencing the mainstream is not only having more women in men's courses, but having male professors focus on gender issues in their own training programmes.
>
> Misrak Elias

Elias undertook a tracer study of women students who had completed courses. There were some surprises:

> 'You would think that a course of one to three weeks could stimulate very little change, but actually there was a lot of change. I remember one very senior woman, a Permanent Secretary, who used to be abrupt and aggressive, and not supportive of other women on her staff. When we followed up on her, her colleagues asked 'What has happened to this woman? She's completely changed. She's supportive and people-oriented in her management style'.

In time ESAMI, co-operating with SADCC, financed national consultants to study the ability of women to advance in the public service sector. Zimbabwe, for example, studied women and men who both started to work at independence time in 1980. 'By 1991 the men were chief executives but women had stagnated at the assistant secretary level', Dirasse said.[39] A needs assessment followed, and Government came up with an affirmative action policy: twenty-five women managers were identified for additional training and promotion.

Credit support systems

Poor women can almost never obtain credit for their entrepreneurial activities because they lack collateral in its traditional form, i.e., land, a house or business assets. Elsewhere in this book I described UNIFEM's response to that issue: adding community revolving-loan funds as integral components of productivity projects. Because RLFs became a very common practice, needing a reservoir of experience and expertise, UNIFEM opened a credit window headed by Teckie Ghebre-Medhin in the early 1980s–not just for Africa but for projects worldwide. It included the credit support systems component of the Africa Investment Plan that had three objectives: to give women's groups access to loans for specific types of enterprises; to help women learn about and obtain credit from conventional sources; and to familiarize them with financial management.[40]

Not all credit funds were small ones. A $4 million trust fund project entitled Credit Scheme for Productive Activities of Women was created through a partnership between the Government of Denmark, UNIFEM, and the Government of Tanzania, with the co-operation of the ILO.[41] UNIFEM's 1988 project design team was constituted with its own technical officer, an experienced researcher from the Grameen Bank in Bangladesh, an international expert, and Tanzanian experts. The project's goal was 'to establish and stabilize viable women's groups and improve their agricultural, technical, managerial and marketing skills.' Secondarily it sought to 'strengthen the capabilities of national institutions for implementing, monitoring and evaluating the credit delivery–recovery system; mobilize indigenous savings; and to document its methodology and the process of credit delivery–recovery.' Mid-term evaluations in 1993 pronounced the project a success to date, in particular: its peer-pressure credit system; its training of women, project staff, counterparts, banks and the government; and the creation of Associations of Rural Women Enterprises.[42]

On the mainland, the impact of the project has been 'tremendous on the lives of the individual women and the community', according to the evaluators. A questionnaire among 139 women in seven villages found 54 per cent of them registered considerable improvement in their incomes, while 30 per cent–farmers–had not yet harvested their products. Employment was created: 318 jobs, or an average of three employees per entrepreneur. As regards the community, women now cultivate up to eight acres rather than the one or two cultivated before the project. Savings and Credit Societies were formed in the participating villages. The evaluation report on the Zanzibar project said that 361 women in 68 groups received nearly 11 million URT shillings in credit, and the repayment rate varied between 81 per cent and 100 per cent. Note was taken of the 'very impressive' impact of the project on the individual family and the community.[43]

'Mainstreaming': linking women with major development resources

A Brainstorming Seminar was organized by UNIFEM in Niger in 1986, just before UNDP's biannual meeting of its senior representatives in Africa.

The seminar was to review the progress of one of the key mechanisms of the Africa Investment Plan: linking women with major development programmes and resources. This 'mainstreaming' initiative had begun in a formal way late in 1984, with the goal of developing methodologies on how to incorporate women's concerns in major programmes, the results of which could be systematized by UN organizations. Akerele intensified our work in this area because we knew that there were very few women in high government or UN agency posts, where policy and projects were designed to influence millions of people; women were easily overlooked under such circumstances.

The new approach led to an explosion of UNIFEM participation in multidisciplinary programming and project formulation missions, donor-round table exercises, national development planning by governments, and UNDP country programming for investment of its resources.[44] The first of the round-table exercises for UNIFEM was in The Gambia, where the Fund was able to witness the procedure which the Minister of Planning presided over in the company of the World Bank and UNDP representatives. Major policy issues were discussed and project proposals reviewed with bi- and multi-lateral donor representatives who had an interest in giving financial support to the country. (Hence the term 'round-table').

In Togo, UNIFEM 'caught the train midway', as Ki-Zerbo expressed it, and participated earlier in the process than was possible in The Gambia. In the sectoral committee on rural development, Committee members were sensitized to the fact that Togolese women play major roles in the food chain; similar presentations were made by UNIFEM in the education and health sector groups. The participation in Togo started a process that continued to evolve over several years. UNIFEM worked with UNICEF in a situation analysis on women in the country's economic and social sectors. Then in 1988, Togo hosted a UNIFEM-financed Conference on mainstreaming that was attended by members of the Economic Community of West African States (ECOWAS) from 16 countries and from two other countries of Central Africa.

The Togo round-table exercise had set the tone for Chad, Niger and Burkina Faso, where UNIFEM assisted the UNDP field offices and the governments in implementing recommendations adopted in Lomé. In Chad, Ki-Zerbo proposed that rural women be given access to improved agricultural tools. The response took the form of an appropriate technology centre, set up to produce equipment such as stoves, oil presses, and manually operated grain mills.

Asked about any special experiences she had when participating in the round-tables, Ki-Zerbo said that donors and host governments repeatedly told her that there was no need for special programmes or special decisions concerning women 'because we know that women work a lot and they participate in African development'. On hearing this, Ki-Zerbo would agree with them and add: 'Yes, we participate when it comes to working, but we would like to participate also in sharing development resources'.[45]

Mainstream initiatives were expanded to the wider UN system and outside it. UNIFEM joined the World Bank's project formulation mission to The Gambia; that resulted in the Bank's first 'free-standing' women's project, a multi-million dollar one. The Fund then supported a seminar hosted by the African Development Bank to design its women and development strategy and also assisted the European Economic Community in identifying ways to incorporate women in its Nigeria programme. It continued to work with the UN Economic Commission for Africa and SADCC, among other regional and subregional organizations. Consultants were assigned for national planning in Niger, Togo, Zambia, and Burkina Faso. A few of those experiences were published in 1987 as Occasional Paper No. 5: *UNIFEM's Mainstream Experiences,* and in *Development Review.*[46]

Attentive as always to the 'innovative' aspects of its projects, UNIFEM created another approach: the appointment of national resource persons. Seeing that one of the major blocks to policy implementation was the weakness of the national machineries' operational capacities, we financed resource persons (nationals) as planning assistants in Burkina Faso, Chad, The Gambia, Niger, Senegal and Togo. During my 1993 visit to Burkina Faso I learned of the slow but sure results of the resource person's work. The Minister for Social Action and the Family told me:

> Just this year (April 1993) the Burkina Faso Government adopted the National Plan of Action for Strengthening Women's Roles in the Development Process. An inter-ministerial co-ordinating group was set up in 1986, to guide the production of a document. It was led by the Ministry of Social Affairs. The ministries of agriculture, social action, planning, environment, education and political co-ordination were represented. With a national resource person financed by UNIFEM, a national Women and Development Strategy was produced; it formed the basis for the *Plan of Action* that was launched at a national seminar in September this year.[47]

Having adopted the Plan, Government set up a national Commission chaired by the Minister of Planning, with the Minister of Social Action as Vice-Chairman. The Commission meets twice a year to monitor the implementation of the Plan by the various technical ministries. A small secretariat in the Planning Ministry backstops the Commission.

A recap on the Africa Investment Plan

UNIFEM concluded that there was a great deal of goodwill about directing resources to women, but that neither governments nor technical assistance officers were quite sure how to provide that assistance; in addition, it could easily be neglected. We therefore continued to have a unique advocacy role, and getting statements in official documents was not enough. It was crucial to take part in programming and project formulation missions at the time when 'development objectives are defined, when financial and technical supports are planned, when resources are mobilized and allocated.'[48]

Thus 'mainstreaming' took place not just in formal forums such as donor

Reactions from the field: What UNDP representatives said about UNIFEM participation in donor round-tables and country programming exercises in Africa.

Togo The participation of UNIFEM in the preparations for the round-table resulted in a study of the conditions of rural women in Togo, which formed the basis for a project financed by UNDP. UNIFEM participation also crystalised the attention of other agencies such as UNFPA and UNICEF, who now take UNIFEM recommendations into account in their programmes. The contribution of women to the economic development of the country and to food production is now officially recognised.

Togo The Government of Togo thanks UNIFEM for its assistance with the success of the sectoral meeting of donors. We request your assistance with the Preparatory study for the operationalisation of a revolving fund that will aid 100 rural women groups.

Niger UNIFEM's contribution will be most welcome for the Niamey meeting.

Chad Your [Ki-Zerbo] participation as the only woman in that meeting, was very remarkable and I congratulate you for having so brilliantly defended the cause of the Chadian women. I am sure that the delegates present at the meeting were sensitized and that the governments and organisations they represent will contribute more resources to promoting the activities of Chadian women.

Burundi UNIFEM's participation in the national assessment (NAT-CAP) greatly facilitated drawing attention to women's issues as part of national human resource development.

Sierre Leone The UNIFEM mission noted *inter alia* establishing marketing associations; credit and savings associations; providing the necessary training to make these viable and setting up appropriate technology groups to design methods to ease women's burdens. Pipeline projects, especially in the agricultural and rural development areas will (also) benefit from these recommendations.

The Gambia UNIFEM's recent mission to Gambia played an important role in formulating a women component in UNDP's new project assistance cycle . . . We expect a strong linkage to emerge between the role of women in development and the employment generation activities in The Gambia.

The UN UNIFEM prepared a training module for UNDP's training of senior economists; ILO scheduled a seminar with its staff in Geneva for UNIFEM to present its experiences; UNIDO and UNCTAD planned similar events.

September 1988

round-tables and country programming. It was the primary objective in supporting national machineries, as discussed in the preceding chapter on political participation. Such government and civil society organs sought to assist setting the national agenda. Mainstreaming also happened when officials were exposed to women's use of fuel-saving stoves, fish smokers and grinding mills. That experience underlined the importance of constantly interrelating macro and micro activities with policies and actions.

Ellen Johnson Sirleaf of Liberia, in her paper *Some Observations on Structural Adjustment and the African Woman,* summed up the value of the AIP as she addressed governments and the international community:

> Eighty-five per cent of rural women work in agriculture and eighty per cent of the food consumed by the family is produced, processed and stored by women. Women thus manage all aspects of the food system from production to consumption . . . It is the women who do the work, while men own the land and control the money. In these circumstances, African women cannot be mentioned merely in the footnotes and subparagraphs of modern plans for African agriculture development. Women are African agriculture; they are the embodiment of subsistence and survival agriculture. They will be the agents for meaningful development and food security in the future–but only if they are given proper education, training, resources, support and decent prices.[49]

AIP became the model for UNIFEM's policy frameworks and programmes in other geographical regions. Once formulated, those programmes brought to light the cross-regional nature of many of the priorities in the fight against poverty: food technologies and credit systems were the first to become visible.

My field visits in preparation for this study revealed once again that despite some progress, women's centrality to economic development continues to be neglected by governments and aid agencies–a quarter-century after hard facts became available on the gendered division of labour in economic activity.

I conclude that today, in 1995, it is still painfully clear that UNIFEM is absolutely necessary. The 'success stories' that the major funds and agencies point out as evidence of their concern for women are the exception, not the common practice. 'Mainstreaming' is the long-range goal that we all share; strategies to reach that goal must include women's units inside the major funds and a greatly empowered UNIFEM to leverage change from outside. That is one of the several conclusions that we shall consider in the following, final chapter of this book.

CHAPTER ELEVEN

Valuable Lessons for an Uncertain Future

Without addressing the livelihood needs of women as half of humanity it is not possible to achieve the human-centred development that is needed to sustain us through the next century.

Noeleen Heyzer
UNIFEM Director, 1994

What significance does UNIFEM's experience in overcoming poverty have for world development and for women? To answer that question, we first make a comparative analysis of the activities earlier described, with the aim to uncover common elements.

The goal of development–to reverse the effects of global poverty–is our lens for appraising the three variables: empowerment, sustainable institutions, and innovative/catalytic effects. Empowerment is measured both by enhanced income and by self-esteem and self-reliance. What empowerment is to individual strength, sustainable institutions are to organizational strength: the capacity for self-reliance and durability. The innovative/catalytic effects of projects are those which open or augment women's access to mainstream resources and provide opportunities for becoming involved in shaping the future of society; the term is used in both qualitative and quantitative ways. The variables are inter-dependent, i.e. there is little gain in enhancing incomes without creating a lasting system. The ultimate goal, human well-being, depends upon the existence of sustainable institutions.

After looking at the field activities in terms of the three variables and drawing some specific lessons from them, we shall reach some overall conclusions about the Fund and its work and about the relevance of its experience to world development. Then we will look at the future through the eyes of those whom I interviewed in the course of my research. Table 11.1, How effective is UNIFEM as an agent of development?, provides the reader with a reference to the activities discussed in this chapter.

Empowerment

Earlier in this book I spoke of UNIFEM's promotion of economic democracy (the broad-based access to the means to create wealth and decide upon its dispostion) as the most frequently used strategy for countering poverty. UNIFEM seeks to meet women's livelihood needs by creating wealth, not just redistributing it; everything in this book depends upon comprehending that reality. Important lessons learned from the application of that strategy are about the two-track approach, market emphasis, disposition of income, entry point and scale of projects, addressing the massiveness of poverty,

246

Table 11.1: How effective is UNIFEM as an agent of development?

Activity	Anti-poverty effectiveness variables		
	Empowerment	Sustainable institutions	Catalytic effects
Economic Productivity			
China Tailoring	*	*	–
India Mahila Haat	*	*	*
India Sericulture	***	**	***
Laos Textiles	**	***	***
Mauritius Arts	**	***	***
Philippines San Miguel	***	***	**
Philippines Root Crops	***	***	**
Swaziland Credit	**	***	***
Social Justice			
Barbados Food	***	**	***
Bolivia Pottery	–	–	–
Bolivia Milk	***	***	*
E. & S. Africa Management Training	***	***	***
Kenya Water	**	***	**
Oman Communities	***	***	**
Sahel Stoves	**	***	***
Syria Literacy	***	***	**
Tanzania Technologies	***	**	**
West Africa Fish Smokers	***	**	***
WAND Caribbean	***	***	***
Yemen Biogas	***	*	***
Participation in Decision-making			
Kenya Green Belt	***	***	***
Peru Workers	***	***	***
Peru NGO Network	***	***	**
Peru Technology	*	*	**

Key:
*** Highly Effective
** Effective
* Partially Effective
– Ineffective

and the invisible external influences on the effectiveness of the interventions. I address those first.

Empowerment goals have been best achieved through two-track projects, i.e. those that set out to increase incomes (growth) through non-traditional technologies, credit systems, and marketing plans, and provide women-specific group training for solidarity and self-reliance (toward equity). The two-track approach is meant to generate both income and the self-confidence and respect from others that are preconditions for participation in decision-making in the home, in co-operatives, and in communities. Agriculturalist Profulla Nagar of TADD called that 'the UNIFEM system' which we will now review and assess.

Laotian women's situation improved and their income from the manufacture of cloth doubled because the government and the Association of Lao Patriotic Women joined in sponsoring the industry. Although the Bolivian milk producers did not reach that specific doubling goal, annual income was significantly increased in a country where 86 per cent of rural dwellers have to survive under severe poverty conditions and where GNP per capita is $680. The co-ordination of technical agency inputs and the extra group-training the women got from the NGO, SETAM prepared them to become active in mixed-gender milk producers' associations (they are still active in 1995) and to take pride in what they saw as their greatest achievement: 'Our husbands respect us more!' That comment contrasts like day and night with the comments of the women in Cochabamba whose husbands got the ceramics training that was meant for wives. Such favouritism had an economic cost in terms of low incomes as well as a social cost relative to the women's low self-esteem.

A sample index of participants' income in Swaziland showed that it compared favourably with, and at times surpassed, the average income in the informal sector of that country's economy. The training centres imparted skills and introduced labour-saving technologies to lessen workloads. Not only did women get the gift of time but they immediately found income opportunities in manufacturing some of the technologies themselves, such as the water storage jars. The revolving-loan fund was an integral element of project effectiveness in Swaziland as elsewhere because, once trained, the women had capital to invest in start-up costs and operations for their enterprises. Interestingly, over time some women's groups adapted the idea and created their own revolving funds.

A 30 per cent to 40 per cent increase in family income was experienced in San Miguel when UNIFEM's loans were taken to raise pigs. Later, those same women were wise enough to switch their production of toys to manufacturing garments when the international market became oversupplied with toys. The expansion to home-based clothing industries found 800 women earning about $68 a month, surpassing the annual GNP per capita of $770. However, the end of that story has yet to be told because the process was converted to a factory-based rural industry, an extremely high-risk decision.

The Indian sericulture project offers a classic example of the significance of the two-track approach. In the early years of that project incomes were multiplied seven-fold, but cash crops edged out food crops, family nutrition suffered and alcohol abuse rose. An evaluation of the project showed that the primary input by the government agency TADD transferred sericulture production and processing technology–but that was not sufficient for realizing a long-range improvement in peoples' lives. The community mobilization training for 500 women, aided by the NGO Aastha, succeeded in earning them respect in their homes. Women were also empowered to use their vote more judiciously and to risk having a say in community and family social problems. Their empowerment eventually spread to villages whose 2500 women had none of the additional group training.

In Argentina a series of training courses prepared three trainers and four promoters to deal with numerous co-operating agencies and with the farm women themselves. That intense preparation made the difference between an earlier, problem-ridden small project and the one that affected 53 000 families and still continues. The same strategy worked in Huancayo in Peru, where the participants saw themselves as 'dynamizing agents' in their communities and became skilled financial managers. Two other communities in the project lacked the second track–which may explain their lesser strength.

The timing for introducing elements of the two tracks may vary but two lessons are clear: first, that creating income must have a very high priority when assistance to poor women begins; and second, that technical skills must be supplemented with opportunities to increase group solidarity and personal confidence.

The experience of SEWA teaches a related lesson. There, women already had the skills for a meagre livelihood. The point was to promote groups organized along economic lines so that they could make demands as trade unionists from positions of strength, to increase their incomes and to improve their working conditions. Flora Tristan used the same methodology with wage workers in Lima.

The massive nature of poverty–which affects one billion people world-wide–calls for simultaneous intervention at both the level of national policy and at the grassroots level. The Indian, Omani, and Argentinian projects responded to the need to reach large numbers of the poor by assisting the poorest people–women. UNIFEM was effective by being a partner with the only institution that can work on such a scale, the government. That finding is of special importance in the 1990s, when the power of the free market has become so ascendent that the downsizing of governments and privatization are often the conditions for getting international bank credit. That shrinkage can actually cripple governments from playing as strong a role as they did in the achievement of the 'East Asian Miracle'.[1]

Despite the rise in personal income in many countries, a weak linkage between production and market demand can be an obstacle to greater income. Marketing skills must be an integral component of training or else economic initiatives will fail. In Syria the problem was foreseen but the solution–an ILO expert from overseas–was ineffective. (However, UNIFEM was able to introduce a promising marketing approach in the region in 1993.) The technology project in Peru is young and could still invite co-operating agencies to provide strong marketing and also solidarity components. Mahila Haat's major thrust was marketing, yet only in the very beginning did it have a business management and marketing specialist to develop that sector. In contrast, SPES in Mauritius found overseas markets for its products, and the National Organization of Women in Barbados created local markets for preserved food where previously there

249

were none. In Swaziland, 81 per cent of credit users reported no difficulty with marketing. TADD in Udaipur continues to work with the sericulturists as they learn the intricate procedures of the silk auction; they got better prices in 1994.

The disposition of earned income is of compelling significance to overcoming poverty. How is income used? In Bolivia, 25 per cent of the cash received by men was spent neither on the family nor on the farm. In sharp contrast, women spent 100 per cent of their income for those purposes. In Tanzania, women's earnings from a mill went to increase their productive assets or to improving the family home. In the Philippines and Syria as well, women's earnings were invested in better nutrition or schooling–the needs of the family. This finding is reinforced by innumerable other studies.[2] Its importance is multiplied by the rising incidence of single breadwinner families headed by women. The proportion of such families in the project areas was and remains high; even traditionally conservative national statistics cite growing rates, coincident with the increasing rate of poverty.

Going back to the San Miguel experience we can see that it points up some of the controversial issues relating to micro-enterprise, income generation and empowerment that arose during my research. Among them are the merits of home-based industries and of teaching 'traditional skills'. The San Miguel evaluators made salient points: 'Medium-scale enterprises are not necessarily more efficient than home-based enterprises . . . Rural women's efficiency is not necessarily increased by putting them to work in a professionally managed environment'. The younger, more mobile workers had a further impact on the development of medium-scale industries; San Miguel experienced an out-migration of its younger workers into the urban and overseas industrial sector. 'When they get knowledge, they go to another place', said Santa Ana.

Most rural and some urban women who have family responsibilities see home-based industry as their only practical option; they may work in their own or a neighbouring home. For many, the point is a straightforward one: either a home-based income or no supplementary income at all. Two foundations, KBBLF and FAFW, in the Philippines learned a difficult lesson when most of Toy City's potential workers opted to continue their knitting and sewing at home rather than joining the central factory. Earning less money was a tradeoff they were willing to make in order to meet their primary family responsibilities while continuing to get their farm income. In Syria, many women were constrained by societal traditions that included their doing 90 per cent of the farm work. Home-based Laotian women were a key factor in the transformation of a significant area of the country's industrial sector.

The choices of those women may in fact have been the most economically efficient ones at the time. Rural women are not sitting idly on the farm. More often than not they have multiple responsibilities as sole managers of the farm enterprises, particularly when a husband works for wages off-farm or is otherwise absent. A new home-based small enterprise is just one of several potential sources of income: crops, crafts, and small animal husbandry are others.

The women in our study are among the millions of home-based workers around the world who either do piece-work or are small producers and own-account workers. When they work in isolation from one another they can easily be exploited. SEWA has taken a lead world-wide as advocate for social and legal protection of homeworkers, and to form a global network to promote their organization in co-operatives, trade unions or other groups. The network is already in action, building international and national policy; they are seeking an International Convention on Home-workers through the International Labour Organization. The network also encourages new grassroots alternative types of productivity and encourages women to take economic leadership. Social and economic justice for home-based workers is a critical dimension of economic democracy.

One thing is certain; critics of 'those small projects' (and there are many) can learn from the preferences of poor women. Mary Racelis's point is relevant here: The popular economy is a huge number of individuals and small groups doing a great variety of activities. We can use the experienced Racelis's insight to identify one problem that often occurs in entrepreneurial projects directed to women: the failure to link one producer to another and to sources of raw materials, expertise and markets. Mahila Haat set out to create such linkages and to influence government policy through the power of village market groups, but that effort has yet to succeed on its intended scale. On the other hand, small projects can be more than just linked; they can also grow. Swaziland's ended up country-wide; Kenya's Green Belt Movement is now transnational; SEWA has national and global outreach.

Teaching women 'traditional skills' like sewing has also come under harsh criticism. On this subject, Christabel Zondo's point about strategies bears repeating: Sometimes starting with traditional skills is 'not the worst thing you can do'. She said further that the really significant things– brickmaking, welding, the revolving-credit fund–were added on gradually, and by that time were quite acceptable. Soon, attitudes had changed about women's work and their access to credit, not only in the project but in the whole of Swaziland.

For some women, learning in groups can be empowering in itself, and easier to initiate through a traditional skill. Such learning can be liberating because it provides women with opportunities to work with their peers and get out of their houses. For example, in Oman, after learning in groups, women who had never attended public events were soon speaking at microphones and, as an added bonus, raising family incomes 15 per cent. Syrian women found a sense of freedom in being able to read the labels of medicine bottles and the signs on buses, and, above all, helping their children with their schooling.

Thoraya Obaid insisted on 'getting women out of their houses' to do something not just for their husband or children but for themselves. In the Yemen, secluded women grasped the initiative to build biogas digesters and benefit from extension services despite the men's initial reluctance;

251

they were imbued with strength through group classes at their social centres. Most home-based workers spend part of their time in the work-rooms of neighbours; that is often their first step toward community participation.

The approach of teaching 'traditional skills' was the correct first step in several projects and has no doubt contributed to the projects' sustainability and expansion over the years. Nonetheless, I hasten to remind the reader that UNIFEM's assistance for augmenting income most often introduced non-traditional technologies and credit funds. The point is always to take local circumstances, including potential markets, into account. Catherine Mwanamwambwa said it well: 'We should go to where women are and start with the skills they have, then improve those skills. There is no need to take a village woman who is cultivating sunflower and tell her to form a club to knit and sew. Give her an oil press to process and sell her sunflower. Teach her to take the cake left from the sunflower and feed the chickens'.[3]

I would reiterate the importance of taking advantage of very large-scale government, and some private initiatives, by injecting a good-sized invest-ment for training, technologies, credit and other inputs directed specifically to women, as was done in Argentina, Bolivia, Oman and the India sericulture project. The point is to have more than what has been called a 'women's component' in a mainstream project; it is to make a significant investment and then have a voice in the overall policy, design, implementa-tion and monitoring of the whole effort.

Major challenges that still remain for women lie in the realm of the external political and economic factors that the project management could not control, and that often weakened or destroyed the gains of economic empowerment projects. India's adjustment programmes impacted on the sericulturists incomes in a visible way as lower tariffs unleashed a flood of imports of cheap but high-quality silk from neighbouring countries. National policies that led to the export of raw materials and import of finished goods in the programmes also left many Mahila Haat entrepre-neurs without income; they could neither get raw materials nor compete in the market.

The country in our study that was hit hardest by man-made negative influences was Peru, where economic downturn and disease were exacer-bated by the civil strife that immobilized the society. Further, as in countless other countries, the government policies that were intended to stimulate economic growth have thrown many people out of work. Under those dire circumstances both adults and children would have been severely under-nourished had it not been for the ingenious popular kitchens and glass-of-milk groups. UNIFEM's recognition of their creative response to poverty attracted other international agencies such as UNICEF to add support.

In neighbouring Bolivia where government is privatizing parastatal organizations, the costs of milk collection in the project's Tiawanaku area can be expected to be prohibitive to a market-oriented entrepreneur for whom maximizing profit is the incentive. That would be shortsighted if the government's goal is to expand the long-term income-generating capabilities of the people of the area. In China, the factory workers' income rose significantly for several years until what appears to be a combination of external market forces and management mobility nearly closed the business.

Another effect of global market-centred policies has been to return low-income countries to the colonial-type trade pattern of exporting raw materials and importing manufactures. In Zambia, and many other countries, the down-sizing of government, combined with the elimination of textile tariffs, has pushed innumerable women, and men, too, into an as yet undeveloped informal marketplace and left many girls and boys outside the school door. Another face of the problem was evidenced in Tanzania where imported food drove local farmers off the land to seek livelihoods in an unfamiliar and hardly existent marketplace. Policies that promote jobless growth without human development increase poverty and desperation.

The civil strife and wars that are scattered across the developing world destroy any semblance of progress and propel millions of people backward into total poverty. We saw that in Peru. Violence of that visible kind has most recently plagued projects in the Middle East and Africa. In Kenya, for example, tribal clashes have interfered with the Green Belt's tree planting and the incomes women got from it. They have brought fear to the movement. In Wangari Maathai's words: 'Organizing ordinary people, poor people, and telling them they can cause positive change in their environment and they can do it on their own, can appear threatening to the status quo'. Yet the Movement has managed to influence national and global environmental and human rights policy. 'These are subtle things which, multiplied several times, create an attitude in society that changes the society positively. That is an indirect influence UNIFEM has had', said Maathai.[4]

Violence is destructive of development–both violence against individuals and that which affects whole societies. The latter can be caused by conflict or by the poverty that short-sighted policies induce. It is time for women to be concerned with these issues in a bigger way. UNIFEM's new African programme–Women in Crisis–speaks to issues of violence and wants women from the North and the South to have louder voices as peacemakers. It is a start.

Sustainable institutions

Our second variable for analysing the capacity of projects and programmes to make significant inroads on poverty is the creation or strengthening of sustainable institutions that will function over the long term as vehicles for advancing women's–and society's–concerns. As has earlier been explained, UNIFEM became unique in the UN system for channeling money to NGOs (fully 50 per cent of projects by 1985); beyond that, it provided institutional support as distinct from project support. At the same time, UNIFEM has been an important source of assistance to governmental women and development machineries, the national commissions and women's bureaux. A third institutional target of the Fund was the regional economic and social commissions of the UN.

In addition, among the Fund's most important partners were governments, regional development banks, sub-regional organizations and other influential institutions that targeted UNIFEM's interventions at some of the massive numbers of the poor. The strategy works when the intervention on behalf of women is of a size commensurate with the scale of the host project and the task to be accomplished. Then one can expect an institutional impact.

One of the first non-governmental organizations to which UNIFEM gave an institutional as distinct from a project grant was the Women and Development Unit (WAND) at the University of the West Indies. With a strengthened central capacity for management, training and the dissemination of information, WAND was positioned to continue its evolution without the distractions of never-ending fundraising for small amounts.[5]

Ada Balcazar of MAI (Women in Industry) in the Dominican Republic and Wangari Maathai of the Green Belt Movement added their praise for that kind of support, because the grants they received were large enough to make their organizations' institution-building possible. The size of the initial grant is important because a too early expectation that a group or organization will soon be self-sustaining burdens the executing agency with fund-raising at a time in the life of the project when intense attention must be given to developing it.

Not infrequently, project assistance led to the creation of new institutions. At San Miguel, group solidarity enabled not only a village-based organization (KBB) but a foundation (KBBLF), that made it possible for the local women to take into their own hands the responsibilities that were earlier entrusted to a Manila-based foundation. In the root-crop project, also in the Philippines, co-operatives were formed for management and for marketing the women's products. Flora Tristan in Peru created a network of rural women's organizations (including those of the glass-of-milk and community kitchen types) whose basic units were described by Nora Galer as unique in Latin America: 'In no other country do you find grassroots organizations as empowered and autonomous and massive'. In Swaziland, the effectiveness of the 'economic roles of women' project led to its expansion into a lasting programme: the government now finances 39 posts and the project operates in five regions of the country.

Institution building at government level to ensure consideration of women in policies and programmes first took the form of training and teaching women the techniques of national planning (26 UNIFEM-assisted multi-country projects in the four regions in the late 1970s and 1980s). In 1992 the evaluator of the South Pacific development planning project found that mainstreaming women in development was a 'complex and time-consuming objective demanding a great deal of institutional development'. That is a conclusion with which my findings fully agree, and it underlay our provision of support to institutions that are capable of that long-term effort.

Strengthening national commissions and women's bureaux was the object of 17 projects by 1986. Terry Kantai, first head of the Kenya Women's Bureau, said that the project helped her to articulate priorities for the Bureau at a time when there were no precedents in the Africa region. Assistance in The Gambia preceded the involvement of the Womens Bureau in designing a multi-million dollar World Bank project for rural women–the first of its kind. The National Commission on the Role of Filipino Women strengthened its hand by preparing a Development Plan for Women: 1987–92 that interfaced policy recommendations with government's sectoral plans.

The impact of institution-building activities can be difficult to measure, but UNIFEM's evaluator of the programme, F. Joke-Bangura, expressed her conviction that in numerous countries the national machineries, despite their weaknesses, were the only organizations to challenge government planners to take up the question of programmes for women. She strongly recommended that UNIFEM continue to augment its support, with the objective to enhance the capacity of the national machineries to influence decisions in respect to women's issues and help them to gain political power and authority.[6]

Seventeen years after UNIFEM first financed senior women's programme officer posts, the UN regional commissions have sustained (but not expanded) their programmes for women. ECA and ECLAC have moved them from social development divisions to the offices of the Executive Secretary. The Commissions bring women and the UN closer to each other at a working level in their respective regions by supporting regional conferences and activities such as ECA's entrepreneurs' network. Of particular importance is the access that they give women to their regional governing bodies, the Conferences of Ministers. My great disappointment, however, is in knowing that UNIFEM support should have been stronger, with more posts than the two senior ones we gave, and have lasted longer, for a decade or more.

The duration of external assistance is a question that arises when speaking of development planning and regional commissions but it is also a vital concern for other types of assistance. I cannot emphasize enough that the time it takes to achieve sustainability has long been under-estimated by donors and project executers alike. We were continuously pressured to either complete projects in a short time or turn them over to other donors. During my recent country visits I judged time and again that phased assistance over a longer period could have multiplied the effectiveness of the project. Alternatively, continued contact after official assistance ends could lead to support–perhaps just moral support or policy interventions–at appropriate times of the project life-cycle. We are, after all, engaged in a social revolution.

The history of the projects discussed here shows clearly that, with few exceptions, a minimum of seven years, and preferably ten, are necessary to create sustainable institutions. Human organizations have life-cycles just as people do, and some periods in that cycle are more complex than others; that fact can create recurring needs for external inputs. Mariam Krawczyk at ECLAC insisted that ceasing support at too early a stage in the project life-cycle was a major cause of some researchers' judgements that income-generating projects benefiting women had failed during the 1980s. Care must be taken, however, to achieve a delicate balance between giving specialized assistance at certain points and creating a crippling dependency. Eremina Mvura of Zimbabwe put it well: assistance should be given 'not to make people dependent, but self-reliant with dignity'.

Continuous leadership is even more critical to sustainability. Ela Bhatt of SEWA, Emma Santa Ana of San Miguel, Peggy Antrobus at WAND, Margaret Mwangola of KWAHO, Wangari Maathai of the Green Belt, Gina Vargas of Flora Tristan, and Linda Vilakati of Swaziland are testaments to that truth; it may be said that they themselves grew in stature together with the growth of the organizations. Feminists sometimes fear individual leadership, perhaps justly when it drowns out democratic participation. Strong, knowledgeable and committed leadership is very often a central feature of effectiveness when it simultaneously fosters participation. In sharp contrast to activities having continuously involved leadership, Mahila Haat's lack of that strength relates to its failure, as yet, to reach its excellent goals.

The most powerful and visible evidence of how group solidarity in conquering adversity can generate sustainable institutions and movements comes from India and Peru. SEWA's 55 000-member trade union, with its credit and social security systems, is a truly remarkable instrument for mitigating the violent effects of poverty. Women who earn paltry incomes as junksmiths, carpenters and cigarette-rollers began to bargain for more money; then they took ownership of productive assets such as technologies, or of a workplace that is also their family home. The bank they started is owned by its 40 000 (mostly illiterate) depositers who have saved 70 million rupees ($ 2.27 million). But SEWA is much much more than just a direct alleviator of poverty; it has also influenced policy time and again. The National Commission on Self-Employed Women and Women in the Informal Sector, for example, has had a profound influence on government economists by alerting them to the vastness of the informal sector's contribution to the nation's economy and the potential it offers as a basis for economic democracy. SEWA has also led home-based workers everywhere in seeking an international convention on their behalf through the International Labour Organization.

The industrial and other workers' weekly sessions, under the leadership of the Flora Tristan organization in Peru, stimulated those workers to join the trade unions at their workplaces. Together with some men, the women helped to raise wages and gain benefits for all workers. More than that, several of the women became officials in major trade unions and together they promoted the adoption of national legislation on women workers' specific concerns. What stopped their progress was their country's economic collapse, acute civil disturbance, and economic adjustment programmes that drove people out of formal sector employment.

What is impressive is to learn that determined Peruvian women found ways to reduce the cost and time for feeding their families during the years of deepest depression and civil unrest. The popular kitchen and glass-of-milk committees were uniquely strengthened by their solidarity in the face of violence, hunger and poverty, to the point of meeting death, as two of them did. Their courage contributed to the creation of sustainable movements that have flourished everywhere in their country.

UNIFEM as innovator and catalyst for change

In pursuing its mandate to reach out to poor women in low-income countries, UNIFEM has been an innovator and a catalyst in three ways. It created new approaches to development co-operation such as replacing handouts with community credit funds; it pushed other organizations–governments, international funds and banks–into action on behalf of women; and it gave women access to mainstream decision-making. The innovative and catalytic role it plays is our third variable in analysing UNIFEM's impact on poverty.

UNIFEM's experience and effectiveness are impressive. As we saw earlier in this book, over a three-year period (1985–88) it attracted more than double its own investment in projects it assisted: two dollars or more for every dollar of its own. The country case studies and their analysis relate one continuous story of the Fund as catalyst. I will review some highlights.

ESAMI, the Eastern and Southern African Management Institute, experienced 'firsts' that transformed it as an inter-governmental institution. ESAMI was the first African management programme to raise women's issues in a sustained way. The women and development programme brought women to the campus for the first time as students or professional resource persons. The project attracted many other contributions, including $500 000 from UNDP. Impressively, ESAMI's enrolment of women went from less than one per cent to 30 per cent of all students during the early years of the programme.

Another inter-governmental organization, CILSS, with UNIFEM-financed senior staff person Jacqueline Ki-Zerbo, integrated governments' concerns for fuel-saving stoves into their energy-conservation policies in the Sahel. The project brought the stoves out of the kitchen to become a public concern and made ordinary women into experts. It attracted UNFSTD, UNSO, the World Bank and other funders. By 1993, Burkina Faso had 400 000 improved stoves. A third African inter-governmental organization, SADCC, held a Ministerial Conference on Women and Food Technology thanks to UNIFEM's women and food technologies (WAFT) project and its representative based in Zimbabwe. That Conference was followed by financing SADCC's own food technology officer.

Other experimental projects of the Africa Investment Plan proved catalytic: the Chorkor fish smoker was replicated in many countries and in Guinea it was instrumental in opening development resources to women. The national resource person's effectiveness took time but, after seven years, Burkina Faso produced a National Plan of Action for Strengthening Womens Roles in the Development Process, co-ordinated and monitored by an inter-ministerial group.

For the first time in Bolivian history, in the milk project, extension services not only went to women but women were hired as extension

257

workers. Rural women in Argentina became participants in the credit and training programmes of projects for the first time ever in 1987 when two projects reached out to a total of 53 000 families. The biogas project in the Yemen so intrigued people from government and academia that the University of Aden now offers an engineering course in renewable energy, emphasizing biogas. A biogas project was launched in Damascus, too.

The Laos textile ateliers attracted over $3 million from UNDP, CDF, Sweden, Austria and Belgium on the basis of Daw Aye's consultations with the national women's organization. Those discussions were financed by UNIFEM, as was the follow-up technical feasibility mission.

In Syria the government became the executing agency of a UN project for the very first time when UNIFEM offered $50 000 and leveraged five times that much from UNDP; in-kind support plus $85 000 from government; and then $263 000 from the Kuwaiti AGFUND, plus small contributions from UNFPA and the World Food Programme. The project got literacy and garment-making classes under way for rural women. The government continues to employ the 139 teachers who were trained (and in turn trained 2080 women in nine-month courses) and to finance the classes. The project created what has been cited as a most unusual and effective institutional partnership among government, the NGO/GUSW and the UN (UNDP and UNIFEM).

In India the Udaipur sericulture project had a multiplier effect in the project area itself–transforming 2500 families. It also captured the attention of the World Bank, which had seventeen sericulture projects with 70 000 rural people involved but which paid no attention to empowering women until it found that productivity was below the set target. When the Bank's India staff learned how the NGO Aastha had transformed the effectiveness of the Udaipur project they requested Aastha to train women from the Bank project as well.

The community revolving-loan fund in Swaziland legitimized women as users of credit not just within the project but nationwide; that about-face in attitude led other programmes and banks to open credit to women, and men became supportive of the initiative. When the RLF was given over to the Bank (SCSB) for management, it released four times its own value. In Colombia, banks loaned seven times the UNIFEM guarantee deposit. The success of those early credit funds not only permanently changed the approach to poor women from welfare to financial management but also resulted in UNIFEM's including loan systems in most of its projects thereafter.

Margaret Mwangola testified to UNIFEM as a catalyst for change: 'UNIFEM shared our risk, and that was most unusual for a UN agency. UNIFEM backed KWAHO at a crucial point in our formation'. She added that UNIFEM funding gave KWAHO status in the donor world 'and that has opened the door for us in numerous places, including UN agencies.'

Two final, important points. First, despite all the gains made by UNIFEM as catalyst and innovator, along with other concerned organizations, the need continues for a catalyst for change working with mainstream organizations on a case-by-case basis, as the Senegal study confirmed when it found a nearly total absence of consideration of women in mainstream projects, except in the social sector. Regretably, that finding is not unusual.

During my country visits my queries to the major funds about activities either directed specifically to or involving women were often met with anxious efforts to think of something; there was very little. A quarter-century of directives to international funding organizations has not yet been institutionalized. Such facts are not surprising when one reviews staffing: in 1985, UNDP had six women heading its developing country offices and in mid-1994 there were 12–of a total of 119![7] And at field level when UNIFEM does not have its own staff and depends on UNDP, it is with few exceptions that the youngest and least-experienced member of UNDP staff is assigned to monitor and assist activities concerned with women. That is not good enough. The only option is for UNIFEM to have its own staff specialists in countries; they make a far-ranging difference in the quality of the work.

My second point is a related one and worth re-emphasizing; it is about the scale of UNIFEM's investment when seeking to direct mainstream activities to women. Argentina is a case in point: a \$264 600 investment by UNIFEM influenced a \$20 million investment by IDB and IFAD. Similar situations prevailed in Oman and with the inter-governmental organizations CILSS and SADCC. In those cases the Fund's investment was most often in the hundreds of thousands of dollars. The point is that a token UNIFEM investment would have been useless. That reality has implications for the long-term future size of UNIFEM.

That completes our comparative analysis of the variables in activities assisted by UNIFEM. In the section that follows, I shall reach some conclusions and look into the future.

From risk to secure livelihoods

We know that the globalization of the economy, ethnic and racial strife and wars, and the economic adjustment measures prescribed for poor countries reach all the way down to the household and impose additional poverty and suffering on women. Cold statistics verify that statement: the number of rural women in poverty has nearly doubled in the past decade. Those realities underlie UNIFEM Director Noeleen Heyzer's call for 'a new ethics of global security based on secure livelihoods'. Heyzer sees UNI-FEM as 'a vehicle of change for sustainable livelihoods and women's empowerment'.[8]

One irony in the prevailing situation is that we try to salvage children without a commensurate concern for the women who are their mothers; we forget that if we help 100 000 women become self-reliant, we help 400 000 children.[9] A second irony is that in a world where no population group can remain uninfluenced by another, the chances of spreading war and disease from conditions of poverty and unemployment are very high. Yet we have neglected economic democracy while pursuing political democracy.

Economic security–secure livelihoods for all–must become our overriding and passionate concern.[10]

The profound failure to internalize the reasons for involving women in development decisions and programmes comes as no surprise when we recall that the international community continues to use economic models that fail to factor–in the most fundamental of all development goals: the quality of human life (which, not incidentally, can be quantitatively measured to a reasonable extent through social statistics if one so chooses). Development is still measured by the outdated concept of GNP growth alone, not by the creation of wealth for the sake of people's well-being.

UNIFEM offers an alternative model that generates economic growth while improving the quality of people's lives. The 'UNIFEM system', as India's Profulla Nagar called it, works just like that. It promotes access to productive resources, knowing that the income produced will be invested in better nutrition and education for the young. It does that by starting with women among the poor, and from their perspective, seeing the entire society.[11] Often working in partnership with major funds, non-governmental organizations and/or governments, UNIFEM has learned how to reach both small and very large groups of people. Thoraya Obaid praised that approach to women because 'it is not just conceptual, in plans of action or otherwise on paper, but it is operational'.[12] Mary Racelis saw the Fund as 'a real force' for women who don't have access to anything; it produced a model that gave them a very important entry-point.[13]

UNIFEM's record of achieving economic democracy contrasts sharply with those of many other organizations. More than twenty years after the women and development concept and movement began and organizations made political commitments to it, the large-scale funds seldom devise their development strategies from the perspective of the poor or act on the potential transformation of development that women offer. Attitudes die hard and bureaucratic attitudes are deeply embedded: despite clear proof to the contrary, the myth still persists that benefits of GNP growth will trickle down to the poor and to women. It is flagrant deception. History tells us that donors ought to look for results, and not be fooled by phrases about women that are written into project documents, and that are no guarantee that a project or programme will actually be enriched by women and their capacity to overcome poverty.

A human development conscience and 'how-to' resource such as UNIFEM embodies the capacity not only to correct that neglect but also to transform the end result of development itself. By risking change it has learned that the combination of expertise and a strategic investment of its own or as a partner with another fund, an NGO or a government, benefits the whole family, community and nation. Poor women themselves make that happen.

Vivian Mota described the vision of UNIFEM's founders as 'affirming the need to improve the quality of life through women. Their idea was not to separate men and women but to understand that as long as women remain poor, illiterate and powerless, the quality of life in the family and in society was not going to improve', she said.[14]

UNIFEM's experience has special importance today, when the donor country public is discouraged with the massive 'white elephant' projects of the past decades. Medium-scale investments offer a proven alternative; not only are the activities of manageable size but also half of them are executed by NGOs and most of them are about creating wealth, not just redistributing it. In addition, the Fund's areas of experience are of great international concern today: human development, environment, enterprise, technology, credit, food security. Thus UNIFEM experience, often gained at high risk, is arguably more useful than that of any other UN fund at this time.

Valuable lessons from UNIFEM's experience with empowering the poor have the potential for a far wider application; they rest on the premise of this book that the prevailing prescriptions for economic growth miss out on the vast potential for creating wealth that poor women represent. Those prescriptions are 'morally indefensible and economically absurd'[15] when tested alternative paradigms exist.

I conclude by identifying some of those lessons. They are set out in three groups: economic empowerment; social justice (human development); and sustainable institutions.

Economic empowerment

o When development policy for economic growth takes account of the potential productivity of the poor, starting with poor women, it can succeed over the long term. Enhancing people's access to productive resources to earn their own livelihoods also expands the consumer base and offsets the need to provide safety nets for those who have been made victims of unconscionable policies that destroy the social sector, the education and health of the present generation and the future work force.

Peggy Antrobus expressed deep concern over present trends: 'We are at different paradigms now. One is market-oriented economic growth, with privatization and structural adjustment . . . We realize that is leading us away from poverty alleviation, away from meeting people's needs, and more and more women are going to be left behind.'[16] Marva Alleyne urged that financial and technical resources be used in areas which 'give women clear indication of being able to alleviate poverty and give them a greater say in national decision-making.'[17]

o Economic growth can be achieved through through economic democracy when 'income-generating' activities are viewed as enterprises and turn a profit. That goal demands a standard of excellence in the transfer of technology, credit systems, management, market linkages and policy support. It calls for continuous and committed leadership and a multi-year duration of the investment at a scale which does not leave the participants begging instead of planting. The executing and co-operating agencies need more than goodwill; they need knowledge and experience.

To convert community development extension agents into business

261

and marketing advisers is as slow and difficult as transforming images of women from objects of welfare to productive agents. In fact it is better to distinguish between community and enterprise development. Until new agents are trained to give extension services on business and credit, projects will have to engage technical organizations and individuals for those tasks.

The International Coalition on Finance and Credit, and the Once and Future Consortium: Women, Science and Technology that UNIFEM supports can make those organizations strong vehicles of both the technical excellence and the policy change that I am advocating here.

○ Because women spend their earnings to lift their families from poverty, getting money into their hands is a proven investment not just in women but in human development. This finding is consistent with innumerable others; women almost inevitably re-invest their incomes in their children, in their homes and their productive activities.

The importance of income is intensified now, at a time when economic responsibility for the family is shifting from men to women and the number of female-headed households–at least a third of all households–is multiplying worldwide. When we add to that figure the numbers of households in which about half of the income is provided by women, the popular phrase that 'women supplement the family income' loses its validity.

Whether group or individual entrepreneurship is preferable depends upon local circumstances, but keeping ownership of productive assets with an individual woman or her family is often the best starting point. What we have seen is that co-operative purchasing and marketing can benefit small- and medium-scale producers even when productive responsibility is in the hands of individual women.

○ Research that situates projects in a wider environment that relates micro to macro, local to international, political and economic factors is the model for the future. When monitoring and evaluation reports also focus on that wider context they will make it possible to identify the supports and constraints of the village, country, and global political economy.

Social and personal empowerment

○ Women need more than income to improve the quality of life of their families and communities. Training for group participation and solidarity can have a transforming effect when it is combined with access to productivity-enhancing resources. Assistance that was most effective started with income and then became multi-faceted.

Women everywhere point to a specific moment in their lives when they became empowered: they agree that it was often the time when they were able to speak in public. Ela Bhatt's description was particularly poignant: Women who were afraid to speak their own names 'had nothing inside like their own identity' until they joined economic

262

organizations. 'I did it !' can be heard from the Philippines to Barbados and from Oman to India.

o Partnerships empower; partnerships between the illiterate and the educated; trilateral partnerships among politicians, NGOs and civil servants; partnerships among women and others who are marginalized by race, class, nationality, origins; partnerships between men and women. 'We are poor but we are many' must ring loudly in every woman's ears.

After a generation of the women and development movement, women now have more than a collection of NGOs or of networks; they have a strong and complex global system that can be tapped to create a transnational power system. UNIFEM has played a key role in that network-building and in creating cadres of leaders of popular movements and other development organizations over the years; many of them are now at the cutting edge of development thinking. That is one of the most important roles of a women-specific institution.

o Women are poised to intensify their political participation at all levels. As we have seen, the best of projects cannot escape the harsh effects of external political and economic factors at transnational and national levels that are outside the projects' control but strongly influence their effectiveness. New agendas and new paradigms can be created to conquer poverty when women's voices join the decision-makers. We have seen the types of linkages that women's economic groups can have with their governments, to influence policy; more of that influence is necessary and possible.

Sustainable institutions

o Governments have central roles in attacking poverty and promoting development in poor countries where the private sector is as yet weak or non-existent. International bankers judge that government protection of nascent national industries took many effective forms in the growing East Asian economies.[18] Influencing government policy and practice is thus key to attacking poverty in a broad-based way.

National machineries in the governmental sector have achieved a great deal in the face of unbelievable resource constraints, and they have learned to focus on specific, attainable goals. With continuous institutional support, these machineries, together with NGOs, trade unions, co-operatives, and other grassroots groups and research organizations can transform development.

o The futile and distracting debate over 'women-specific versus integrated (mainstream)' activities and institutions can be put to rest permanently. Both are required. Sustainable women-specific groups and institutions continue to be essential not only to empower but also to generate policies, and public and private actions to eliminate poverty, to 'prevent slippage' from those commitments, to train cadres for mainstream institutions, and to avoid the co-option of resources intended for women by powerful organizations that will not in fact use those scarce resources

most responsibly for women. As was said in UNIFEM's Forward Looking Assessment: there is a clear danger that the resources, rather than the
women, will be 'integrated' or 'mainstreamed'.

Economist Sundarshan confirmed that notion from a man's perspective: 'Often you may have the most sensitive of bureaucrats, who go for
gender-sensitizing courses and will be able to hold forth on women's
concerns. But there is a whole world view, and no gender-sensitizing
course can substitute for knowing what it is to be a woman.'[19]

○ Hard evidence shatters our dream that organizations like the World
Bank, UN and bilateral agencies will in the near future adopt a holistic
view of development that transforms their lending practices into human-
centred ones that recognize women as half of productive humanity.
Women's units in those organizations do heroic work but they have
only small victories. Administrators and experts, still mostly men, still
don't know how to involve women. (Every programme or project design
team should be composed of 40–60 per cent women experts; a stronger
UNIFEM can make that possible).

Those organizations still need strong influence from outside as well as
inside; UNIFEM is strategically placed in the multilateral family of
organizations to wield such influence and continue the UN's role as
the principal advocate and guardian of the global women and development movement. The implication here is that, if economic development
is to be achieved, some of the taxpayers' money that has until now been
entrusted to the larger funds and banks will have to be put under
women's management.

○ The power of global economic institutions such as transnational corporations and the Bretton Woods lending organizations speaks to women's
need for an economic power centre of their own to create wealth and to
leverage their fair share of existing wealth. An empowered UNIFEM
could establish a credit institution that might also operate internationally
as a savings bank to promote individual and family business as well as
co-operative enterprise.

○ Because it is a proven catalyst, risk-taker and innovator in the battle
against world poverty, with full autonomy and enough resources to have
clout, UNIFEM can play a global role such as UNICEF does for children
and UNFPA for population. That role demands a size that is adequate to
meet the needs of women and to fully utilize the Fund's proven
capability. Because women use money well does not mean that they
need little of it; it means that they should have enough of it to transform
society. In addition, the value of innovative and experimental activities
will persist as long as human societies exist.

With the exception of its innovative experiments, UNIFEM's investments need to be of a scale and duration to build sustainable institutions
and effect lasting change. In the case of partnerships with mainstream
funds, the UNIFEM investment must be of a size commensurate with the
size of the task of transforming the project. Put another way: bread will

not rise without enough yeast.

'We have marginalized the women's issue for so long . . . it has never had a central focus', says Catherine Mwanamwambwa. 'It is not enough to do a conference every five years; women as a central issue should be addressed at all levels. We must have structure.'[20] A power centre.

'UNIFEM's success will depend on how sensitive it is to the pulse of the people, on whether it speaks the language of the people or the language of New York' says Obaid. With a rich experience of listening to grassroots women, UNIFEM can increase opportunities for women's voices to be heard. As a global power-centre it can be the human development conscience of the major funds and a 'how-to' resource to promote that goal in addition to building women's solidarity groups. It is women themselves who will act upon the three priorities that were most often cited during my interviews over the past two years: education, economic empowerment, and political participation. With them, UNIFEM can help to create the world's agenda, not just follow it. One condition for effectiveness was wisely pointed out: the availability of resources is critical because you have to have a certain level of resources for people to take you seriously.

This book's major thesis has been that the experience in development co-operation with women provides a basis for reversing global poverty trends, thereby fostering self-reliance and increasing the prospects of global security. UNIFEM seeks to meet the needs of women and families through a broad-based access to the means of creating wealth, and deciding on its disposition, not just redistributing it. That is what I mean by economic democracy and the transformation of development. Isn't it worth a try?

Annexes

Annexe 1: Resolution adopted by the General Assembly
31/133. Voluntary Fund for the United Nations Decade for Women

The General Assembly,

Recalling its resolution 3520 (XXX) of 15 December 1975, in which it proclaimed the period from 1976 to 1985 United Nations Decade for Women: Equality, Development and Peace,

Recalling also that it decided at its thirtieth session that the voluntary fund for the International Women's Year, established by Economic and Social Council resolution 1850 (LVI) of 16 May 1974, should be extended to cover the period of the Decade,[1]

Aware that some countries, particularly the least developed ones, have limited financial resources for carrying out their national plans and programmes for the advancement of women and for the implementation of the World Plan of Action for the Implementation of the Objectives of the International Women's Year[2] adopted by the World Conference of the International Women's Year, held at Mexico City from 19 June to 2 July 1975,

Recognizing the necessity for continuing financial and technical support for these programmes,

Having considered the report of the Secretary-General on the Voluntary Fund for the Decade,[3]

1. *Adopts* the following criteria and arrangements for the management of the Voluntary Fund for the United Nations Decade for Women:

   (a) **Criteria:**
   The resources of the Fund should be utilized to supplement activities in the following areas designed to implement the goals of the United Nations Decade for Women: Equality, Development and Peace, priority being given to the related programmes and projects of the least developed, land-locked and island countries among developing countries:
   (i) Technical co-operation activities;
   (ii) Development and/or strengthening of regional and international programmes;
   (iii) Development and implementation of joint interorganizational programmes;
   (iv) Research, data collection and analysis, relevant to (i), (ii) and (iii) above;

(v) Communication support and public information activities designed to promote the goals of the Decade and, in particular, the activities undertaken under (i), (ii) and (iii) above;

(vi) In the selection of projects and programmes, special consideration should be given to those which benefit rural women, poor women in urban areas and other marginal groups of women, especially the disadvantaged;

(b) Arrangements:

The General Assembly endorses the arrangements for the future management of the Fund contained in the annex to the present resolution;

2. *Requests* the Secretary-General to consult the Administrator of the United Nations Development Programme on the use of the Fund for technical co-operation activities;

3. *Requests* the President of the General-Assembly to select, with due regard to regional distribution, in the first instance for a period of three years, five Member States, each of which should appoint a representative to serve on the Consultative Committee on the Voluntary Fund for the United Nations Decade for Women to advise the Secretary-General on the application to the use of the Fund of the criteria set forth in paragraph 1 above;

4. *Requests* the Secretary-General to report annually to the General Assembly on the management of the Fund.

102nd plenary meeting
16 December 1976

---

[1] See *Official Records of the General Assembly, Thirtieth Session, Supplement No. 34* (A/10034), p.100, items 75 and 76.

[2] *Report of the World Conference of the International Women's Year* (United Nations publication, Sales No. E.76.IV.1), chap. II, sect. A.

[3] E/5773.

ANNEXE
Arrangements for the management of the
Voluntary Fund for the United Nations Decade for Women

1. The Secretary-General shall apply the following arrangements for the management of the Voluntary Fund for the United Nations Decade for Women:

I. Solicitiation and Acknowledgement of Pledges and the
Collection of Contributions

2. The Controller, in consultation with the Under-Secretary-General for Economic and Social Affairs and the Assistant Secretary-General for

Social Development and Humanitarian Affairs, shall determine the responsibility and procedures for soliciting voluntary contributions to the Fund.

3. Any prospective donor desiring to make a voluntary contribution to the Fund shall submit a written proposal to the Secretary-General; the request for acceptance should contain all relevant information, including the amount of the proposed contribution, the currency and the timing of payments, and may indicate the purposes and any action expected of the United Nations.

4. The proposal, with the comments, inter alia, of the Under-Secretary-General for Economic and Social Affairs and the Assistant Secretary-General for Social Development and Humanitarian Affairs, shall be forwarded to the Controller, who shall determine whether or not any proposed gift or donation might directly or indirectly involve additional financial liability for the Organization. Before acceptance of any gift or donation involving such liability, the Controller shall request and obtain the approval of the General Assembly through the Advisory Committee on Administrative and Budgetary Questions.

5. The Contoller shall acknowledge all pledges and shall determine the bank account or accounts in which contributions to the Fund should be deposited; he shall be responsible for collecting contributions and following up on payments of contributions pledged.

6. The Controller may accept contributions in any national currency donated for the purpose of the Fund.

II. Operations and Control

7. The Controller shall ensure that the operation and control of the Fund shall be in accordance with the Financial Regulations and Rules of the United Nations; he may delegate responsibility for the operation and administration of the Fund to the heads of departments or offices designated by the Secretary-General to execute activities financed by the Fund; only officials so designated may authorize the execution of specific activities to be financed by the Fund.

8. Subject to the criteria for disbursements from the Fund endorsed by the General Assembly, the Controller may, after consultation with the Department of Economic and Social Affairs, allocate resources of the Fund to a specialized agency or another United Nations body for the execution of projects financed by the Fund; in such an event, the administrative procedures of the executing body would apply, subject to such provisions for periodic reporting as the Controller may specify. Before making disbursements for technical co-operation activities, the Controller should consult the Administrator of the United Nations Development Programme.

9. In respect of activities conducted by the United Nations, requests for allotments of Funds shall be submitted to the Controller by the Department of Economic and Social Affairs, accompanied by such supporting information as the Controller may require. After review,

allotments to provide for expenditures of the funds received shall be issued by the Director of the Budget Division, and certifying officers for the Fund shall be designated by the Controller in accordance with established procedures.

10. The Controller shall be responsible for the reporting of all financial transactions concerning the Fund and shall issue quarterly statements of assets, liabilities and unencumbered Fund balance, income and expenditure.

11. The Fund shall be audited by both the Internal Audit Service and the Board of Auditors, in accordance with the Financial Regulations and Rules of the United Nations.

III. REPORTING

12. An annual report showing funds available, pledges and payments received and the expenditures made from the Fund shall be prepared by the Controller and submitted to the General Assembly and, as appropriate, to the Commission on the Status of Women.

Annexe 2: Resolution adopted by the General Assembly

39/125. Future arrangements for the management of the Voluntary Fund for the United Nations Decade for Women

The General Assembly,

Recalling its resolution 31/133 of 16 December 1976, containing the criteria and arrangements for the management of the Voluntary Fund for the United Nations Decade for Women,

Recalling also its resolution 36/129 of 14 December 1981, in which it decided that the Fund should continue its activities beyond the United Nations Decade for Women: Equality, Development and Peace,

Stressing the urgency of determining at its current session the most effective arrangements for continuing the activities of the Fund beyond the Decade in view of the need for ensuring the long-term stability of the Fund,

Recalling further its resolution 38/106 of 16 December 1983, in which, inter alia, it decided that, when considering the reports of the Secretary-General on the future of the Fund, all possible options would be reviewed in depth,

Reaffirming that the Fund has a unique contribution to make to the achievement of the goals of the Third United Nations Development Decade, and even beyond it,

Recognizing the important actual and potential contribution by women to development, as evidenced in the forward-looking assessment of the activities assisted by the Fund and the crucial role of the Fund as a specialized resource base for development co-operation, and the need for continued assistance to activities directly benefiting women,

Considering it, accordingly, to be of paramount importance to establish a future organizational framework that will secure the ability of the Fund to act as a catalytic agent on the main United Nations development co-operation system,

Considering also the innovative and experimental activities of the Fund directed to strengthening both governmental and non-governmental institutional capacities to ensure access for women to development co-operation resources and their full participation at all levels in the development process,

Stressing that general questions of development and access of women to development resources have, as a common objective, to create conditions which will improve the quality of life for all,

Welcoming the completion of the forward-looking assessment of the activities assisted by the Fund and the findings and conclusions with regard to women and development and their implications for technical co-operation agencies and organizations,[1]

Conscious of the highly specialized professional competence of the Fund in the area of development activities for women and the need for strengthening that competence,

Aware of the broad range of linkages of the Fund with national Governments, national women's groups, non-governmental organizations and women's research institutes, besides its close co-operation with United Nations development agencies, including the regional commissions,

Taking into consideration the moderate size of the Fund and its continued need to draw on the operational capacity of other agencies and, in this regard, expressing its appreciation to the United Nations Development Programme for its continuing technical and resource assistance to the Fund,

Expressing appreciation to the Department of International Economic and Social Affairs of the Secretariat and its Centre for Social Development and Humanitarian Affairs for their contribution to the work of the Fund during its initial operational years,

Taking note of the reports of the Consultative Committee on the Voluntary Fund for the United Nations Decade for Women on its fifteenth and sixteenth sessions, referred to in the report of the Secretary-General,[2]

Taking note also of the reports of the Secretary-General on the Fund,[3]

1. *Decides* that the activities of the Voluntary Fund for the United Nations Decade for Women shall be continued through establishment of a separate and identifiable entity in autonomous association with the United Nations Development Programme, which will play an innova-

tive and catalytic role in relation to the United Nations over-all system of development co-operation;

2. *Endorses* the modalities for the future management arrangements between the Fund and the United Nations Development Programme, as contained in the annex to the present resolution, and decides that these arrangements shall enter into force at the latest on 1 January 1986;

3. *Reaffirms* the criteria laid down in its resolution 31/133 on the use of the resources of the Fund and the guidelines established on the advice of the Consultative Committee on the Voluntary Fund for the United Nations Decade for Women, emphasizing the use of these resources for technical co-operation benefiting women;

4. *Requests* the Consultative Committee at its seventeenth session, to propose an appropriate future title for the Fund;

5. *Stresses* the need for close and continuous working relationships between the Fund and the bodies, organs and organizations of the United Nations system concerned with women's issues and development co-operation, in particular with the Department of International Economic and Social Affairs of the Secretariat and its Centre for Social Development and Humanitarian Affairs;

6. *Expresses its appreciation* for the contributions to the Fund made by Governments and non-governmental organizations, which have a vital role to play in maintaining and increasing the financial viability of the Fund and the effectiveness of its work;

7. *Notes with concern* that contributions to the Fund have not been sufficient to enable it to respond to all the deserving requests for technical assistance that it has received;

8. *Urges*, accordingly, Governments to continue and, where possible, to increase their contributions to the Fund, and calls upon those Governments that have not yet done so to consider contributing to the Fund;

9. *Requests* the Secretary-General, after consultation with the Consultative Committee at its seventeenth session, to report to the General Assembly at its fortieth session on the arrangements he has made with the Administrator of the United Nations Development Programme for the future of the Fund;

10. *Requests* that the Consultative Committee monitor the process of implementing the arrangements for the management of the Fund contained in the annex to the present resolution and that the Committee's views on this matter be reflected fully in the annual report on the Fund to the General Assembly, particularly in its initial years.

101st plenary meeting
14 December 1984

[1] See A/39/569, sect. II.

ANNEXE

Arrangements for the management of the ( ) Fund

1. The (name) Fund (acronym), hereinafter referred to as "the Fund", is hereby established as a separate and identifiable entity in autonomous association with the United Nations Development Programme. The Administrator of the United Nations Development Programme, here-inafter referred to as "the Administrator", shall be accountable for all aspects of the management and operations of the Fund. There shall be a Consultative Committee to advise the Administrator on all policy matters relating to the activities of the Fund in accordance with paragraph 13 below. The following arrangements for the management of the Fund shall apply:

I. TRANSFER OF EXISTING RESOURCES, SOLICITATION AND ACKNOWLEDGEMENT OF PLEDGES AND COLLECTION OF CONTRIBUTIONS

2. The Voluntary Fund for the United Nations Decade for Women and its subsidiary Supplementary Trust Fund, which was established by a memorandum of understanding between the Secretary-General of the United Nations and the Administrator on 25 June 1980, are hereby liquidated and their assets transferred to the Fund.

3. Governments, intergovernmental and non-governmental organizations and other donors may contribute to the Fund.

4. The Fund shall be included among the programmes for which funds are pledged at the annual United Nations Pledging Conference for Devel-opment Activities. The Administrator shall assist with the mobilization of financial resources for the Fund. The contributions to the Fund and the bank accounts into which they are deposited shall be in accordance with the applicable Financial Regulations and Rules of the United Nations Development Programme.

II. OPERATIONS AND CONTROL

5. All operations of the Voluntary Fund for the United Nations Decade for Women are hereby transferred to the Fund.

6. The Administrator, in consultation with the Consultative Committee on the Voluntary Fund for the United Nations Decade for Women, shall appoint a Director of the Fund, hereinafter referred to as "the Director", bearing in mind the relevant qualifications and experience with technical co-operation, including those benefiting women. The Administrator shall appoint the staff of the Fund in consultation with

the Director, pursuant to the Staff Regulations of the United Nations and the relevant provisions of the Charter of the United Nations.

7. The Administrator shall delegate the management of the Fund and its administration, including responsibility for the mobilization of resources, to the Director, who shall have the authority to conduct all matters related to its mandate and who shall be accountable directly to the Administrator.

8. The operations of the Fund shall be conducted taking into account the innovative and catalytic nature of its development co-operation activities for women and its existing criteria and operational procedures. The present procedures of the Fund, including those governing the identification, formulation, approval, appraisal, execution and evaluation of projects established in accordance with the requirements set out in the criteria adopted by the General Assembly in its resolution 31/133 and on the advice of the Consultative Committee, shall remain in force. Subject to the provisions of this annex, the regulations, rules and directives of the United Nations Development Programme shall be applied to the operations of the Fund.

9. The resources of the Fund shall be used mainly within two priority areas: first, to serve as a catalyst, with the goal of ensuring the appropriate involvement of women in mainstream development activities, as often as possible at the pre-investment stages; secondly, to support innovative and experimental activities benefiting women in line with national and regional priorities. Fund resources should be a supplement to and not a substitute for the mandated responsibilities of other United Nations development co-operation organizations and agencies, including the United Nations Development Programme.

10. All the administrative and programme support costs of the Fund shall be met from its own resources.

11. The regional bureaux, other organizational units and field offices of the United Nations Development Programme shall continue to assist the operations of the Fund, inter-alia by joint programming missions to ensure the involvement of women in technical co-operation activities financed by the United Nations Development Programme and by supporting the project cycle activities of projects financed by the Fund. For its part, the Fund shall participate in existing machineries for co-ordination of technical co-operation at headquarters and field levels.

12. The proposed biennial budget for the administrative costs of the Fund shall be reviewed initially by the Consultative Committee prior to its submission by the Administrator for approval by the Governing Council of the United Nations Development Programme.

III. The Consultative Committee and the Relationship of the Fund to Other Organizations

13. The President of the General Assembly shall designate, with due regard for the financing of the Fund from voluntary contributions

and to equitable geographical distribution, five Member States to serve on the Consultative Committee for a period of three years. Each State member of the Consultative Committee shall designate a person with relevant expertise and experience in development co-operation activities, including those benefiting women, to serve on the Committee. The Committee shall advise the Administrator on all matters of policy affecting the activities of the Fund, including the application of the criteria set forth by the General Assembly in respect of the use of the Fund.

14. The Fund shall establish and maintain close and continuous working relationships with other United Nations organs, in particular the Department of International Economic and Social Affairs of the Secretariat and its Centre for Social Development and Humanitarian Affairs, the regional commissions, the United Nations Children's Fund, the United Nations Fund for Population Activities and the International Research and Training Institute for the Advancement of Women, as well as through the Administrative Committee on Co-ordination and with the specialized agencies and other United Nations entities concerned, in particular the International Fund for Agricultural Development. Co-operation shall also be established for the sharing of information with the Commission on the Status of Women and other relevant global and regional intergovernmental bodies concerned with development and with women. As appropriate, the activities of the Fund may be drawn to the attention of the Committee on the Elimination of Discrimination against Women.

IV. REPORTING AND AUDITING

15. The Director shall prepare substantive and financial progress reports on the use of the Fund for the Administrator to submit to the Consultative Committee.

16. Taking into account the advice of the Consultative Committee, the Administrator shall submit to the Governing Council of the United Nations Development Programme an annual report on the operations, management and budget of the Fund. He shall submit a similar report to the General Assembly, to be referred to the Second Committee for consideration of its technical co-operation aspects and also to the Third Committee.

17. The Commission on the Status of Women shall also be provided with the annual reports referred to in paragraph 16 above.

18. The Administrator shall be responsible for reporting all the financial transactions of the Fund and shall issue annual financial statements in accordance with the Financial Regulations and Rules of the United Nations Development Programme.

19. The Fund shall be subject to the internal and external auditing procedures provided for under the financial regulations, rules and directives of the United Nations Development Programme.

Annexe 3: National committees for UNIFEM*, 1993

AUSTRALIA
Beverly Perel

GERMANY
Annelies Muller

SWEDEN
Ulla Jonsdotter

BELGIUM
Lily Boeykens

ICELAND
Sigridur Lilly Baldursdottir

SWISS/LIECHTENSTEIN
Danielle Bridel

CANADA
Valerie Hume

JAPAN
Mitchiko Nakamura

UNITED KINGDOM
Thelma Leeuw

DENMARK
Annette Winther

NEW ZEALAND
Mary Sinclair

UNITED STATES
Hope S. Miller

FINLAND
Eila Kivekas

NORWAY
Elin Bruusgaard

WORLD UNIFEM
Helvi Sipila

FRANCE
Danièle Refuveille

PHILIPPINES
Erlinda J. Villanueva

* Committees forming:
Ireland, Italy, Luxembourg,
the Netherlands, Portugal,
Spain

Annexe 4: Founding Members of the NGO Advisory Committee on UNIFEM

Convener: Claire Fulcher (IFBPW)
Recording Secretary: Anne Yedowitz (Soroptimist)
Treasurer: Margaret Corey (WAGGGS)
Corresponding Secretary: Doris Vaughn (ZI)

American Association of Retired Persons (AARP)	Virginia Hazzard
Associated Country Women of the World (ACWW)	Mildred Talbot
	Eleanor Roberts
Bahai International Community (BIC)	Mary S. Power
Int. Alliance of Women (IAW)	Kay Fraleigh
Int. Council of Women (ICW)	Emma Broisman
	Dorothy Willner
Int. Fed. of Business and Professional Women (IFBPW)	Claire Fulcher
	Esther Hymer
Int. Fed. of Home Economics (IFHE)	Ruth Norman
Int. Fed. of University Women (IFUW)	Virginia Maynard
Int. Fed. of Settlements and Neighbourhoods Centres	Carol Lubin
Int. Institute of Rural Reconstruction (IIRR)	Pam Levin
Int. Society for Community Development (ISCD)	Mildred Leet
Pan-Pacific Southeast Asia Women's Association	Leoni Pynappel
(PPSEAWA)	Terry Singh
Society for International Development (SID)	Caroline Pezzullo
Soroptimist International (SI)	Anne Yedowitz
World Association of Girl Guides/Girl Scouts (WAGGGS)	Margaret Corey
World Union Of Catholic Women's Organizations (WUCWO)	Alba Zizzamia
World Union for Progressive Judaism (WUPJ)	Norma Levitt
World Young Women's Christian Association (WYWCA)	Mildred Persinger
	Mildred Jones
Zonta International (ZI)	Doris Vaughn

Annexe 5: Members of the Consultative Committee, 1977–93

YEAR	SESSION	COUNTRY & REPRESENTATIVE
1977	1st 2nd 3rd	Philippines, Mrs. Leticia R. Shahani, Chair German DR, Mr. Horst Keilau Jamaica, Dr. Lucille Mair Nigeria, Mr. Bayo Ayeni UK, Dr. Teresa Spens
1978	4th	(Not available)
1979	5th	German DR, Mr. Horst Keilau, Chair UK, Dr. Teresa Spens, Rapporteur Jamaica, Miss Marcella Alexandra Martinez Nigeria, Miss Olajumoke Oladayo Obafemi Philippines, Mr. Josue L. Villa
	6th	GDR: Dr. Rolf Lammerzahl replaces Mr. Keilau Jamaica: Ms. Evadne Coye replaces Miss Martinez Nigeria: Mr. A.E. Bayo Ayeni joins Miss Obafemi Philippines: Ms. Caroline Villa replaces Mr. Villa
1980	7th	German DR, Dr. Rolf Lammerzahl, Chair India, Mr. T.C.A. Rangachari Jamaica, Ms. R.V. Evadne Coye Nigeria, Ms. Olajumoke Oladayo Obafemi UK, Dr. Teresa Spens
	8th	Same
1981	9th	German DR, Dr. Rolf Lammerzahl, Chair India, Mr. T.C.A. Rangachari Jamaica, Ms. R.V. Evadne Coye Nigeria, Ms. Olajumoke Oladayo Obafemi UK, Dr. Teresa Spens
	10th	Jamaica: Jennifer Sharpe replaced Ms. Coye
1982	11th	India, Mr. T.C.A. Rangachari, Chair GDR, Mr. Norbert Poerschke Jamaica, Ms. Maureen Stephenson-Vernon Nigeria, Mr. John O. Aje UK, Dr. Teresa Spens
	12th	Jamaica: Ms. Ava Mignott replaced Ms. Stephenson-Vernon
1983	13th	India: Mr. T.C.A. Rangachari, Chair GDR: Mr. Norbert Poerschke Jamaica, Ms. Ava Mignott Kenya, Ms. Rose Arungu-Olende

1983 (Cont.)	14th	Norway, Ms. Range Birte Lund Jamaica: Ms. Ava Mignott, Chair GDR: Mr. Norbert Poerschke India: Mr. Rajendra S. Rathore Kenya: Ms. Rose Arungu-Olende Norway: Ms. Bjorg Leite
1984	15th	Jamaica: Ava Mignott, Chair GDR: Mr. Norbert Poerschke India: Rajendra S. Rathore Kenya: Ms. Rose Arungu-Olende Norway: Ms. Bjorg Leite
	16th	Jamaica: Ms. Patricia Durrant replaces Ms. Mignott as Chair India: Mr. Banbit A. Roy replaces Mr. Rathore Norway: Ms. Cecilie Landsverk deputises for Ms. Leite
1985	17th	Jamaica: Ms. Ava Mignott, Chair GDR: Mr. Norbert Poerschke India: Mr. Kumwar Bahadur Srivastava Kenya: Ms. Rose Arungu-Olende Norway: Ms. Bjorg Leite
	18th	India: Mr. Arif Khan replaces Mr. Srivastava
1986	19th	Kenya: Ms. Rose Arungu-Olende, Chair Colombia: Dr. Fanny Umana GDR: Dr. Norbert Poerschke India: Mr. Arif Khan Norway: Ms. Bjorg Leite
	20th	Same
1987	21st	Kenya: Ms. Rose Arungu-Olende, Chair Colombia: Dr. Fanny Umana GDR: Dr. Norbert Poerschke India: Ms. Bhaswati Mukherjee Norway: Ms. Bjorg Leite
	22nd	GDR: Mr. Heinz Duehring replaces Dr. Poerschke
1988	23rd	Kenya: Ms. Rose Arungu-Olende, Chair Colombia: Dr. Fanny Umana GDR: Mr. John Ruediger India: Ms. Bhaswati Mukherjee Norway: Mr. Baard Hopland and Ms. Ingeborg Stofring
	24th	India: Mr. Virendra Gupta replaces Ms. Mukherjee Norway: Ms. Bjorg Leite replaces both Mr. Hopland and Ms. Stofring
1990	27th	India: Sujata Mehta, Chair Netherlands: Ms. Susan Blankhard

277

1990 (Cont.)		Senegal: Khardiata Lo Ndiaye GDR: Mr. John Ruediger Mexico: Ms. Margarita Dieguez Armas
	28th	GDR departs the committee. Bulgaria: Mr. Peter Kolarov
1991	29th	India: Sujata Mehta, Chair Bulgaria: Mr. Peter Kolarov Netherlands: Ms. Susan Blankhart Mexico: Ms. Margarita Dieguez Armas Senegal: Ms. Khardiata Lo Ndiaye
	30th	
1992	31st	Bahamas: A.Missouri Sherman-Peter, Chair Denmark: Ms. Ulla Lehmann Nielsen Poland: Ms. Eva Calczynska Indonesia: Ani Santhoso Uganda: Ms. Rosemary Semafumu
	32nd	
1993	33rd	Bahamas: A. Missouri Sherman-Peter, Chair Denmark: Ms. Ulla Lehmann Nielsen Poland: Ms. Eva Calczynska Indonesia: Mr. Achie Luhulima Uganda: Ms. Rosemary Semafumu

Annexe 6: Testimonials of world leaders on the occasion of UNIFEM's tenth anniversary, 1987

"The Tenth Anniversary of UNIFEM presents a welcome opportunity for us to join our voices with the millions of women in the world and salute the fine contributions which this new Development Fund of the United Nations has made to the poorest countries, through its innovative programmes. Further, we wish UNIFEM continued success in its recognition of the roles of women in the struggle for development."

Abdou Diouf, President of the Republic of Senegal

"The work of UNIFEM is important for women as well as for the economic future of all developing countries and indeed, for all those who believe that people should have the opportunity to create an economic future for themselves, their families, and their nations."

Corazon Aquino, President of the Republic of the Philippines

"The integration and full participation of women in the development process are fundamental requirements for progress: objectives which UNIFEM has so effectively promoted in the developing countries over the decade of its existence. I appreciate its significant role and hope that UNIFEM, in performance of its responsibilities, would be contributing to the efforts to ensure a better future for the women of the world and all its peoples."

Hussain Muhammad Ershad, President of the People's Republic of Bangladesh

"In order to obtain justice and well-being for all it is essential to insure full participation of men and women in the development process of their countries, especially among the poorest sectors of the population. Recognition of the role of women in this process is a priority issue for the Colombian Government. In its first ten years of existence, UNIFEM has helped to promote this recognition. The solemn celebration of the Fund's Tenth Anniversary during the Forty-Second Session of the General Assembly is a well-deserved tribute to UNIFEM. I hope that this occasion will encourage the international community to redouble its efforts to strengthen the work of the Fund."

Virgilio Barco, President of Colombia

"I greatly welcome UNIFEM's continuing efforts to encourage a strong commitment of development funds to projects which benefit women as well as men and send my congratulations on its Tenth Anniversary."

Margaret Thatcher, Prime Minister of the United Kingdom of Great Britain and Northern Ireland

"The UN Development Fund for Women has helped women around the world become economically self reliant. The Fund has played a catalytic role in designing and promoting programmes for women. It is the only Fund of its kind which is mandated to serve the needs, specifically, of women."

Rajiv Ghandhi, Prime Minister of India.

"In a world where the importance of women and their contributions to development is so easily neglected, I see UNIFEM as a unique instrument for strengthening the position of women in the developing world and for the practical realization of their potentials."

Gro Harlem Brundtland, Prime Minister of Norway

"It is the unique achievement of UNIFEM that it constantly reminds us that women, all over the world, have a legitimate right to participate in and to benefit from the economic and social achievement of their countries. The crucial role of women, in this respect, is demonstrated in numerous countries by the projects initiated by UNIFEM."

Yvonne van Rooy, Minister for Foreign Trade, The Netherlands

"On this occasion of the Tenth Anniversary of UNIFEM, I would like to offer my congratulations on your efforts to increase attention to women in development. I share your commitment and wish you success in the future."

Barber B. Conable, President, The World Bank

279

"UNIFEM stands as a beacon of hope for all the world's women. No project is too small – or too large – for UNIFEM to tackle when it comes to drawing women into development activities. Entering its second decade, UNIFEM will continue to inspire and encourage creative use of all human potential."

Nancy Landon Kassebaum, United States Senator

"We highly appreciate the unique role played by UNIFEM over the last ten years in providing financial support for various development projects focusing on particularly the promotion of women's participation in the self-reliant efforts of many countries. We hope that UNIFEM's activities will be enhanced so as to make a greater contribution to the advancement of women, particularly to the full and effective participation of women in development."

Mayumi Moriyama, Chairperson of the Standing Committee on Foreign Affairs, House of Councillors, Head of the Japanese Delegation to the World Women's Conference in Nairobi

"UNIFEM, an outstanding achievement of the UN Decade for Women, has stimulated a global effort for the advancement of women, so that they, together with men, can commit their creative energies to the quest for global peace, stability, and the well-being of all our peoples."

"I congratulate UNIFEM on their valuable contribution to the full development of our human resources and anticipate its even more successful future."

Senator Jeannette Grant Woodham,
Minister of State in the Ministry of Foreign Affairs, Trade and Industry,
Jamaica

"The delegation of Barbados believes the United Nations Development Fund for Women (UNIFEM) is a valuable support in the development of women's potential. It requires considerable increase in funding if it is to carry out its mandate. It is to be hoped that there will be an increase in contributions of Member States despite other calls upon their resources. We welcome the progress made in the preparation of regional priority strategies and support the recommendation of the Consultative Committee to establish a UNIFEM presence at the sub-regional level.

"We believe that this tiered approach will help in the efficient implementation of the Fund's mandate and facilitate the presentation and implementation of valuable projects from Member States. This will only be possible if a serious attempt is made by Member States to increase their contributions."

Dame Ruth Nita Barrow, Permanent Representative of Barbados to the UN

"On behalf of the Ford Foundation, I offer congratulations to UNIFEM as it celebrates its Tenth Anniversary. Your work empowers the poor women of the developing world, and, by providing such critical resources as technology, training and credit for small businesses, recognizes the pivotal role women play in the economic life of their countries. Your contribution rests not only in your support of specific projects but also in the vision you hold up to all of us of a world in which the productive capacity of every human being can be realized. Best wishes for UNIFEM's continued success."

Franklin A. Thomas, President, Ford Foundation

"In the extreme poverty of the poorest regions, women are still the most deprived. Since its creation, UNIFEM has been taking specific development actions on behalf and with which women are closely associated.

"The successes already obtained are not sufficient. A lot still remains to be achieved so that women can gain a certain level of knowledge and a minimum of resources which will enable them to fulfill the role that is theirs.

"That is the condition for success of any development policy."

Simone Weil of France

"We cannot afford to waste half our human resources. My guess would be that investments in basic education for girls probably produce the biggest benefits per dollar spent. If we are going to win the race for survival, then – all at the same time – we must learn to count women, and we must learn to make women count, and we must learn to count on women."

Maggie Catley Carson, President, Canadian International Development Association (CIDA)

"The Associated Country Women of the World congratulates UNIFEM on its 10th Anniversary celebration and looks forward to the possibility of working constructively together to improve the status and living conditions of women and their families worldwide."

Jennifer Pearce, General Secretary, Associated Country Women of the World

Annexe 7: Source table for country statistics

Statistical data come from sources listed below unless otherwise indicated on particular country table. Where data were not available, country table shows 'na.'

Source Table		Source	Date Data Collected
Demographics	Population	Wistat	1995 projected
	% rural	Wistat	1995 projected
	% urban	Wistat	1995 projected
Income	GNP per capita	World Bank, Table 1, 1992	
	% in absolute poverty*	UNDP, Table 18, 1980–90	
	% of rural population	UNDP, Table 18, 1980–90	
	% of urban population	UNDP, Table 18, 1980–90	
Health	Life expectancy	Wistat	1990–1995 projected
	Infant mortality	Wistat	1990–1995 projected
	Maternal mortality	Wistat	Latest, no earlier than 1986
	Access to safe water	Wistat	1990–1992
Education	Illiteracy of women and men	Wistat	1991
	Girls as % of boys in secondary school	Wistat	Latest, no earlier than 1985
	Girls as % of boys in tertiary school	Wistat	Latest, no earlier than 1986
	Girls as % of tertiary science/engineering students	Wistat	Latest, no earlier than 1986
Work	Households headed by women (%)	Wistat	Latest, no earlier than 1987
	Women as % of labour force	Wistat	Latest, no earlier than 1985
	Female wages as % of male	Wistat	1990, non-agricultural
Representation	Parliamentary seats occupied by women	Wistat	1993

* Note that the data on demographics and income are from different sources; as a result, the urban/rural poverty data may appear to be inconsistent with the urban/rural population breakdown.

Wistat: U.N. Women's Indicators and Statistics Database (Wistat), Version 3.0, produced by the U.N. Statistics Division, Gender Statistics Unit.

UNDP: *Human Development Report 1994*, by the U.N. Development Programme. New York: Oxford University Press, 1994.

World Bank: *World Development Report 1994*: Infrastructure for Development, by the World Bank. New York: Oxford University Press, 1994.

Notes

Introduction

1. The debt crisis is 'a fundamental problem, and without drastic reductions in their debt the debt-distressed countries will find that the 1990s are a decade of economic catastrophe and socio-political disaster', said the President of a debt-bound country. (Yoweri Museveni of Uganda, 25 February 1991.)
2. *Poverty Reduction and the World Bank: Progress in 1993*, Washington, 1994, and *Africa Recovery*, Vol.8 No.1/2, 1994, p.8.
3. Ibid.
4. Bradford Morse, 1985. 'Address to the Nairobi Mid-Decade Conference on Women'. Nairobi.
5. *Evaluation Report* 3.9, Oslo, 1991.
6. Ministry of Foreign Affairs, 1991. *A World of Difference: A New Framework for Development Co-operation in the 1990s*. The Hague, Netherlands. pp 203–204.
7. A/RES/40/104
8. Margaret Snyder and Mary Tadesse, 1995. *African Women and Development: A history*. London, ZED Books.
9. Ibid.
10. Because of the excellence of the available documentation, in no instance did I personally conduct a formal 'evaluation' of projects.

Chapter One

1. World Bank, Washington DC, 1990.
2. The definition of a person who is in 'absolute poverty', as used in 1994, is 'anyone who earns less than a dollar a day', according to Inge Kaul, Director of the UNDP team for the Human Development Report, 31 October 1994.
3. *Human Development Report 1994*, Oxford University Press, New York, 1994.
4. The Report has also received a barrage of criticism from developing countries for other reasons.
5. The 'Fifty Years is Enough' campaign has put up much evidence of the poverty that accompanies the Bretton Woods prescriptions.
6. It has been widely demonstrated that working women use their money first of all for their children's needs, and that the same is not true of fathers. See Daisy Dwyer and Judith Bruce, 1988, *A Home Divided: Women and Income in the Third World*, Stanford University Press, Stanford, California; see also Marilyn Carr, 1984, *Blacksmith, Baker, Roofing Sheet Maker*. IT Publications, London.
7. Grassroots Organizations Operating Together in Sisterhood (GROOTS), Caroline Pezzullo, 1994.
8. Gita Sen and Karen Grown, 1987, *Monthly Review Press*, New York.
9. Environmentalists define sustainable development as 'development that fulfills the needs of the present without limiting the potential for meeting the needs of future generations.' *The World Commission on Environment and Development*.
10. Robert Chambers, 1983, *Putting the Last First*. Longmans, London.
11. *Women Farmers and Rural Change in Asia*, Asia Pacific Development Centre, Kuala Lumpur, 1987.

12. *Innovative and Catalytic Projects: Criteria for their Selection*. CRP/UNIFEM/ CC.22/7.a.iii, 1987.

Chapter Two

1. See Margaret Snyder, forthcoming 1995. 'The Politics of Women and Development', in *Women and Politics in the United Nations*, Anne Winslow, (ed.) Greenwood Publishing Group, Westport, Connecticut.
2. When European countries are included, a total of 64 countries joined the UN in the 1950s and 1960s.
3. Telcon, Gindy and Snyder, 28 March 1992. CSW grew out of the Human Rights Commission in 1946, and remained heavily influenced by legal perspectives. Its concern was later defined as the equality of rights and opportunities for women and men, and the contribution that women make as individuals to development. One of its major feats was the *Declaration on the Elimination of Discrimination Against Women*, adopted in 1967. The Commission on Social Development, in contrast, was concerned with human resources for development, including women, and was a firm advocate of the community development approach. See E/CN.5/493 para. 186.
4. ECOSOC, *Report of the 16th Session of the CSW*, 1963, p.22.
5. E/CN.6/527, January–February 1969.
6. A/RES/2716 (XXV), 15 December 1970.
7. Letter from Helvi Sipila to Snyder, 19 April 1991.
8. The following references relate to that history:
   ○ Helen Diner, 1965, *Mothers and Amazons: The First Feminine History of Culture*, New York: the Julian Press, Inc.
   ○ Kamla Bhasin and Nighat Said Khan, *Some Questions on Feminism and its Relevance in South Asia*, New Delhi: Kali for Women.
   ○ *Slave of Slaves: the Challenge of Latin American Women*, Latin American and Caribbean Women's Collective. London: Zed Books, 1977;
   ○ 'The Latin American Women's Movement: Reflections and Actions', *Isis International Women's Journal* no. 5, 1986. See also June E. Hahner, 1980, *Women in Latin American History: Their Lives and Views*, Los Angeles: UCLA Latin American Center Publications;
   ○ Juliet Minos, 1981, *The House of Obedience: Women in Arab Society*, London: Zed Books;
   ○ Soon Mau Rhim, 1983, *Women of Asia: Yesterday and Today*, New York: Friendship Press.
   ○ *The Status and Role of Women in East Africa*, Social Development Section, UNECA, Addis Ababa 1967. E/CN.14/SWSA/6.
9. Interview, Kenyatta and Snyder, Nairobi, November 1993; See also Margaret Snyder and Mary Tadesse, 1995, *African Women and Development: A History*, London: Zed Books.
10. *Report of the Kenya Women's Seminar*, Nairobi 1962.
11. Conversation, Mulimo and Snyder, Lusaka, November 1994.
12. Conversation, Asiyo and Snyder, Nairobi, June 1993, The conventional wisdom that the impetus for the movement arose from the UN Commission on the Status of Women and the US Women's movement does not pass the test of history. See Irene Tinker, 1990, *Persistent Inequalities*, Oxford University Press, New York, p.28.
13. Interview, Racelis, Francisco and Snyder, Manila, February 1994.
14. See John Kenneth Galbraith, 1979, *The Nature of Mass Poverty*, Harvard

University Press, Cambridge, Mass., pp. 24–27. It was a time when 'As a different field of study, the special economics of the poor countries was held not to exist,' according to economist Galbraith.

15. *Let the Word Go Forth: the Speeches, Statements and Writings of John F. Kennedy, 1947–1963.* Delacorte Press, 1988, p.12.

16. Gunnar Myrdal, 1971, *The Challenge of World Poverty*, page xiii; see also *Asian Drama: An Inquiry into the Poverty of Nations*, NY: Pantheon.

17. *Annual Report of the ECA, 1965–1966*, E/CN.14/393, p.3.

18. Conversation, Adagala and Snyder, Nairobi, November 1993.

19. On these subjects see Atul Kohli, (ed.) 1986, *The State and Development in the Third World*, Princeton University Press, p. 15. See also Jan Pronk, 1990, *Solidarity Against Poverty*, The Evert Vermeer Foundation, Amsterdam, Chapter 2.

20. See Margaret Snyder, 'The Politics of Women and Development' in *Women and Politics in the United Nations*, Anne Winslow, (ed.), *op. cit.* See also *The New International Economic Order: What Roles for Women?* ECA, Addis Ababa, 1977.

21. E.CN.5/441 *Report of the 20th Session of the CSD*, 1969.

22. *Ibid*, pp. 27–28.

23. A/RES 2626 (XXV), 24 October 1970.

24. Discussion, Scott and Snyder, Washington DC, 1991.

25. John Lewis refers to 'populism' in *Development Strategies Reconsidered*, ODC: Washington, 1986, and in *Strengthening the Poor: What Have we Learned?*, ODC, 1988.

26. *Employment, Growth and Basic Needs*. See *Report on a Tripartite Conference on Employment, Income Distribution and Social Progress and the International Divisions of Labour*, ILO, Geneva, 1976, Volumes I and II.

27. FAO's landmark World Food Conference of 5–17 November 1974 also contributed strong and clear evidence of rural women's centrality to development and the consequent urgency of directing resources to them. FAO's Jean Delaney, who was working closely with the ECA Women's Programme and was a co-founder of ATRCW, was an author of the FAO directives.

28. Ester Boserup, 1970. *Women's Role in Economic Development*, St. Martin's Press, New York.

29. Boserup drew extensively on resources like ECA's *The Status and Role of Women in East Africa*, which in turn drew on the findings of the East African Women's Seminars of the early 1960s.

30. United Nations, *Integration of Women in Development: Report of the Secretary-General*, E/CN.5/481, 14 November 1972.

31. United Nations, *Report of the 25th Session of the Commission on the Status of Women*, E/CN.6/589, February 1974, p.58.

32. Karin Himmelstrand, 'Can an Aid Bureaucracy Empower Women?' in Kathleen Staudt, 1990, *Women, International Development and Politics: the Bureaucratic Mire*, Philadelphia, Temple University Press, p.104.

33. Betty Friedan, 1963. *The Feminine Mystique*, New York: Norton.

34. Mary Hilton, deputy director of the US Women's Bureau and Kay Wallace, special assistant for international affairs, travelled to ECA for consultation with the Women's Programme. Letter Wallace to Snyder, April 26 1992. The Percy Amendment mandated special attention to programmes, projects and activities which tended to integrate women in the national economies of developing countries.

35. Lucille Mair, 'Address to a Research Conference', 18 April 1986, Vermillion,

South Dakota. Mair was a founding member of the Fund's Consultative Committee and the Secretary-General of the Copenhagen Conference, 1980.

36. This is not to ignore the seminal and often valiant work of several individuals and groups within organizations of the UN system. Betsy Johnstone of ILO; the FAO Home Economics Programme; Ulla Olin of UNDP, and others. ECA's was the first comprehensive programme centre of its kind in the UN system.

37. See *Recommendations of Regional Meetings for Africa on the Role of Women in Development*, UNECA, Addis Ababa, 1975.

38. *Status and Role of Women in East Africa*, ECA, Addis Ababa, 1967, E/CN.14/SWASA/6. The publication drew heavily on the Reports of the Kenya and East Africa Women's Seminars.

39. J. Riby-Williams, Opening Address by the Chief, Human Resources Development Divison, on behalf of the ECA, *op. cit.*

40. 'The Data Base for Discussion on the Interrelationships Between the Integration of Women in Development, their Situation and Population Factors in Africa', ECA, Addis Ababa, 13 May 1974, E/CN.14/SW/37; and *Women of Africa Today and Tomorrow*, ECA, Addis Ababa 1975. Such documents led Kathleen Staudt to credit the ECA for the increased visibility of women farmers in Africa. She wrote in the *Canadian Journal of African Studies*: 'In 1972, (ECA's) Human Resources Development Division prepared 'Women: the Neglected Human Resource for African Development' for the *Canadian Journal of African Studies* . . . Drawing on data from country reports, regional meetings, and UN documents, the article argued that women, 'responsible for 60 to 80 per cent of the agricultural labour', go unrecognized, unresourced and unrewarded. ECA's later companion pieces quantified women's overparticipation in labour and underparticipation in access to agricultural resources; its figures were widely disseminated and nearly etched in stone.' *Canadian Journal of African Studies*, Vol 22, No 3, Toronto, 1988.

41. ECA, Addis Ababa 1972.

42. ECA/FAO/SIDA: *The Impact of Modern Life and Technology on Women's Role: Implications for Planning*, ECA, Addis Ababa, 1972, p.15.

43. 'Women and Development in African Countries: Some Profound Contradictions' in *African Studies Review*, XVIII, 1975.

44. Kathy Larin interview with Terry Kantai, Nairobi, December 1992.

45. Interview, Hafkin and Snyder, Addis Ababa, November 1993.

46. See Margaret Snyder in Winslow, *op. cit.*

47. United Nations, *The Nairobi Forward-Looking Strategies*, New York, 1985, para 8.

Chapter Three

1. See M. Snyder and M. Tadesse, 1995 *African Women and Development: a History*, London, Zed Books; see also 'The Politics of Women and Development' in Anne Winslow, (ed.), 1995. *Women and Politics in the UN*, Greenwood Press, Westport.

2. See Mexico City Conference Resolutions 10, 16, 18, 21, 22, 27.

3. United Nations, *Report of the Conference on IWY*, New York, 1975, pp. 48–50, and resolution 27 entitled 'Measures for the Integration of Women in Development'.

4. World Conference of IWY: 'Speech by Dr Shirley Summerskill MP.' Further

conditions for the UK grant were set out in the Annexe to a letter to Helvi Sipila, ASG/CSDHA shortly after the IWY conference.

5. See Margaret Snyder, 'The Politics of Women and Development' in Winslow, *op cit.*

6. Report of the Conference of IWY, *op. cit.*, para 43.

7. Resolution 12, co-sponsored by Afghanistan, the Dominican Republic, Nepal, the UK, and later Indonesia and the Netherlands. See E/CONF.66/C.2/L.63: *Establishment of a UN Fund for Women.* This draft was rewritten as Resolution 12: *Special resources for the integration of women in development,* after it was learned a fund could be started with an estimated one million dollars that might be left over from the IWY Conference.

8. General Assembly decision on Item no. 76, 15 December 1975.

9. 6 December 1976.

10. Report of the Consultative Committee on VFDW, Eighth Session, p.2.

11. *Ibid.*

12. Report of the Secretary-General, A/32/174, 26 August 1977.

13. *Ibid.* The balance between principle and political expediency in promoting decentralization to the regions may remain blurred. Some delegations believed that Sipila, a Finn, would support anti-Zionist activities, and for that reason the Fund ought to be well-removed from her control.

14. Before the second session of the Committee was convened, in June 1977, the Economic Commissions for Africa (ECA) and Asia/Pacific (ESCAP) sent replies and proposals, and Latin America (ECLA) agreed to send further information following its regional women's conference.

15. A/RES/32/141, March 1978.

16. A/32/174; para 15c.

17. ESCAP, *Report of the Regional Conference on the Integration of Women in Development,* Tokyo 1984.

18. Interview, Krawczyk and Snyder, Santiago, September 1993.

19. Interview, Tadesse and Snyder, New York, November 1994.

20. The very competent and committed secretary to the Fund was Menelea Lao. In 1979 Aldwin Harvey joined as the accounts clerk, and later that year an additional post was added for a research clerk, Alice von Buskirk.

21. Joan Bunche of UNDP was consistently helpful as was Richard Duncan of CSDHA.

22. *Report of the Eleventh Session of the Consultative Committee,* 29 March–2 April 1982.

23. Specifically, AMS's Thompson said: 'I have never in my UN experience, found a more dedicated and hard working group of staff. They have achieved a great deal, with relatively little resources, and in spite of the organizational difficulties arising as a result of the transfer of CSDHA to Vienna.' Memo 24 December 1982, Thompson to Yolah. Aldwin Harvey was Accounts Clerk and Alice von Buskirk Research Clerk at the time.

24. *Report of the Seventh Session of the Consultative Committee,* p.45.

25. A/RES/33/188. Over those six years, four requests were made to provide posts through redeployment. 33/188 was followed up with resolutions 35/137, 37/162, 38/106 and 39/127. The matter of posts was also discussed in A/C.3/38L42 and A/39/569/Add. I of 1993.

26. Rafael Salas, 1977. *People: An International Choice,* Pergamon Press, New York

27. UNFPA's income was $220 million in 1993.

28. In the case of the Fund for Science and Technology for Development

(UNIFSTD) administrative costs were 28.8 per cent of total expenditures, and of the UN Fund for Natural Resources Exploration, 19 per cent. See *Financial Report and unaudited financial statements for year ending 31.12.81*, UNDP.

29. Dudley Madawela, 1981. *Administration of the VFDW*, CSDHA.
30. *Report of the Eighth Session of the Consultative Committee*, para 22.
31. *Report of the Secretary General*, A/35/523, 14 October 1980, para 22.
32. A/RES/39/125.
33. Conference Room Paper: UNIFEM/CC22/7.a.iii.
34. UNIFEM/CC 22/INFO paper 12.
35. Dr. Marilyn Carr developed a project idea to establish a Business Advisory Service for Women in Malawi to enhance the direct participation of women in the modern economy; UNDP funded it at $668 000. A credit system for productive activities in four countries was developed: UNIFEM contributed $200 000 and UNDP $2.7 million.
36. Conversation, Mwangola and Snyder, Nairobi, November 1993. See also: *Why they called me Mama: KWAHO, 1980–1993*, Nairobi, 1995.
37. Information by telephone from UNDP Personnel office, June 1994. Of note is that the number of women holding those top level positions moved only from six to twelve over a decade.

Chapter Four

1. All publications appeared in English, French and Spanish.
2. Interview, Hafkin and Snyder, Addis Ababa, November 1993.
3. *Memorandum of Understanding, 25 June* 1980. Under a new agreement with UNDP, projects having no direct input from the regional commissions and those prepared by governments, non-governmental organizations or UN organizations were initially reviewed by the UNDP resident representative in the country. In the case of projects to be carried out by voluntary organizations, it was also the UNDP representative's responsibility to determine that the concerned government had no objection to the project being carried out. S/he then forwarded the request directly to VFDW at headquarters, with a copy to the regional commission for any comments it might wish to make.
4. *UNIFEM Project Manual*, New York. Not surprisingly, field staff resisted gathering the base-line data and my time as Director ran out before the *Knowledge Bank* could become operational.
5. *Memorandum of Understanding* between the UN Controller and the UNDP Administrator, *op. cit.* We paid an administrative fee of 1.5 per cent of project value to UNDP for its services.
6. UNDP/ADMIN/FIELD/657, 1980.
7. In 1977 UNDP had issued Olin's thirty-three page draft *Programme Guidelines on the Integration of Women in Development* to all headquarters and field offices. CS100–1/TL.2, 25.2.1977, UNDP, New York. The *Guidelines* followed-up on earlier communications that discussed the fact that 'women's role in development is far from fully understood'.
8. *Rural Women's Participation in Development*, Evaluation Study No. 3, New York, June 1980; *Women's Participation in Development: An Inter-Organizational Assessment. Evaluation Study no.13*, New York, 1985. See also DP/1985/10, paras 74 and 109.
9. *Report of the Secretary-General on the Voluntary Fund for the UN Decade for Women*, A/35/523, 14 October 1980.
10. *Ibid.*

11. UNDP/PROG/79/Add.1.
12. UNDP's work with developing countries is phrased over four-year periods called programming cycles.
13. Decision 87/41, UNDP Governing Council.
14. We also assisted Inge Kaul of UNDP Central Evaluation Office to identify and share the costs of two consultants, Sarah Lukalo and Birget Madsen, both of whom had assisted UNIFEM earlier. They reviewed and analysed a series of evaluations of UNDP projects.
15. See UNIFEM Occasional Paper No. 5. There were obvious limitations to the study, which reviewed evaluations that had a different intent than the NGO-focused one. Nonetheless, the study revealed a number of interesting points to pursue.
16. *Ibid.*
17. Norwegian Review of UNIFEM, 1987, and my field interviews 1993–4.
18. UNIFEM/CC.20/3.d; and a formal publication, New York 1987.
19. UNIFEM, 1988.

Chapter Five

1. United Nations, *Report of the World Conference of the United Nations Decade for Women: Equality, Development and Peace*, New York, para 244. Resolution 42 expressed appreciation to the Fund and appealed for additional contributions.
2. 'A Success Story', *AAUW Journal*, 1982.
3. United Nations, *op. cit.* See para 223. See also Resolution No. 42.
4. Leimas, *op. cit.*
5. In 1981, a continuing resolution of the Congress allocated the same amounts as the previous FY; thus it was only in 1982 that new priorities could be set, on the basis of recommendations by the Executive Branch, i.e., the President of the United States.
6. Record of a meeting with Abrams, Assistant Secretary of State, Bureau for International Organizations Affairs, US Department of State, in the first half of 1981, as quoted in *Global Negotiations Action Notes*, No. 15, 6 July 1981, Church Center, New York.
7. Letty Cottin Pogrevin, 'Antisemitism in the Women's Movement', *MS Magazine*, June 1982, p.45.
8. In May, 1983, the UK delegate to the CC, Dr. Spens, who represented Western European countries and others, met with leaders Leet, Barbara Leslie, and Rita Solberg. (From informal discussion with concerned persons, 1993, and personal records.)
9. See *Report Language on the UN Voluntary Fund for the Decade for Women*, Mr. Lehman, undated.
10. *Ibid.*
11. Personal notes on the meeting. Dorothy Binstock, President of B'nai B'rith Women, in cable No. 4–0335935101, 11 April 1993, wrote to Congressman Zablocke on behalf of 120 000 members of her organization, opposing the funding of UNIFEM.
12. Snyder, personal records.
13. *Global Negotiations Action Notes*, No. 15, Church Center, New York, 6 July 1981.
14. Report of the Sixth Session of the Consultative Committee, p.35.
15. A/34/612.

16. See para 39 of the first study; both studies are summarized in the CC Report, footnote 18.
17. CRP IESA/SDHA/VFCC. *9/8 Report of the CC*, p.13.
18. A/36/647. *Report of the Secretary-General on the VFDW*. This document was mentioned above in relation to the Copenhagen controversy and the US position that VFDW should remain in New York and affiliate more closely with UNDP.
19. *Ibid.*
20. *Ibid.* para 49.
21. *Ibid.* para 56.
22. Information conveyed personally.
23. The Capital Development Fund (CDF), the UN Sahelian Fund (UNSO), the UN Fund for Science and Technology for Development (UNFSTD) were all associated with UNDP under different arrangements.
24. See Rafael Salas, *People: An International Choice*, Pergamon Press, New York, 1976.
25. Olubanke King-Akerele, Kyo Naka and I constituted the professional staff at the time. A/RES/37/62 notes the view of the Consultative Committee 'that there were still grounds for concern regarding administrative matters . . . and hopes that specific and concrete measures would be taken on an urgent basis'.
26. A/RES/37/62, December 1982.
27. UK delegation, comments in the 37th Session of the GA.
28. See Report of CC 13. Martha Cabal (Colombia) and Jim Djeu (China) joined staff.
29. Report of CC 15.
30. United Nations, *Development Co-operation with Women: the Experience and Future Directions of the Fund*, New York, 1985, E.85.IV.6.
31. *Ibid.* Further, it was found that many of the larger scale projects had secondary economic impacts on more people than just the immediate project beneficiaries. Even small-scale projects helped to raise the profile of women and to demonstrate the centrality of women's contributions to development, thereby influencing national policy. By helping to include women in large-scale, mainstream development projects. the Fund contributed to the restructuring of traditional, inequitable systems and institutions.

   Technical co-operation activities supported by the Fund received special attention in the assessment. When technical co-operation was linked with mainstream development resources, such as universities and national ministries of health and education, the impact of the projects was enhanced. Long-term sustainability of projects was also increased when national agencies took responsibility for project execution. The evaluation emphasized the importance of including women and local organizations in the continuous monitoring and evaluation of projects to ensure that they were responsive to changing needs and circumstances.
32. *Ibid..* p. 7.
33. *Ibid.*, p. 7.
34. *Report of the Secretary-General*, A/39/569.
35. Report of CC 16.
36. Representatives of the UN organizations at the informal sessions included Nissam Tal, UNDP; Stafford Mousky, UNFPA; Akerele and myself. Salimatu Diallo Khan of the Organization of African Unity was very helpful.
37. As 'mainstreaming' became a catchword in the women and development vocabulary, UNIFEM would find it necessary to define it. In document A/

43/643: *Forward Looking Strategies for the Advancement of Women to the Year 2000: UN Development Fund for Women*, para 3, we said: 'Mainstream has been accepted by UNIFEM as indicating the macro concerns and goals of national governments and the international community. The term also refers to the development resources available from the large-scale, central financing and technical co-operation organizations and bodies (banks, ministries of finance, World Bank, UN specialized agencies, etc.) Thus the concept of 'mainstreaming' indicates the strengthening of women's active involvement at all levels of development by interfacing their capabilities and contributions with macro issues and goals such as the environment, critical poverty, population, food security, energy, urbanization, debt and adjustments, and appropriately considering the implications of these issues for women. Strategies for mainstreaming also require the establishment of linkages between national and international development policies and programmes in such priority areas and those policies and programmes which are specific to women. They call for the full and appropriate consideration both of women and of men in all financial and technical assistance programmes and projects.

38. For the first time, we would report directly to the General Assembly. UNIFEM's autonomy far surpassed that of CDF and UNSO, two UNDP-associated funds that were administratively placed deep in the UNDP bureaucracy.

39. Report of the CC, IESA/SDHA/VFCC.17/8, 25–29 March 1985.

40. Report of the Secretary-General, A/40/727, 14 October 1985.

41. UNIFEM/CC.19/8 *Report of the Consultative Committee, 19th session*, 17–21 March 1986.

42. *Ibid.*

43. Memo of 26 March 1987.

Chapter Six

1. Private information from records.

2. CC, 1981.

3. The Norwegian evaluation was controversial because it was released to major donors before Consultative Committee members saw it, and because the composition of the evaluation team, having no geographical balance, was atypical for a United Nations study. Report of CC 21, 30 March–8 April 1987, pp.12–13.

4. For example, when we had a Fund balance of US $8.8 million only $2.3 million was available for new projects if we had existing commitments of $6.5 million. This reserve had to be maintained despite the fact that major donor countries expected to continue or raise their annual contributions, as had been demonstrated by their record over more than a decade, and, in addition, interest would be earned from the reserves. The full-funding system was applied to all trust funds of the United Nations at the time.

5. A/RES/31/137.

6. *Report of the Secretary-General to the General Assembly*, A/35/523, 14 October 1980.

7. We were taken aback at receiving the actual contribution – so much so that Debbie Czeglady, my secretary at the time, put the cheque in her shoe to take it to the UNDP office for safekeeping.

8. Five of us met around a very small table at the offices of the Austrian Association of University Women, hosted by Dr. Adelheid Schinak. (Pat Hutar of the new US Committee and Lily Boeykens sent regrets). The

Swedish Committee was formed later that year by Ula-Liza Blum. UNIFEM staff and I invited representatives of the National Committees to an informal dinner at the Nairobi Conference in 1985.

9. Observers came from Australia, Canada, Ireland, Jamaica, the Netherlands and Spain. Among the speakers were the Secretary of State for Development Co-operation, the Ambassador of the Philippines to the European Economic Community and a representative of the Africa, Caribbean and Pacific States Organization. There were also Belgian members of the European Parliament and representatives of the Ministry of Foreign Affairs.

10. The opening session was addressed by Minister of Finance Ulla Puolanne and YKNK Chairman Pirkko Tyolajarvi, and Helvi Sipila chaired the working sessions. By then Pida Ripley chaired the UK Committee; Virginia Allen attended for the USA. Observers represented Argentina, Austria, Greece, Germany, Hungary, Iceland, Israel, Malaysia, Mexico, the Netherlands, New Zealand, Nigeria, Norway, Phillipines, Poland, and the USSR.

11. YWCA, OEF, AAUW, NCNW and professional organizations.

12. ZONTA, Soroptomists and AAUW, among others, also published articles on the Fund.

13. 1. The Committee would be known as the NGO Committee on UNIFEM;
    2. Membership would be comprised of NGOs in Consultative Status with ECOSOC;
    3. The purposes of the Committee were:
       – to serve in a consultative and supportive capacity and to exchange information with UNIFEM;
       – to provide a forum for exchange of information and discussion among international NGOs on subjects and activities related to UNIFEM; and
       – to facilitate communication between UNIFEM and NGOs at regional and field levels.
    4. The Committee would elect its Convenor and Secretary.

14. Among their actions would be encouraging their national affiliates at country level to press their governments to pledge to UNIFEM and initiating an international NGO campaign for UNIFEM at the time of the annual Pledging Conference. They would also support the possibility of National Committees being formed in developing countries.

15. A/36/646. At the time, the Government of Denmark and Church Women United were co-financing approved projects.

16. Produced by the Department of Public Information and Cusack Productions of Chicago.

17. In 1983, with technical advice from an adviser to the Smithsonian Museum in Washington DC, improved, fuel-saving stoves were brought from the Sahel, together with firewood, for an environment exhibit in the Visitors Lobby of the UN. Jacqueline Ki-Zerbo, whom the Fund financed at the headquarters of CILSS to promote energy-conserving activities, was present to explain the technical and social aspects of the stoves. The Director-General of the UN lit the fire (a can of sterno) on behalf of the Secretary-General, closely supervised by UN guards.

18. UNICEF spent 2.9 per cent or less of its income for external relations. For UNIFEM in 1983, 2.9 per cent would have allowed us $90 000; we were allowed $16 000.

Chapter Seven

1. *Shramshakti: A summary Report of the National Commission on Self-Employed Women and Women in the Informal Sector.* SEWA, Ahmedabad, 1991, p.iii.

2. The informal sector (also called the popular economy) is defined as all units operated by own-account (self-employed) workers with or without family labour, in return for a profit. It also includes micro-enterprises, which utilize a few hired workers, apprentices, or family labour but employ a total of ten persons or less per unit. See M. Snyder, 1991. *Gender and the Food Regime: Some Transnational and Human Issues.* 'Transitional Law and Contemporary Problems.' University of Iowa.

3. See Acción International, 1988. *An Operational Guide for Micro-Enterprise Projects.* The Calmeadow Foundation, Toronto.

4. Interview, Racelis and Snyder, Manila, February 1994. Mary Racelis, a scholar and former official of UNICEF in Eastern and Southern Africa, now represents the Ford Foundation in her home country, the Philippines.

5. United Nations, *The World's Women: 1970–1990*, New York, 1991.

6. *Gender and the Food Regime, op. cit.*

7. Shramshakti, *op cit.* pp.13, 16, 23.

8. *Ibid*, p.iii.

9. *Ibid*, p.vii.

10. *Interview*, Racelis and Snyder, *op. cit.*

11. *Ibid.*

12. United Nations, *Development Co-operation with Women*, pp.144, 145.

13. Interview, Letta Dlamini and Snyder, Ludzeludze, Swaziland, November 1993.

14. Data for the above obtained from Sarah Murison, *UNIFEM Experience of a Revolving Loan Fund*, UNIFEM Occasional Paper No. 4, UNIFEM, New York 1986; Sheila Reines and Ngozi M. Awa, *Draft Report, Evaluation Mission: Woman in Development Project*, UNDP; Mbabane, December 1990; and UNDP: 25 Years of Service, Mbabane, 1993.

15. Interview, Motsa and Snyder, Mbabane 1993. (All quotations from Motsa in this chapter.)

16. Vilakati died in 1983 in Nairobi while returning from briefings at UN headquarters.

17. UN Radio, *op. cit.*

18. Occasional Paper, *op. cit.*

19. Sheila Reines and Ngozi Awa, *Swaziland Women in Development Project Evaluation Mission, draft report*, December 1990.

20. *Report of the Credit Consultancy on Women and Development Project SWA/ 92/003*, Stephen Mirero, credit consultant, Nairobi, 15 September 1993.

21. *Ibid.*

22. Interview, Simelane, Lomahoza and Snyder, Mbabane, November 1993. (All quotations in this chapter.)

23. *Ibid.*

24. Interview, Motsa and Snyder, *op. cit.*

25. Interview, Katamzi and Snyder, Mbabane, November 1993.

26. Interview, Racelis and Snyder, *op. cit.*

27. Leonore M. Briones. 'Debt and Poverty: Mal-development and Misallocation of Resources' in *Review of Women's Studies*, Vol II, No. 2, 1991–1992, University of the Philippines, Quezon City. NGOs allege that some $3.5 billion of the government borrowing during President Marcos' regime was

293

fraudulent. The most dramatic example they give is a $2.67 billion loan for a nuclear plant to be built by the Westinghouse Corporation. That kind of state-controlled development, with its massive projects, excluded the people from the process and was accompanied by a great deal of corruption. On top of that, the stabilization programmes instituted with the advice or conditionality of the World Bank and IMF drastically reduced levels of social and other investment expenditure. They did *not* reduce payment of debts to lenders.

28. Data from UNDP, 1993.
29. See Giovanni Andrea Cornea *et al.*, 1987. *Adjustment with a Human Face*, Oxford University Press, New York.
30. Discussion with Josefa S. Francisco, Director, at the Women's Resource and Research Centre, concerning their joint study with the Asia Pacific Development Centre, February 1994.
31. Briones, *op. cit.* p.22.
32. Interview, Ancheta and Snyder, Pampanga Province, February 1994.
33. Interview, Jiminez and Snyder, Pampanga, March 1994.
34. *Ibid.*
35. Interview, Popatco and Snyder, Pampanga 1994.
36. Interview, Nagrampa and Snyder, Pampanga 1994.
37. Discussion with project participants and Jiminez.
38. Jiminez, *op. cit.*
39. *Monitoring of the Project*, PH1/88/WO1, Technology and Livelihood Resource Centre, Manila 1993, p.48.
40. *Ibid.*
41. Interview, Santa Ana and Snyder, San Miguel 1994.
42. Interview, Ordonez and Snyder, Manila 1994.
43. *Ibid.*
44. Conversation with Ordonez and with participants, San Miguel, February 1994.
45. See Carlos A. Fernandez, *Lessons in Self-Reliance and Empowerment from the Rural Women of the Philippines*, Foundation for the Advancement of Filipino Women, 1985. p.10. See also UN Development Fund for Women, *Philippines: National Women's Co-operative Development Programme*, November 1985.
46. External Evaluation of the San Miguel Stuffed Toy Co-operative Project (PHI/89/W01), by the Asian Social Institution, Manila, March 1993.
47. The project's three partners were the FAFW, TLRC, and KBB. They soon met with problems in evolving into a medium-scale rural industry. KBBLF sub-contracted with a big factory in Manila and got ready-cut materials from them. Toy City provided the labour, and the Manila group did the marketing. Unfortunately, the Manila-based exporter had to close due to flooding, leaving the women 10 000 pesos short. They considered and even tried direct export, but withdrew from that in the face of its cost and of the 'nerve-wracking bureaucratic red tape encountered.' In 1993 it took 34 signatures to clear imports in the Philippines. Subcontracting then seemed to be the only viable option.
48. Interview, Santa Ann and Snyder, February 1994.
49. Interview, San Miguel 1994.
50. The women leaders sing that theme song at their meetings.
51. Interview, San Miguel 1994.
52. Ordonez, *op. cit.*
53. *An Evaluation of the San Miguel Stuffed Toy Co-operative Project* (PHI/89/W01) by Asian Social Institute, Manila, March 1993.
54. *Ibid.* pp.74–75.

55. *Ibid.*
56. Evaluation, *op. cit.* 1993, p.61.
57. *Business Ideas Magazine*, Manila, February 1988, p.19.
58. The data on access to water and maternal mortality is from WISTAT, Version 3, 1994. The communications figures are from the UNDP's *Human Development Report 1994*, published by Oxford University Press in New York.
59. Project No. LAO/83/PRO1, *Development of Women's Textile Ateliers*. See also Project No. LAO/82/WO1.
60. These figures as well as the description of the production process in the following paragraph are from the four-page UNDP brochure: *Lao Women's Pilot Textile Centre*. Undated, but appears to be from 1988.
61. Projected by Women's Indicators and Statistics Database (WISTAT), Version 3, UN Statistics Division, Gender Statistics Unit (1994).
62. Literacy figures from WISTAT, 1994. Education data is from *UNDP Human Development Report 1994*. New York: Oxford University Press.
63. Beijing Municipal Women's Federation, 1987.
64. All China Women's Federation, 1994 interview.
65. Post-Project Monitoring Visit Project CRP/82/WO1: *Establishment of a Tailoring, Knitting, Spinning and Weaving Factory for Women and a Revolving Loan Fund for other Income-Generating Activities*. Authored by J.W. Swietering, Senior Planning and Co-ordination Officer, UNDP, 5 October 1987.
66. UNDP World Development, May 1988 issue.
67. Beijing Municipal Women's Federation, 1994 interview.
68. *Ibid.*
69. See Jiuzhai Garment Mid-Term Evaluation Project, Submitted July 1993, p.27. This project was spearheaded by the Women's Federation of Mengyin County.
70. All China Women's Federation, 1994 interview.
71. 1992 Law of the People's Republic of China on the Protection of Rights and Interests of Women.
72. Francis Rey, SPES.
73. Proposal for Silk-Screening and Hand-Printing project, 1980.
74. Monsieur Francis Rey.
75. Application Form to Voluntary Fund (UNIFEM) for a pottery project, July 1980.
76. Langlois to Snyder, April 1993.
77. Monsieur Francis Rey writing in a Mauritian newspaper. Forwarded to Margaret Snyder by UNDP Resident Representative of Mauritius Olubanke Y. King-Akerele, 6 April 1993.
78. At an award ceremony on the occasion of the 10th Anniversary of UNIFEM, 1987, Vina Mazumdar, head of the Centre for Women's Development Studies accepted an award for the Role of Public Specialized Agencies Project.
79. Interview, Nath and Snyder, New Delhi, 1994.
80. *Shramshakti: A Summary of the Report of the National Commission on Self-Employed Women and Women in the Informal Sector*, Ahmedabad, 1991.
81. *Ibid.*
82. The 1981 census had concluded that a mere 14 per cent of women participated in the workforce, as against 51.6 per cent of males; in 1990 the figure was raised to 29.6 per cent of women. Demographers expect an increase of 20–25 per cent in fast-growing populations; the 44 per cent increase is thus attributed to the revised census question.
83. United Nations, 1991. *The World's Women 1970–1990*, New York.

84. New York *Times*, 27 August 1994.
85. Interview, R. Sundarshan, Senior Economist, UNDP, and Snyder, 1994.
86. Data are from the 1980s.
87. IND/80/WO5 The full project valued at $271700 was not funded; rather, UNIFEM supported the Udaipur sub-project.
88. See UNIFEM project document.
89. IND/88/WO1.
90. *Ibid.*
91. WFP gave $38500 and UNFPA $3482.
92. Lucy Creevey, (ed.) 1994, *Changing Women's Lives and Work*, final report to UNIFEM, New York, p.195; see also 'The Silk Route to Development' in *Choices*, UNDP, New York, December 1993.
93. *The Silk Route*, *op. cit.*.
94. Interview, Nath and Snyder, Udaipur 1994.
95. Interview, Dixit of the Tribal Area Development Department (TADD) and Snyder, Udaipur 1994.
96. Interview, Parfulla Nagar, TADD, Udaipur 1994.
97. Interview, Fommu Shrivastava, Aastha, Udaipur 1994.
98. Communication, Nath to Haslett, 6 February 1991.
99. Madhu Bala Nath, *Integrated Development of Women in Sericulture*. Undated.
100. Follow-up of Case Studies under Project IND/88/W01, September/October 1993. UNIFEM, Delhi.
101. Interview, Shrivastava and Snyder, *op. cit.*
102. Creevey, *op. cit.* p.204 ff.
103. *Follow-up of Case Studies*, *op cit.*, 1993.
104. Interview, Nath and Snyder, *op cit.*
105. Creevey, *op. cit*, pp.358–9.
106. See Madhu Bala Nath paper: *Integrated Development of Women in Sericulture, op. cit.* for data in the following summary.
107. *Ibid.*
108. Nath to Haslett, *op. cit.*
109. Mahila Haat brochure, 1988.
110. IND/84/W01 Mahila Haat Facilitation Centre for Poor Women Producer Groups.
111. IND/87/W02.
112. Strategic Planning and Review, ISST, May 1993.
113. *Project Proposal for UNIFEM Assistance*, 6 March 1987.
114. Conversation with evaluator Madhu Bala Nath and Snyder, Delhi, February 1994.
115. Meeting at Mahila Haat, March 1994.
116. *Ibid.*
117. *Ibid.*
118. Interview, *op. cit.*
119. *Ibid.*
120. Discussions in India, February 1994.
121. Sundarshan, *op. cit.*

Chapter Eight

1. Interview, Mota and Snyder, Santiago, September 1993.
2. See Jeanne Vickers, 1992. *Women and the World Economic Crisis*, Zed Books,

London. See also United Nations, 1991. *The World's Women: 1970–1990*, New York. Note that girls often help their mothers either after school, when their brothers are allowed to do homework, or by staying out of school.

3. The World Bank, 1994. *Adjustment in Africa: Lessons from Country Case Studies*, Washington D.C., p.185.
4. *Ibid.*
5. *Etude sur l'integration de la femme dans les plans et programmes de dévéloppement: Cas du Senegal*, Republique du Senegal, Ministere du Developpement Social, Dakar, September 1988. The research team was composed of two persons from the Ministry of Planning, two from the Ministry of Social Development, and one from the Ministry of Rural Development; four were female and one male.
6. *Ibid.*, p.41.
7. The National Development Plan for 1991–6 did have a section on women. But the most important document on women in Senegal was published by the Ministry of Woman, Child and Family: *Femmes Seneglaises a l'Horizon 2015*, Ministere de la Femme, de l'enfant et de la famille, Dakar, July 1993. A long-term, future-oriented study, it does not focus on specific programmes, but does draw lessons from the experience of two large-scale women-specific projects of international agencies. One of them, to establish pre-co-operatives, was recognized as the first such project to consider women as economic actors but it actually included only a few of the 3600 women's groups in the countryside. It made no provision for women's illiteracy and consequent inability to read instructions for using technologies; a credit scheme component was never established.
8. Interview, Jefferson and Snyder, Bridgetown, September 1993.
9. Social services, including hospitals, clinics, schools and day-care centres are inadequate. The general worsening of Caribbean country economies has led women to seek alternative strategies of development and to challenge government policies. See *A Historical Profile of the Women and Development Unit*, WAND, UWI, January 1993, p.3.
10. *Ibid.*
11. UN Radio Interview with Peggy Antrobus, 1983.
12. *Ibid.*
13. *Women on the Move in Grenada*, 1 February 1988. UNIFEM contributed $37 800 to the motor mechanics project.
14. *Ibid.*
15. Telephone interview, Stapleton and Snyder, Barbados 1993.
16. *Ibid.*
17. *Ibid.*
18. Jane T. Benbow, 1991. *Women Doing Development: An Impact Evaluation of a Pilot Project for the Integration of Women in Rural Development*, University of Massachusetts, Center for International Education, Barbados.
19. Interview Stapleton, *op. cit.*
20. *The Barbadian Family with Specific Reference to the Woman as Head of Household*, Marva Alleyne, Director, Bureau of Women's Affairs, Bridgetown. September 1993.
21. Currently, the unemployed women who are trained are given a government stipend of 100 BBD dollars a week to help pay their bus fare and other expenses. Several institutions provide trainers.
22. Interview, Fraser and Snyder, Bridgetown 1993.
23. Interview, McIntosh and Snyder, Bridgetown, September 1993.

24. Alicia Modesire and Associates, *Evaluation of the Women and Development Unit (WAND)*, Trinidad and Tobago, January 1993; the evaluation was presented to UNIFEM.
25. *Ibid.*
26. Interview, Bridgetown, *op. cit.*
27. *Ibid.*
28. DAWN is noted for its vision of a world 'where inequality based on class, gender and race is absent from every country, and from the relationships among countries . . . a world where basic needs become basic rights and where poverty and all forms of violence are eliminated.' Gita Sen and Caren Grown, 1987. *Development, Crises and Alternative Visions*, Monthly Review Press, New York.
29. *A Historical Profile of the Women and Development Unit*, WAND, Barbados, 1993.
30. *Ibid*, p.15.
31. Evaluation, *op cit.*, p.43.
32. *Ibid* p.55.
33. *Ibid.*
34. *Bolivian Times*, 10 September 1993. Data in the same paragraph are from WISTAT, Version 3, UN Statistical Office, New York 1995.
35. CEPAL, *Feminization of the Informal Sector in Latin America and the Caribbean?* Women and Development Series, Santiago, 1993. The 1993 inflation rate is from UNDP La Paz.
36. Interview, Krawczyk and Snyder, September 1994.
37. For a more complete description of the area, see *UNIFEM Women's Milk Project*, La Paz, undated but *circa* 1992–3.
38. UNIFEM, *Increase Milk Production by Rural Women*, Project Document BOL/83/WO1, 5 January 1983.
39. *Ibid.*
40. Interview, Yara Carafa and Snyder, Altiplano 1993.
41. IBTA judged that up to 15 cattle could be maintained with improved technology, but it appears that they overestimated the carrying capacity of the improved pasture, according to the 1992 evaluators.
42. Before it had even begun, the project was hit by the hyper-inflation that plunged the average per capita income in Bolivia from $510 to $200 in a single year. In combination with severe drought and then floods, inflation strained the government's resources and reduced the possibility of a government contribution to the Milk Project. That constraint was felt by innumerable projects in many countries in the world during the economic crisis of the 1980s.
43. UNIFEM's Women's Milk Project, *op. cit.*, p.8.
44. There were also studies of subjects such as the comparative value of fresh milk and cheese, the former fetching one boliviano per litre and the latter fifty centaros.
45. Carafa, *op. cit.*
46. Discussions with Yara Carafa and Cristina Albertin of WFP, Altiplano, September 1993.
47. *Ibid*, p.12.
48. PIL also demanded that the project communities provide their own collection truck and build their own collection centres–something not asked in other areas.
49. Danida.

50. Cornelia Flora, *UNIFEM Women's Milk Project: An Evaluation*, 1992, p.15 ff.
51. *Ibid.*
52. *Ibid*, pp.22–23.
53. *Ibid*, p.23
54. *Ibid*, p.24.
55. Interviews, Osco and Quisepe, with Snyder, Altiplano 1993.
56. *Ibid.*
57. *Evaluation, op. cit.*, p.28.
58. Interview, Cristina Albertin, WFP and Snyder, Altiplano, September 1993.
59. *Ibid.*
60. FSE's mandate is to mobilize internal and external funds to finance decentralized projects dealing with employment and social services. CEPAL, *Feminization of the Informal Sector in Latin America and the Caribbean*, pp.28–29.
61. *Ibid.*
62. Interview at Tiawanaku, 1993.
63. Interview Quisepe, *op. cit.*
64. *Evaluation* 1992, *op. cit.*
65. Statistics based on research conducted in Mizque which is close to Cochabamba: Susan Paulson, *Women of Mizque: the Heart of Household Survival*, November 1991, IDA Working Paper No. 76.
66. The grant was $165 222.
67. Interview with 15 of the 45 male artisans involved in the project, 1993.
68. *Report of the Evaluation and Continuation*, UNIDO, July 1993.
69. Interview with women potters, September 1993.
70. *Ibid.*
71. 2. *Proyecto de Fortalecimiento de la Alfareria Tradicional en el Valle Alto-Huayculi*, US/BOL/86/232. *Informe, asunto de evaluacion del proyecto* per el senior Karl Heinz, 11–15 July 1993.
72. Paulson 1991, *op. cit.*
73. Interviews, Altiplano 1993.
74. *Evaluation, op. cit.*
75. Interview, Obaid and Snyder, Amman 1994.
76. *Ibid.*
77. *Ibid.*
78. ESCWA, *Survey of Social Trends and Indicators in Countries of the ESCWA Region*, Amman, 1993, p.12.
79. *Ibid.*
80. Obaid, *op. cit.*
81. Survey, *op. cit.*, pp.26–27.
82. *Ibid.*, and also ESCWA, *Survey of Economic and Social Developments in the ESCWA Region*, Amman, October 1993.
83. Today, Oman's GNP per capita is more than $6000 (the GDP rose from $256 million in 1970 to $11 520 million in 1992, of which 16.4 per cent is spent on the military; WISTAT and UNDP *Human Development Report*, 1993); the US spends 5.6 per cent of its GDP and Germany 2.8 per cent on military.
84. Obaid, *op. cit.*
85. *Ibid.*
86. ESCWA, *Survey of Social Trends*, Amman, 1993.
87. UNDP, *Human Development Report*, New York, 1994.
88. Interview, Hla and Snyder, Damascus, March 1994.

89. *Ibid.* See *New York Times*, 25 December 1994; some UN agencies had done otherwise.
90. *Ibid.*
91. Interview, Muhamed and Snyder, Bosra, March 1994.
92. Hla, *op. cit.*
93. Statistics are from WISTAT, Version 3 as well as from *Survey of the Economic and Social Developments in the ESCWA Region 1992*, published by ESCWA in October 1993.
94. UNESCWA, *Biogas Technology and the Development of Rural Woman in Yemen* (E/ESCWA/SC/1993/1 and E/ESCWA/NR/1993/11), New York, 1994, p.10.
95. Interview, Obaid and Snyder, Amman, February 1994.
96. *Op. cit.*, ESCWA 1994, p.83.
97. Interview of Dr. Mahmoud Saleh, ESCWA Regional Adviser, and Snyder, Amman, February 1994.
98. *Op. cit.*, ESCWA, 1994, p.67.
99. Interview, Saleh and Snyder, *op. cit.*
100. *Op, cit.*, ESCWA 1994, p.83.
101. *Ibid.*, p.42 and p.67.
102. Interview, Saleh and Snyder, *op. cit.*
103. PDY/84/W01 was later disbursed as PDY/88/W01
104. PDY/86/W01, *Introduction of Biogas Technology*, $20000 from UNIFEM, $300 from UNDP, $2600 from ESCWA.
105. RAB/86/005 from the Netherlands Fund-in-Trust at ESCWA.
106. PDY/88/W01, *Diffusion of Biogas Technology in Democratic Yemen*. The government contributed $73 500 in-kind and ESCWA contributed $39 000 in-kind; UNIFEM provided $194 000.
107. *Op. cit.* ESCWA, 1994, p.78.
108. Interview, Saleh and Snyder, *op. cit.*
109. The manure required by one family biogas unit is measured as two 'cow units,' where one camel, ten sheep. or a hundred chickens produce the same quantity as a cow.
110. *Op. cit.*, ESCWA 1994, p.83.
111. *Op. cit.*, ESCWA 1994, p.82.
112. Interview, Saleh and Snyder, *op. cit.*
113. *Ibid.*
114. Margaret Mwangola and George Orich, *Why they called me Mama: KWAHO 1980–1993*, p.2. 1994.
115. UNIFEM, CC20, Info 4c.
116. UN General Assembly Economic and Social Council, *Progress in the Attainment of the Goals of the International Drinking Water Supply and Sanitation Decade.* 6 March 1985, A/40/108, E/1985/49.
117. Margaret Mwangola and George Orich, *op. cit.*
118. Interview with Virginia Hazzard in Mwangola and Orich, *op. cit.*
119. Mwangola and Orich, *op. cit.*, in Chapter entitled 'Organizing KWAHO'.
120. KEN/83/W01, *Training of Women in Hand-pump Operations and Maintenance.*
121. Mwangola and Orich, *op. cit.* 'Organizing KWAHO' chapter.
122. Deepa Narayan-Parker, *Achieving a Fit: People, Technology, and Agencies in the South Coast Hand-Pump Project.* Prowess/UNDP, New York, May 1988.
123. Bibi Hamisi's speech at UNIFEM's 10th Anniversary, 1987.
124. Deepa Narayan-Parker, p.11.

125. Mwangola and Orich, *op. cit.*, Chapter on 'Organizing KWAHO.'
126. The before date is 1985, after is 1987; from Deepa Narayan-Parker.
127. Mwangola and Snyder, *op. cit.*
128. Mwangola and Orich, *op. cit.*, Kwale chapter.
129. Deepa Narayan-Parker, *op. cit.*, Introduction.
130. Mwangola and Orich, *op. cit.*, Kwale chapter.
131. Mwangola and Orich, *op. cit.*, Kisumu 12.
132. Quoted in UNDP *Source*, December 1992.
133. UNDP *Human Development Report 1994*. New York, Oxford University Press.
134. MEX/85/W01, *Socio-Economic Development for Women's Organizations*, 156 000. The Ministry of Agriculture (SAHR) also donated $5000 in kind, and UAIM gave $14 000 in kind; executing agencies were UAIM, Women's Associates of Huasteca (AMCHAC), SARH, and the Instituto Nacional de Capacitacion del Sector Agropecuario (INCA).
135. Klaus Bethke, *Economic Adjustment and Revolving Loan Funds*, UNIFEM, October 1988.
136. English version of the *Executive Summary of the Evaluation Report: Program in Support of Tempoal Women*, June 1992.
137. *Ibid.*
138. UNDP *Source*, December 1992.
139. Klaus Bethke, UNIFEM's regional representative, quoted in UNDP *Source*, December 1992.
140. UNDP *Source*, December 1992.
141. WISTAT, Version 3. UN Statistics Division, Gender Statistics Unit.

Chapter Nine

1. Ela Bhatt, *The Grind of Work*, SEWA, Ahmedabad, 1989.
2. Interview, Alleyne and Snyder, Barbados 1993.
3. ECLAC, *Support provided to the ECLAC Women's Programme by the Voluntary Fund*, Santiago, 1984.
4. RLA/80/W01.
5. Interview, Mota and Snyder, Santiago, September 1993. Mota was Senior Women's Programme Officer for women and development at ECLAC at the time of the development planning training.
6. *Women as Recipients of Services from Resources Allocated in the National Budget*, RLA/84/W02. Additional support was provided to the budget analyses by the IDRC of Canada.
7. ECLC Series no. 16, UN Sales Publication E.82.II.G.10. UN, New York, 1982.
8. RLA/80/22, RLA/81/41.
9. Caroline Pezzullo, UN publication 5.84.II.G, New York, 1983.
10. RAB/78/01, RAB/78/06 and RAB/83/W03.
11. Interview, Obaid and Snyder, Amman, February 1994.
12. RAS/78/02, RAS/78/03, RAS/81/06, RAS/83/03.
13. Workshop on Programme/Project Development, RAS/78/08; the third and final phase of the projects was entitled *Assistance to Governments in Project Identification and Formulation Phase III*, RAS/81/W07.
14. *The Establishment of the Women in Development Pacific Planning Team: Regional Mission Undertaken by UNIFEM, UNDP, UNFPA*, September 1988.
15. *Ibid.*, p.1.

16. Dr. Lorraine Corner, *Mainstreaming Women in Development Planning*: UNDP/UNIFEM/AIDAB Project PMI/89/W01, 11 December 1992.
17. *Ibid.*
18. UNECA, *Report of the Regional Conference on Education, Vocational Training and Work Opportunities for Girls and Women in African Countries*, Addis Ababa, 1971.
19. UN/ECOSOC/IWY *Interregional Seminar on National Machinery. E/CONF.66/BP/4* 18 April 1975. p13.
20. Interview, Moriyama and Perdita Huston, Tokyo 1993.
21. Interview, Alleyne and Snyder, Barbados 1993.
22. Assistance went to Burundi, The Gambia, Ghana, Ivory Coast, Kenya, Lesotho and Zimbabwe in Africa; Belize, Dominica, Grenada, and Jamaica in the Caribbean; the Marshall Islands and Sri Lanka–2 projects–in Asia.
23. *Research on Rural Programmes for Women's Bureau*, KEN/78/05. $26 700. The grant was managed by ECA.
24. Interviews in Nairobi: Kantai and Kathy Larin, 1992; Oeri and Snyder, 1993. Oeri explained that it is now easier for women to get access to credit. Bankers know that 'a woman is not going to use the money to get another husband' she said.
25. With the Jamaica Women's Bureau and the National Commission on the Role of Filipino Women, it was one of the first in developing countries.
26. Interviews, Accra, 1993.
27. GAM/84/W03 *Strengthening the Women's Bureau.*
28. UNIFEM, *Experiences and Lessons in Joint World Bank/UNIFEM Mission to The Gambia, 25 January–10 February 1988.* See also AWA, publication of The Gambia Women's Bureau Volume 1, Number 4, May 1990.
29. Interview, Barrow and Snyder, Barbados, 1993.
30. UNIFEM Occasional Paper Number 2, June 1986, pp.8, 26.
31. Interview, Opoka and Snyder, Kampala 1993; and Alleyne, *op. cit.*
32. Galvez *op. cit.* pp.8–9.
33. Galvez *op. cit.* pp.14, 54
34. Daw Aye: unpublished document, *UNIFEM in Asia and the Pacific: 1977–1987.*
35. Daw Aye, *op. cit.*
36. Interview, Obaid and Snyder, Amman, February 1994.
37. *Ibid.*
38. *Ibid.*
39. Interview, Adegala and Snyder, Nairobi 1993.
40. Interview, Racelis and Snyder, Manila, 1994.
41. The UNIFEM project is RLA/88/WO1; Interview, Weinstein and Snyder, Santiago, September 1993.
42. RLA/85/W02.
43. Interview, Jere and Snyder, Lusaka, November 1993.
44. *Ibid.*
45. *Ibid.*
46. *Report of the National Census of Women's Groups in Kenya*, Women's Bureau, Ministry of Culture and Social Services, Nairobi, September 1993.
47. Interview, Mota and Snyder, *op. cit.*
48. Interview, Ela Bhatt and Snyder, Ahmedabad, February 1994. The reader is advised that SEWA is a co-operator with UNIFEM, not a beneficiary.
49. *Ibid.*
50. Interview, Vyas and Snyder, Ahmedabad, February 1994.
51. *Ibid.*

52. Interview, Bhatt and Snyder, *op. cit.*
53. SEWA Executive Committee, February 1994.
54. Interview, Jhabvala and Snyder, Ahmedabad, February 1994.
55. Interview, Bhatt and Snyder, *op. cit.*
56. *Ibid.*
57. Interview by Geoffrey Lean, undated.
58. Wangari Maathai, 1988, *The Green Belt Movement: Sharing the Approach and the Experience*. Nairobi: Environment Liaison Centre International, p.17.
59. *Op. cit.* 1988. p.22.
60. *Op. cit.*, 1988.
61. As reported in an interview of Wangari Maathai by United Nations Radio in 1983 (Women Eighty-Three, No. 199).
62. *Op. cit.*, 1988.
63. *The Green Belt Movement*, a nine-page mimeo published by the movement, apparently in 1990, indicates that there are 1500 nurseries.
64. *Op. cit.*, 1988.
65. *Op. cit.*, 1988, p.39. A high level task force was appointed by Kenya's president in 1993 to study the laws of Kenya which affect women.
66. Interview with Professor Maathai on 'Women Eighty-Three' for UN Radio, 1983.
67. *Ibid.*
68. *New York Times*, Wednesday, 6 December, 1989.
69. *Letter to New York Times*, Martin Kilson and Clement Cottingham, 10 January 1990.
70. *The Weekly Review*, January 12 1990.
71. *New York Times*, 6 December 1989.
72. *The Weekly Review*, 12 January 1990.
73. *The Economist*, January 13 1990.
74. *Ibid.*
75. Interview by Daphne Topouzis in *Africa Report*, November-December 1990. See also letter dated January 14 1992 from Dorothy Thomas of Human Rights Watch to Daniel T. arap Moi, President of Kenya.
76. *The Observer*, Sunday, 8 March 1992.
77. In 1990 California's Resource Renewal Institute awarder her the Green Century International Award for Courage. *Conde Nast Traveller* magazine gave her their first environmental award that same year. She also received the Right Livelihood Award, and the Goldman Environmental Award. In 1991, Maathai was awarded The Africa Prize for Leadership by the Hunger Project. In 1992, she received honorary degrees from Williams College and from Le Moyne College in New York, as well as from Justus-Liebig University in Germany.
78. From fax cabled on 14 January 1992. The other senators were Nancy Kassebaum, Patrick Leahy, Paul Simon, Barbara Mikulski, Ted Kennedy, Paul Wellstone, and John Chafee. Amnesty International and Africa Watch were among the many international organizations that supported Maathai.
79. *Op. cit.*, 1988.
80. 'A Statement on Global Values' by Wangari Maathai at the Public Symposium on Issues of Global Governance, UNU, Tokyo, 18 April 1994.
81. Interviews in Kenya, 1991.
82. Discussions with members of Flora Tristan, Lima, September 1993.
83. Andrew Maskrey, Country Director for Peru of the Immediate Technology Development Group, in an interview in 1993.

84. UNIFEM project number PER/86/WO1, Comedores Populares. The proceedings of this workshop are published in Nora Galer and Pilar Nunez, (ed.) 1989 *Mujer y Comedores Populares*, UNIFEM.
85. Cecilia Olea Mauleon, 1990. *Feminist Training's Contribution to the Democratization of Labor Unions*, Lima.
86. Interview, Galor and Snyder, Lima, September 1993.
87. The numbers for these UNIFEM projects are as follows: PER/82/W01 was the study of women workers in the electronics industry; PER/84/W01 was entitled, *Promotion of Women Workers in Metropolitan Area*; and PER/88/W01, *National Network to Assist NGOs Involvement in Rural Women's Projects*.
88. Cecilia Olea Mauleon, *Feminist Training's Contribution to the Democratization of Labor Unions*, Flora Tristan, Lima, March 1990, p.6.
89. Interview with Flora Tristan leaders, Lima, September 1993.
90. Interview with Flora Tristan leaders, Lima, 1993.
91. *Ibid.*
92. Cecilia Olea Mauleon, March 1990, *op. cit.*
93. Interview, Galer and Snyder, 1993, *op. cit.*
94. Domestic problems include children's issues. When a Flora Tristan writer interviewed boys 8 to 14 years of age who carry groceries for people in the markets or sell newspapers, after persistent questioning she learned that their small sisters are engaged in prostitution–at the age of 10 to 12 years.
95. *The Economist*, 12 December 1987.
96. Cecilia Olea Mauleon, 1990, *op. cit.*
97. From Nora Galer and Pilar Nunez (eds.) *Mujer y comedores Populares*, UNIFEM, 1989; particularly, from the chapter 'Los Comedores y La Promocion de la Mujer' by Violeta Sara-Lafosse.
98. Interview Galor, *op. cit.*
99. From Chapter 3: 'Peru – Alternative Technologies for Food Processing in Rural Areas' in *Changing Women's Lives and Work: A Comparative Study of the Impacts of Different Strategies in Projects to Support Small and Medium Scale Enterprises* by Lucy Creevey for UNIFEM, 1994.
100. Educational Services for Promotion and Rural Support—this is the organization with experience of empowering women.
101. Centre for Farmer's Services.
102. Interview, Maskrey and Snyder, Lima 1993.
103. Victor Raul Begazo, Lucila Caceres, Francisco Verdera, *Evaluation del Proyecto*, March 1992, p.21.
104. 'Mientras sus ingresos reales y niveles de vida caian y faltaban empleos, el proyecto se proponia lo opuesto.' Begazo, Caceres, Verdera, March 1992, p.21.
105. As reported in Creevey (1993) based on field notes from Huancayo by Marisela Benavides.
106. *Ibid.*
107. Interview, 1993.
108. Interview 1993.
109. Interview in Lima, September 1993.

Chapter Ten
1. The Lagos Plan sought to reduce post-harvest losses, achieve food security, increase food production and strengthen extension services. It emphasized the

need for special attention to women when undertaking situation analyses and planning for food self-reliance. See Snyder and Tadesse, *African Women and Development: A History*, 1995.

2. News Release, 11 June 1986, Minister for External Relations, Canada.

3. *Ibid.*

4. WAFT collaborators included FAO, ILO, UNICEF, ECA, German Appropriate Technology Exchange, Groupe de Recherche et d'Exchanges Technologiques, Royal Tropical Institute, International Development Research Centre, Tropical Development Research Institute, Appropriate Technology International, Institute of Development Studies, and Save the Children Fund. AIDOS, the Italian Association for Women in Development assisted the production and translation of the books into French and Portuguese. Each of the books has sections on traditional and improved processes and technologies, case studies, a checklist for planners of enterprises, facts and figures on equipment, a bibliography and a list of contact institutions.

5. SADCC was reorganized and renamed SADC (the Southern African Development Community) in 1993.

6. Mbilinyi, Marjorie, 'Women and the Pursuit of Local Initiatives' in W. Gooneratne and M. Mbilinyi, 1992, *Reviving Local Self-Reliance*, Nagoya Japan, UN Centre for Regional Development, pp. 51–52. Mbilinyi considers the rise in female-headed households as a 'sign of crisis in the community and of female resistance' to marriage when the economy was so poor that young men could not afford to marry.

7. *Ibid.*, from FAO 1984 data. Like other poor countries, Tanzania suffered severely from external shocks in the 1970s: quadrupling oil prices; depressed income from commodities sold on the global market; and a severe drought in 1973–4. Then came the war with Uganda. A foreign exchange crisis cut off imports of farm and manufacturing equipment, and by the early 1980s rural householders – among them women – were seeking incomes off the farm as self-employed or casual workers. Ignoring Tanzania's proven food production capacity noted above, the World Bank held that food security in Africa would be achieved most efficiently through importing excess food produced in the North and expanding wage employment in the South.

8. The economic downturn and the macro-economic policies such as stabilization and adjustment programmes of the 1980s and 1990s caused havoc by eating into the value of many credit funds and micro-enterprises. The cost of machinery and other inputs rose, currency was devalued, inflation rates of 20–30 per cent a year killed profits, and middlemen made gains. A grain mill in Tanzania, for example, cost shs T 720 000 in mid-1988 and 930 000 just six months later. See Occasional Paper No 10: *Preliminary Assessment of Impact of Stablization and Structural Adjustment Programmes on Selected UNIFEM-Supported Projects*, UNIFEM, New York 1990. See also World Bank, 1986. *Poverty and Hunger*, Washington, DC.

9. UNICEF gave $20 000; UN Volunteers, $10 000; and Government $12 000 in cash and kind. The long-range goals of the project were to improve women's socio-economic status while contributing to the national goal of food self-sufficiency, and to improve rural women's food processing activities through the dissemination of successful low-cost technologies, with a support system that included training in operation and maintenance, basic management skills and credit through a revolving loan fund. See project document, URT/87/WO1, 1987.

10. One hundred and ten villages were to be reached in the pilot phase of the project; only 26 village women's groups could receive revolving fund credit.
11. Valerie Autissier in 'Tanzania Food Processing' in Lucy Creevey, 1994, *Changing Women's Lives and Work*, UNIFEM, p.302.
12. Personal notes, 1989. The exchange rate of Shs 150/ to one US dollar in 1989 rose to shs 450/ in 1993. In order to repay their loan, the women planned to charge Shs 4/ to mill a tin and Shs 70/to mill 20 kilos of grain.
13. See Marja-Lisa Swantz, 1985, *Women in Development: a Creative Role Denied?*, St Martins Press, New York.
14. Autissier and Creevey, *op. cit.*, p.310.
15. *Ibid.* p.316.
16. In her book, *op. cit.*, Swantz noted that with the introduction of private ownership of property '. . . fundamental changes in the situation of women took place through the new conception of land as a possession instead of a means of common utilization for common needs'. She hoped that participation in village co-operatives would restore women's rightful place in society. Curiously, UNICEF, which had $22 million for Tanzania in 1989, worked mostly with men and regarded them as the decision-makers in the countryside because women, they said, did not chair village committees. Personal information from Letitia Van den Assum, Dsm 1989.
17. The World Bank, *Adjustment in Africa: Lessons from Country Case Studies*, Washington DC, 1994, pp.355, 407–413.
18. A publication, *Women and Food Security: the Experience of the SADCC Countries* contains a compilation of the papers presented at the Meeting. Marilyn Carr, (ed.), 1991. IT Publications, London. The project was URT/88/W01: Conference on Women and Food Technology in the SADCC Region.
19. Report of VFCC.5/11, para. 44.
20. *Ibid.*
21. *Women and Fuel in Rural Areas: A Preliminary Examination of Opportunities for a Programme Focus*, 1979, 20 pages plus Annexes. The paper found few actions taken within the UN system to alleviate the burdens of fire-wood supply in wood-poor areas – a task that usually fell to women. 'Not only has the impact of wood scarcity on women, the family and the community not been studied, but no efforts have been reported that would determine how women can contribute to the alleviation of the scarcity of wood'. There were some projects in afforestation, biogas and solar energy. NGOs had experimented, successfully, with fuel-efficient cookstoves.
22. In 1989 the European Economic Community financed through CILSS a regional programme to promote the use of bottled butane gas for cooking. We were told by Richard Gataroum of CILSS that while the price of a big bag of charcoal is 1500 to 2000 francs, and lasts seven days for a family of eight to ten persons, butane costs 1840 francs for six kilos, and lasts 15 days, but it is not practical for rural areas.
23. Interview, Ki-Zerbo and Snyder, Ouagadougou, 1993.
24. UN Radio Interview 1983.
25. Interview, Ki-Zerbo, November 1993.
26. BEN/81/W01; UNIFEM's grant was $251 000.
27. *Study on UNIFEM's Experience in Food Technology Projects*, UNIFEM, New York, 1988. The Netherlands and Denmark contributed to the projects.
28. *Ibid.*
29. Anne Marie Goetz, 'Feminism and the Claim to Know', in Rebecca Grant and Kathleen Newland, 1991. *Gender and International Relations*, Open Univer-

sity Press, Buckingham. Information on the actual design of the project was provided to me by FAO home economist Jocelyn Lopez and technologist Bill Brownell, who assisted Government with its design and execution. The Guinea project was GUI/81/W03, $229 000.

30. Interview, Sandhu and Snyder, Dakar, December 1993.
31. *Co-operation in Fisheries in Africa: Report of the Secretary General*, A/47/279, United Nations General Assembly, 24 June 1992. The UN Convention on the Law of the Sea gives nations jurisdiction over use of fishery resources up to 200 nautical miles off their coasts, a provision intended to ensure a rich source of protein and income for many citizens, and to be a foreign exchange earner for governments.
32. Interview, *op. cit.* Dakar, November 1993; see also two evaluations noted above.
33. Interview Sandhu, *op. cit.*
34. Laketch Dirasse, *Women Managers in Eastern and Southern Africa*, ESAMI, 1991. The project was RAF/80/WO4, for $190 444. Later $21 500 was added by RAF/84/W07.
35. Interview, Elias and Snyder, New York, September 1994.
36. *Ibid.*
37. Interview, Laketch Dirasse and Snyder, Nairobi, November 1993.
38. Interview Elias *op cit.*, and following quotations.
39. Interview Dirasse, *op. cit.*
40. United Nations, *Forward Looking Assessment*, UNIFEM, New York 1984, p.145. For these purposes, UNIFEM's *Guide to Community Revolving Loan Funds* was succeeded by a trial set of *Guidelines* to be adopted nationally and finally the publication of *An End to Debt: Guidelines for Credit Projects*. UNIFEM, New York, 1982, 1984, 1993. UNIFEM's credit support officer, Teckie Ghebre-Medhin served as adviser to our own projects and adviser/designer for credit activities of other organizations.
41. Thanks to the Government of Denmark sending Members of Parliament to the GA's discussions on women and their request for meetings with UNIFEM's staff.
42. *Mid-Term Project Evaluation: Draft Report on URT/89/W01 Credit Scheme for Productive Activities of Women in Tanzania*, 3 November 1993, and Mid-Term Project Evaluation Review, URT/92/WO2 *Credit Scheme for Productive Activities for Women*, October 1993. Note that the project has been separated into a mainland and a Zanzibar component – hence the two evaluations.
43. *Ibid.*
44. Ki-Zerbo had left CILSS in Ouagadougou and worked from Dakar thereafter. The Government of the Netherlands financed her post and many of the activities.
45. Interview Ki-Zerbo *op. cit.*
46. UNIFEM 1987.
47. Interview, Ouagadougou 1994.
48. *UNIFEM's Approach to Country Programming and Round Table*, undated.
49. Ellen Johnson Sirleaf, *Some observations on Structural Adjustment and the African Women*, UNIFEM, New York, 1988. Johnson Sirleaf was the first woman to head a UNDP Regional Bureau when she became head of the Africa Bureau after a distinguished career in banking and politics.

307

Chapter Eleven

1. *The East Asian Miracle: Economic Growth and Public Policy*, The World Bank, Washington DC, 1993. In East Asia, government policy interventions took many forms as they sought to protect nascent national industries. That option all but disappears under many economic adjustment programmes in the poorer countries today.
2. See Daisy Dwyer and Judith Bruce, 1988, *A Home Divided: Women and Income in the Third World.* Stanford University Press, Stanford, California. See also Margaret Snyder, 1991, 'Gender and the Food Regime: Some Transnational and Human Issues' in *Transnational Law and Contemporary Problems.* University of Iowa.
3. Interview, Mwanamwambwa and Snyder, Lusaka, November 1993.
4. Interview, Maathai and Larin, Nairobi, January 1993.
5. WAND's own goal as reformulated in 1993 was 'to contribute to building the human and institutional capacity for a new model of development' in the Caribbean region.
6. UNIFEM Occasional Paper No. 2, June 1986.
7. Data from UNDP Personnel Office, June 1994.
8. Noeleen Heyzer. UNIFEM Director. *Statement to the Third Committee of the General Assembly*, December 1994.
9. *Annual Report*, UNIFEM, 1988.
10. Ministry of Foreign Affairs, *A World of Difference: A New Framework for Development Co-operation in the 1990s.* The Hague, Netherlands, 1991.
11. Gita Sen and Karen Grown. *Development, Crises and Alternative Visions.* New York, Monthly Review Press, 1987.
12. Interview, Obaid and Snyder, Amman, February 1994.
13. Interview, Racelis and Snyder, Manila, February 1994.
14. Interview, Mota and Snyder, Santiago, September 1993.
15. Bradford Morse, Address to the World Conference at Nairobi, 1985.
16. Interview, Antrobus and Snyder, Bridgetown, September 1993.
17. Interview, Alleyne and Snyder, Bridgetown, September 1993.
18. The World Bank, *The East Asian Miracle, op.cit.*
19. Interview, Sundarshan and Snyder, Delhi, February 1994.
20. Mwanamwambwa and Snyder, *op.cit.*

Index

310

imports 90, 117, 122, 131, 137, 252
incomes 85–6, 93, 95, 125, 126, 130, 236
   disposal/use of 108, 110, 158, 229, 250,
     262
   increased 103, 108, 118, 120, 129, 134,
     157, 248
   see also wages
independence (post-colonial) 9, 10, 11, 12,
   13, 145
India 86, 124–40, 201–5, 248, 250, 252, 256,
   258
industrialization 13
inflation 152, 189, 210, 218, 221
informal sector (popular economy) 85–7,
   101–2, 125, 126, 136, 152, 212, 251
infrastructure 116–17, 133, 135, 158, 160,
   170–1
inheritance 200
innovative activities (Fund) 7, 161, 257–9
institutions 7, 26, 27, 145, 194–200, 254,
   255
   see also bureaux, women's; groups,
     women's; organizations
Isis International, Chile 199
Islam/Muslims 169, 170, 185
isolation/exclusion of women 163, 165, 166,
   218, 251
ISST (Institute of Social Studies Trust) 136
ITDG (Intermediate Technology
   Development Group) 22, 219, 220, 221,
   222, 225
IWY (International Women's Year) 22,
   25–27, 195, 266

jam-making 218
jar-making 95
jobs 101, 120, 134, 170, 211, 215, 216, 236
   see also work
Jordan 169–70, 173

KBB (Village Women) 109, 111, 114, 254
KBBLF (Kababaihang Barangay Livelihood
   Foundation) 109, 114, 250, 254
Kenya 13, 183–7, 195, 205–10, 253
knitting 110–11, 114, 120, 177
Knowledge Bank (VFDW) 46, 47
KWAHO (Kenya Water for Health
   Organization) 183, 184–5, 186, 187,
   258

land ownership/rights 88–9, 152, 188–9,
   197, 202, 207–8
language 71, 154, 156, 157, 199
Laos 116–18, 248, 250, 258
Latin America 55–6
leaders/leadership 52, 111, 114, 184–5, 205,
   213–16, 256, 278–81
legislation 17, 121, 127, 200, 204, 212, 214

Lesotho 230
literacy/illiteracy 118–19, 128, 152, 156,
   157, 175–8, 180–1
livestock 104, 105–9, 154, 155, 159, 182
loan repayment 86–7, 92, 97, 104, 108, 203,
   236
loans & credit 91, 92, 93, 94, 201–2, 229,
   241
location of Fund 35, 62–7, 70

magazine/newsletters 60, 144, 170, 213,
   216–17, 233
Mahila Haat (village markets) 135–40, 249,
   251
Mahila Mandal (village organizations) 129,
   133, 135
mainstreaming 7, 38, 191, 194, 196, 239–43,
   245, 258–9, 263–4
management course 239–40
management (Fund) 28, 31–3, 74, 267–74
   see also administration; bureaucracy
mandate/priorities
   UNIFEM 36, 37–8, 49–50, 53, 55, 56, 57,
     69
   VFDW 28, 29, 36–8, 58, 68, 69
markets/marketing 131, 132, 134, 135–40,
   190, 249–50
Mauritania 235
Mauritius 122–4, 138, 249
mechanization 13, 131, 133, 134–5, 137,
   164
medium-scale production 112, 120, 130, 250
men 163, 164, 165, 189, 240
   attitudes of 67, 108, 118, 121, 146, 159,
     162, 214
   changes in attitudes of 90–1, 92, 162,
     165–6, 180, 181, 190
   income disposal 158, 250
   support from 52, 92, 97, 105, 146, 156,
     180
   work done by 16, 118, 161–2, 166
   see also gender issues
Mexico 187–90
Mexico City Conference (IWY) 25–7, 266
micro-enterprise 22, 87, 119, 122–4, 125,
   147–9, 152, 203, 220
migration see emigration; out-migration
milk production 152, 154–5
milling 133, 227–9, 231, 238
mortality 170, 180
Mothers Clubs, Bolivia 153, 156, 165,
   217–18, 220
motor mechanic scheme 145

national committees 76–7, 126, 275
national machinery/development planning
   192–7, 200, 254, 255, 263
natural disasters 90, 100, 103

311